Battleground

Battleground

Electoral College Strategies, Execution, and Impact in the Modern Era

Daron R. Shaw, Scott L. Althaus, and Costas Panagopoulos

OXFORD
UNIVERSITY PRESS

Oxford University Press is a department of the University of Oxford. It furthers the University's objective of excellence in research, scholarship, and education by publishing worldwide. Oxford is a registered trade mark of Oxford University Press in the UK and certain other countries.

Published in the United States of America by Oxford University Press
198 Madison Avenue, New York, NY 10016, United States of America.

CIP data is on file at the Library of Congress
ISBN 978–0–19–777437–3 (pbk.)
ISBN 978–0–19–777436–6 (hbk.)

DOI: 10.1093/oso/9780197774366.001.0001

Contents

Preface vii
Acknowledgments ix

1. **A New Look at Presidential Campaigns in the Modern Era** 1
2. **Strategy, Time, and Presidential Campaigning** 19
3. **Wholesale Campaigning (1952–1972)** 49
4. **Zero-Sum Campaigning (1976–2000)** 99
5. **Micro-Targeted Campaigning (2004–2020)** 139
6. **Tracking Electoral Strategy Over Time** 168
7. **Tracking the Allocation of Resources Over Time** 187
8. **Putting It All Together: Resource Allocation and Vote Outcomes** 209
9. **The Past, the Present, and the Future of Presidential Campaigns** 240

Appendix: Strategy Categorization, Candidate Appearances, and Ad Spending by State, 1952–2020 247
Notes 267
References 279
Index 289

Preface

We have a confession to make: We like presidential campaigns. As caring citizens and scholars dedicated to the substance of American politics, we know that we should be more interested in the nuts and bolts of policy-making. We should recoil from the boilerplate and repetitive stump speeches. We should smirk and roll our eyes at the simplistic television advertisements, which avoid context and emit an oily sense of salesmanship. We should join the chorus of voices that lecture voters about the vapidity of modern election campaigns and yearn for a more edifying and nutritious process for selecting the leader of the free world. But we don't. Instead, we are drawn to them. They are our guilty pleasure.

Here is another heretical notion: We suspect that we are hardly alone. Between 10% and 20% of the electorate that cannot be bothered to show up for midterm elections turns out for the presidential contest. The news media—broadcast, cable, digital, and traditional print—spend more time reporting and opining on these races than on all others combined. The personalities that emerge from presidential campaigns—the candidates, families, friends, strategists, and surrogates—drive news coverage, comedic satire, and even popular conversation. Tell-all and insider books about these campaigns are gobbled up by millions of readers. We believe the reason is that they engage us at two levels. At a visceral level, they are fun. The drama and the personalities. The narrative quality of the campaign as every day unfolds. At an intellectual level, the subtle complexity of the presidential contest is utterly compelling. It is a high-stakes chess game, except much more complex.

It is this last point that we take up here. What the candidates say, to whom they say these things, and where they choose to deploy their precious resources is interesting and important. Our point of departure is that we do not seem to know much about these things, especially decisions concerning where the candidates campaign. To be sure, we know a great deal about messaging (what candidates say) and targeting (whom they say it to), both within certain elections and even across time. And we know a great deal about the dispensation of resources and even Electoral College strategy in some specific elections. However, we have not leveraged the historical record in a way that substantively informs what we know about which states draw the lion's share of attention, nor can we speak to broader issues of bias or neglect. These issues and questions are of utmost importance in a democratic society. Thus, our focus in this volume is on Electoral College strategy.

This project has been more than twenty years in the making. We began nosing around campaign archives in presidential libraries and a few candidate collections in the late 1990s and early 2000s. What we found at the LBJ Library in Austin and at a few other facilities confirmed our belief that a treasure trove of data was available for investigating past presidential campaigns. The professionalism—and even the brilliance—of the operatives who have run presidential campaigns was perhaps the most striking finding. We never ceased to be amazed at how smart these people were. Our initial forays also confirmed our assumption that compiling these data would often be difficult and frustrating. In the end, the pull of our enthusiasm outweighed our reticence, and we have been plugging away ever since, ever cognizant of our own limits as well as the limits of historical research and social scientific methods. The humbling nature of this research notwithstanding, we think the result advances the conversation about how presidential campaigns are conceptualized and executed, how these dynamics have been affected by changes in society and technology, and about the broader impact of these campaigns on representative democracy.

Acknowledgments

This project began in the late 1990s and, at the time of this writing, is old enough to buy itself a drink. It would be inaccurate to say that we have been continuously working on these ideas and data every day since then, but they have never been too far from our minds. Given this long and winding road, it should come as no surprise that numerous people have contributed substantially to the book and its contents. Indeed, a book reaching this far into the past and this deep into specific election campaigns cannot be but for the efforts and assistance of many individuals.

We would first like to recognize the tremendous aid we received from our graduate research assistants over the years: collecting, organizing, cleaning, and compiling the voluminous archival evidence amassed for this project was done by Sarah Castle, Philip Habel, Matt Harrington, Jake Jensen, David Paul, Lauren Ratliff, Emily Renwick, Paul Richardson, Ulric Shannon, Paul Testa, Kaye Usry, and especially Jason Rittenberg, who accompanied Scott Althaus on numerous trips to archive locations around the country. Brian Arbour, Seth McKee, Mathieu Turgeon, Josh Blank, Nadine Gibson, and Cornelia Lawrence helped with some of the core data analyses and conference papers that presented preliminary or partial results. Perhaps most notably, Lindsay Dun-Guaglianone conducted key statistical analyses of Electoral College strategies. In addition, undergraduate research assistants Ian Adams, Amanda Carne, Jelena Tiosavljevic, Roma Tragon, and Tessa Walter provided invaluable aid in compiling and verifying data on television ads, candidate appearances, and overall Electoral College strategies.

We would also like to express our gratitude to the wonderful assistants at the various presidential libraries and other archives that we relied on. The professionals at the National Archives in Washington, D.C., made us aware of resources associated with reports from the Federal Communications Commission that we had only dreamed of prior to our interactions with them. Similarly, the experts at the George H. W. Bush, Jimmy Carter, Dwight Eisenhower, Gerald Ford, Lyndon B. Johnson, John F. Kennedy, Richard Nixon, and Ronald Reagan presidential libraries were tremendous resources for our specific interests in their presidential campaign materials. Among a universe of helpful stars, Mary Lukens shines especially bright. A long-time assistant to Republican pollster Robert Teeter, Mary was incredibly useful to several of our searches. Frank Palumbo of Nielsen Media Research provided valuable assistance in locating historical data on the geographic boundaries of television media markets from 1972 to 1988, and the library staff at the University of Georgia at Athens provided important assistance in locating historical data on the geographic boundaries of television media markets from 1952 to the late 1970s using Arbitron archival records.

We also benefited from the help of various stalwarts associated with the archives of Adlai Stevenson, Barry Goldwater, Hubert Humphrey, George McGovern, Walter Mondale, and Michael Dukakis. For example, Ruth Rowley, special assistant to Dukakis, allowed us to recover TV ad data from the governor's campaign that would have been nearly impossible to replicate without her assistance.

Our ability to analyze all this voluminous archival data would not have been possible without the computational expertise of Kalev Leetaru, who constructed the project's first document repository system for the Cline Center for Advanced Social Research, as well as that of Joseph Bajjalieh and Loretta Auvil, who built the project's second document repository system.

Beyond these repositories, we reaped the benefit of the wisdom of people who participated in many of these campaigns. Accordingly, we wish to thank David Axelrod, Robert Beckell, Joel Benenson, Donna Brazille, Charlenne Carl, Matthew Dowd, Anita Dun, Tucker Eskew, Susan Estrich, Ken Mehlman, Robby Mook, Bill Moyers, Bill Murphy, Jen O'Malley, Jen Palmieri, David Plouffe, Gerald Rafshoon, Scott Reed, Michael Shannon, Robert Shrum, Ted Sorensen, and Bill Wilson. Their stories, leads, and occasionally their records allowed us to significantly enhance the data and theory we bring to the table in this account. At the head of this list are Karl Rove, Fred Steeper, and Robert Teeter. Our debt to those three individuals is immense.

Generous funding for this project came from many sources over the years, including the Cline Center for Advanced Social Research at the University of Illinois Urbana-Champaign, the Research Board at the University of Illinois Urbana-Champaign, and the Frank C. Erwin, Jr. Chair of State Politics at the University of Texas at Austin.

Even a cursory glance at this volume would reveal that we draw on the truly outstanding existing research done by journalists, political scientists, and historians who have specialized in presidential campaigns. It is nearly impossible to identify all our influences and data sources, and we will surely leave some out in any effort to offer even a partial list. But we feel particularly obliged to acknowledge our debt to the work of journalists like Richard Ben Cramer, John Dickerson, Elizabeth Drew, Jack Germond, Mark Halperin, John Heilmann, Sasha Issenberg, Ezra Klein, Joe McGinnis, Evan Thomas and the reporters associated with *Newsweek*'s campaign narratives, Hunter S. Thompson, Jules Witcover, Bob Woodward, and especially Theodore White. Then there is an array of stellar political scientists whose research and insight have shaped this project, including (but not limited to) Alan Abramowitz, Herbert Alexander, Robert Axelrod, Larry Bartels, Paul Boller, Steven Brams, James Campbell, Jonathan Cervas, George Edwards, James Enelow, Robert Erikson, Paul Freedman, James Gimpel, Ken Goldstein, Bernard Grofman, Michael Hagen, Melvin Hinich, Thomas Holbrook, Kathleen Hall Jamieson, Richard Johnston, Lawrence Longley, Jennifer Merolla, Michael Munger, Sam Popkin, John Sides, Lynn Vavreck, and John Wright. We literally could not have done this without you.

The assistance and support we have received from our colleagues and friends in our departments and throughout political science have also been invaluable. Foremost among them is Peter Nardulli, who was an early champion and valued founding collaborator of this project and coauthor of several papers as well as an article (Althaus, Nardulli, and Shaw, 2002) that was the first and only academic publication to arise from this multi-year effort prior to the one that you are reading now. In this category we also wish to credit Bethany Albertson, Stephen Ansolabehere, James Henson, D. Sunshine Hillygus, Shanto Iyengar, Gary Jacobson, Robert Luskin, Eric McDaniel, Arnon Mishkin, John Petrocik, Tasha Philpot, Brian Roberts, Chris Wlezien, and John Zaller for their comments and criticisms, advice and questions, and unfailing professionalism.

Along these lines, we are especially grateful to the two anonymous reviewers who read entire drafts of the manuscript on behalf of Oxford University Press. They didn't always tell us what we wanted to hear, but they showed us what we needed to do to make this book much better than it was otherwise going to be. We have no doubt that the book you are reading now bears the hallmark of their constructive feedback. We are deeply grateful for the time and careful attention that these reviewers took with the entire manuscript.

Last but certainly not least, our deepest and most important acknowledgement goes to our respective families. Without their love and support, none of this would ever have come to pass.

1
A New Look at Presidential Campaigns in the Modern Era

From popular accounts of recent American presidential campaigns, strategy and execution seem to be key when it comes to winning elections. In the aftermath of these elections, detailed reportage documents the key decisions that led one campaign to triumph over the other. Losers are scorned, legends are born. Academic studies of the same campaigns tell a vastly different story. In these accounts, neither strategy nor execution matters much to outcomes because the vote is largely determined by fundamentals such as the state of the economy and the current popularity of the incumbent president. This book charts a middle course between the journalistic Scylla and the academic Charybdis. We show how and why strategies as well as execution can contribute to success in presidential elections, but also how they have been evolving over the last seventy years in systematic ways that make presidential campaigning in the early twenty-first century quite different in purpose and payoff from the way such campaigning looked in the mid-twentieth century. Prussian Field Marshall Helmuth von Moltke may have been right when he said in 1871 that "no plan of operations extends with any certainty beyond the first encounter with the main enemy forces."[1] But we show that when it comes to winning elections for the American presidency, these plans and the efforts of campaigns to follow them help us understand who wins and who loses.

American presidential campaigns have long been a spectator sport. And like other sports, it seems that everybody who watches them makes claim to expertise. From the comfort of television studios, living room couches, or even classroom podiums, journalists, academics, elected officials, and social media users pontificate about what the candidates did right and (more commonly) did wrong. Sometimes the assessments are compelling. Other times they are banal. Occasionally, someone will offer an insightful tidbit and, just maybe, leaven their appraisal with some charity about the enormity and complexity of the task. In the heat of the moment, however, most of us feel free to treat the presidential candidates and their campaigns as if they were players and teams in the National Football League: How could they throw that interception on

Battleground. Daron R. Shaw, Scott L. Althaus, and Costas Panagopoulos, Oxford University Press.
 DOI: 10.1093/oso/9780197774366.003.0001

the final drive, and what was the coach *thinking* by going for it on fourth down when a field goal would have tied the game?

Yet after the game has ended, even diehard fans can grow reflective. When the stadium lights have dimmed, reason can sometimes creep in to temper passion. We realize that the players and coaches are professional and competent. Deep down, we understand that very few of us could ever play the game at that level. More broadly, we appreciate that specific actions and decisions matter, but that outcomes result from the interactions of dozens of discrete choices and events. Moreover, we know that players cannot easily overcome the fundamental circumstances that constrain and condition their choices and their performances. Perhaps poker is a more apt comparison than football: skill in playing cards is necessary for winning, but even champions are constrained by the hands they've been dealt. So it is with presidential campaigns. Strategies are developed and executed, but perhaps their effects on election outcomes are overrated because larger and more powerful forces shape results. This is the key insight of detached and cool-headed academics and academically-inclined journalists. Their perspective suggests that while presidential campaigns are certainly entertaining, the decisions and actions made by campaigners rarely have a decisive influence on who wins the White House.

But is this cold-eyed assessment correct? Do the strategies and campaign decisions of key players really have so little bearing on Election Day results? To answer this question, we need to take stock of what we know—*really* know—about presidential campaigns from the last seventy years or so of modern electoral experience. Despite the musings of campaign insiders and the detached analyses of academic experts, the answer is that we know vanishingly little, and certainly less than either of these perspectives admits to being the case. If the president of the United States is the most powerful person in the world, then how we select this individual is the most consequential process that students of politics can consider. Yet there are surprisingly few attempts to analyze in systematic ways how major party candidates go about winning this office.

This book aims to fill this gap. We draw on seven decades of data from public and private sources to reveal the Electoral College strategies of presidential campaigns, the execution of these plans, and the attendant effects of this execution on statewide outcomes and electoral vote totals.[2] Across the modern political era from 1952 through 2020, we find that presidential campaigns are strategic, sophisticated, and effective. However, we also find that broader contextual changes define and divide these eighteen elections such that they sort coherently into three distinct eras. Yet both across and within these three eras we find differences in how (and how well) specific campaigns approached their tasks.

Our perspective thus offers a different assessment than those of journalists or other academics. For the most part, we agree that sometimes the fundamentals crowd out the best laid plans of campaigners, as many academics tend to believe. But sometimes those Electoral College strategies and how effectively they are implemented become the crucial keys to electoral success, and in these cases the truth is not inconsistent with journalistic accounts. Beyond the argument we advance, what distinguishes this project is the scope and quality of the underlying data: We draw on insider campaign memos, ad buy records detailing how much money was spent on advertising in particular media markets, and a complete reconstruction of daily, public appearances by major party candidates from 1952 to 2020 across eighteen presidential contests spanning the modern era. This unique vantage point allows us to not only gauge when and how campaigns matter but more importantly why they can sometimes push candidates over the line against all the odds and sometimes fail miserably to carry the day even when the fundamentals are all pointing in the right direction. We conclude that campaigns matter, usually by providing a small boost in one or two states that make a difference in the Electoral College tally.

One at a Time: Previous Studies of Presidential Campaigns

It is not as though pundits, practitioners, and political scientists have ignored the question of what presidential campaigns attempt to do or how effective they are at accomplishing their goals. Journalistic accounts of presidential campaigns go back at least as far as the mesmerizing work of Theodore White and the 1960 Kennedy-Nixon campaign (White, 1961). The tradition encompasses Joe McGinnis's classic *The Selling of the President 1968* (McGinnis, 1969), Hunter S. Thompson's narrative of the 1972 Nixon-McGovern campaign (Thompson, 1973), the quadrennial work of Jack Germond and Jules Witcover from 1980 through 1992 (Germond and Witcover, 1981; Germond and Witcover, 1985; Germond and Witcover 1989; Germond and Witcover, 1993) and books by the intrepid *Newsweek* teams from 1992 through 2008 (Goldman, et al. 1994; Thomas, et al., 1997; Thomas, et al., 2005; Thomas, 2009), as well as a heroic novel about the 1988 campaign by Richard Ben Cramer (Cramer, 1993). More recently, we have John Heilemann and Mark Halperin's accounts of the 2008 and 2012 contests (Heilemann and Halperin,

2010; Halperin and Heilemann, 2013), and numerous stand-alone novels about the 2016 and 2020 elections. In addition to these colorful and eventful documentary tomes, a small handful of books offer stories and anecdotes from a range of presidential campaigns across time, most notably Paul Boller's *Presidential Campaigns: From Washington to George W. Bush* (Boller, 2004) and John Dickerson's *Whistlestop: My Favorite Stories from Presidential Campaign History* (2017). These books, however, only occasionally venture beyond any one election. They offer terrific details yet rarely identify important patterns or broader themes.

Beyond journalistic accounts, practitioners have actively retold the stories of recent campaigns. Among others, James Carville and Mary Matalin (Clinton 1992 and Bush 1992, respectively), Stuart Stevens (Bush 2000), Karl Rove (Bush 2000 and 2004), David Plouffe and David Axelrod (Obama 2008), and Roger Stone (Trump 2016) have authored books detailing their thoughts about, and experiences in, presidential campaigns. These endeavors typically proceed chronologically, giving the reader a sense of what the campaign wanted to do when, and how it was done. They often praise the candidate and campaign staff, occasionally leavening these accounts with a dash of humor and self-effacement. Oftentimes useful data or empirical evidence emerges in support of a specific point or argument, but there is rarely any effort to present a comprehensive account of the campaign plan, let alone how well it was executed or what its effects were. To be fair, this is understandable; practitioners regard the details of a successful campaign as professional secrets and reveal them only to future candidates (or clients). As will become clear, our book brings previously hidden details to light for all to see, spanning every presidential major party campaign from 1952 through 2020.

The most instructive and open discussions featuring the participants of presidential campaigns are from the post-election conferences hosted by Harvard's Kennedy School of Government. From 1980 through 2020, these two-day affairs featured a series of panel conversations on different elements of the recently completed presidential campaign. Transcripts from these conferences were published as part of the Campaign for President book series. Similarly, for the 2000–2012 presidential elections, a series of books was published under the eponymous title of Electing the President, based on similar post-election conferences held by the University of Pennsylvania's Annenberg School of Public Affairs. These books offer rare insight into the campaign from those who were there, and occasionally provide tantalizing bits of polling or television advertising data. On several occasions, they also proffer discussions of electoral strategy. However, they rarely reference any presidential campaigns other than the one that just ended.

If journalists and practitioners give us only a scattered set of clues about presidential campaign strategies, academics (as suggested earlier) tend to downplay their significance altogether. The Ivory Tower has produced a few notably broad projects examining presidential campaigns and their effects. Foremost among these is James Campbell's *The American Campaign* (2008), which amasses survey and voting data from modern elections to estimate the effects of campaign events, such as conventions and debates, as well contextual variables, such as the state of the economy and presidential approval. Campbell concludes that campaigns have only minor effects on the vote distributions and the outcomes of presidential elections. The concept of the "campaign" in that analysis is coincident with major events and specific occurrences. Yet even in this astute overview there is no attempt to define, measure, or estimate the impact of strategy on the constituent activities of the campaign.

Also of note is Robert Erikson and Chris Wlezien's *The Timeline of Presidential Elections*, which relies on extensive polling data—close to two thousand national polls covering every presidential election from 1952 through 2008—to assess the role of the campaign in shaping opinions and preferences (Erikson and Wlezien, 2012). They show that over the course of an election year the presidential campaigns help to make voters aware of both candidate positions and fundamental factors (like the state of the economy). In this sense, campaigns typically work to bring about gradual changes in voters' perceptions, but only rarely produce major or sudden shifts. The campaign is viewed as a purveyor of information, one whose impact accrues over time as the election nears.

There are other important studies, as well. For the 2012, 2016, and 2020 elections John Sides and Lynn Vavreck, along with their co-authors, provide detailed analyses of the impact of a wide array of candidate and campaign activity on voters (Sides and Vavreck, 2013; Sides, Tesler, and Vavreck, 2018; Sides, Vavreck, and Warshaw, 2022). They use daily polling data—along with appropriate controls for potentially confounding variables—to isolate the effects of presidential campaigning. This research realizes the dream of political scientists to have sufficiently detailed, granular data to assess the effects of a given campaign effort amid the cacophony of noise associated with the presidential campaign. Their project refines the work of Johnston, Hagen, and Jamieson (2004), who pioneered the "rolling cross-section" survey to analyze campaign effects in the 2000 presidential election. It also builds on the work of Freedman, Franz, and Goldstein (2004) and Shaw (1999, 2006), who were among the first to acquire and analyze detailed information on television advertising buys made by presidential campaigns. Although these analyses engage the larger question of the nature and magnitude of presidential campaign effects, they do not attempt to systematically classify or measure campaign strategy, nor do they leverage over-time data to make broader inferences about campaign effects across different elections.

One study that does these things is Lynn Vavreck's *The Message Matters* (2009), which offers a theoretical and practical definition of *messaging strategy* and then measures it across roughly the same time period as we consider here. Vavreck takes research demonstrating the power that economic performance has on the attitudes of the electorate and uses it to craft and test theoretical expectations about how incumbents and challengers will approach presidential elections given extant circumstances. She posits that when the economy is good, incumbents will run a "clarifying" campaign, while challengers will run an "insurgency" campaign and attempt to focus voters' attention on other issues. Theoretically, Vavreck builds on Sam Popkin's notion of "low-information rationality," articulated in *The Reasoning Voter* (Popkin, 1994). Empirically, Vavreck collects data from news stories and campaign speeches across multiple campaigns to operationalize her core concepts and put them to the statistical test.

Though necessarily less historical and comprehensive than Vavreck's project, another impressive effort to define and measure campaign strategy is Eitan Hersh's *Hacking the Electorate* (2015), which focuses on targeting strategy. More specifically, Hersh details the revolutionary impact that voter file databases have had on modern elections—presidential and nonpresidential—with extensive data on the habits and preferences of individual voters now available to campaigns. Hersh shows how data analysts use this information to craft individualized appeals to voters to persuade and/or mobilize them on behalf of their candidates.

Note the distinction between these works and the present one: Vavreck considers presidential campaigning from the perspective of messaging strategy; Hersh considers it from the perspective of targeting strategy; we consider it from the perspective of Electoral College strategy. Messaging strategy focuses on *what campaigns say*, targeting strategy focuses on *who campaigns say it to*, and Electoral College strategy focuses on *where campaigns say it*. Each of these approaches is theoretically and empirically interesting, and we believe that the work of Vavreck, Hersh, and others complements what we are doing. Put a slightly different way, our book focuses on the strategic allocation of scare campaign resources to create messaging impact affecting key states in the Electoral College framework—what is sometimes called *macro-targeting* (e.g., Hillygus and Shields, 2008; Ridout et al., 2012). Vavreck focuses on the *messaging themes*—themes that campaigns use to win voters in those macro-targeted states, while Hersh focuses on *micro-targeting*—how campaigns reach particular kinds of people within macro-targeted states using personalized appeals aligned with the campaign's messaging theme that individually motivate voters to support a preferred candidate.[3]

Like these other scholars, we endeavor to bring greater theoretical cohesion and empirical depth to the study of campaigns. Equally important, their work has expanded our understanding and appreciation of what constitutes campaign "effects," which is something that our project also aims to do. But it is also worth reiterating that despite our intuition, we do not know nearly as much about Electoral College macro-targeting strategies as we do about messaging strategies or micro-targeting tactics. This is partly because the work of scholars such as Vavreck and Hersh has filled some of the previous gaps regarding the last two. It is also partly because presidential campaigns are distinct among American election campaigns with respect to their rules and construction. The impact of the Electoral College on strategy only matters for U.S. presidential elections, but these contests are so important that we believe a better understanding of their strategic underpinning is critical to truly understanding American democratic processes.

Even acknowledging the work of Vavreck, Hersh, Campbell, and a handful of others, to the extent that scholars have used over-time data to analyze the impact of presidential campaigns, this has mostly come in the form of presidential vote "models" in which other factors drive outcomes while campaign factors account for "residual variance" in the results.[4] Most research in this vein observes that economic performance is a strong predictor of support for the party of the incumbent president (Tufte, 1978; Fair, 1978), while campaigns have relatively limited substantive independent effects on voters and elections. The attendant rule of thumb here is straightforward: the better the economic models, the less room there is for campaign effects. It is important to observe that although this strand of research systematically considers a range of presidential elections, it only indirectly tackles the issue of how much *campaigns* matter. Indeed, subsequent prediction models incorporate factors that are, at least in part, dependent on the campaign, such as poll support and presidential approval. Gelman and King (1993), for example, observe that the "predictability" of presidential elections is at odds with the observed variance in trial ballot results from pre-election polls, arguing that survey results tend to converge on predictions as voters tune into the campaign. For many, this is an unsatisfying take on the impact of campaigns, because some of the exogenous factors that influence presidential elections in these models are, as already noted, not exogenous to the campaign.

We would also opine that the prevalence of economic and forecasting models in the presidential election literature has decreased since the early

2000s. In addition to the handful of comprehensive studies of presidential campaigns and their effects, numerous scholarly articles have been published in recent years examining the impact of forms and elements of campaigning. A quick perusal of the top journals in American politics, for example, yields studies of television advertising, radio advertising, online advertising, door-to-door canvassing, direct mail, phone calls, emails, text messages, candidate visits, debates, conventions, gaffes, and scandals. Many of these consist of field experiments or survey experiments, allowing researchers to specify causal relationships and effects (Green and Gerber, 2023). While these studies offer compelling and worthy contributions to our understanding of specific campaign effects, they do not necessarily acknowledge each other or explicitly consider the broader question of how much campaigns affect election results overall.[5]

In sum, past work on presidential campaigns largely consists of narrative accounts of what happened in a specific election, or scholarly analyses of specific types of campaign activity, usually in one election only. The former tends to see campaigns as critical for explaining outcomes, while the latter tends to see them as mechanisms by which the impact of broader, contextual factors is realized. However, there have been several notable efforts dedicated to establishing and explaining patterns of strategy, execution, or effects over time. This book follows in this tradition, while focusing more exclusively on Electoral College strategy.

The clear and obvious gap in the literature is that few have attempted to define, measure, and assess presidential Electoral College macro-targeting strategies over the past few decades. One notable exception is Christopher Devine's recent book tracking presidential and vice presidential campaign visits and their effects between 2008 and 2020 (Devine, 2023). Overall, Devine finds that campaign visits rarely influence voting behavior and that, when they do, they generally do so by persuading undecided voters rather than by mobilizing voters (Devine, 2023) While analyses such as these are instructive, the contracted time frame leaves open questions about longer-term developments and impact over time. As a result, we contend that both political scientists and the cognoscenti have much still to learn about patterns or trends in the approaches, actions, and effects of presidential campaigns, especially over a longer time horizon. This project aims to fill this gap. More specifically, we ask three questions. First, what do presidential election campaign strategies look like? Second, to what extent do candidates and campaigns follow their strategies? Third, and perhaps most importantly, do these strategies have any effect on election outcomes? We also grapple with how answers to these questions may have changed over time.

We conclude that campaign strategies from 1952 to 2020 discriminated between and among states, and often among media markets, based on their potential to contribute to an Electoral College majority; that the candidates and their campaigns executed those strategies by allocating the lion's share of their resources in states and media markets most critical to their winning coalition of states; and that these efforts usually produced modest but plausibly important effects in targeted states and media markets. These conclusions, however, mask differences across time, and it is toward this key point that we now turn our attention.

Main Arguments of This Book

Our examination of the Electoral College strategy documents and resource allocation patterns evident in our data leads us to posit that the strategic context of presidential campaigns has changed over time, with three distinct eras since 1952: wholesale campaigning (1952–1972), zero-sum campaigning (1976–2000), and micro-targeted campaigning (2004–2020).

Wholesale Campaigning: 1952–1972

Our nomenclature here notes that this first era is distinguished by the rise of broad-based, mass advertising (especially television), which assumed a place alongside more traditional person-to-person, "retail" outreach. Indeed, over the course of this initial era, TV *overtook* radio and newspapers to become the dominant form of communication with voters, through both paid advertisements and news broadcasts. In this sense, "wholesale" denotes a shift in the *scope and reach* of campaigns as well as a shift in the *mode* of information dissemination and politicking.

Beyond the broad contours that animated each era, the three periods are also distinguished by unique circumstances with respect to information, resources, and connection to other campaign actors (most notably, political parties and interest groups). In the era of wholesale politics, we see the development of polling and an uneven tendency toward systematically collecting and analyzing data. The fruit of these seeds will be fully realized in the second and third eras. With respect to campaign contributions and expenditures, there were few rules in this first era. And because money flowed freely into presidential campaigns, there were inequities in the mix of resources that competing campaigns could use to win elections. Finally, political parties still maintained substantial—though not complete—control over the nominating process, which meant that broader goals (focusing on the success of the party beyond the presidential contest) remained relevant for presidential candidates and their campaigns.

Zero-Sum Campaigning: 1976–2000

The notion of "zero-sum" campaigning refers to the rational choice perspective often associated with the study of economics, whereby resources are assumed to be constrained such that allocating them in one place necessarily comes at the expense of allocating them somewhere else. Although one could hold that all American campaigning is zero-sum, in this second era campaign finances came to be regulated and constrained in ways that made the zero-sum dynamic especially pressing and relevant. The Federal Election Campaign Act (FECA) of 1971[6] redefined campaign finance by placing limits on campaign spending that obviated the need to fundraise during the fall campaign and that created a level playing field for the major party candidates in the general election.

With public funding and caps on expenditures, information from polls, focus groups, and other data sources became more valuable than ever, as presidential campaigns sought to efficiently target their limited resources toward television and radio advertising. The catch-22 was that these campaigns were also often reluctant to invest scarce resources in empirical research that would allow them to more effectively allocate those scarce resources. Along with public funding, changes in the rules for the parties' nominating processes lessened the power of officeholders and party elites.[7] Beginning in 1972, securing the nomination required winning delegates in statewide primary elections and caucuses. This created new incentives for candidates to build their own national campaign organizations rather than primarily mobilizing support among state and local party officials, as had been done in the past. Consequently, the goals of the party became less important in this second era given their increasingly marginal relevance to deciding the nominee.

Micro-Targeted Campaigning: 2004–2020

The title of our final era is meant as a counterpoint to the title of the first. While presidential campaigns remained wholesale—outreach was still broad and television was still an important mode of communication—the development of the internet, big data, and social media transformed campaign communication into something more akin to its old retail form. That is, the information revolution affected electoral politics by enabling campaign outreach to specific individuals rather than merely to geographically targeted areas. Handheld digital technologies became an important means of communicating with voters and the dominant means by which campaigns entered, received, and used data about voters.

These new informational and technological possibilities were accompanied by the passage of the Bipartisan Campaign Reform Act (BCRA) in 2002,[8] which also helped to transform fundraising by increasing limits for individual contributions.[9] Presidential candidates and their campaigns were thus once again positioned to raise and spend hundreds of millions of dollars, rendering the previous era's public financing system obsolete. Unless one was willing to run the risk of being swamped by an opposing campaign that might raise a billion dollars, presidential candidates opted out of funding. This shifted the focus of presidential campaigns away from obsessively worrying about not "wasting" resources to finding better and more effective ways to identify and contact potential (supportive) voters. Despite the enhanced role of interest groups in the wake of BCRA and the *Citizens United* decision,[10] the proliferation of money and information further exacerbated the tendency of candidates and campaigns to develop and rely on their own organizations rather than those of parties or interest groups.

Furthermore, we argue that in each of these eras presidential candidates and their campaigns tended to take different approaches to the nature of Electoral College strategy, its execution, and its targeting goals and tactics. Our specific expectations are summarized in Figure 1.1.

Implicit in these arguments is our theoretical assumption that presidential candidates and their campaigns are strategic actors seeking to win the White House. They are affected by the rules of the game, by the nature and mood of the electorate, and by the actions of their opponents. As these conditional factors shift from election to election—and evolve over longer spans of time—what we expect from our presidential candidates and their campaigns will change in predictable ways.

Note also that while we have some intuitions and make some educated guesses, we do not offer explicit expectations with respect to the impact of campaign efforts on Election Day vote totals across our eras. This is because the developments across eras produce contrary impulses when it comes to how campaigns might (or might not) impact voters. Put succinctly, in the earlier eras there are more persuadable voters, but the means of targeting them with visible and credible messages are limited; while in the later eras,

	Wholesale Campaigning 1952–1972	Zero-Sum Campaigning 1976–2000	Micro-Targeted Campaigning 2004–2020
Strategy	Medium sophistication. Set by national and some state polls. Raising money is key. Communicating with certain voters in a set of critical states in person and via TV.	High sophistication. Set by national and statewide polls and focus groups. Strict campaign finance rules make raising money less important. Communicating with certain voters in a set of critical states in person and via TV.	Very high sophistication. Set by statewide polls, micro-targeted databases, and complex modeling. Raising money is again key. Communicating with voters wherever necessary in person, via TV, and digitally.
Execution	Imperfect, due to limits on communication, transportation, and available voter data.	Improved, as data gets better and reaching voters gets easier through transportation and TV improvements.	Still better, as money is no object and the mechanisms for identifying persuadable voters and delivering salient messages improve.
Targeting Goals and Tactics	Persuading groups of undecided voters identified from aggregated prior election result data using geographically targeted mass media.	Persuading groups of undecided voters identified from polling and focus group data using geographically targeted mass media.	Mobilizing individual likely supporters identified from registered voter lists, personalized contacts, and commercial databases using individually targeted niche media.

Figure 1.1 Presidential Campaign Characteristics across Three Eras.

campaigns have greater ability to target and reach these voters, but there are fewer of them due to polarization. These complicating factors make it difficult to predict how much presidential campaigns might influence partisan vote totals and outcomes, as well as whether this influence (whatever its magnitude) shifts over time.

Novel Sources of Data Underlying Our Analysis

We test these arguments by analyzing detailed data on the Electoral College strategies of Democratic and Republican presidential campaigns between 1952 and 2020. As will be detailed in chapter 2, over the past two decades we have visited numerous libraries and special collections—both public and private—to amass information on the strategic plans of presidential candidates, and to compile data on the two most critical modes of campaigning: candidate appearances and television advertising. In addition to information from these sources, we have examined a comprehensive array of journalistic and academic accounts, which help fill in gaps in the records and validate data from our primary sources. These serve as our main explanatory variables of interest, and we describe them for each election year as well as across time.

Since presidential elections are decided by winning enough states to achieve a majority of votes in the Electoral College, our fundamental unit of analysis is the state. That is, we describe how campaigns categorize states and then how candidate appearances and television advertising are distributed across the states. However, we also offer more granular data and analysis. In U.S. elections, political communication—and especially campaign communication—often occurs at the level of the media market. Broadcast television ads are purchased at the market level, and major sources of local news (including local television news, radio news, and newspapers) publicize candidate appearances at the market level. Therefore, in chapter 8 we look at the campaign and its effects not only in each of the 50 states, but also in each of the country's 210 media markets.[11] This enhances our ability to assess the nature and impact of campaign activity.

There is an extremely large and complex academic literature exploring the potential effects of political campaigns on voters. Some scholars look for campaign effects in the results of opinion surveys, for example by tracking changes over time in the perceived favorability of one candidate or another as recorded in polls and then seeing if the changes in favorability shift immediately following major campaign events like televised presidential debates (e.g.,

Sides, Tesler, and Vavreck, 2018; Stimson, 2004). Other scholars prefer experimental approaches, either bringing voters into laboratory settings to expose them to campaign messages in controlled settings and then measuring immediate opinion changes that might result (e.g., Lau and Redlawsk, 1997), or else randomly selecting groups of voters (e.g., Green and Gerber, 2023) or entire geographical areas (e.g., Shaw and Gimpel, 2012; Gerber et al. 2011) for message "treatments" that happen in real-world campaigns to see what bearing they might have had on later voting patterns. These are excellent approaches for tackling complex problems of causality and, when well-designed, can even reveal which of several possible psychological mechanisms such campaign effects might be operating through. But they are less useful for understanding what happened across an entire electorate on any particular Election Day. For this reason, our approach to assessing campaign impact will focus on state- and market-level presidential vote results.

Focusing on Election Day vote totals across geographic units is the obvious way to gauge what impact presidential campaigns might have on winning an election, but this approach has an important shortcoming that limits its appeal for academic scholarship: researchers using vote totals to assess impact can tell if state-by-state differences in candidate appearances and television ad buys are correlated with Election Day results, but they can't say why, and answering "why" questions is what butters the bread for academics. Like our fellow academics, the authors of this book would also like to know which specific messages and psychological processes might be changing the minds of voters. Towards this end, we are deeply interested in sorting out whether placing ads or candidates in one state versus another influences elections by persuading the undecided or by mobilizing each side's already committed partisans to actually show up and cast a ballot. However, settling a more basic and fundamental question matters even more to us: Does it matter at all on Election Day if campaigns have put their advertising and candidates in some places but not others? Is all the effort and money lavished on the task of moving voters simply a big waste of time? These have been the driving questions behind seven decades of sustained campaign effect research in the disciplines of communication and political science and—at least for the question of presidential elections in the United States—this book presents a definitive answer for the Election Day impact of television spot advertising as well as candidate appearances. We do so by offering simple (to academic researchers, at least), controlled analyses of how strategic categorizations and resource allocations influence shifts in statewide and market-wide votes.

While we are excited to share what we have learned—insights that could not have been produced without several years of painstaking analysis of internal campaign documents retrieved from presidential libraries and limited access archives across the United States—we freely acknowledge that the geographic allocation of scarce campaign resources is only one of many ways a campaign might affect an election. Candidate appearances and television advertising can affect the flow of donations and volunteers (among other things), which themselves might be responsible for any downstream effects on the vote. It is also possible that these campaign activities are designed mainly to influence perceptions of the candidates or their signature issues in ways that make voters more receptive to subsequent outreach by campaign volunteers. Of course, the most basic messaging decision that a campaign can make is its "positioning strategy": how they will characterize what's at stake for the country if the voter chooses their candidate rather than the opponent (e.g., Newman, 1994). Unfortunately, we cannot directly speak to these possibilities in this study. We are content to offer a broader, more clear-eyed examination of the correlation between fundamental aspects of the campaign and the vote. When placed alongside an impressive academic literature that uses more refined and nuanced methods to draw related conclusions about campaign effects using single-election studies, our small and very incomplete step is nevertheless a major leap forward in the field's understanding of how presidential campaigns matter, and whether their impact is different today than in past decades.

Chapter Outlines

This book is comprised of two parts. The first part of the book encompasses the current chapter, as well as chapters 2–5, and focuses on describing strategies as well as chronicling candidate appearances and television advertising in the three eras. The second part encompasses chapters 6–9 and offers statistical analyses of campaign strategies and Election Day effects of these campaign activities, as well as a concluding chapter.

Chapter 2—Strategy, Time, and Presidential Campaigning. Our second chapter presents what we think we know about presidential campaign strategies and their effects on voters and elections. This review draws not only on political science research, but also on relevant journalistic and insider accounts. The dominant perspective is that presidential campaigns are mostly strategic in their allocation of resources, but that campaign outreach is not decisive. Instead, the underlying distribution of party preferences and broader conditional variables such as the state of the economy determine the vote. From this perspective, campaigns function mainly as catalysts that bring about a predictable outcome. We contend that this perspective is temporally limited and that we need more data and analysis to understand properly the role of presidential campaigns in elections over time.

We then present our alternative perspective and our main arguments, which include the three-era model and attendant expectations for strategy, execution, and goals and tactics.

Chapter 3—Wholesale Campaigning (1952–1972). The first empirical chapter of the volume presents Electoral College strategy data for both major party candidates in each election across this initial era. We find surprising levels of sophistication with respect to classifying states as more or less crucial and allocating resources accordingly. The sheer volume of candidate appearances during the fall campaign is also remarkable given transportation limits of the era. Television advertising begins in earnest during this time and allocation patterns are more locally targeted than many contemporary experts assume.

Chapter 4—Zero-Sum Campaigning (1976–2000). This chapter chronicles the second era of presidential campaigns. Again, we present major party strategies and campaign resource allocations in detail, with campaigns in the second era showing an even greater tendency toward identifying battleground states and piling campaign resources into those states. This tendency is consistent with expectations borne of greater information about public opinion and campaign spending limits associated with FECA.

Chapter 5—Micro-Targeted Campaigning (2004–2020). This chapter focuses on the most recent era of presidential campaigning. The new century brought significant changes to the context of these contests, creating additional possibilities for precise targeting and outreach, but also alleviating the resource constraints that pushed campaigns toward concentrating exclusively on narrow segments of the electorate while ignoring others. Once again, we offer detailed descriptive information about the Electoral College strategies of major party campaigns and state- and media market-level data for candidate appearances and television advertising.

Chapter 6—Tracking Electoral Strategy Over Time. In this first chapter of the book's second part, we analyze the factors that explain Electoral College strategies. We consider the role of past competitiveness, electoral votes, the presence of a governor from your party, and other factors in predicting how Republican and Democratic presidential campaigns view individual states. We conduct these statistical analyses for each of our eras, allowing us to test the significance of posited differences over time. We find that the number of battleground states has decreased over time, although this tendency is not as stark as one might think. Similarly, factors that influence whether a state is targeted by presidential campaigns are significant and important but are not perfectly predictive. Our concluding discussion offers reasons for these findings.

Chapter 7—Tracking the Allocation of Resources Over Time. In this chapter, we analyze the extent to which presidential campaigns actually allocate resources according to their strategic plans. Are some states and media markets "zeroed out"? Do candidates visit states and media markets that are not battlegrounds? If so, when, and why? We examine this adherence to strategy between major party campaigns, as well as across time. The analysis is statistical, with assessments of resource allocation across different strategic categorizations. We find that presidential candidates and their campaigns have always allocated their most important resources strategically, although this tendency was particularly evident in the second and third eras of "zero-sum" and "micro-targeted" campaigning. While still adhering to their electoral plans overall, presidential candidates in the micro-targeted era do occasionally appear in electorally "safe" states and media markets to raise money. Due to their swollen war chests, they will also sometimes spend money outside of their battleground universe.

Chapter 8—Putting It All Together: Resource Allocation and Vote Outcomes. In our final empirical chapter, we consider the impact of candidate appearances and television advertising buys on vote outcomes in the states and in media markets. We estimate effects using statistical models that account for confounding variables—most notably past votes—and current national trends. We provide these estimates for Republican and Democratic campaigns within each of the three eras. We find modest effects associated with state-level analyses and slightly larger effects associated with available market-level data. Consistent with a "middling" perspective of campaign effects, similarities in Electoral College strategies and high levels of execution—especially in the most recent era—limit the ability of the campaigns to significantly affect statewide results or Electoral Vote totals. Still, we show that close elections such as 1960, 1968, 1976, 2000, 2004, 2016, and 2020 might have tipped the other way with shifts in how television ads and candidate appearances were allocated across battleground states.

Chapter 9—The Past, the Present, and the Future of Presidential Campaigns. We end our book with a look at presidential campaigns moving forward. Our crucial point, one that animates our approach throughout this project, is that politics is not static and that political actors respond rationally to changes in strategic incentive structures. The state of politics is dynamic in the 2020s, but it is not yet clear how this will affect campaigns substantively or normatively. On the one hand, the ability of presidential campaigns to slice and dice the electorate is at an all-time high, which may lead to narrower outreach. On the other hand, we are witnessing a proliferation of both campaign resources and communicative modes, which may lead to broader outreach. We think both things can be true at the same time: that is, more voters will receive more narrowly tailored campaign messages. Is this atomization of campaign issues and messaging a good thing? That depends on the party system and the ability of the major parties to frame politics in a way that is substantive and compelling for the salient groups in American society.

As we transition to the following chapters, we think it relevant to point out that although we systematically identify hypotheses and test them empirically with statistical models, we attempt to do so in a way that is accessible to a wide range of readers. Whenever possible, we use simple charts and tables to make our results as clear as possible. We find politics captivating. Presidential campaigns are especially exciting and mysterious. This is not something we wish to lose as we look under the hood at the engine of elections. We want our audience to follow our arguments without getting lost in the weeds of specification and modeling issues. We provide the underlying analyses in a technical appendix, so that those who are interested can assess the particulars of our modeling strategies. With this stated, let us move to chapter 2 and the particulars of our study.

2
Strategy, Time, and Presidential Campaigning

A Brief History of American Presidential Campaigns

American presidential campaigns are unique in the history of the world. This uniqueness stems both from the nature of the office and how presidents are selected. The notion of executive authority was, of course, somewhat anathema to many of those charged with crafting a national government in the wake of independence from Great Britain. Nevertheless, the utter weakness of the president under the initial Continental Congresses and then under the Articles of Confederation became one of the key issues addressed at the Constitutional Convention (Berkin, 2003). There was general agreement among the Framers that there should be a single executive. However, a minority of delegates opposed this position because they feared the return of a British-style monarchy. In addition, those supporting a stronger president disagreed over the selection process. Some wanted Congress to elect the president to a lengthy, single term. Others favored popular election but for a shorter period with no term limits (Klarman, 2018). Ultimately, the convention settled on the basic structure that is still (mostly) in place today: the president is to be elected to a four-year term by electors chosen in a manner prescribed by the state legislatures. To win election, a candidate must have the support of a majority of the total number of electors, with no limit on the number of terms the president could serve.[1]

This compromise was hotly debated during the ratification period. On the one hand, Antifederalists charged that "the President would become an elected monarch, that cabals would develop to ensure his reelection, and that the presidential veto power would be abused. They further feared that presidential power to grant pardons would allow the president to conspire with others in treasonable activities with impunity."[2]

On the other hand, Federalists defended the newly redesigned presidency. They argued the United States needed a separate and independent president with sufficient power to enforce federal laws and conduct foreign policy. They

Battleground. Daron R. Shaw, Scott L. Althaus, and Costas Panagopoulos, Oxford University Press.
 DOI: 10.1093/oso/9780197774366.003.0002

also pointedly observed that the American president was limited, checked by the Congress and the Judiciary, and that the president would be accountable to both the people (through re-election processes) and Congress (through impeachment powers).[3]

The ratification of the Constitution initiated the new system and its innovative, unprecedented system for selecting a president, but the particulars of the selection process took time to develop (Klarman, 2018). Notably, the nearly unanimous election (and re-election) of George Washington provided important precedents for the office but masked the true nature of presidential elections. This nature only became apparent in the 1800 presidential contest between John Adams and Thomas Jefferson. In fact, it is our view that the 1800 campaign gave rise to several fundamental and enduring characteristics of U.S. presidential campaigns: these affairs are (1) lengthy, (2) expensive, (3) candidate-centered, and (4) negative. It is not enough, however, to simply assert that campaigns are as we say. In what follows, we carefully document and discuss each of these characteristics, as well as their relevance for the present study of Electoral College strategy.

Presidential Campaigns Are Lengthy

An enduring characteristic of American presidential campaigns is that they are lengthy. In contemporary politics, the discussion of the next election—and preparation for it—often begins right after Election Day. Although the exact length of presidential campaigns has ebbed and flowed throughout the years, the guiding precedent for this tendency was first evident in the 1800 contest. In the 1796 campaign that preceded it, John Adams and Thomas Jefferson had both sought to succeed George Washington as president. Although the former friends distrusted one another and had deeply divergent views about the proper course for the new nation, neither campaigned actively (Larson, 2007). The contest resulted in victory for Adams, with Jefferson—who had the second-most electoral votes—winding up as the vice-president.[4] Jefferson chafed at the limits of the vice-presidency and soon began clandestine machinations to affect the results of legislative races in key states. The formation of the Democratic-Republican Party in the 1790s (or "Jeffersonian Democrats") in response to the Federalist Party (represented by John Adams but led by Alexander Hamilton) ushered in the first party system in the United States—a development Washington opposed and vehemently warned against in his farewell address to Congress. As a practical matter, candidates for legislative and executive office came from one of these two camps in 1800 (Larson, 2007).

This development profoundly affected presidential electioneering in ways that would only surface for the first time in 1800. In the presidential elections of 1788, 1792, and 1796, presidential electors had often been selected directly by voters within the states' congressional districts. Electors were then empowered with two electoral votes each, which would presumably be cast for their preferred presidential and vice-presidential candidates. Mostly, electors were men of distinction, chosen because of their reputations within their local communities: it was hardly a partisan affair (Schudson, 1998). Nevertheless, after 1796, the process for choosing electors became the focus of tremendous inter-party conflict.[5] In states where one party had a legislative majority, that party often sought to change the rules so that the state's electoral votes would be determined and cast as a block (the so-called "unit rule"). In other words, a majority in a state legislature had the potential to deliver all the state's votes for one party's candidate. The minority party, by contrast, often sought to have electors determined by votes within the individual districts. Thus, the Federalists and the Democratic-Republicans waged fierce battles to win control of state legislatures—and the rule-making processes—in the long run-up to the election of 1800. Indeed, the first battlegrounds in American presidential campaigns were actually swing districts in competitive states, such as Delaware, New Jersey, New York, Pennsylvania, and South Carolina.[6]

Although not every presidential election campaign spans a Jeffersonian three and a half years, a lengthy timeframe has remained an important feature of many of these contests. For example, after his controversial defeat in the 1824 presidential election, Andrew Jackson's supporters famously identified county-level organizers in the early days of 1827, roughly two years before the 1828 contest (Meacham, 2008). Abraham Lincoln began positioning himself among different factions of the new Republican Party after the 1858 midterms for a run at the White House in 1860 (Kearns Goodwin, 2006). William McKinley, under the tutelage of Mark Hannah, began lining up supporters for the 1896 Republican primary contests in late 1894 (Rove, 2016). Again, this is not to say that all candidates began two or three years in advance of the presidential election. Rather, the point is that presidential campaigns have generally tended to be longer than those for lower-level U.S. election contests, and they are on average much longer than presidential contests in other democracies.

It is also worth observing that American presidential contests have tended to run even longer since 1968, when the process for determining the major parties' nominees shifted to emphasize the results of a series of primary elections. Prior to that time, party officials controlled the nomination, and the forum for selecting the candidate was the national convention, held in the summer of the presidential election year. But then the Democratic and Republican parties changed the rules: by the 1970s delegates were selected based on the results of statewide caucuses or primary elections in the winter of the presidential election year so that candidates were incentivized to begin organizing earlier than ever. Consider the 2020 election. On January 17, 2017, Donald Trump submitted a letter to the Federal Election Commission stating that he qualified as a candidate for the 2020 presidential election. By late December 2018, Congressman John Delaney, businessman Andrew Yang, Senator Elizabeth Warren, and former Housing and Urban Development Secretary and San Antonio Mayor Julian Castro had formed exploratory committees as they positioned themselves for the Democratic presidential nomination. By the time former vice-president Joe Biden announced his candidacy on April 25, 2019, nineteen other Democrats had declared their candidacies. The election was still more than eighteen months away.

There are, of course, good reasons why presidential campaigns in the United States have tended to be relatively long, especially compared to other contests in the U.S. and even to other countries. First, as already noted, presidential races for most of U.S. history have actually been comprised of two distinct processes—one to select a nominee to represent each eligible party, and a separate contest to select a final winner. Second, in our constitutional structure only presidents have a national constituency, and it takes time to appeal to voters, electors, and supporters across the country. It was even harder to do this before communication became easy and instant. Networks of donors, supporters, and operatives must be cultivated and managed across the whole nation. Third, time may even serve strategic purposes, as wounds conceivably created in bruising, intra-party nomination battles often need time to heal. Whatever the explanation, long campaigns have important implications for Electoral College strategy, as candidates and their advisors not only have to think about *where* to allocate scarce resources, but also *how* to allocate them strategically and in a timely manner so that money and energy are not spent unwisely, too early, or too late. This temporal feature of strategy is even more obvious in the pre-nomination stage—there are many examples of presidential campaigns that have fizzled out in large part because they ran out of money (as well as some failed attempts that left money on the table). One example was in late March 1992 when Massachusetts Senator Paul Tsongas bowed out of the Democratic presidential race claiming his campaign had run out of money, a decision that essentially delivered the nomination to then-Governor of Arkansas Bill Clinton (Toner, 1992). Campaign cash flow problems in the 2004 Democratic nomination battle forced then-Senator John Kerry, who was trailing Vermont Governor Howard Dean for the Democratic nomination, to take out a mortgage on his family home in order to loan his campaign $6 million to keep it afloat. Many analysts believe that, without this infusion of cash, Kerry would not have gone on to become the 2004 Democratic nominee, though he ultimately lost to President George W. Bush in the general election. In sum, timing is important, and long campaigns are different from short campaigns, for many reasons.

Presidential Campaigns Are Expensive

A second enduring characteristic of presidential campaigns is that they are expensive. In part, this relates to their length. The more time spent campaigning, the more money a campaign is likely to need. In part, it relates to the need to reach out to voters in a variety of ways. For example, for one of his presidential campaigns George Washington used his personal cache of liquor and port wine to ply voters with drink on Election Day (Pogue, 2011). This tactic was not unusual; in fact, throughout most of American history candidates and their campaigns were expected to provide hard spirits for voters when they came into town to vote. Washington learned his lesson as a candidate for the Virginia House of Burgesses in 1755, when his "moral" objections to drunkenness (and thus toward providing alcohol for his supporters) was partly to blame for his loss. In the 1758 election, however, he reportedly provided 28 gallons of rum, 50 gallons of rum punch, 34 gallons of wine, 46 gallons of beer, and 2 gallons of cider royal (Pogue, 2011). Despite providing nearly half a gallon of liquor per elector, Washington feared that he had not been lavish enough, telling his campaign manager James Wood that he "spent with too sparing a hand" (Pogue, 2011).

Besides drink, presidential candidates historically relied on sympathetic partisan sources to publish political pamphlets or newsletters promoting their candidacies. The "pamphleteer" contest between supporters of Jefferson and Hamilton in 1800 remains the exemplar (although a case can be made for the 1840 election, as well). Jefferson relied heavily on letters, in which he articulated arguments and crafted messages, which were then distributed to obliging journalists and publishers (Larson, 2007). Perhaps most notably, Jefferson also relied on the notorious James Callender, a writer who had previously penned personal and vitriolic attacks on Washington, Adams, and (especially) Hamilton. Callender wrote, and then published and disseminated, a 183-page pamphlet, "The Prospect Before Us," a scathing screed that mercilessly attacked the sitting president (Dickerson, 2017). Federalist outlets responded in kind, with newspapers such as the *Hudson Bee* and the

New England Palladium quoting liberally from letters often traced back to Hamilton.

Nevertheless, campaigns were most often funded by the candidates themselves and by sympathetic, wealthy contributors. Most campaigns relied on both sources, although the balance often tilted in one direction. Abraham Lincoln went into debt financing his presidential campaign in 1860, though he also received funds from other leaders of the Republican Party. All told, Lincoln spent the equivalent of an estimated $3.2 million in 2020 dollars.[7] But Lincoln's efforts paled in comparison to subsequent campaigns. For instance, in the 1896 presidential campaign, Republican Party candidate William McKinley often collected more than $100,000 in single donations (unadjusted for inflation), thanks to the implementation of an organized, corporate system of fundraising by party leader Mark Hanna (Urofsky, 2020). McKinley's total expenditures were between $6 and $7 million, which equates to over $170 million in 2020 dollars (Chandler, 1998). This led to the passage of the Tillman Act in 1907, which banned corporations from making campaign donations and demanded the filing of financial reports after every election cycle.

However, the banning of corporate money did not dissuade candidates from raising and spending substantial sums. In 1932, Franklin D. Roosevelt and Herbert Hoover raised and spent a combined total of roughly $100 million in 2020 dollars (Alexander, 1992). The 1968 election set a record for presidential campaign spending when Richard Nixon, Hubert Humphrey, and George Wallace raised and spent a combined total of approximately $276 million in 2020 dollars (Alexander, 1992). The flow of money into the 1968 presidential campaign was so concerning that Congress passed the 1971 Federal Election Campaign Act (FECA), which was later amended in 1974, to sharply limit the amounts that could be raised and spent in federal elections. FECA campaign finance reforms succeeded somewhat in containing expenses, but only for a few decades. After the turn of the twenty-first century, contributions and expenditures once again went through the roof as candidates eschewed the public financing system to break every fundraising and spending record on the books. In 2008, Barack Obama and John McCain raised and spent a combined total of roughly $1.7 billion in 2020 dollars.[8] Combined spending in 2020 by Joe Biden and Donald Trump exceeded $1.7 billion. When added to spending by outside groups in 2020, total expenditures in that presidential contest soared above $5.3 billion.[9]

The ever-increasing need for money to promote their candidacies has important implications for campaign strategy. For instance, in contrast to the second era when presidential candidates received equal, lump-sum payments for election expenses so they could focus on campaigning, White

House contenders today must run parallel campaigns for cash as well as votes right through Election Day (and beyond, if needed, to pay off campaign debts). Since candidates' time is not infinite, decisions about whether to focus on votes or dollars tend to involve potentially consequential tradeoffs. Increased transparency, media scrutiny, and near-instant reporting of campaign fundraising requires campaigns to remain competitive in the contest for dollars: falling behind on fundraising not only means fewer resources but could also be perceived as electoral weakness. Fundraising demands also often require candidates to have a presence in financial epicenters (like New York and Los Angeles) they might otherwise overlook because these places are not generally located in pivotal states. Finally, increased transparency in how campaigns spend their money almost in real time provides hints about competitors' strategies that candidates can use to adapt or hone their own macro-targeting efforts.

In sum, American presidential campaigns have always been expensive. Therefore, effectively competing for the office often requires candidate strategy and behavior to reflect the need for raising money, quite apart from the need for attracting votes. However, the impact of money on presidential candidates and their campaigns varies based on the legal circumstances and the costs associated with relevant modes of communication.

Presidential Campaigns Focus More on Candidates than Issues

A third characteristic of U.S. presidential campaigns is that they have generally emphasized whatever is most likely to move voters rather than articulating a coherent set of policies and programs. Campaigns therefore tend to focus on the personal characteristics of candidates (e.g., war hero or flip-flopper, family man or lothario) rather than around specific policies they would implement if elected. In this way, American elections have always been distinct from those in most European countries, where programmatic imperatives often exceed strategic impulses. This is not to suggest that presidential candidates lack important policy differences, nor do we claim that policy positions are taken or discarded based on the latest opinion polls. Rather, the *primary* goal of presidential candidates in the United States is, and has always been, to win the election. Issues are merely a means to that end.[10]

This is no modern development. In the elections of the early 1800s it was considered unseemly for candidates to make promises that might bind them unduly in the discharge of their duties. Rather than running on a platform of policies, these early contests were defined by personality traits and character issues. This dynamic proved frustrating to candidates who preferred a fight over ideas. In the bitter contest of 1828, for example, supporters of John Quincy Adams repeatedly tried to "smoke out" Andrew Jackson's take on Henry Clay's program of congressional aid for economic development through transportation subsidies and protective tariffs. Jackson assiduously avoided any pronouncements on this (or any other) policy question (Meacham, 2008). In 1860, Abraham Lincoln famously avoided being pinned down by his Democratic detractors on the issue of slavery, preferring instead to focus on his desire to preserve the union at any cost (Kearns Goodwin, 2006). This tradition is evident even in more modern times, as with the candidacy of Dwight D. Eisenhower who won two presidential elections based largely on his enormous appeal as the leader of allied forces in World War II. Ironically, until the announcement of his candidacy in January 1952 it was unclear whether Eisenhower was even a Republican (Dickerson, 2017). The candidacy of Donald Trump in 2016 is another excellent example: Americans knew about Trump as a real estate mogul from his media appearances during the 1990s and 2000s and then again as the head of a company from his television show, *The Apprentice*. It was the power of his celebrity and personality rather than his detailed issue positions that drove his appeal. In this regard, Donald Trump's seemingly unusual candidacy was in many ways a continuation of the historical norm.

Despite this consistent tendency, during the time period we are examining an expectation developed among voters and journalists that the candidates should have clear and well-thought-out positions on a wide array of domestic and foreign policy issues.[11] Even by the 1960 election, campaign staff for both sides included notable policy experts who helped develop and articulate both broad programmatic themes as well as detailed positions on a range of issues. The detail and specificity of these positions, however, tends to be somewhat illusory. In fact, candidates may have incentives to be as ambiguous about their policy positions as possible to maximize their appeal to voters (Alvarez, 1997; Alesina and Cukierman, 1990). Moreover, when they do offer specific new programs with attendant details on costs and funding sources, these often hinge on unrealistic economic and political assumptions. At the same time, these positions can also be bland, featuring boilerplate promises to "do more" on a certain issue. For example, in 2020 Joe Biden promised "to get Covid-19 under control." According to *Politifact*, Biden's standard stump speech contained the following "pledge": "I'm never going to raise the white flag and surrender. We're going to beat this virus. We're going to get it under control, I promise you."[12]

Issue promises such as these are crafted to appeal to all people, frequently at the expense of ideological or philosophical coherence.

Perhaps more to the point, campaigns use policies to create and reinforce "positioning strategies" that aim to sharpen the contrast between opposing candidates using broader character images (Powell and Clowart, 2002): Joe Biden is experienced and steady; Donald Trump is a straight talker who gets things done; Barack Obama is young, dynamic, and hopeful; George W. Bush is compassionate and decisive. Note that the candidate-centered nature of American presidential campaigns is more directly relevant for messaging and micro-targeting strategies. It is less important for macro-targeting Electoral College strategies, although candidate images can vary considerably by geographic regions and, more importantly, by states.

The takeaway point is that presidential campaigns see issues as weapons to be wielded in the service of raising money, gaining votes, and winning elections. There are some limitations, as candidates that embrace nonsensical or obviously contradictory issue positions risk inviting journalists and voters to draw negative conclusions about their competence or seriousness. But in deciding which issues to emphasize and then in deciding what positions to take on those issues, candidates and campaigns are thinking first and foremost about improving their chances for election. These strategic decisions about messaging often consider the campaign's macro-targeted Electoral College plan along with the distinctive preferences of voters in the plan's critical states and media markets.

Presidential Campaigns Are Negative

A fourth and final characteristic of American presidential campaigns is that they are relatively negative and, at least after 1796, always have been. That is, presidential campaigns generally prioritize moving voters away from the opposition more than toward their own candidate. Partly, this is because negative information can be more memorable and powerful than positive information. No one remembers the time they *weren't* involved in a car accident on the way home from work; everyone remembers the time they were. In fact, Mattes and Redlawsk (2015) argue that negativity is not only accepted by voters as part of the political process but may even be necessary to convey valuable information that would not otherwise be revealed.[13] Partly, campaigns are negative because both candidates tend to enter a contest with high levels of popularity. Not only do most presidential candidates win their party's nomination because they have a favorable record and are well-liked, but winning the nomination further boosts this favorable reputation. From this perspective, it makes sense for each side to attack the other in order to soften them up.

Consider the incentives from the perspective of both the challenger and the incumbent. Challengers must make the case that the incumbent should be defeated because change is needed. Doing this requires pointing out for voters what the incumbent has done wrong. This virtually assures that there will be a strong critique of the policy decisions and the personal behavior of the incumbent. Incumbents, on the other hand, must defend their record, which they will certainly do. But holding office means taking positions and making decisions that will assuredly offend some portion of the electorate. It is usually in the interest of the incumbent to make the election a comparison of the candidates—rather than a referendum on the incumbent—and that requires "defining" the challenger in an unflattering light. Defining the challenger usually consists of highlighting their lack of experience, their controversial positions and decisions, and their personal shortcomings and failures.

Because of these incentives on both sides, American presidential campaigns nearly from the beginning have been intensely negative, and to such a degree that it remains unclear whether they might have become more (or less) negative over time. To be sure, the 2016 and 2020 elections were fierce affairs. But they hardly seem more so than the election of 1800, during which James Callender wrote that Adams was a rageful, lying, warmongering fellow; a "repulsive pedant" and "gross hypocrite" who "behaved neither like a man nor like a woman but instead possessed a hideous hermaphroditical character" (Dickerson, 2017; Larson, 2007). Meanwhile, the influential president of Yale University publicly suggested that were Jefferson to become president, "we would see our wives and daughters the victims of legal prostitution." Similarly, an influential—and highly partisan—Connecticut newspaper warned that electing Jefferson would create a nation where "murder, robbery, rape, adultery and incest will openly be taught and practiced" (Larson, 2007).

The 1800 election is hardly anomalous. The election campaigns of 1840, 1860, 1876, 1888, 1912, and 1936 all stand as contenders for most outrageously negative (Boller, 2004). Perhaps the strongest contender for the post-1800 negativity throne was the 1828 contest, during which headlines levelled charges of murder, adultery, and pimping against the main candidates. These headlines appeared in highly partisan newspapers that remind us how little today's media have on those of the 19th century when it comes to pursuing a political agenda. To fuel scandal in that election cycle, supporters of incumbent president John Quincy Adams pondered publicly whether Andrew Jackson's wife had been properly divorced from her first husband before marrying Jackson. They accused the Democratic challenger of shacking up with another man's wife and labeled Mrs. Jackson as a bigamist (Meacham, 2008). In response to these allegations, the Jackson campaign fired back with accusations that Adams had lined up an American girl for the pleasure of the Russian Czar during Adams' time as ambassador to Russia. This was in the century before anything like legitimate journalistic investigation would appear in the United States, so newspaper content was largely produced by editors, who often simply republished verbatim anonymous letters addressing issues of the day. The authors of these letters were sometimes the very candidates that the newspapers were defending or decrying. In the case of 1828, candidate Andrew Jackson was known to write letters to the editors of sympathetic newspapers himself, not only to provide material for editors to use in launching scurrilous attacks on the sitting president he was contesting, but also to give them guidance about how to effectively counter opposition attacks made against his own candidacy (Meacham, 2008).

Long before the thirty-second television ad was developed in the mid-20th century, presidential campaigns were getting the word out by publishing campaign songs for their supporters to boisterously sing in public parades. These songs sometimes extolled the virtues of the crowd's preferred candidate, but often focused on the vices and shortcomings of the opposing candidate in the most scathing language possible. Consider this ditty issued in 1840 by the William Henry Harrison campaign against incumbent president Marin van Buren:

> Who rules with an iron rod, who moves at Satan's beck and nod,
> Who heeds not man, who heeds not God? Van Buren!
> Who would his friend, his country sell, do other deeds too base to tell,
> Deserves the lowest place in Hell? Van Buren! Van Buren![14]

Twenty-first century campaigns may be increasingly negative, but they have nothing on those of the mid-nineteenth century. It is hard to tell if Harrison's in-your-face depiction of the sitting president had any impact on van Buren's loss in his bid for re-election in 1840, but it certainly has been a while since any major party candidate depicted their rival as the Antichrist incarnate. Negativity is nothing new.

Nevertheless, negativity can affect campaign messaging and targeting strategies in powerful ways. Attacks, especially those with teeth, require immediate responses before their damage can be allowed to calcify. In the 1992 campaign, for example, Bill Clinton's campaign famously set up a "war room" to allow for rapid response to attacks. Thinking about Electoral College strategy, it is often the case that well-timed or potent attacks can throw off candidates' campaign implementation plans, requiring them to pivot in order to defend themselves or respond in ways that can temporarily or even permanently shuffle their strategic priorities. For instance, campaigns may need to shore up support from their bases in the face of damaging attacks, diverting attention and resources from persuadable voters or pivotal states.

Setting aside whatever normative qualms one might have about negative campaigns, the historical prevalence of negativity is important for our understanding of presidential contests. The distinctiveness of negative information leads presidential candidates to emphasize it when seeking to persuade undecided voters or to mobilize ambivalent partisans. A powerful negative message has potential to influence a campaign's decision whether to target or contest a certain state. Furthermore, the attractiveness of negative information comes at the expense of grand policy visions. Relying on attacks or counterattacks is often an easier, more effective way to draw a sharp contrast between oneself and one's opponent than explaining policy differences. This "ease" creates significant strategic incentives to "go negative," especially when time and resources are limited.

What History Does (and Does Not) Tell Us about Campaigns

This historical review reminds us that American presidential campaigns are lengthy, expensive, candidate-centered, and negative. But what else do we know about them? Less than meets the eye, we argue, because despite the plethora of outstanding studies and data from specific presidential cycles, we still lack a unifying theory of presidential campaigns. This seems to be a curious function of two contrary facts. The first is that presidential campaigns occupy a unique and powerful place in the American consciousness. They are the main course of the American political family's dinner. References abound not only in contemporary news media coverage of politics, but also in popular culture, such as music and film.[15] Comedians routinely roast politicians, of course, but this is especially the case for the presidential candidates as the election nears.[16] Most Americans can recall (or at least recognize) specific lines or gaffes from past presidential campaigns. They mark our collective political memory.

The second fact is that presidential campaigns are too big, too noisy, and too context-dependent to make simple sense. Every four years, they come at us with dozens of characters, plotlines, and memorable events. Even in the context of a single election, they are dizzying affairs where we can scarcely remember what happened last week, let alone last month. Imagine trying to explain to someone who was not there, what the 1992 Clinton-Bush-Perot contest was like. Now imagine creating a coherent theory of presidential campaigns while considering 1992 along with the seven elections that have occurred since that contest. The cacophonous nature of presidential campaigns creates confusion and bias as we seek to parcel out lessons and meaning.

Thus, we are left with a lacuna and a conundrum. On the one hand, we care deeply about presidential election campaigns as a country and as a people. We find them entertaining and important. They create a shared communal experience, even though people have very different feelings about that experience. On the other hand, these campaigns are overwhelming. Connecting them to prior campaigns is difficult because of their sheer complexity and because each is unique in many respects to its moment in history.

Yet we contend that we can leverage the range of presidential elections and the attendant data to create a broader and more compelling understanding of Electoral College strategy and, thus, of American campaigns. To do this, however, we first need to identify more clearly our theoretical expectations about how campaigns think and behave. It is toward this end that we now turn.

Theorizing about Electoral College Strategy, Execution, and Targeting

As alluded to earlier, there is no "grand theory" of presidential campaigns, and there never has been. This much is obvious even to the casual observer. There are, however, several relevant theories about particular aspects of presidential campaigns, the vast majority of which derive from single election studies. Although these theoretical perspectives do not perfectly fit within our three-fold distinction of campaign strategy, execution, and targeting, they are an appropriate starting point for a project seeking to use these distinctions to shed light on the broader endeavor. What follows is an outline of some of the relevant building blocks from past research efforts that shape our theoretical conceptualization of Electoral College strategy and presidential campaigns.

Campaign Strategy

> If you know the enemy and know yourself, you need not fear the result of a hundred battles. If you know yourself but not the enemy, for

> every victory gained you will also suffer a defeat. If you know neither the enemy nor yourself, you will succumb in every battle.
>
> —**Sun Tzu, *The Art of War***

Most research on presidential campaigns begins with the assumption that presidential candidates and their campaigns are strategic actors seeking to win office so they can control policy (Downs, 1957; Riker, 1962).[17] The context of U.S. presidential elections dictates that this goal requires winning a sufficient number of states to secure 270 electoral votes.[18] This strategic task is influenced by the fact that campaigns have limited resources with which to persuade voters to support their candidates. Given these conditions, some scholars have posited that campaigns macro-target states according to their importance in a hypothetical winning coalition. In other words, campaigns are thought to rank-order states according to their predicted two-party vote and then focus resources on the so-called pivotal states, where victory is most uncertain but where winning is most critical to amassing a 270 electoral vote majority (Mann and Shapley, 1960; Longley and Dana, 1984, 1992; Smith and Squire, 1987; Wright, 2009). This approach has a common-sense appeal: journalistic narratives of presidential campaigns often identify and comment on the one state that will supposedly decide the election, such as Ohio in 2004, Florida in 2000, or Michigan in 1960.[19]

Early research along these lines assumed each possible coalition is a particular random ordering of states, leading scholars to argue that a state's power in the Electoral College is the proportion of all possible coalitions in which the state is pivotal (Mann and Shapley, 1960). Subsequent studies often assumed that all coalitions are equally likely to form, and thus suggested a slight bias in favor of larger states (Longley and Braun, 1972; Longley and Dana, 1984, 1992; Longley and Peirce, 1999; Smith and Squire, 1987). This thinking has more recently given way to approaches that amend the (dubious) assumption that all coalitions are equally likely to form. Instead, some recent research has assumed that coalitions form "in the order of their popular vote shares for the winning candidate, where states with the largest within-state vote shares for the winner commit first" (Wright, 2009: 25). A state "pivots" if it changes rank-order in this type of coalition such that it becomes the state critical for an electoral majority. Under this definition, states that commit early, *even if large*, will not be pivotal. Neither will competitive states be pivotal if those states do not supply enough electoral votes to be required in a campaign's minimum winning coalition. Consider New York in Reagan's 1984 campaign. As we explore later, even though the Empire State was highly competitive, Reagan already had such a massive margin of victory nationally that New York did not occupy the pivot position in states committed to his coalition.

In our view, there is something to this notion of pivotal states. Later chapters will confirm that practitioners think this way and that the basic logic of this approach is strategically sound. In this instance, we believe that the existing literature is on to something, although we argue that rank-orderings of the states have a probabilistic character that has not yet been adequately understood. We return to the notion of pivotal states later in this chapter.

Campaign Execution

> To fight and conquer in all your battles is not supreme excellence; supreme excellence consists in breaking the enemy's resistance without fighting.
>
> —**Sun Tzu, *The Art of War***

Rather than describing or predicting Electoral College strategies, another important recent theoretical strand of research assesses Electoral College strategies with an eye toward clarifying whether campaigns make "mistakes" in their classification of states and subsequent allocation of resources. For example, it has been observed that presidential contests under the Electoral College can take one of three game-theoretic forms: lotto, blotto, or frontrunner games:

> Under a Lotto outcome, the probability that a candidate wins a state is a draw from an unknown distribution. In this context, candidates cannot make mistakes, since strategic behavior has no impact on electoral outcomes. According to Blotto . . . outcomes are a product of the resolution of strategic uncertainty. These games have no pure strategy equilibrium, which means that the loser, by definition, made one or more "mistakes," which were unpredictable ex ante. Finally, in a Frontrunner setting, one of the candidates has an advantage that the opponent cannot overcome, assuming best play by the frontrunner. The candidate with the lead always wins, unless s/he makes a mistake; thus, mistakes are identifiable ex ante. Given that candidates can identify mistakes ex ante, we should not witness mistakes often in this class of outcomes. (Merolla, Munger, and Tofias, 2006: 2–3)

In other words, in two of the three scenarios it is either impossible (lotto) or extremely unlikely (frontrunner) for a campaign to make a strategic mistake, while in the remaining scenario (blotto) the impossibility of discerning a winning strategy beforehand makes the notion of a "mistake" essentially meaningless (Merolla, Munger, and Tofias, 2005, 2006).

Although this work is refreshing both theoretically and in its admonition against post-hoc judgments about campaign mistakes, we think its broader conclusions are somewhat overstated for three reasons. First, one can only identify strategic mistakes when one understands *how* strategies are developed. Judging execution therefore requires knowledge of how the campaigns themselves saw the "task at hand." Otherwise, as the aforementioned studies suggest, there is a post-hoc quality to the assessment. Second, we think using static cumulative resource allocation totals as the sole measure of Electoral College strategy is too limiting. Again, as noted in the previous criticism, one must recover the *actual strategies* of the campaigns to thoughtfully comment on execution. Third, we question the assumption that both major party campaigns, in all instances, have similar information and resources. Asymmetries on both dimensions exist in presidential campaigns and could affect both strategy and execution. Put another way, it is problematic to assess strategic execution unless one has information and data on (a) what the campaign knew at the time strategies were developed and implemented, and (b) how much time and money the campaign had to execute its strategy.

In sum, while we agree that post-hoc judgments of campaign strategy and execution are problematic, we disagree with the (implicit) idea that they are beyond assessment. We simply need more data to treat them on their own terms. If we know how the campaigns thought they could get to 270 electoral votes, as well as what was known when they made their plans, we could appropriately assess the execution of campaign strategy. Indeed, a fundamental driver of this book is our belief that the paucity of systematic, empirical data on presidential campaign strategy prevents rigorous testing and refinement of the theories developed by political scientists.

Campaign Targeting

> Let your plans be dark and impenetrable as night, and when you move, fall like a thunderbolt.
>
> —**Sun Tzu, *The Art of War***

The main contribution of recent political science research is the notion that presidential campaigns have become more precisely—if not necessarily more narrowly—focused. This observation merits unpacking. Two core facts inform our thoughts here. First, the main goal of any major party presidential campaign is to secure a majority of electoral votes to win the White House.[20] To do this, candidates and their campaigns must persuade and mobilize enough voters in pivotal states to win those states (Shaw, 2006; Panagopoulos, 2020). The second (and related) fact is that candidates and their campaigns must identify the "correct" states, as well as the "correct" voters within those states, and then obtain their support (Hersh, 2015; Sides and Vavreck, 2013). The first point pertains to the campaign's macro-targeting goals, whereas the second point pertains to the campaign's opportunities for identifying "moveable" voters through specific messaging targeted at particular media markets and individual voters.

Academic studies and journalistic accounts of campaigns have claimed that presidential campaigns falling within our third era (2004–2020) have focused almost exclusively on a small number of pivotal states (Shaw, 2006). This is possible for campaigns because of the increasing prevalence of reliable data on the probability of winning specific states, and the primary implication of this claim is that the number of states in play should have decreased over the 1952–2020 time period. This seems plausible to us, although campaigns—even those in the 2000s—appear to be sensitive to all the errors and uncertainties endemic to estimating election outcomes, which suggests flexibility and inclusivity when it comes to determining which states to contest.

Other studies have charted the rise of individual-level voter targeting based on statistical modeling of statewide voter files (Hersh, 2015; Panagopoulos, 2020). These micro-targeting opportunities have made it possible for campaigns to identify specific voters in pivotal states, and to reach them with messages that have been estimated to have the greatest probability of persuading or mobilizing them. If this conclusion holds, then presidential campaigns in the 2000s and beyond are not only likely to have targeted a smaller number of voters than those of earlier eras, but also to have done so with more precision than past campaigns. There is a contrary possibility here as well: recent campaigns might well be targeting more voters than ever before. Because previous eras tended to target voters based on the political complexion of their geographic location, many voters who might have been receptive to outreach were left untouched back then because they lived in unpromising territory. Think of a Republican voter in Manhattan or a Democratic voter in rural west Texas who would have been ignored in the first and second eras but actively sought in the third. Another reason to expect wider outreach in recent campaigns rather than narrower targeting is the proliferation of money in presidential campaigns from 2004 through 2020, which provides resourcing to expand campaign targeting and outreach beyond what was possible in earlier eras.

Thus, while we are sensitive to the possibility that presidential campaigns may have become more focused and less inclusive, it is also conceivable that the actual proportion of voters who are targeted by a presidential campaign has increased over time.

What about Campaign Effects?

Perhaps the most well-known political science research on presidential campaigns considers the fundamental question of whether candidate strategies and targeted activities—broadly defined—have any meaningful effects on voters or election outcomes. Intuition suggests presidential campaigns persuade voters to support candidates and are therefore critical to elections (see, among others, de Tocqueville, 1835; Berelson, Lazarsfeld, and McPhee, 1954). Nevertheless, in the 1950s and 1960s political science research based on election surveys—most notably the American National Election Study (ANES)—found that while campaigns might persuade a few voters, most voters identify with one or the other major political party and vote in accordance with that identity regardless of what the campaign says or does (Campbell et al., 1960). Thus, persuasive effects should be confined to independent voters and some cross-pressured partisans. Furthermore, independent voters tend to be as susceptible (if not more so) to short-term forces as they are to persuasive campaigns (Berelson, Lazarsfeld, and McPhee, 1954; Campbell et al. 1960). In 2020, for example, exit polls estimated that Joe Biden carried independent voters by thirteen points, and this advantage correlated with expressed attitudes among this group such as fear and hardship caused by the Covid-19 pandemic and attendant economic problems, many of which were blamed on President Trump and Republican leadership.[21] Subsequent work in the 1970s and 1980s acknowledged this basic storyline, even as it explored how much political and economic context might matter for shaping election outcomes (e.g., Nie, Verba, Petrocik, 1976; Fiorina, 1981).

As polls and survey data proliferated in the late 1980s and 1990s, some scholarship raised the possibility that even this reduced role for campaigns in presidential elections might be overly sanguine. These studies emphasized how campaigns largely serve to remind voters of their partisan predispositions (Gelman and King, 1993). In this sense, presidential campaigns may be important to outcomes, but mostly by activating latent partisanship rather than changing hearts and minds. This view suggests that in any given election, campaigns have little ability to move electorates more than a point or two away from a political reality determined by the distribution of partisan identities and short-term political forces (Campbell, 2000; Holbrook, 1996). This research received indirect support from several studies proposing presidential election forecasting models that completely ignored campaign activity by predicting the vote (to varying degrees of accuracy) using economic and political performance variables alone (Tufte, 1978; Fair, 1978; Lewis-Beck and Rice, 1982; Holbrook, 1996).

By the late 1990s, this prevailing sense that presidential campaigns had limited ability to affect outcomes produced a vigorous response from a new generation of political scientists who thought the argument had swung too far in the direction of minimal effects. This response leveraged newly available data and innovative analytic techniques—lab and field experiments, detailed data on campaigning, daily polling estimates, etc.—to estimate campaign effects more precisely. Laboratory experiments showed that negative advertisements could affect both turnout and persuasion (Ansolabehere and Iyengar, 1995). Media market-level data on television advertising by the campaigns showed that these ads could have significant effects on turnout and (occasionally) partisan vote choice (Freedman, Franz, and Goldstein, 2004; Shaw, 1999, 2006). A national rolling cross-sectional survey provided detailed daily polling data in 2000 and 2004 that allowed scholars to isolate the effects of policy pronouncement and campaign events on voters (Johnston, Hagen, and Jamieson, 2004). In addition, more fulsome statistical models were developed to analyze aggregate-level data, and these tended to show campaigning could have statistically significant effects (Finkel, 1993; Holbrook, 1996; Campbell, 2000). The new view coming out of this research was that campaigns were far more powerful drivers of turnout and even vote choice than previous studies had given them credit for.

Since the early 2000s, the pendulum has swung yet again back toward the "modest effects" side of the spectrum. Many recent studies can be sorted into two broad categories, each with its own distinct approach to engaging with the question of presidential campaign effects. First, there are field experiments. This research uses random assignment of subjects to either a campaign treatment group (sometimes mode of outreach, other times message) or a control group to assess the impact of electioneering. When properly done, these studies produce extremely powerful insights on the causal effects of campaign activity. In general, they have shown that effects can occasionally be large, sometimes small, but often fleeting or non-existent (see Green and Gerber, 2023; Gerber et al., 2011). In particular, these studies show that campaigns can have statistically significant effects on turnout even when they have only modest persuasive effects (Kalla and Broockman, 2018).

In the second category, we have careful statistical analysis of cross-sectional and panel polling data (Sides, Tausanovitch, and Vavreck, 2022; Sides, Tesler, and Vavreck, 2018; Sides and Vavreck, 2013) or voter file data (Panagopoulos, 2020). These studies confirm mostly modest effects associated with campaign events and activities. Instead, the data point to the far more determinative role of broader conditions (such as the economy) and contextual variables (such as party identification) in determining voice choice for a particular contest. Consistent with the field experiment studies, the emphasis in this new wave of methodologically advanced studies is on the mobilizing rather than the persuasive effects of campaigns.

One of our main interests in adding to this expansive literature on campaign effects is assessing whether and how often Electoral College strategies, execution, and targeting might move enough votes to affect statewide election results by shifting how many television ads and candidate appearances go to each state. As such, a primary goal is assessing the impact of any differential *volume* of campaigning in a specific statewide contest, rather than the differential *quality* of campaigning (which, at any rate, our novel forms of data cannot ultimately measure). Later, we also consider the possibility that a campaign might overcome a television advertising or candidate appearance disadvantage by simply doing more with less.

Some Practical Theoretical Perspectives on Presidential Campaigning

Our takeaway from this overview of the scholarly research on presidential electioneering is that while political scientists have developed theories of outreach in singular campaigns, these insights have rarely been expanded—let alone tested—across multiple elections.[22] Nor have researchers attempted to acquire systematic information on Electoral College strategies, which seems necessary to us if we want to evaluate the nature and effectiveness of these plans. All of this reinforces our motivation for this book: there is a crying need for research that expands the scope of inquiry into presidential campaigns. Specifically, we need more data on what candidates and campaigns are attempting to do, and we need that data from more than a few presidential elections.

Yet, while previous studies are not definitive, they do provide us with some important and useful insights. Perhaps the most relevant finding in this regard is that contemporary campaigns use information from surveys, past elections, and current voter files to estimate their position in each state and to develop a rank-order of states (Shaw, 2006). We believe that this rank-order determines a campaign's macro-targeting priorities. For example, Table 2.1 offers a

Table 2.1 Hypothetical Rank-Order of States by Estimated Republican Presidential Vote Potential

Rank	State	Current Vote Standing	EVs	Cumulative EVs
1	UT	+48	6	6
2	WY	+41	3	9
3	OK	+34	7	16
4	ID	+32	4	20
5	ND	+30	3	23
6	WV	+26	5	28
7	AR	+24	6	34
8	KY	+23	8	42
9	AL	+23	9	51
10	KS	+22	6	57
11	TN	+20	11	68
12	TX	+18	38	106
13	SD	+18	3	109
14	LA	+17	8	117
15	AK	+14	3	120
16	MT	+13	3	123
17	MS	+12	6	129
18	SC	+11	9	138
19	AZ	+10	11	149
20	MO	+10	10	159
21	IN	+10	11	170
22	GA	+8	16	186
23	**NC**	**+3**	**15**	**201**
24	**FL**	**0**	**29**	**230**
25	**VA**	**−2**	**13**	**243**
26	**OH**	**−2**	**18**	**261**
27	**CO**	**−4**	**9**	**270**
28	IA	−6	6	276
29	NV	−7	6	282
30	WI	−8	10	292

Notes:

"EVs" stand for "electoral votes." Shaded rows indicate states close to being the pivot state. Boldened rows indicate states both close to being the pivot state and contributing to the Republican candidate's electoral majority.

hypothetical presidential election, in which states are rank-ordered based on their estimated current support for the Republican candidate. Again, in practice, the estimates of support, which drive the rank-order, would be based on a statistical model incorporating the most recent polling data, state-level historical vote tendencies, and individual-level voter file records. The estimates and rankings are therefore dynamic, with states perhaps moving slightly in the rankings as new data flows into the models. Overall, however, these changes would be minimal.

Let us focus therefore on this hypothetical snapshot in Table 2.1. Under these circumstances, we expect that the Republican campaign would classify North Carolina, Florida, Virginia, Ohio, and Colorado as "battleground" states. This is because the most viable path to a 270 electoral vote victory consists of carrying these states, but it is also because they are the weakest/riskiest states in this minimum winning coalition.

If we were *only* focused on pivotal states—those most likely to be decisive to our winning majority—we would stop there. However, we expect that a campaign facing the posited hypothetical rank-order would also designate states such as Iowa, Nevada, and Wisconsin as "battlegrounds." This is because we assume that presidential campaigns prize strategic flexibility. Campaigns understand that (1) electoral politics are dynamic, which means differences in rank-orderings are often tiny and subject to change, and (2) the information used to develop rankings is imperfect. This creates uncertainty. The result is that targeting states such as Iowa, Nevada, and Wisconsin could provide alternative paths to a majority if something goes wrong with the minimum winning coalition.[23]

Note our use of the word "battleground" in the preceding description. Recently, it has become common to refer to states critical to winning an Electoral College majority as "battleground" or "swing" or even "pivot" states. We use "battleground" here, however, to identify states designated by a presidential campaign as being of the highest priority. We further use "lean" to identify states designated as being consequential but not of the highest priority, and "base" to identify states designated as safely Republican or Democratic and therefore relatively "out of play" because the partisan advantage in these states is so large and unlikely to change in the short run.[24] These terms—or, more precisely, their attendant categories—allow us to standardize the strategies of presidential campaigns and facilitate over-time comparisons. We elaborate on this methodology shortly, but it is important to reiterate that *battleground states are not always competitive states*. In a nationally tight presidential election like 1976 or 2000 the states most likely to provide a candidate's 270th electoral vote are also likely to be electorally competitive. But in a race where one candidate is a decided underdog, as in 1984 or in 1996, the states around the 270 electoral vote threshold—the battleground states, according to the campaigns—are likely to tilt decidedly toward the national favorite.[25]

In such cases, the battleground states needed to secure the underdog's victory may tilt lopsidedly toward the opponent. Despite being less competitive than would be preferred, for the underdog these are the states that are needed to win. We return to this point later.

To be clear, the theory underpinning our strategic categories of states is that presidential campaigns use rank-orders for establishing "cut-points" to classify states into a small number of distinct categories that broadly determine the types and amounts of attention they will receive. As suggested earlier, where these cut-points fall in the rank-order of states presumably depends on a number of factors, including the estimated vote, uncertainty about the vote, and the overall competitiveness of the race. An important task for this book is to measure the influence of these (and other) factors to better understand how strategy informs execution on the campaign trail.

Our theory with respect to strategic execution on the part of presidential campaigns follows directly from the logic sketched earlier. Candidates and campaigns should tend to allocate resources based on their strategic plans, but they might fail to do so for any of three reasons. First, because the strategic plan is unclear or there are organizational impediments to implementing it. Second, because they lack the resources in money or candidate time to implement the plan. Third, because other strategic priorities come into play that require diverting from the plan. For example, a presidential candidate might campaign in a competitive congressional district—one that is not in a battleground state—to help his party win a majority in the House of Representatives (Bartels, 1984). With these three reasons in mind, we still expect that campaign resource allocations should tend to adhere closely to campaign strategies.

Up to this point, our theoretical perspective has assumed that candidates and their campaigns are rational actors seeking to maximize their prospects for winning the election. When we consider campaign effects, however, our focus expands to encompass voters. As such, we have both micro- and macro-level theoretical assumptions for this aspect of the campaign. At the micro-level, we assume that voters are exposed to the presidential campaign, yet because most voters also identify with one party, they are therefore only somewhat open to persuasion (Campbell, et al. 1960). Independents are the most movable, but they are also the most unpredictable because they tend to be least interested in politics and least likely to vote. At the macro-level, this set of assumptions constrains the net effect of persuasion because the most persuadable segment of the electorate is unlikely to cast a ballot on Election Day.[26] Similarly, net campaign effects are also constrained by the fact that persuasion runs in different directions: for every Republican who can be persuaded to vote for the Democrat, there is a Democrat who can be persuaded to vote for the Republican.

Persuasion is, however, only one aspect of what we mean by campaign effects. We also have theoretical assumptions about mobilization. At the micro-level, we assume that voters are differentially likely to participate, owing to varying interests, unique perceptions of the candidates, and different personal circumstances that make it more or less costly to cast a ballot. We further assume that campaign outreach can increase the perception that the election is important and can decrease the informational costs that impede participation. At the macro-level, this creates incentives for campaigns to identify and target voters who would probably support the candidate if they could be motivated to cast a ballot at all. As with persuasion, the net effects of mobilization activities are likely to be constrained. So, when we use the term "campaign effects" throughout this book, we are thinking of both persuasion effects and mobilization effects. Indeed, our most basic definition of a campaign effect is any detectable Election Day difference in popular vote totals that can be reasonably attributed to geographic variation in campaign allocations of advertising dollars and candidate appearances across the Electoral College map.

Ultimately, while the detailed evidence of Election Day impact across the 1952 to 2020 period that we bring together in this book can tell us when and how often campaign activities might change election outcomes, our reliance on Election Day vote totals as the key measure of campaign influence leaves us unable to distinguish between persuasion effects and mobilization effects that might be associated with where campaigns put their ads and candidate visits during the general election campaign. A recent study of candidate visits in presidential election cycles between 2008 and 2020 suggests that while effects overall tend to be muted, visits are most likely to affect outcomes by persuading undecided voters than by mobilizing supporters (Devine, 2023). While we find these results to be quite plausible, we concede that the data at our disposal do not allow us to separate these two kinds of impact with any confidence. We can tell if turnout is higher or lower than last time and whether the Republicans or Democrats received more or less votes than in the previous election, but the aggregate Election Day vote totals at the heart of our analysis cannot reveal whether these year-over-year differences are due to mobilized co-partisans or changed minds. We nonetheless can say whether a campaign's decision to spend ad dollars in one state or to send candidates to another makes any detectable difference to what happens on Election Day. And we will, in chapter 8.

Research Questions and Arguments

As outlined in chapter 1, this book asks three questions. First, what do presidential election campaign strategies look like? Second, to what extent do candidates and their campaigns follow their strategies? Third, do they work? Again, our main argument is that the strategic context has changed over time, such that there have been three distinct eras of presidential campaigns since 1952. To assess this claim and to answer our questions, we have amassed an unusually rich array of data to help us unpack the story of modern presidential campaigns.

Data and Design

A consistent theme of this book is that past studies of presidential election campaigns have been limited by a lack of information on Electoral College strategies. Even though they play out in plain sight, the strategies that guide these campaigns are closely guarded secrets. We offer an unprecedented examination of presidential campaigns by reconstructing and analyzing Electoral College strategies across all 18 elections of the television era, from 1952 to 2020.

Building this dataset required us to visit the presidential libraries of Dwight Eisenhower, John Kennedy, Lyndon Johnson, Richard Nixon, Gerald Ford, Jimmy Carter, Ronald Reagan, George H. W. Bush, Bill Clinton, and George W. Bush to view campaign documents pertaining to the candidates' Electoral College strategies. We also visited the libraries (or viewed the official papers) of defeated presidential candidates Adlai Stevenson, Barry Goldwater, Hubert Humphrey, George McGovern, Walter Mondale, Michael Dukakis, and Robert Dole, as well as special collections (including the Robert Teeter Papers at the University of Michigan and the several collections at the Hoover Institution Library) that offered relevant information from the Goldwater, Nixon, Reagan, and G.H.W. Bush campaigns. Figure 2.1 offers an example—from the 1980 presidential campaign of Ronald Reagan—of the strategy documents we found at these sites. The "Reagan for President" plan is not unusual and provides explicit corroboration of our assumption that campaigns have sophisticated Electoral College strategies.

To cross-check information from the libraries and collections, we also reviewed post-election presentations as well as journalistic and insider narratives for information on strategy. As noted already, the election debriefing conferences sponsored by Harvard University and by the University of Pennsylvania often offered information on presidential electoral strategies. In addition, the narrative accounts of presidential campaigns from journalists were occasionally instructive, as were insider accounts from people such as Gary Hart (McGovern), Martin Schram (Carter), and Stephen Shadegg (Goldwater). Finally, the first author of this book helped develop Electoral College strategies in the 1992, 2000, and 2004 election campaigns and was able to provide insight into those elections.

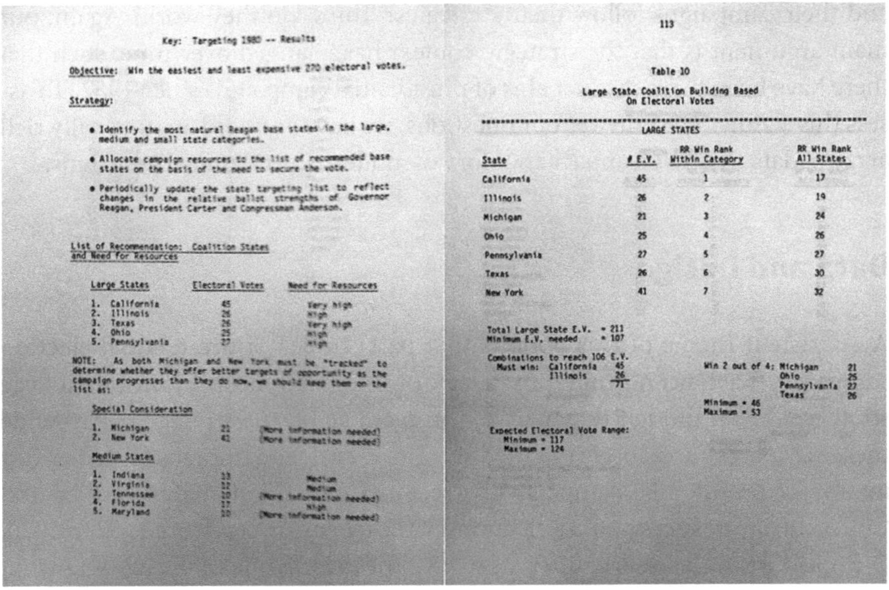

Key: Targeting 1980 -- Results

Objective: Win the easiest and least expensive 270 electoral votes.

Strategy:

- Identify the most natural Reagan base states in the large, medium and small state categories.
- Allocate campaign resources to the list of recommended base states on the basis of the need to secure the vote.
- Periodically update the state targeting list to reflect changes in the relative ballot strengths of Governor Reagan, President Carter and Congressman Anderson.

List of Recommendation: Coalition States and Need for Resources

Large States	Electoral Votes	Need for Resources
1. California	45	Very high
2. Illinois	26	High
3. Texas	26	Very high
4. Ohio	25	High
5. Pennsylvania	27	High

NOTE: As both Michigan and New York must be "tracked" to determine whether they offer better targets of opportunity as the campaign progresses than they do now, we should keep them on the list as:

Special Consideration		
1. Michigan	21	(More information needed)
2. New York	41	(More information needed)

Medium States		
1. Indiana	13	Medium
2. Virginia	12	Medium
3. Tennessee	10	(More information needed)
4. Florida	17	High
5. Maryland	10	(More information needed)

113

Table 10

Large State Coalition Building Based On Electoral Votes

LARGE STATES

State	# E.V.	RR Win Rank Within Category	RR Win Rank All States
California	45	1	17
Illinois	26	2	19
Michigan	21	3	24
Ohio	25	4	26
Pennsylvania	27	5	27
Texas	26	6	30
New York	41	7	32

Total Large State E.V. = 211
Minimum E.V. needed = 107

Combinations to reach 106 E.V.
Must win: California 45
Illinois 26
71

Win 2 out of 4: Michigan 21
Ohio 25
Pennsylvania 27
Texas 26
Minimum = 46
Maximum = 53

Expected Electoral Vote Range:
Minimum = 117
Maximum = 124

Figure 2.1 Strategic Plan for the 1980 Ronald Reagan Campaign

Source: Reagan for President, Campaign Plan, 6-29-1980 (Draft 2), Richard Wirthlin—Political Strategy (Series IV), Planning and Strategy Files (Sub-Series A), Box 177, Ronald Reagan 1980 Presidential Campaign Papers, 1964–1980. Ronald Reagan Library.

Based on this information, we develop summary measures of Electoral College strategies, which we present for each major party candidate for every presidential election from 1952–2020. There was, of course, considerable variability in the nomenclature used by different campaigns. Our goal, however, is to discern similarities and to develop a plausible, consistent classification scale. After examining data from each campaign, we create a common scale encompassing five categories: Republican Base (+2), Republican Lean (+1), Battleground (0), Democratic Lean (−1), and Democratic Base (−2). We adopt this scale based on input and advice from several former presidential campaign consultants.[27] To code each campaign's strategy, two different researchers independently classified the states using this five-category scale.[28] We discussed differences in coding and resolved them by consensus. Depending upon the analytic task at hand, we can also jettison the partisan direction of categories by recoding −2 or +2 states as 0 (safe), −1 and +1 as 1 (lean) and 0 as 2 (battleground).

Table 2.2 offers an example of this coding based on 1976 data from Jimmy Carter's campaign. In this case, Carter's team identified 21 states worth 213 electoral votes as likely (base or leaning) Democratic. They viewed 8 states, worth 210 electoral votes, as battlegrounds. Carter therefore needed to win 57

Table 2.2 1976 Electoral College Strategy—Jimmy Carter

# of states	Base Democratic	Lean Democratic	Battleground	Lean Republican	Base Republican
1	Alabama (9)	Florida (17)	California (45)	Connecticut (8)	Alaska (3)
2	Arkansas (6)	Maryland (10)	Illinois (26)	Delaware (3)	Arizona (6)
3	D.C. (3)	Missouri (12)	Iowa (8)	Indiana (13)	Colorado (7)
4	Georgia (12)	Texas (26)	Michigan (21)	Montana (4)	Idaho (4)
5	Hawaii (4)		New Jersey (17)	Nevada (3)	Kansas (7)
6	Kentucky (9)		New York (41)	Oregon (6)	Maine (4)
7	Louisiana (10)		Ohio (25)	South Dakota (4)	Nebraska (5)
8	Massachusetts (14)		Pennsylvania (27)		New Hampshire (4)
9	Minnesota (10)				New Mexico (4)
10	Mississippi (7)				North Dakota (3)
11	North Carolina (13)				Oklahoma (8)
12	Rhode Island (4)				Utah (4)
13	South Carolina (8)				Vermont (3)
14	Tennessee (10)				Washington (9)
15	Virginia (12)				Wyoming (3)
16	West Virginia (6)				
17	Wisconsin (11)				
# of States	**17**	**4**	**8**	**7**	**15**
# of EVs	**148**	**65**	**210**	**41**	**74**

Notes:

Electoral votes are indicated in parentheses.

votes from this pool of 210 to get to a 270 electoral vote majority. California, worth 45 electoral votes in 1976, was the obvious prize in this election, as a win in the Golden State opened the door to numerous other winning combinations. But even without California, Carter's campaign had a range of strategic options.

Our measures of campaign resource allocations are in-person candidate appearances and television advertising. There are, of course, many other ways that presidential campaigns reach out to voters. Visits from the presidential or vice-presidential candidates are the most time and labor intensive investments, while television advertising is the most capital intensive. From even a cursory glance at internal records or news media coverage, one can see that these two categories of effort also command more attention than other campaign activities. For tracking in-person campaign appearances by presidential and vice-presidential candidates, we confine ourselves to the traditional September 1 to Election Day general election campaign timeframe.[29] Within that (roughly) ten-week and quadrennial period, we have amassed a complete dataset of public appearances made by every Democratic and Republican presidential and vice-presidential candidate from 1952 through 2020. In building our database of appearances, we consulted both campaign documentation as well as local news media coverage. For incumbent presidents (and vice-presidents) seeking re-election, we also referred to the daily calendar of the White House. To fill gaps in the calendar and to cross-check our data, we referenced the daily digital newspaper archives of the *New York Times* and *Chicago Tribune*, both of which consistently and comprehensively tracked the campaign appearances of presidential candidates. Although we record the city or town of the appearance, we code these at the county, media market, and state levels in our datasets. We should also note that what we are estimating here are public appearances in a specific locale, as opposed to "days" in that locale. For example, a candidate could give Florida speeches in Gainesville, Orlando, and Miami on a single day, and would tally three appearances in our dataset. We do not consider time at work (say, in the White House or Senate) as a candidate appearance, nor do we count time at home or in preparation for a debate or major speech. In short, our candidate appearance count variable requires a public appearance, one that presumably had at least a chance of being covered in a local newspaper or on a local television or radio news broadcast. Finally, and by extension, we do not count fundraisers unless they are public events.

Statewide estimates of television advertising by the campaigns and parties are more difficult to come by. Our trips to archives and libraries as well as (occasionally) personal connections allowed us to fill this gap. We compiled a comprehensive record of spot advertising buys for each major-party campaign in every general election from 1952 through 2020 except for 1960, sometimes coming from the Federal Communication Commission (FCC), as in 1952, 1956, and 1972 for every media market in the country, and in several other years at the state level,[30] sometimes from the records of one or more of the campaigns themselves, as in 1952, 1956, 1976–2004, sometimes from the Campaign Media Analysis Group, as in 2000–2016, and sometimes from Advertising Analytics, as in 2016 and 2020. The raw data are most often in the form of advertising expenditures at the media market level.[31] When available, we analyze market-level activity and its influence on votes (more on this shortly), but we also aggregate these to the state level. These data complement those for candidate appearances; candidate schedules allow us to analyze how Electoral College strategies affect the allocation of labor, while television advertising allows us to analyze how they affect capital.

A final, critical piece of the puzzle involves collecting data on election results. These allow us to gauge how campaign strategy and resource allocation affect election outcomes. Retrieving statewide election results for specific years is straightforward, although it is important to account for third party and independent candidate support, as well as for ballot quirks in some states during the early years of our period.[32] Calculating media market-level results is far more difficult, but we have done this going back to 1952. Aggregating county-by-county results into media markets was necessary for us to leverage fully the more granular data we have for candidate appearance and television advertising.

Preview of the Analysis

With these data in hand, our analysis proceeds on two distinct levels. On one level, we emphasize basic descriptive statistics for both Electoral College strategies and the allocation of resources within and across strategic categories. For example, we examine which states were most often classified as battlegrounds across our period. Is there a "big state" bias? We also consider whether the number of battleground states is decreasing across our period. Are the number of targets shrinking as information (polls, voter file analyses) and polarization become more pervasive? We look at strategies versus outcomes. Do campaigns make "mistakes" in their classifications? We consider symmetry and overlap in strategy. Do Republican and Democratic campaigns size up the election in the same ways? Finally, yet importantly, we assess the execution of campaign strategies. Did the campaigns adhere to their strategic plans in allocating precious resources? To the extent that they deviate from a strict reading of those plans, we try to explain why. Moreover, we look at these issues within and across the three eras, mindful of the impact that shifting politics and resources can have on campaigning. These analyses occupy the first three empirical chapters of the book.

On the second level, we specify and estimate statistical models to assess a different set of key questions. Once again, given that we distinguish conceptually between and among campaign strategy, execution, and targeting, three specific analyses are critical for this study. First, we seek to understand the development of campaign strategies. Second, we seek to understand the efficacy of strategy on resource allocation. Third, we seek to understand the impact of campaign resource allocation on election outcomes. For each analysis, we specify and estimate regression models with appropriate controls. These correlational analyses—conducted within and across our three campaign eras—allow us to assess the distinctive and dynamic impact of different factors on macro-targeting strategy, of macro-targeting strategy on the allocation of campaign activity, and of campaign activity on the distribution of Election Day votes. These more sophisticated analyses animate the final three empirical chapters of this volume.

With this design in mind, we now turn to our empirical and historical overview of presidential campaigns, beginning with the first era, which starts with Eisenhower-Stevenson and culminates with Nixon-McGovern.

3

Wholesale Campaigning (1952–1972)

Of Madison Avenue and Slush Funds

For our analysis, the first era of the modern American presidential campaign begins with the Eisenhower elections of the 1950s and ends with Nixon's decisive (if retrospectively tarnished) triumph in 1972. While any designation of campaign eras involves some subjective appraisal, based on our review of our data as well as the historical record, we think this categorization is imminently plausible. To see why, let's first consider the election that occurred right before the start of our first era.

The 1948 presidential campaign occupies a special place in the heart of American election lore. Harry Truman's 1948 "whistle stop" campaign—marked by the Democrat's extensive use of personal appearances and speeches made from the back of a train—is often cited as an example of electioneering that changed the trajectory of presidential voting dynamics. Trailing badly in the polls, Truman took to the hustings in the summer and fall of 1948 to reframe the contest against Republican nominee Thomas Dewey (Figure 3.1). He traveled a total of 31,000 miles on train rides across the country, making 352 speeches (White, 2015). Truman's campaign paid the news media to print and publicize these speeches, running out of money several times and having to replenish their campaign coffers with appeals on the trail (White, 2015). His blistering attacks on the Republican Party and the Dewey-Warren ticket gave rise to the famous call to "Give 'em hell, Harry!" (to which the president supposedly replied, "I only give 'em the truth . . . they just think it's hell!") (Boller, 2004). Because recalcitrant New Deal Democrats were flirting with the idea of voting Republican based on a set of grievances with the incumbent Democratic president, the goal of the campaign was to remind base voters why they identified with their party and rejected the GOP. Setting aside the intriguing question of how much the whistle-stop campaign moved voters, it is important to note that this was the last campaign to focus on railroads and partisan newspapers.[1] It is legendary, but somewhat archaic in ways that mark it as the end of an earlier era of campaign style.

Battleground. Daron R. Shaw, Scott L. Althaus, and Costas Panagopoulos, Oxford University Press.
 DOI: 10.1093/oso/9780197774366.003.0003

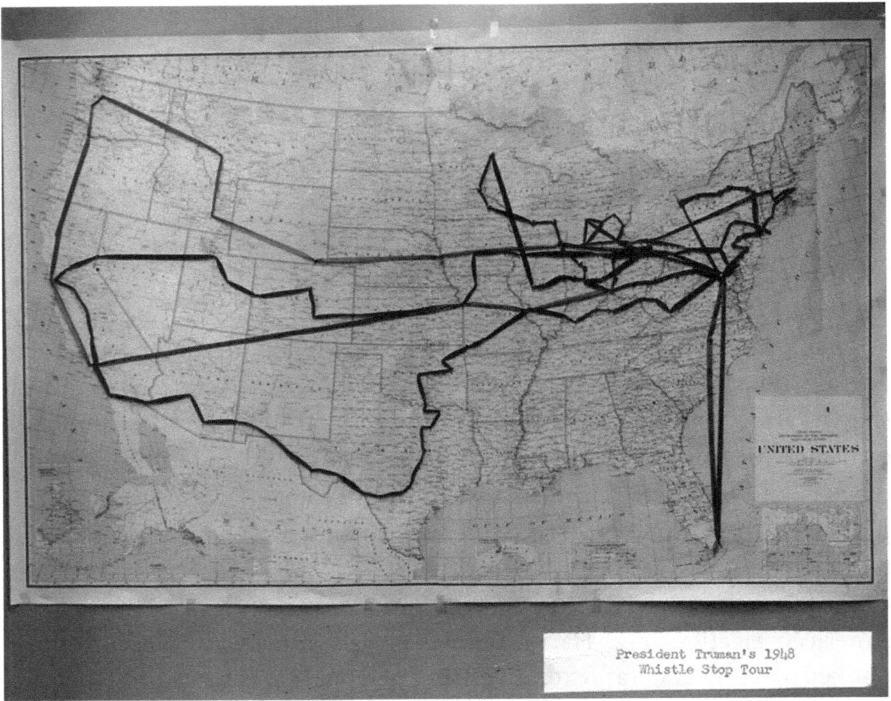

Figure 3.1 Harry Truman's "Whistle-Stop" Campaign Tour
Credit: Harris & Ewing.
Source: Harry S. Truman Library (Accession Number: 2006-175). https://www.trumanlibrary.gov/photograph-records/2006-175

So, what changed between 1948 and 1952? Most critically, the 1950s ushered in the era of television. In Figure 3.2, we use county-level data on the percentage of households with televisions to show the rapid proliferation of the new medium from 1953 to 1960. The spread of television from the urban areas of the country to the farthest reaches of the continent occurs within a single decade.

In terms of campaigns, personal appearances remained an important mechanism for communication, but the potential for reaching mass audiences with persuasive visual messages made television advertising an increasingly important part of presidential elections alongside the more traditional radio advertising, which had been used by national campaigns since the 1930s. In addition, while the national and state party organizations remained powerful players in the nomination process, starting in the 1950s primaries and caucuses began to become more important as venues for demonstrating a candidate's national viability within the convention-driven nomination

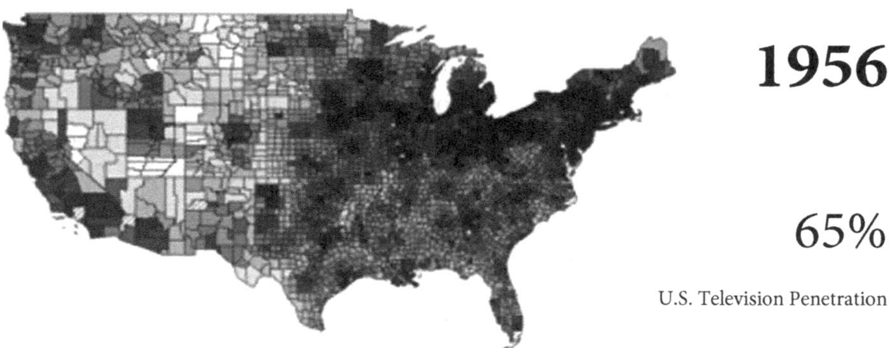

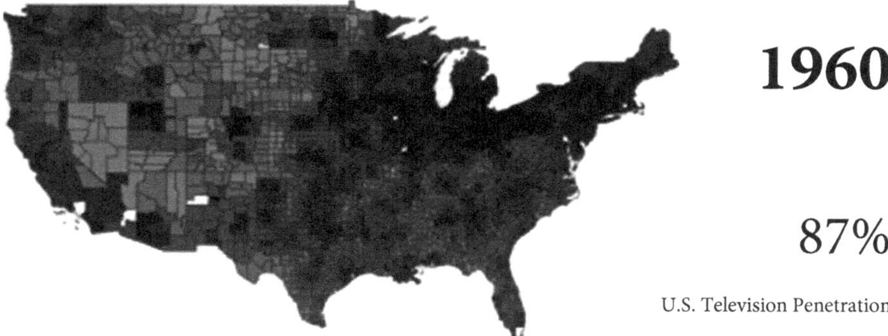

Figure 3.2 Rapid Growth in Television Penetration from 1953 to 1960
Source: Columbia Broadcasting System, *Television Magazine*

system. For example, winning a small number of crucial primary contests was key to Kennedy's 1960 nomination strategy for convincing party insiders that a Roman Catholic candidate could appeal to a wide range of American voters (White, 1961). Although these contests did not become determinative until the 1970s, their increasing relevance—coupled with the ability of candidates to reach audiences directly through television advertising—laid the groundwork for the rise of candidate-centered politics in lower-ticket offices and for the sharpening of the focus on candidate characteristics that had always been part of Electoral College campaigning.

The 1950s also saw significant advances in public opinion polling and marketing research methodologies, as well as their increasingly refined application to political campaigns. In the memos and research files from the Eisenhower and Stevenson presidential campaigns, we see that past election results from the state and county levels were the main basis for determining where the campaigns should focus their messaging efforts. In part this resulted from the polling debacle of 1948, when national pollsters using old-fashioned quota samples predicted a Dewey landslide by failing both to accurately assess Dewey's true level of popular support and to detect Truman's rapid rise in popularity late in the campaign (Converse, 1987). It would take a few election cycles before pollsters using more modern random probability sampling techniques would once again inspire confidence that their methods could accurately predict election outcomes. Despite this temporary hiatus in the respectability of opinion survey data, polling results at the state and national levels were beginning to inform the 1950s campaigns, especially on the Republican side. By the 1960 Kennedy-Nixon contest, we see the targeting of resources by both sides based on polling data integrated with historical voting data and commercial data detailing the preferred broadcast programs and news sources of specific types of voters (Oliphant and Wilkie, 2017; White, 1961). This trend only becomes more pronounced with each subsequent election.

Another element of this new, modern era is the heightened importance of money. To be sure, American presidential campaigns have always required cash, and lots of it. However, the increasing importance of television advertising as the dominant means of political communication along with the rise of modern polling and marketing techniques increased the costs of campaigning for president. This dynamic is most obvious in the campaigns involving Richard Nixon. From the slush fund scandal in 1952 that prompted the famous "Checkers speech" to the slush fund scandal involving payments to those involved in the Watergate break-in, Nixon is an avatar for the general ascension of money to hallowed status in presidential campaigns.

In 1952, the Republican ticket of Eisenhower and Nixon spent roughly $6.6 million ($57.7 million in 2020 dollars) on the general election campaign (Heard, 1962). In 1972, the Republican ticket of Nixon and Agnew spent $37.6 million ($232.8 million in 2020 dollars) (Alexander, 1976). That constitutes well over a five-fold increase in campaign spending. On the Democratic side, the increase was from $5.0 million in 1952 ($48.8 million in 2020 dollars) to $13.0 million in 1972 ($80.5 million in 2020 dollars).

In short, the 1950s saw the emergence of "wholesale" presidential campaigns, in which persuasive messages were disseminated broadly and rather indiscriminately to ideologically diverse audiences through radio and increasingly through the nascent medium of broadcast television. Mobilization was left to the parties' grass roots operations, while Madison Avenue marketing techniques were for the first time routinely applied to the "selling" of presidential candidates.

Expectations in the Era of Wholesale Campaigning

This broad narrative describing the six presidential election campaigns from 1952 through 1972 suggests specific research expectations across our three dimensions. First, with respect to strategy, we expect that these campaigns operated with what we characterize (relative to later campaigns in the second and third eras) as "medium sophistication." We do not, of course, expect that campaigns viewed all states and all voters as equally in play. The relevant question is the extent to which distinctions were made between and among states in Electoral College plans and what types of information served as the empirical basis for those distinctions. We think it likely that presidential campaigns in this era relied on past voting data, especially the most recent presidential and mid-term election, along with some state and national polls. Our expectation is that they did, in fact, identify states as critical for winning the election and that they targeted these states with greater activity and resources as this first era progressed. But the limited types of real-time data available on any current race during this "wholesale campaigning" era probably means that plans were inclusive, with more states on the target list due to the lack of information on the dynamics of the contest at hand and the need for strategic flexibility. It is also likely that they identified and targeted broad groups of voters, selectively mobilizing key constituencies and persuading swing voters. We further presume that there was an emphasis on efforts to raise money, as costly forms of television advertising became increasingly important.

Second, with respect to the execution of strategic plans and goals, we hypothesize that the campaigns were rational but "imperfect." That is, resources such as candidate appearances and television advertising were disproportionately allocated into states deemed most important to the outcome, but that the highest priority states did not necessarily receive attention commensurate with their status because of the financial, communication, and transportation limits of the era. Put another way, candidates and their campaigns needed to raise money, which necessitated time and energy spent on this rather than reaching out to voters. They were also limited by the small number of television network options (CBS, NBC, and ABC) and the scarcity of detailed data on audience habits and preferences in the 1950s and 1960s, which made it difficult to precisely target key constituencies. Finally, due to the limits of air and road travel they were not able to campaign in smaller, harder-to-reach states without a substantial investment of time.

Third, with respect to targeting goals and tactics, we expect that candidates and campaigns in this era focused on persuading undecided voters in key media markets and counties in battleground states through mass media, such as television and radio. That is not to say that campaigns did not use more traditional outreach, such as door-to-door contact, nor do we think they neglected mobilization efforts. The overriding focus, however, is more likely to have been on persuasion with television as the dominant means of communication.

The historical context of the first era has potential implications for campaign effects, as well. Whatever the strategic acumen of presidential campaigns of the era, the ability of campaigns to identify and reach voters was limited. This is certainly so compared to today's campaigns, with their voluminous and granular data on political behavior and consumer habits. On the other side of the ledger, voters in this era were decidedly less partisan than they are today, and more open to candidate and issue appeals. Democrats voted for Republicans, and vice versa, at much higher rates in the 1950s and 1960s than in the 2010s and 2020s.

How do we assess these claims and expectations? We begin by pulling together and analyzing descriptive information on each of the presidential campaigns. As noted in chapters 1 and 2, these data are from the campaigns themselves, either in the form of contemporaneous memoranda and reports or from post-election biographies or analyses. Key players from the campaigns most often house their papers in presidential libraries or along with the political papers of those they served under, and we leverage these to gain unprecedented insight into all the major party presidential election campaigns over this nearly seventy-year period. Based on these records, we classify states into one of five categories: base Democratic, lean Democratic, battleground, lean Republican, and base Republican. In this chapter, as well as in chapters 4 and 5, we simplify these strategies for the reader by sorting them into three more basic categories: base Democratic, battleground, and base Republican.[2] From Eisenhower and Stevenson to Nixon and McGovern, the data bear out several of our expectations, while causing us to re-think others. The bottom line is that campaign managers and operatives from this initial period of the television era were remarkably adept and sophisticated: high-level strategic thinking, we learned, is not a new thing.

In the following sections, we review the specific campaigns that mark this era. It is a pattern we repeat for the other eras in chapters 4 and 5. Our purpose in doing this is to give light to the full range of elections—in all their nuance and complexity—that animate these time periods, as well as to ensure a systematic review of the data we have amassed. In so doing, we consider the entirety of each campaign including the political conditions of the election, the emergence of candidates, the struggle for the nomination, and the general election contest. We believe that these details crucially set the stage for the fall strategies.

We Like Ike: The Eisenhower-Stevenson Elections

It is important to remember that Harry Truman had the option of running for re-election in 1952. He had ascended to the presidency following the death of Franklin Roosevelt in April 1945 and had won election in his own right with a come-from-behind victory in the 1948 contest. Even with the ratification of the twenty-second amendment in 1951, Truman could have run again in 1952.[3] But Truman's popularity, while briefly resurgent in 1948, had dipped to toxic levels by 1952. The Korean War, allegations of corruption within his administration, and the anti-communist red baiting of Joseph McCarthy and his allies in Congress all contributed to the collapse of support for Truman (Boller, 2004; Dickerson, 2017). This created a dilemma for the Democrats and an opportunity for the Republicans to win the White House for the first time in two decades.

Truman himself had lobbied General Dwight D. Eisenhower to run as the Democratic nominee in 1948 and had run for re-election only when the former Supreme Allied Commander spurned his offer. In 1952, the specter of Eisenhower loomed over both parties' nomination contests. Despite his protestations of neutrality and the hopes of most Democrats, however, it was clear by late 1951 that if Eisenhower ran, he would do so as a Republican.

Eisenhower's coyness proved a considerable obstacle, though, as his equivocal statements concerning a potential candidacy made it difficult for his supporters—most notably Rep. Hugh Scott of Pennsylvania, Sen. Henry Cabot Lodge of Massachusetts, and Gov. Thomas Dewey of New York—to gain the commitments of party people around the country. Instead, Sen. Robert Taft of Ohio was gaining Republican organizational support and commitments that made an eventual GOP convention fight all but inevitable (Dickerson, 2017).

Eisenhower's victory at the Republican convention in Chicago in July 1952 is one of the more fascinating and underappreciated nomination fights of the twentieth century. As a non-candidate, Eisenhower was on the ballot for the New Hampshire primary, in which he trounced Taft, 50% to 39%, and garnered 107,000 write-in votes in the Minnesota primary (the so-called Minnesota Miracle). The latter result caused Eisenhower to "reexamine my personal decision and past position" not to actively seek the nomination (Dickerson, 2017). He announced his candidacy on June 4, 1952, one month before the Republican convention. Because he had waited so long to commit, Eisenhower had no chance to win over delegates from the northern states, where Republican officials had rallied behind Taft. But the Republican Party organization was virtually non-existent in the southern states, and the prevalence of "open" nomination contests in those states made them attractive options for a highly popular but somewhat non-partisan candidate like Eisenhower. Unfortunately, the success of Eisenhower's forces at convincing independent and Democratic voters to support Ike in the precinct caucuses and county conventions led to heated fights over delegates. Texas was ground-zero for these fights, as Eisenhower's victory at the county conventions was overturned by the Texas State Republican convention in Mineral Wells, where the Taft-dominated credentials committee seated 519 of the contested delegates for Taft but just 30 for Eisenhower (Dickerson, 2017). Eisenhower forces dubbed this the Texas Steal and used it (and other, similar stories throughout the southern states) as a rallying point for their fight against Taft. "Thou Shalt not Steal" placards and pamphlets were printed and distributed by the thousands at rallies and speeches. A month later at the national convention in Chicago, Taft's forces wilted under the unrelenting pressure of Eisenhower's supporters—along with, for the first time, a national television audience—and ended up losing control of the composition of delegates that would determine the nominee. The particulars are vast and complicated, but the gist is that Eisenhower people won the fight to disallow those delegates whose credentials were questioned to vote on the seating of delegates. This led to more balanced representation of Taft and Eisenhower forces for subsequent votes, with Eisenhower's people having the luxury of a powerful emotional and rhetorical message ("Thou Shalt not Steal"). In the end, Eisenhower won on the first ballot, 845 to 280. He named Richard Nixon as his running mate to mollify the conservative wing of the party that had been attached to Taft.

On the Democratic side, Truman—as the incumbent president—had a great deal of say with respect to who would run as the nominee in his stead. His criteria for the nominee were simple: "Now if we can find a man who will take over and continue the Fair Deal, Point IV, Fair Employment, parity for farmers and consumers protective policy, the Democratic Party can win from now on. It seems to me that the Governor of Illinois has the background and what it takes. Think I'll talk to him" (Epstein, 1968). On the night of January 23, 1952, Truman met with Illinois governor Adlai Stevenson for about two hours. In Stevenson's account, he said that he was honored by the offer but that he had things he wanted to do as governor of Illinois. In Truman's account, Stevenson was "apparently flabbergasted" (Truman, 1960). For the next few months, Stevenson played a high-level, intellectual version of the same game that Eisenhower was playing. He never flatly ruled out running for president, saying only that he did not think he could run for two offices simultaneously and that he still wanted to be governor of Illinois. More prosaically, Stevenson insisted that he "could not" accept his party's nomination for president, but he never said that he "would not" (Epstein, 1968). In a technical sense, one could argue that he was only the third presidential candidate to be "drafted" by his party, the other two being James Garfield in 1880 and Charles Evans Hughes in 1916. But while Stevenson could have stopped the movement at any time, he chose not to.

Stevenson's apparent indecisiveness in pursuing the nomination—and, ultimately, the presidency—was a lingering issue throughout the campaign. To be fair, most pundits and practitioners viewed 1952 as a terrible year to run as the Democratic candidate for president. The Democrats had controlled the White House since 1933, and the country had turned on the sitting president over charges of corruption in his administration, as well as over Truman's handling of the Korean War. Stevenson himself said in 1964 that "To run as a Democrat in 1952 was hopeless, let alone against the No. 1 war hero" (Epstein, 1968).

Yet, the inevitability of Eisenhower's victory is apparent only in retrospect, and Stevenson's public diffidence over his candidacy helped make it so. For the most part, Stevenson hewed to traditional Democratic/New Deal issue positions, though by the end of the campaign he expressed a blistering contempt for charges that he and his party were "soft on communism" (Epstein,

1968). On race and other social issues, though, he was less forceful. For example, he chose as his running mate Alabama Sen. John Sparkman, to balance the ticket regionally and appeal to voters in the South. More generally, Stevenson did not connect his campaign with the incumbent administration, nor did he feel obliged to point out where he and President Truman were in sync and where they differed. Instead, Stevenson and most Democratic strategists believed that their main hope resided in the possibility of a major Eisenhower gaffe or scandal. Furthermore, despite the Republican candidate's popularity and caution, there *were* some opportunities for Stevenson and the Democrats.

First, there was Nixon. While Eisenhower mostly glided above the fray, the young California senator took the lead in actively campaigning for the GOP. This proved a mixed bag. In early September, the hard-charging Nixon turned into a liability due to the disclosure of a slush fund. There were calls for him to be dropped from the ticket, and Eisenhower kept his distance from the controversy. The seriousness of the issue was evident to all, and Nixon took the bold step of making a televised address to the nation on September 23, 1952. The so-called Checkers Speech—named after the dog given to Nixon by supporters, a gift he said he had no intention of returning—quelled the movement to bump him from the ticket.

Still, the prominence of hardline Republicans such as Nixon and Sen. Joseph McCarthy galvanized liberal Democrats around Stevenson's run. And in late October, McCarthy's criticisms of Eisenhower's mentor and friend, General George Marshall, created a second opportunity for the Democrats. Prior to a speech in Wisconsin—McCarthy's home state—Eisenhower scrubbed language praising Marshall in a nod to political expediency. The omission was noted, and the press and public reaction was strongly negative. The backlash was not quelled until Eisenhower's "I will go to Korea" pledge in a speech on October 24 (Boller, 2004).

The record from the campaigns shows that neither side was entirely sure what to make of the post-war, post–New Deal electorate. As shown in Table 3.1, we rely on the papers of Robert Humphreys (publicity director for the Eisenhower-Nixon campaign) and view the Eisenhower campaign's plan as encompassing an expansive list of battleground states.[4] They had 20 states worth a total of 264 electoral votes on their battleground (or "target") list. These included 14 "priority 1" states worth 206 electoral votes and 6 "priority 3" states worth 58 electoral votes. Given that they had 14 states worth 127 electoral votes as their "base", the Republican ticket needed 139 additional electoral votes from 264 possible in the battleground states (53%) to win a

266 Electoral College majority.[5] Despite being favored in the election, the cautious posture of the Eisenhower campaign is also evident in how they classified 5 of the base states, worth 50 electoral votes, as "priority 2" targets. In fact, California, Illinois, and Iowa were each designated as "deserving particular resources" despite being categorized as base states. Note that the Republican campaign conceded only the states of the confederacy, along with two southwestern states (Arizona and New Mexico) and the Democratic stronghold of Rhode Island.

The Stevenson campaign plan is largely gleaned from a retrospective report of Ken Hechler, who served as research director for Stevenson's 1956 campaign. In addition, we consulted the papers of Porter McKeever, Stevenson's publicity director, and Robert Hind, Stevenson's assistant publicity director, as well as a "master plan" written by public relations pioneer Edward Bernays.[6] From the aggregation of these sources, we know that the Stevenson campaign saw 14 states worth 128 electoral votes as their base. They designated 20 states worth 318 electoral votes as "battlegrounds." This means that they needed 138 electoral votes out of 318 (43%) to win the election. Within their battleground categorization, they bifurcated their targets: Stevenson's team identified 9 states worth 237 electoral votes as "primary" states and another 11 states worth 81 electoral votes as "secondary" states. They conceded 14 states worth 85 electoral votes to the Eisenhower-Nixon ticket.

The two main differences between the campaigns were that (1) the Republicans indicated that they intended to sink resources into defending a few key base states, and (2) the campaigns differed in their respective views of California (Nixon's home state) and Illinois (Stevenson's home state). This last distinction may not mean very much, however, since the Eisenhower campaign explicitly notes that they intended to prioritize these states.[7]

The press at the time wrote about the campaign as if Eisenhower were far ahead, based on national polling from the Gallup Organization.[8] The campaigns seem to have done little polling on their own, although both sides reportedly reached out to George Gallup to ask for his analysis (Blake, 2016; Epstein, 1968). They did use some of this data to make broad thematic adjustments, but there is no evidence that they employed statewide polls to much effect. This may be why Stevenson and the Democrats seemed to believe—even late in the game—that they would carry the lion's share of their targeted states.

> Toward the end of the campaign, Stevenson apparently came to believe that he stood a chance of winning. Senator Sparkman has told how, on election eve, on

Table 3.1 1952 Presidential Campaign Plans

	STEVENSON			EISENHOWER		
# of states	Base Democratic	Battleground/ Targets	Base Republican	Base Democratic	Battleground/ Targets	Base Republican
1	Alabama (11)	California (32)**	Colorado (6)	Alabama (11)	*Connecticut (8)**	*California (32)***
2	Arkansas (8)	Illinois (27)**	Delaware (3)	Arizona (4)	Delaware (3)***	Colorado (6)
3	Florida (10)	Massachusetts (16)**	Idaho (4)	Arkansas (8)	*Indiana (13)****	Idaho (4)
4	Georgia (12)	Michigan (20)**	Indiana (13)	Florida (10)	Kentucky (10)*	*Illinois (27)*
5	Louisiana (10)	New Jersey (16)**	Iowa (10)	Georgia (12)	*Maryland (9)**	*Iowa (10)*
6	Mississippi (8)	New York (45)**	Kansas (8)	Louisiana (10)	Massachusetts (16)***	Kansas (8)
7	New Mexico (4)	Ohio (25)**	Maine (5)	Mississippi (8)	*Michigan (20)**	Maine (5)**
8	North Carolina (14)	Pennsylvania (32)**	Maryland (9)	New Mexico (4)	Minnesota (11)***	Nebraska (6)**
9	Oklahoma (8)	Texas (24)**	Nebraska (6)	North Carolina (14)	Missouri (13)***	New Hampshire (4)
10	Rhode Island (4)	Arizona (4)*	New Hampshire (4)	Rhode Island (4)	Montana (4)***	North Dakota (4)**
11	South Carolina (8)	Connecticut (8)*	North Dakota (4)	South Carolina (8)	Nevada (3)***	Oklahoma (8)
12	Tennessee (11)	Kentucky (10)*	Oregon (6)	Tennessee (11)	*New Jersey (16)****	Oregon (6)
13	Virginia (12)	Minnesota (11)*	South Dakota (4)	Texas (24)	*New York (45)****	South Dakota (4)
14	West Virginia (8)	Missouri (13)*	Vermont (3)	Virginia (12)	*Ohio (25)****	Vermont (3)**
15		Montana (4)*			*Pennsylvania (32)****	
16		Nevada (3)*			Utah (4)***	
17		Utah (4)*			Washington (9)***	

18		Washington (9)*				West Virginia (8)*		
19		Wisconsin (12)*				*Wisconsin (12)****		
20		Wyoming (3)*				Wyoming (3)*		
States	14	20	14	48	14	20	14	48
EVs	128	318	85	531	140	264	127	531

Notes:

"EV" stands for electoral votes. State electoral votes provided in parentheses.

For Stevenson's battleground state strategy, ** indicates "primary" states; * "secondary" states.

For Eisenhower's strategy, italics indicate states targeted for significant campaign resources. *** indicates "priority 1" targets; ** "priority 2" targets; * "priority 3" targets.

Sources:

Hechler, Ken. 1956. "Campaign Analysis," Adlai E. Stevenson Papers (8/8/56), Box 280; Princeton University Mudd Manuscript Library.

Humphreys, Robert. 1952. "Campaign Plan," Robert Humphreys Papers (8/31/52), Box 10; Dwight D. Eisenhower Presidential Library.

Joseph Katz Company Advertising Agency. 1952. "Democratic National Committee Expenditures per Thousand Population," Papers of the Democratic National Committee (n.d.), Box 370; John F. Kennedy Presidential Library.

> their way to deliver a final television broadcast, Stevenson began to discuss possible members for their prospective cabinet. And Kenneth Davis reports that in a private pool among his immediate campaign staff Stevenson predicted he would win by an electoral vote of 381 to 150. When the returns were in, of course, Eisenhower had defeated him by a vote of 442 to 89. (Epstein, 1968)

All told, Eisenhower carried thirty-nine states, including Illinois, California, New York, Pennsylvania, Ohio, and all the battleground targets. Stevenson carried nine states, all in the Deep South, with the exceptions of Kentucky and West Virginia. In a sign of things to come, the Republicans broke the Democratic lock in parts of Dixie, carrying Florida, Tennessee, and Virginia.

It is worth noting that the Eisenhower and Stevenson presidential campaigns were the first to use television advertising. Moreover, they did more than simply purchase time on national broadcast programs. On the Democratic side, Stevenson made some limited buys of geographically targeted advertisements but focused primarily on broader distribution of long-form speeches: he was widely thought to be a master of the genre. This was undoubtedly the right mode for large crowds of in-person stadium attendees but decidedly out of step with the new intimacy brought about by televisions in living rooms. The Republicans, meanwhile, pioneered the use of television spot advertising. Two individuals deserve credit for this innovation. First, Bruce Barton was one of the principals of the advertising firm Batten, Barton, Durstine, & Osborn (BBD&O). Barton had advised Republican candidates since Calvin Coolidge in the 1920s about applying the rules of product advertising in the realm of political campaigns. His trademark advice was "short and simple" messages designed to appeal to regular Americans. He had worked with Alf Landon in 1936 and was Thomas Dewey's main publicity advisor in 1948, securing the advertising account from the Republican National Committee (RNC). By 1952, the number of households with televisions had jumped to over 18 million, from less than half a million in 1949. Having argued persuasively but unsuccessfully for a more aggressive use of modern communication techniques in 1948, BBD&O won contracts from both the RNC and Citizens for Eisenhower-Nixon in 1952 (Hollitz, 1982). But while Barton had foreseen the role that television would play in the modern campaign, it fell to a younger man from another agency to figure out how best to use the new medium.

That younger man was Rosser Reeves, and he is the second person worth crediting. Reeves was with the Ted Bates Company, an advertising agency that had an extensive list of clients but little experience in political marketing. Reeves, however, saw the potential.

> In the summer of 1952, three wealthy Republican oilmen were at a country club in Rhode Island discussing the effectiveness of the Democratic slogan, "You Never Had It So Good." They decided to approach a mutual friend and advertising man, Rosser Reeves of the Ted Bates Company, to see if he would work on a similar slogan which the Republicans might use. Reeves told them what the Republicans needed was not a slogan, but an entire advertising campaign. The advertising man said he would work on such a campaign if they would raise the necessary money to finance it. What Reeves had in mind was the use of short one-minute or twenty-second television "spots" as a form of political advertising. (Hollitz, 1982: 30)

"Spots" were the advertisements sold in between the radio and television shows at the time. Popular shows were sponsored by companies, which paid princely sums for the rights to Bob Hope or Jack Benny or Dean Martin and Jerry Lewis. But short advertisements could be purchased and run after one show and before the next for pennies on the dollar. Reeves recommended that the Eisenhower campaign extensively use these in the fall of 1952. Furthermore, he backed his claim with hard data.[9]

> Since the 1940's, the Bates agency had also been a leader among advertising agencies in studying what was referred to in the trade as "penetration," meaning the number of people who actually remembered the message of the commercial. During the television revolution between 1948 and 1952, the Ted Bates Company had set up what it called a "copy laboratory" in which advertisers could show commercials to random samples of people and "scientifically" test the "penetration" of any commercial . . . Reeves had a former Ted Bates employee draw up a political analysis for an intensive nationwide advertising campaign. This analysis determined, among other things, that a switch in voting behavior of a mere 2 per cent in sixty-two designated counties in twelve crucial states could spell the difference between victory and defeat for the Republicans in a close election. (The states were Connecticut, Maryland, New Jersey, New York, Pennsylvania, Ohio, California, Indiana, Michigan, Illinois, Iowa, and Wisconsin.) Reeves proposed that

> a million and a half dollars' worth of television and radio spots be poured, like a tidal wave, into these critical areas. (Hollitz, 1982: 34)

The Republican spot advertising campaign began in early October, with the famous "Eisenhower Answers America" television commercials. Citizens for Eisenhower-Nixon paid $60,000 to produce the spots, and a special finance committee was set up to solicit funds for their broadcast. The committee raised roughly $1.5 million, while local Republican organizations borrowed copies of the spots and ran them with their own funds. Local markets targeted by the campaign—including New York, Los Angeles, Milwaukee, and Denver—were "deluged" with Eisenhower ads, with an estimated 140–150 spots a day running in New York City alone (Hollitz, 1982).

As noted earlier, Stevenson's team was aware of the power and potential of the new medium. In fact, they believed that their candidate's ability to deliver stump speeches on substantive issues played to his strengths compared to the "boring" Eisenhower—these long-form speeches were just the thing to highlight Stevenson's presidential airs. Furthermore, the Stevenson campaign was fully apprised of what the Republicans were doing: the Democrats had a complete copy of the Eisenhower spot buy plan courtesy of a turncoat spy! Our review of the Stevenson campaign documents reveals that his campaign thought the Eisenhower television plan was a gimmick, but they nevertheless counter-programmed to some extent in the counties that Eisenhower was covering with his spot advertising. Beyond this counter-programming, the Democrats emphasized half-hour campaign speeches that ran on Tuesday and Thursday nights at 10:30 p.m.

Still, Stevenson's use of spot advertising was half-hearted: he refused to appear in any of them, and they instead featured single shots or crude cartoon images. In fact, outrage was the main Democratic response to Eisenhower's more polished spots. Stevenson took to the stump to denounce them as an attempt to trivialize the election. George W. Ball, executive director of Volunteers for Stevenson, decried the use of "high powered hucksters of Madison Avenue" (Hollitz, 1982).

Of course, it would be an exaggeration to suggest that Eisenhower won in 1952 because he ran a more sophisticated campaign. It is reasonable, however, to observe that his campaign was quite sophisticated and that this sophistication made it all but impossible for Stevenson to overcome the short-term forces arrayed against him with a superior campaign.

In 1956, the presidential election was a rematch between Eisenhower and Stevenson. The result was virtually identical to the preceding one: Eisenhower won re-election by a 457 to 73 margin in the Electoral College. The Eisenhower-Nixon ticket carried 41 states, compared to 7 for the Stevenson-Kefauver ticket. Despite the familiar results, the 1956 campaign was a different animal than its immediate predecessor. Rather than attacking the Democrats, the incumbent Republican ticket was defending its own record on domestic and international affairs. And unlike 1952—in which the incumbent administration was saddled with an unpopular war and a slowdown in economic growth—by 1956 the country was prosperous and at peace. Eisenhower had signed an armistice ending the Korean War in 1953, and by 1955 the economy had recovered from a brief recession. In addition to these favorable short-term forces, Eisenhower remained personally popular. During 1955, his job approval rating ranged from 68% to 79%.[10]

Against this broad backdrop, three factors complicated what was otherwise a straightforward re-election bid. First, in September 1955 Eisenhower suffered a major heart attack. This episode made it extremely difficult for the Democrats to aggressively confront the president, who was not only personally popular but now facing a life-threatening medical circumstance. Stevenson honored a moratorium on criticism of the ailing president for the remainder of 1955 and well into 1956. Any chance the Democrats had to reduce Eisenhower's stature ahead of the actual campaign was thereby eliminated (Boller, 2004; Shields-West, 1992).

On the other hand, the heart attack also led to the second factor: concerns over the vice-president. Although by all accounts Nixon served admirably in presiding over the government in Eisenhower's absence—and especially in guiding the National Security Council—concerns persisted that he was more of a partisan attack dog than a seasoned statesman. In the months preceding the convention, Eisenhower gently attempted to get Nixon to leave the ticket, suggesting that he might be appointed secretary of defense, which would burnish his credentials for running in 1960.[11] But Nixon refused to take the hint, and deftly maneuvered to remain on the ticket.

The third factor was that Tennessee senator Estes Kefauver (among others) chose to run for the Democratic nomination, forcing Stevenson to commit time and treasure to primary elections. The seriousness of Kefauver's challenge became evident when he handily beat Stevenson in the New Hampshire primary on March 13 and followed this up with victories in the Minnesota and Wisconsin primaries. Stevenson rallied to win primaries in Oregon, California, and Florida, and headed into the Democratic convention with a clear lead in primary delegates. Then former president Truman blindsided Stevenson at the convention by announcing his support for New York governor W. Averell Harriman. Truman said that Stevenson was following the "counsel of hesitation" and lacked the fighting spirit that the Democrats needed to win (Epstein, 1968).

The last of these three factors is the most immediately relevant for our consideration of Electoral College strategy and resource allocation. Although Stevenson prevailed at the convention and carried the Democratic Party's banner into the fall contest, he was not as sharp as he had been in 1952. More than a decade after the fact, a sympathetic portrayal of Stevenson offered this sharp criticism of the candidate's performance in 1956:

> Fatigued from his efforts during the primaries and the Convention, Stevenson was vastly over-scheduled for the regular campaign. This took its toll. His indecisiveness, formerly reserved for grand decisions, now intruded upon petty matters. Crowds of supporters and important politicians would be kept waiting at airports, while Adlai Stevenson's plane circled aloft, the candidate within endlessly touching up his speech. Among his campaign staff, according to James A. Finnegan, his campaign manager, the politicians insisted on acting like intellectuals and the intellectuals like politicians. The result was that on substantive issues Stevenson tended to be vague, ambiguous, sometimes even contradictory. (Epstein, 1968)

As in 1952, the strategic plans developed by the Republican and Democratic campaigns reflected ambivalence about the nature of the electoral map in the aftermath of the New Deal and World War II elections. Most notably, Democratic dominance in the South—still a fact of life in local and most state elections—was no certainty in presidential contests. Based on the papers of Thomas E. Stevens—a confidante of White House Chief of Staff Sherman Adams, who served as an important political advisor in the 1956 campaign—we know that Eisenhower's team saw their base as consisting of 18 states worth 103 electoral votes. Unlike 1952, they gave no indication that these states required any material attention. Rather, they targeted 22 battleground states worth 349 electoral votes. An Electoral College majority of 266 votes thus required the Republicans to win 163 of the 349 battleground votes (47%). They identified eight states as "priority" targets (California, Illinois, Massachusetts, Michigan, New Jersey, New York, Ohio, Pennsylvania, and Texas; worth 237 votes), and eight other states as "secondary" targets (Connecticut,

Florida, Kentucky, Maryland, Minnesota, Missouri, Tennessee, Virginia, and Washington; worth 83 votes). Even a split in these "primary" and secondary states would deliver a victory. Eisenhower's team wrote off 8 deep South states, as well as West Virginia, totaling 79 electoral votes (Table 3.2).

Relying again on the analysis of Democratic strategist Ken Hechler, we see that Stevenson's campaign viewed their base as encompassing 13 states, worth 127 electoral votes. Their plan saw five states as "leaning" Democratic, including four border south states (Missouri, Oklahoma, Tennessee, and Virginia) and stalwart Rhode Island. They targeted 23 battleground states worth 311 electoral votes. This required them to win 47% of the votes within their target universe to gain the White House. Within their battleground category, they identified four states as "greatest concentration" targets (California, Kentucky, New York, and Pennsylvania; worth 119 votes) and another nine states as "lesser concentration" targets (Arizona, Delaware, Idaho, Montana, Nevada, New Mexico, North Dakota, Utah, and Wyoming; worth 33 votes). Carrying their base plus the "concentration" targets would have yielded a 279 electoral vote majority. They classified 12 states as base Republican, with six identified as only "leaning" to Eisenhower.

The most obvious point to be made about the Electoral College strategies of these Eisenhower-Stevenson campaigns is the sheer number of battleground states. Both sides had twenty battleground states in 1952, while in 1956 the Republicans had twenty-two and the Democrats twenty-three. There are several potential reasons for this:

1. The campaigns were not especially strategic in their plans, and included states on their target lists that were not essential to a winning coalition.
2. The campaigns were strategic, but there were many competitive states and/or many states with significant variance in their votes.
3. The campaigns were strategic, but there was not enough timely polling information to exclude states from the target lists.
4. The campaigns were strategic, and broad plans masked a more targeted allocation of resources.

Based on our reading of the strategic memos and the research behind the targeting plans, we reject the first potential reason as implausible. Indeed, we are struck by the sophistication of the discussions and considerations surrounding where and how to campaign. The campaigns clearly saw the election as developing pathways to a majority of Electoral College votes. The fourth explanation has mixed empirical support, something we speak to directly and extensively in chapter 5. The second and third potential reasons for the substantial number

Table 3.2 1956 Presidential Campaign Plans

	STEVENSON			EISENHOWER		
# of states	Base Democratic	Battleground/ Targets	Base Republican	Base Democratic	Battleground/ Targets	Base Republican
1	Alabama (11)	Arizona (4)*	*Colorado (6)*	Alabama (11)	California (32)**	Arizona (4)
2	Arkansas (8)	California (32)**	*Florida (10)*	Arkansas (8)	Connecticut (8)*	Colorado (6)
3	Georgia (12)	Connecticut (8)	*Iowa (10)*	Georgia (12)	Delaware (3)	Idaho (4)
4	Louisiana (10)	Delaware (3)*	Kansas (8)	Louisiana (10)	Florida (10)*	Indiana (13)
5	Mississippi (8)	Idaho (4)*	Maine (5)	Mississippi (8)	Illinois (27)**	Iowa (10)
6	*Missouri (13)*	Illinois (27)	*Maryland (9)*	North Carolina (14)	Kentucky (10)*	Kansas (8)
7	North Carolina (14)	Indiana (13)	Nebraska (6)	South Carolina (8)	Maryland (9)*	Maine (5)
8	*Oklahoma (8)*	Kentucky (10)**	New Hampshire (4)	West Virginia (8)	Massachusetts (16)**	Montana (4)
9	*Rhode Island (4)*	Massachusetts (16)	*New Jersey (16)*		Michigan (20)**	Nebraska (6)
10	South Carolina (8)	Michigan (20)	South Dakota (4)		Minnesota (11)*	Nevada (3)
11	*Tennessee (11)*	Minnesota (11)	Vermont (3)		Missouri (13)*	New Hampshire (4)
12	*Virginia (12)*	Montana (4)*	*Wisconsin (12)*		New Jersey (16)**	North Dakota (4)
13	West Virginia (8)	Nevada (3)*			New Mexico (4)	Oregon (6)
14		New Mexico (4)*			New York (45)**	South Dakota (4)
15		New York (45)**			Ohio (25)**	Utah (4)
16		North Dakota (4)*			Oklahoma (8)	Vermont (3)
17		Ohio (25)			Pennsylvania (32)**	Wisconsin (12)
18		Oregon (6)			Rhode Island (4)	Wyoming (3)

19		Pennsylvania (32)**				Tennessee (11)*		
20		Texas (24)				Texas (24)**		
21		Utah (4)*				Virginia (12)*		
22		Washington (9)				Washington (9)*		
23		Wyoming (3)*						
States	13	23	12	48	8	22	18	48
EVs	127	311	93	531	79	349	103	531

Notes:

"EV" stands for electoral votes. State electoral votes provided in parentheses.

For Stevenson's strategy, italics indicate states leaning toward one side or the other; ** indicates "greatest concentration" states; * "less concentration" states.

For Eisenhower's strategy, ** indicates "priority" targets; * "secondary" targets.

Sources:

Hechler, Ken. 1956. "Campaign Analysis," Adlai E. Stevenson Papers (8/8/56), Box 280; Princeton University Mudd Manuscript Library.

Stevens, Thomas E. 1956. "Information Report from the Closest States in the 1952 Election," Thomas E. Stevens Papers (10/18/56), Box 30; Dwight D. Eisenhower Presidential Library.

of battleground states strike us as more compelling. Presidential elections in the 1950s were precarious from the perspective of party coalitions, as the majority Democratic Party attempted to retain its hegemony in the South while also nurturing its advantage in large Midwest and Mid-Atlantic states. This required walking a tightrope on the issue of race and civil rights: take too liberal a position and the White South bolts, but take too conservative a position and the liberal intelligentsia defects. The other piece of the electoral puzzle resides in the Rocky Mountain West, where the nature and pull of partisan identities was more ephemeral and harder to read; there was an independent, reformist strain to politics in these states that did not match up well with the parties' traditional appeals. These coalitional vagaries could be teased out with detailed and timely survey research, but such data was only beginning to become available. Indeed, we find only sporadic reference to statewide public opinion polls in either the Eisenhower or Stevenson files. Exhaustive and sophisticated analyses of previous election results? Yes. But lots of contemporaneous local polls? No.[12] Finally, the multitude of battleground states may be obviated by a narrower and more precise allocation of actual campaign resources, which we consider in chapter 6.

A final note on the 1956 race: Stevenson and the Democrats seem by this time to have reluctantly embraced the need for a modern television advertising campaign. After a long, somewhat torturous process, they ended up hiring the little-known firm of Norman, Craig, and Kummel to oversee their TV ads, and their spot advertising strategy was more robust than in 1952. Still, resistance remained, and top Democratic officials complained bitterly about the Madison Avenue quality of the Republican campaign.[13] They eventually attempted to tap into some of their own support in Hollywood, including Lauren Bacall and Mercedes McCambridge (Blake, 2016). They even planned a special TV program, in which film and music stars (including Elvis Presley) would explain their opposition to the Republicans' use of celebrities. This plan was never realized (Blake, 2016).

All the Way with JFK and LBJ: the Kennedy-Nixon and Johnson-Goldwater Elections

In the words of the thirty-fifth president in 1960, "the torch is passed." The cautious presidential campaigns of the 1950s, which had employed the new technologies of television and polling as best they could, were succeeded by hard-charging 1960s campaign teams intent on integrating innovative marketing research and television communication techniques. The new era was ushered in by the campaigns of Eisenhower and Stevenson but was given a rocket boost by the 1960 Kennedy and Nixon campaigns.

The context of the 1960 presidential election campaign promoted such an acceleration. While fatigue with Truman and the Democrats and public adoration for the war hero Eisenhower had stacked the deck in the 1950s—and imbued both sides with a sense that the races were foregone conclusions barring a major event—the contest to replace the old general was wide open. The country had suffered a recession in 1958 and another (short) recession in 1960, leading to concerns about the economy. There was also consternation about foreign policy and the threat posed by the Soviet Union. So, while Eisenhower remained personally popular, it was unclear how the electorate would respond to a potential third term for the Republicans.

With all this going on, Vice-President Richard Nixon was the obvious choice to succeed Eisenhower as the Republican nominee. New York governor Nelson Rockefeller considered challenging Nixon, but a national tour to gauge support for his candidacy showed Nixon to be too formidable.[14] Rather than contesting primaries and expending energy fighting off intra-party rivals, Nixon was instead afforded the opportunity to raise funds and to position himself as experienced and statesmanlike, a necessity given his image as a strident partisan in the press and with liberals across the country. Nixon easily won the Republican nomination at the GOP convention in Chicago and named former Massachusetts senator and UN Ambassador Henry Cabot Lodge Jr. as his running mate. Lodge's foreign policy credentials signaled that Nixon was doubling down on the belief that the election would turn on foreign policy expertise.[15] In hindsight, simply becoming the GOP candidate is an underrated accomplishment given that he was the first sitting vice-president to be nominated by his party since John C. Breckinridge in 1860.

Another Massachusetts senator, John F. Kennedy, quickly emerged as the front-runner among a crowded field of Democratic contenders in 1960. As noted earlier, the parties' presidential selection processes were evolving during this new era. But while primaries and other popular mechanisms were becoming more relevant for amassing delegates and successfully seeking the nomination, they were not yet decisive. During this period, multiple paths were available to candidates when it came to seeking the nomination. Kennedy, Minnesota senator Hubert Humphrey, Oregon senator Wayne Morse, and Florida senator George Smathers all sought the nomination by contesting several carefully chosen primaries. Other candidates sought to win their home state primaries and preserve their viability along with a small set of delegates heading into the convention. Meanwhile, Texas senator Lyndon Johnson, Missouri senator Stuart Symington, and Adlai Stevenson each chose not to contest any primaries, but to build their bids around the hope that no one candidate dominated the primaries and that they could capture the support of Democratic delegates as a "compromise" candidate. The trick for

Kennedy, then, was to become the dominant candidate through the primaries (White, 1961).

One obstacle for Kennedy was the idea that he was too young to be president and that he was merely running to position himself as a vice-presidential candidate. Kennedy himself forcefully and directly denied the idea, stating "I'm not running for vice-president, I'm running for president."[16]

A more important second obstacle was Kennedy's religion: Roman Catholicism. Kennedy wanted to draw on the long-standing affinity of Catholic voters for the Democratic Party, but he needed to prove that he could win Protestant votes, as well. And a main concern for Protestants was whether Kennedy could be counted on to exercise independent judgment from the pope on sensitive social and cultural issues.[17] The stakes escalated, ironically, following a major Kennedy victory: although Kennedy defeated Humphrey in the Wisconsin primary, his margin was such that skeptics claimed it was entirely attributable to the Catholic vote. Kennedy, who contested nine of the fifteen Democratic primary elections, decided to roll the dice and campaign in heavily Protestant West Virginia. Humphrey was the early favorite, but Kennedy invested heavily in television advertising and get-out-the-vote operations (and, allegedly, in county-level Democratic officials as well). These efforts, along with a statewide televised debate on May 4, tilted the contest in Kennedy's favor. He ended up winning over 60% of the vote and scoring a resounding victory.[18] Humphrey quit the race afterward.[19]

Yet a third obstacle facing Kennedy was the opposition from senior party leaders heading into the Democratic convention in Los Angeles. Both Johnson and Stevenson announced their candidacies the week before the convention. Former president Truman had already stated that Kennedy was too young and callow to be the nominee and had long supported Symington. Former first lady Eleanor Roosevelt backed Stevenson. But Kennedy and his team had assiduously cultivated the support of key party leaders and at-large delegates in the months before the convention. The feeling was that the party needed a "fresh face" (White, 1961). Johnson, sensing the need for a bold act, went as far as to challenge Kennedy to a televised debate before a joint session of the Massachusetts and Texas delegations, which Kennedy accepted (most observers indicated that Kennedy probably won that debate). In the end, Kennedy not only won the nomination but offered the vice-presidency to Johnson. The inclusion of Johnson on the ticket surprised many but signaled the Democrats' intention to retain their hold on the southern states.[20]

But neither the Kennedy nor the Nixon campaign thought that all the southern states were in play. In fact, a look at their respective electoral strategies reveals that the southern battlefield included only Texas (for both campaigns), Florida (for Nixon), and Virginia (for Nixon). Kennedy's camp considered Florida and Virginia part of Nixon's base, and both sides treated Alabama and Mississippi as "Dixiecrat" states. This last point is important. Voters in Alabama cast their ballots for individual delegates to the Electoral College, rather than for an entire slate pledged to a candidate from a particular party. In Alabama, voters elected five delegates pledged to Kennedy and six unpledged delegates, all of whom cast their electoral votes for the Democrat. In Mississippi, voters cast their ballots for entire slates of electors, but one slate was committed to Kennedy, one to Nixon, and another (unpledged) slate would eventually support Harry Byrd of Virginia. Whereas the Nixon campaign treated Mississippi as a battleground state and Alabama as a Dixiecrat state (therefore, one that was unwinnable), the Kennedy campaign placed both states in the Dixiecrat category.

More generally, Kennedy's plan was as expansive as the Stevenson plans of 1952 and 1956, though with a significantly greater chance of success. From our reading of strategic memos to Robert F. Kennedy from the advertising company of Guild, Bascom, & Bonfligi, Inc., the Democrats saw their base as eight states worth 62 electoral votes. They appear to have identified 21 states worth 339 electoral votes as battlegrounds. Given the majority threshold of 269 votes, Kennedy needed to carry 61% of the electoral votes in his battleground category. The Kennedy campaign further distinguished between and among targeted states based on their relative electoral vote totals. Looking at the biggest prizes, Kennedy had eight "priority 1" states, all battlegrounds and worth 221 electoral votes; carrying these along with the base would have given Kennedy the win. They also identified 12 medium-sized "priority 2" states, worth 109 electoral votes. Based on our review, several of these states—Florida, Kentucky, Oklahoma, Oregon, Tennessee, and Virginia—leaned to Nixon and do not appear to have been sufficiently important to Kennedy's team to be included in the campaign's battleground category. Our decision to exclude them is based on the campaign's view of the (excessive) investment of resources necessary to effectively compete in those states.[21] Similarly, five of the seven small-sized "priority 3" states (worth a total of 37 electoral votes) leaned toward Nixon and did not seem to be integral to the Democratic battleground plan. "Priority 4" states—seven in all—are both small and varied in their underlying partisan tendencies. Louisiana, for example, leaned heavily Democratic, while Vermont and Maine leaned heavily Republican. The Kennedy campaign saw these states as potentially volatile and therefore worth monitoring. All this amounts to an extremely complex and nuanced vision of the election, extremely sensitive to the possibility that multiple and varied pathways to victory could emerge (Table 3.3).

Table 3.3 1960 Presidential Campaign Plans

	KENNEDY				NIXON			
# of states	Base Democratic	Battleground/ Targets	Base Republican	Dixiecrat	Base Democratic	Battleground/ Targets	Base Republican	Dixiecrat
1	Arkansas (8)	California (32)****	*Alaska (3)*	Alabama (11)	Arkansas (8)	California (32)****	Alaska (3)	Alabama (11)
2	Delaware (3)	Colorado (6)	Arizona (4)*	Mississippi (8)	Delaware (3)	Colorado (6)*	Arizona (4)	
3	Georgia (12)	Connecticut (8)	Florida (10)***		Georgia (12)	Florida (10)*	Connecticut (8)	
4	*Hawaii (3)*	Illinois (27)****	Idaho (4)**		Hawaii (3)	Illinois (27)***	Idaho (4)	
5	Louisiana (10)*	Iowa (10)	Indiana (13)		Louisiana (10)	Iowa (10)**	Indiana (13)**	
6	North Carolina (14)***	Kansas (8)**	Kentucky (10)***		Massachusetts (16)	Maryland (9)*	Kansas (8)	
7	Rhode Island (4)	Maryland (9)***	Maine (5)*		Minnesota (11)	Michigan (20)***	Kentucky (10)	
8	South Carolina (8)	Massachusetts (16)	Montana (4)		Mississippi (8)	New Jersey (16)**	Maine (5)	
9		Michigan (20)****	Nebraska (6)**		Missouri (13)	New York (45)****	Montana (4)	
10		Minnesota (11)***	Nevada (3)		North Carolina (14)	Ohio (25)***	Nebraska (6)	
11		Missouri (13)***	New Hampshire (4)**		Rhode Island (4)	Oregon (6)**	Nevada (3)	
12		New Jersey (16)****	New Mexico (4)		South Carolina (8)	Pennsylvania (32)****	New Hampshire (4)	
13		New York (45)****	Oklahoma (8)***		West Virginia (8)	Texas (24)***	New Mexico (4)	
14		North Dakota (4)*	Oregon (6)***			Virginia (12)*	North Dakota (4)	
15		Ohio (25)****	Tennessee (11)***			Washington (9)**	Oklahoma (8)	
16		Pennsylvania (32)****	Utah (4)**			Wisconsin (12)**	South Dakota (4)	
17		South Dakota (4)*	Vermont (3)*				Tennessee (11)	
18		Texas (24)****	Virginia (12)***				Utah (4)	
19		Washington (9)***	Wyoming (3)**				Vermont (3)	

20		West Virginia (8)**						Wyoming (3)		
21		Wisconsin (12)***								
States	8	21	19	2	50	13	16	20	1	50
EVs	62	339	117	19	537	118	295	113	11	537

Notes:

"EV" stands for electoral votes. State electoral votes provided in parentheses.

For Kennedy's strategy, **** indicates "priority 1" states; *** "priority 2" states; ** "priority 3" states; * "priority 4" states; italics indicate Alaska or Hawaii.

For Nixon's strategy, **** indicates "priority 1" states; *** "priority 2" states; ** "priority 3" states; * "priority 4" states.

Sources:

Guild, Bascom, and Bonfligi, Inc. 1960. "Media Buying Report," Robert F. Kennedy Papers (8/28/60), Box 38; John F. Kennedy Presidential Library.

Guild, Bascom, and Bonfligi, Inc. 1960. "Suggested Political Research for the 1960 Presidential Campaign," John F. Kennedy Papers (n.d.), Box 447; John F. Kennedy Presidential Library.

Haldeman, Robert. 1960. "Tentative Priority List of States for Campaign," Robert Haldeman Papers–White House Special Files (8/1/60), Box 45; Richard M. Nixon Presidential Birthplace and Library.

Haldeman, Robert. 1960. "Intensity of Campaigns by State," Robert Haldeman Papers—White House Special Files (8/1/60), Box 45; Richard M. Nixon Presidential Birthplace and Library.

Based on strategy and media memos archived in the papers of Bob Haldeman, we see that the Nixon campaign strategy employed a similar nomenclature, also recognizing priority 1–4 states. The difference is that the prioritization occurred within the broader context of battleground states. In other words, the GOP campaign was more focused and (perhaps) less flexible with respect to "leaning" states becoming more consequential targets. The Nixon team viewed the Republican base as 20 states worth 113 electoral votes. They identified 16 states worth 295 electoral votes as battlegrounds. This means they needed to win 53% of the battleground electoral votes to deliver the election. They saw the three most populous states (California, New York, and Pennsylvania; worth 109 votes) as "priority 1." The next four most populous states (Illinois, Michigan, Ohio, and Texas; worth 96 electoral votes) were "priority 2." The six (relatively small) "priority 3" states contained 66 electoral votes, while the four (even smaller) "priority 4" states contained 37 electoral votes. From our reading of the data, only Indiana stands out as a "priority" state that was not also a battleground state.

Both campaigns clearly distinguished between and among targets based on competitiveness and contribution to a potential winning Electoral College coalition. In other words, bigger and more competitive states were the most obvious targets. However, they also seem to have been sensitive to the possibility of relative cost asymmetries; that is, they discussed how bigger states usually required more money and more effort, such that campaigning in those states might not be as efficient as campaigning in several "smaller" but less expensive states. This is something that all modern presidential campaigns grapple with, and we clearly see it in 1960.

We also see differences in the strategic plans of the major party campaigns. Although the campaigns identified many of the same states as priorities, Kennedy had 33 "priority" states compared to Nixon's 17. There are two plausible reasons for the flexibility of Kennedy's plan. First, Kennedy was not as constrained by financing concerns as Nixon. Joseph Kennedy's willingness to use the Kennedy family fortune for his son's candidacy allowed the Democratic campaign to explore opportunities in states that otherwise might have been on the chopping block. Second, Kennedy was receiving extensive national and regional polling data from Lou Harris. This gave his team better insight into trends that might bring some states into (and out of) play. Nixon's archives reveal that he also benefitted from consistent and extensive polling data, but it does not seem that his campaign engaged in comparable modeling. Whether Kennedy actually invested campaign resources in these states is something we explore in chapter 6.

The 1960 election was one of the closest in American history, with Kennedy defeating Nixon by less than 0.4 percentage points in the popular vote, and by a 303 to 219 total in the Electoral College. Kennedy's slim—as well as controversial—margins in Illinois (0.2 percentage points) and Texas (2.0 percentage points) were enough to carry the day. Given the razor thin margin, specific campaign decisions such as Nixon's insistence on honoring his pledge to visit all 50 states as well as specific campaign events—such as the four presidential debates—are often revisited and reconsidered by political scientists and historians. But in an election that close, anything is potentially decisive. More to the point, the main lessons from the 1960 campaign go far beyond the specific outcome. The importance of money (as noted above, Kennedy had benefitted from the largesse and connections of his wealthy father) and of television (Kennedy's debate appearances were slick, professional, and showed the handsome young candidate in the best possible light) was firmly established in the minds of partisan practitioners and party professionals everywhere, even if the debates had no discernable impact on candidate support dynamics (Stimson, 2004) and in the absence of any clear contemporaneous evidence that conclusively demonstrated any differential impact across radio and television audiences (Bruschke and Divine, 2017; Kraus, 1996).

Finally, when considering the strategic sophistication of the campaigns, one last point merits mention. Although both Kennedy and Nixon employed numerous spot ads in 1960, their organizational approaches to television advertising were distinct and instructional. Kennedy employed two different agencies for his TV ads and ended up producing nearly two hundred separate spots. These ads differed wildly in content and style, allowing for a variety of approaches across different contexts and circumstances. For example, Kennedy's team produced and aired a one-minute ad featuring Jackie Kennedy appealing directly to Hispanic voters in Spanish. At the same time, they also aired an eleven-minute speech given by JFK to Protestant ministers in Houston. Meanwhile, Nixon pioneered an approach that became standard for subsequent GOP campaigns: rather than hire an ad agency, he formed a group (Campaign Associates). Then he placed Carrol Newton (one of Eisenhower's top ad men) and Ted Rogers (who had produced the Checkers Speech) at the head of the group, gaining expert consultants while allowing the campaign to retain control over ad content and placement.

Of course, Kennedy never had the opportunity to run for re-election. His assassination in 1963 dramatically altered the political landscape for the 1964 campaign. Kennedy's decision to run with Lyndon Johnson in 1960 meant that Johnson was elevated to the presidency upon Kennedy's death; the delicacy of opposing Kennedy's heir—however much members of Kennedy's inner circle resented Johnson—all but insured the Texan would be the nominee in 1964. Interestingly, Johnson did not have a vice-president as he served out Kennedy's term; he picked Minnesota senator Hubert Humphrey as his running mate at the Democratic convention (White, 1965), after carefully assessing the field and gaining the support of both Democratic party leadership across the country and his own cabinet (which included many Kennedy holdovers, among them Attorney General Robert Kennedy).

Beyond the implications for the Democratic nomination, the broader political context was also altered, as the martyred president's shadow loomed over issues that might have otherwise been intractable. Most notably, the 1964 Civil Rights Act was passed by the Congress, effectively ending almost a hundred years of Jim Crow laws in the South and also curtailing discriminatory practices throughout the nation. Less notably, yet also of critical importance, Johnson was able to push the Gulf of Tonkin Resolution—expanding the executive's ability to prosecute the war in Vietnam—through Congress just three months before Election Day. Aside from allowing him to claim the mantle of Kennedy as well as the bully pulpit itself, the momentum that the assassination provided for policies passed in the name of Kennedy allowed Johnson to claim significant substantive victories in advance of the 1964 election. What may have been another closely fought contest shaped up as a coronation for the new king.

For their part, the Republicans contributed to the electoral mismatch. Even before the assassination, the GOP nomination fight shaped up as a donnybrook between establishment forces and an emerging conservative block. Leading the conservatives was Arizona senator Barry Goldwater, who began organizing in the summer of 1963 (Shadegg, 1965). New York governor Nelson Rockefeller appeared to be a formidable centrist threat after winning re-election in 1962, but moderate Republican organizations declined to rally behind him due to concerns about his personal life.[22] Other mainstream, moderate Republicans—such as Henry Cabot Lodge Jr., Pennsylvania governor William Scranton, Maine senator Margaret Chase Smith, and former Minnesota governor Harold Stassen—drew interest, but none emerged as a unifying candidate capable of defeating Goldwater.

In the late fall of 1963, during the self-imposed campaign moratorium following Kennedy's assassination, Republican Party leaders studied the implications of nominating Goldwater. They concluded that Goldwater would probably lose the Northeast and split the South with Johnson (Shadegg, 1965). On December 7, Dwight Eisenhower called on Lodge to enter the race as a compromise candidate. Others mentioned Richard Nixon as a possibility, though Nixon's star had dimmed after his loss in the 1962 California gubernatorial election. But Lodge refused to bless the efforts to draft him, and Nixon never got in. That left Goldwater alone as the conservative candidate amid a fractured sea of moderate opponents. Although he fared poorly in Republican primaries in the New England and Mid-Atlantic states, he cruised to the nomination by winning the delegate vote at the party convention.

Prior to formally accepting the GOP nomination at the San Francisco convention, Goldwater steered the party faithful to select New York representative William E. Miller as his running mate. Miller had been chairman of the RNC and was known as a fierce and articulate opponent of Johnson's policies during his time in the House. Generally, however, his elevation to the ticket was viewed as an effort to make Goldwater more appealing in New York and other eastern states (White, 1965).

If observers thought this was an indication that Goldwater was maneuvering to the center of the political spectrum, they were sadly mistaken. With the business of the vice-presidency settled, Goldwater's fall campaign was effectively launched with the memorable lines from his convention speech: "Anyone who wants to join us in all sincerity, we welcome. Those who do not care for our cause, we don't expect to enter our ranks in any case. And let our Republicanism, so focused and so dedicated, not be made fuzzy and futile by un-thinking and stupid labels. I would remind you that extremism in the defense of liberty is no vice. And let me remind you also that moderation in the pursuit of justice is no virtue."[23] Given the reticence of many moderate Republicans to embrace Goldwater's new brand of conservatism, this was hardly the sort of palliative rhetoric one might have expected.

Johnson pounced on Goldwater's refusal to back down. His campaign proceeded on two tracks. The first track was to highlight the "extremism" of Goldwater's policy positions, especially on foreign policy and how to deal with the Soviet Union. The most remembered example of this is the famous "Daisy Girl" ad, in which a young girl counting petals she was picking from a flower was transposed with a countdown for a missile launch, presumably ordered by "President Goldwater" to deliver a nuclear weapon.[24] The ad was produced by the New York ad company Doyle Dane Bernbach, in collaboration with sound designer and ad creator Tony Schwarz. It aired only once but was emblematic of the provocative and powerful style of Johnson's spot advertisements. Less widely remembered but every bit as controversial was a Johnson ad suggesting Goldwater was being endorsed by the Ku Klux Klan.[25] Johnson's second track was to lay claim to the legacy of the slain President Kennedy, emphasizing himself as both the guardian of Kennedy's policy legacy and an experienced, compassionate leader during turbulent times. The more uplifting nature of this second track should not obscure the ominous

Table 3.4 1964 Presidential Campaign Plans

	JOHNSON			GOLDWATER		
# of states	Base Democratic	Battleground/ Targets	Base Republican	Base Democratic	Battleground/ Targets	Base Republican
1	Alaska (3)	California (40)*	Alabama (10)	Alaska (3)	Alabama (10)**	Arizona (5)
2	Connecticut (8)	Florida (14)**	Arizona (5)	D.C. (3)	Arkansas (6)	Colorado (6)
3	D.C. (3)	Illinois (26)*	Arkansas (6)	Delaware (3)	California (40)***	Idaho (4)
4	Delaware (3)	Indiana (13)*	Colorado (6)	Hawaii (4)	Connecticut (8)	Indiana (13)
5	Hawaii (4)	Maryland (10)*	Georgia (12)	Iowa (9)	Florida (14)**	Kansas (7)
6	Iowa (9)	Massachusetts (14)*	Idaho (4)	Massachusetts (14)	Georgia (12)**	Kentucky (9)
7	Kentucky (9)	Michigan (21)*	Kansas (7)	Michigan (21)	Illinois (26)*	Montana (4)
8	Maine (4)	Minnesota (10)*	Louisiana (10)	Minnesota (10)	Louisiana (10)**	Nebraska (5)
9	Nevada (3)	Missouri (12)***	Mississippi (7)	Missouri (12)	Maine (4)	North Dakota (4)
10	New Hampshire (4)	New Jersey (17)*	Montana (4)	Nevada (3)	Maryland (10)	Oklahoma (8)
11	New Mexico (4)	New York (43)*	Nebraska (5)	New Mexico (4)	Mississippi (7)*	South Dakota (4)
12	Oregon (6)	Ohio (26)*	North Carolina (13)	Oregon (6)	New Hampshire (4)	Utah (4)
13	Rhode Island (4)	Pennsylvania (29)*	North Dakota (4)	Rhode Island (4)	New Jersey (17)	Wyoming (3)
14	Tennessee (11)	Texas (25)**	Oklahoma (8)	Washington (9)	New York (43)	
15	Vermont (3)	Wisconsin (12)*	South Carolina (8)	West Virginia (7)	North Carolina (13)**	
16	Washington (9)		South Dakota (4)		Ohio (26)*	
17	West Virginia (7)		Utah (4)		Pennsylvania (29)	

18			Virginia (12)			South Carolina (8)**		
19			Wyoming (3)			Tennessee (11)**		
20						Texas (25)***		
21						Vermont (3)		
22						Virginia (12)*		
23						Wisconsin (12)*		
States	17	15	19	51	15	23	13	51
EVs	94	312	132	538	112	350	76	538

Notes:

"EV" stands for electoral votes. State electoral votes provided in parentheses.

For Johnson's strategy, * indicates "12-state strategy"; ** "expanded 12-state strategy"; *** "expanded 12-state strategy plus Missouri".

For Goldwater's strategy, *** indicates "priority 1"; ** "priority 2"; * "priority 3".

Sources:

Abraham, G. 1964. "Memo from G. Abraham of DDB, Inc. to Bill Moyers," Lyndon B. Johnson Papers-DNC (8/6/64), Box 224; Lyndon B. Johnson Presidential Library.

Doyle Dane Bernbach, Inc. 1964. "Media Recommendation for Democratic National Committee, 1964 Election,"

Lyndon B. Johnson Papers—Democratic National Committee (7/24/64), Box 225; Lyndon B. Johnson Presidential Library.

Middendorf, J. William, III. 2006. *A Glorious Disaster*. New York: Basic Books: see especially 150, 188.

Shadegg, Stephen, 1965. *What Happened to Goldwater? The Inside Story of the 1964 Republican Campaign*. New York: Holt, Reinhart, and Winston. (See especially pages 195-196, 216.)

US News and World Report, 1964. "Barry's Chances against LBJ: Issues Abound Once Goldwater Takes on Johnson in Presidential Campaign," US News and World Report, 56, June 22, 1964: 31–33.

Wentworthy, E. W. 1964. "Campaign—Goldwater's Strategy Takes Shape," *New York Times*, August 2, 1964: 131.

tone that permeates the initial track: having noted the persistent negativity of presidential campaigns over time, we would be remiss if we did not also note that the 1964 campaign featured more overtly threatening language and content than its immediate predecessors in this era. In this way, it was a harbinger of what was to come.

Beyond themes and broad messages, Johnson's campaign was confident though wary of how the mercurial candidacy of Goldwater might upset the electoral map. The Democratic team, like the Republican Party leadership, concluded that Goldwater would seriously compromise the GOP's ability to compete in the northeastern states. However, Johnson and the Democrats were worried about Goldwater's appeal in the southern states, as well as the possibility that he could be appealing in the Rocky Mountain and western states. Based on strategic memos to LBJ press secretary Bill Moyers—many from the TV ad agency, Doyle Dane Bernbach—Table 3.4 shows that the Johnson campaign saw their base as consisting of 17 states worth 94 electoral votes. The battleground category encompassed 15 states worth 312 electoral votes. Johnson thus needed to win 56% of the votes within this category to achieve re-election. Our category of battleground states encompasses the campaign's more targeted "12-state strategy," as well as their subsequent expansions on this strategy, which brought Florida, Texas, and finally Missouri into the mix. The Democrats wrote off 19 states worth a collective 132 electoral votes. It is worth noting that Johnson's campaign largely conceded the southern states to Goldwater and the Republicans; a stunning shift historically and one especially notable given that Johnson himself was a southerner.

Based on strategic memos from Goldwater's advisors—many archived at the Hoover Institute's library—as well as insider accounts like Stephen Shaddeg's and journalistic work from reporters following the campaign, we know that the Goldwater campaign figured their base was 13 states worth a total of 76 electoral votes. They did not see the South as part of their base; rather, they considered those states as battlegrounds. Their larger battleground classification included a whopping 23 states worth a total 350 electoral votes. In our view, this expansive plan does not reflect a lack of strategic acumen. Rather, it seems to reflect the odd coalitional dynamics associated with a strongly conservative candidate at that point in American history: opportunities in the South, but a need to defend turf in the Northeast. It also reflects their underdog status: the daunting short-term forces arrayed against them required a concerted effort in many places. At any rate, the lengthy list of battleground states still required the GOP ticket to carry 55% of the available electoral votes, which seems a tall order given the Democrats' advantages. Within the battleground category, the Republican campaign identified two "priority 1" states

(California and Texas); seven "priority 2" states (Alabama, Florida, Georgia, Louisiana, North Carolina, South Carolina, and Tennessee); and five "priority 3" states (Illinois, Mississippi, Ohio, Virginia, and Wisconsin). The "priority" distinctions appear to reflect both size and geography: priority 1 are the most populous; priority 2 states are middle sized and southern; priority 3 states are populous or southern (e.g., Mississippi). Goldwater's team conceded 15 states, mostly in the upper Midwest, worth 112 electoral votes.

The election of 1964 was a landslide for the Johnson-Humphrey ticket. They carried 61% of the popular vote and 45 states worth 486 electoral votes. The Democrats swept California and the key states of the industrial Midwest, and even dominated in the Republican strongholds of New England. Goldwater managed to win his home state of Arizona (by a single percentage point) and the five Deep South states of Alabama, Georgia, Louisiana, Mississippi, and South Carolina.

With the benefit of hindsight, an argument can be made that the disastrous result for the Republicans laid the groundwork for their subsequent success: they won four of the next five presidential elections, largely by dominating in the southern and border South states. But such a viewpoint would have seemed pollyannaish in the immediate aftermath of LBJ's great triumph. It also diminishes the fact that the Republicans seemed to have lost whatever strategic advantage they had in the 1950s with respect to innovative television advertising. Specifically, Goldwater's campaign had de-emphasized spot ads in favor of more traditional half-hour televised speeches. In addition, the spot ads they produced were stilted and old-fashioned.[26] This was something the Nixon campaign would correct in subsequent election campaigns.

The Return of Tricky Dick: Nixon-Humphrey and Nixon-McGovern Elections

One of the most tumultuous years of American history deserved an equally tumultuous and chaotic presidential campaign, and 1968 gladly obliged. The war in Vietnam, which had been a consequential but quiescent issue in 1964, was now a major dividing line in American politics. President Johnson, who had continued to score major legislative victories in the aftermath of his 1964 triumph, including the Voting Rights Act and the "Great Society" bills, was now beset by criticism over his handling of the conflict. The national economy continued to expand at a rapid rate—following a pattern of growth begun in 1961—but signs of weakness were beginning to show, as a chronic imbalance of payments resulted in a speculative run on gold in March 1968 (Collins, 1996). Most obviously, the social fabric of the country was fraying over divisive issues such as civil rights, crime, and drugs in addition to the national discord over the Vietnam War.

It was widely assumed that Johnson would run for re-election in 1968 and that the election would serve as a referendum on his policies, domestic and foreign. His job approval ratings had fallen from the 70s to the 40s by the time of the 1966 mid-term elections.[27] Furthermore, by the fall of 1967, signs of internal strife were evident among a vocal yet still small anti-war constituency within the Democratic Party. Still, the only figure bold enough to openly declare for the Democratic nomination was Minnesota senator Eugene McCarthy, and Johnson's lead in national opinion polls ranged between 50 and 70 points (White, 1969).

But in January 1968, the Tet Offensive shook the nation's confidence in the war effort. Opposition to Johnson came from both sides of the partisan aisle: Republican "hawks" thought that Johnson was using half-measures to win the war, while Democratic "doves" thought the war was immoral as well as unwinnable. Whispered concerns became full-throated opposition. McCarthy then scored a major public relations victory by almost upsetting Johnson in the March 12 New Hampshire primary (Johnson won by a 49% to 42% margin). New York senator Robert Kennedy, brother of the assassinated president, declared his candidacy on March 16. Johnson decided he could not win the nomination without a considerable effort. Facing an intractable war and declining health, Johnson decided to drop out and use his control of the party apparatus to help his vice-president, Hubert Humphrey, win the nomination. The president withdrew from the race in a televised address to the nation on March 31. Humphrey declared his candidacy on April 27.

The shape of the contest was unique. On the one hand, Humphrey (and Johnson) skipped the primaries, using "favorite son" candidates to win delegates who would then serve as surrogates for Humphrey at the convention. On the other hand, Kennedy and McCarthy battled across the primary states to win the hearts and minds of liberal Democrats. This latter battle came to a crashing halt during the early morning hours of June 5, when Kennedy was assassinated after defeating McCarthy by four points in the critical California primary. Kennedy's death meant that his delegates splintered; some going to McCarthy, who shared their anti-war views, and some going to Humphrey, who had not directly opposed their fallen hero (White, 1969). Humphrey was thus assured of the nomination.

Unfortunately for the Democrats, the 1968 national convention, where Humphrey's triumph was officially validated, reflected the disaffection and rancor of the primary season. Hundreds of anti-war protestors agitated outside of the convention hall in Chicago. They were brutally beaten by Chicago police, as the world watched on television (Boller, 2004). Inside the hall,

Chicago mayor Richard Daley used strong-arm tactics to intimidate those who voiced opposition to the actions of his police force outside (Troy, 1996). Ultimately, Humphrey was nominated, and the convention chose Maine senator Edmund Muskie as his running mate.

The Democratic contest marked the end of the old nomination system: the party's 1968 convention fiasco ushered in new reforms recommended by the McGovern-Fraser Commission, starting initially in 1972 and culminating in a complete shift by 1976. Never again could a candidate win the party's nomination without actively contesting caucuses and primaries.[28] The 1968 race also marked the end of the old New Deal coalition for the Democrats: labor unions and big city bosses sided with Humphrey; white students and intellectuals sided with McCarthy; Catholics, Blacks, and Latinos sided with Kennedy; and white southerners sided with George Wallace (Boller, 2004).

On the Republican side, the nomination process resulted in the phoenix-like resurrection of Richard Nixon. Left for dead after his loss in the California governor's election of 1962, Nixon spent the next five years carefully rebuilding his reputation and cultivating the support of Republican leaders across the country (Boller, 2004). Over the course of the spring of 1968, he systematically dispatched all challengers to the Republican nomination. One by one, he defeated Michigan governor George Romney, New York governor Nelson Rockefeller, and California governor Ronald Reagan. Nixon sailed into the Republican convention with a commanding lead and was easily nominated after Rockefeller and Reagan forces could not agree upon a plan to unite in opposition. Rather than reach out to his defeated co-partisans, Nixon chose as his running mate the relatively unknown Maryland governor Spiro Agnew. This move no doubt reflected Nixon's own insecurity as well as the belief that he could call the shots because the Democrats were in disarray.

For both sides, but especially for the Republicans, the greatest complication in a complicated election was the nomination of Alabama governor George Wallace—who had unsuccessfully sought the Democratic nomination—as the standard bearer for the American Independent Party. Wallace supported segregationist policies in the 1950s and 1960s and championed "states' rights" in his 1968 campaign. He was popular in the South, especially with men, and appealed to blue-collar whites in many northern states because of his populist views asserting collusion among elite forces in the country. Wallace chose retired four-star general Curtis LeMay as his running mate, mostly to bolster his credentials on foreign policy and to appeal to voters with strong anti-communist attitudes. The Wallace-LeMay ticket was on the ballot in all fifty states, though not in the District of Columbia.

The electoral plans of the campaigns are laid out in Table 3.5. We do not consider Wallace's plans in detail, although we know that his overall strategy was

Table 3.5 1968 Presidential Campaign Plans

	HUMPHREY				NIXON			
# of states	Base Democratic	Battleground/ Targets	Base Republican	Base Wallace	Base Democratic	Battleground/ Targets	Base Republican	Base Wallace
1	Connecticut (8)	Alaska (3)*	Arizona (5)	Alabama (10)	Connecticut (8)	California (40)	Alaska (3)	Alabama (10)
2	D.C. (3)	California (40)*	Delaware (3)	Arkansas (6)	D.C. (3)	Florida (14)	Arizona (5)	Arkansas (6)
3	Hawaii (4)	Colorado (6)**	Florida (14)	Georgia (12)	Delaware (3)	Illinois (26)***	Colorado (6)	Georgia (12)
4	Maine (4)	Illinois (26)***	Idaho (4)	Louisiana (10)	Hawaii (4)	Michigan (21)***	Idaho (4)	Louisiana (10)
5	Massachusetts (14)	Maryland (10)**	Indiana (13)	Mississippi (7)	Maine (4)	Missouri (12)***	Indiana (13)	Mississippi (7)
6	Michigan (21)	Nevada (3)**	Iowa (9)		Maryland (10)	New Jersey (17)	Iowa (9)	
7	Minnesota (10)	New Mexico (4)**	Kansas (7)		Massachusetts (14)	New York (43)**	Kansas (7)	
8	Missouri (12)	North Carolina (13)*	Kentucky (9)		Minnesota (10)	North Carolina (13)	Kentucky (9)	
9	New Jersey (17)	Ohio (26)**	Montana (4)		Rhode Island (4)	Ohio (26)***	Montana (4)	
10	New York (43)	Oregon (6)**	Nebraska (5)		Tennessee (11)*	Pennsylvania (29)***	Nebraska (5)	
11	Pennsylvania (29)	South Carolina (8)*	New Hampshire (4)		West Virginia (7)	South Carolina (8)	Nevada (3)	
12	Rhode Island (4)	Washington (9)**	North Dakota (4)			Texas (25)	New Hampshire (4)	
13	Texas (25)	West Virginia (7)**	Oklahoma (8)			Virginia (12)	New Mexico (4)	
14		Wisconsin (12)**	South Dakota (4)			Wisconsin (12)	North Dakota (4)	
15			Tennessee (11)				Oklahoma (8)	
16			Utah (4)				Oregon (6)	
17			Vermont (3)				South Dakota (4)	

18			Virginia (12)					Utah (4)		
19			Wyoming (3)					Vermont (3)		
20								Washington (9)		
21								Wyoming (3)		
States	13	14	19	5	51	11	14	21	5	51
EVs	194	173	126	45	538	78	298	117	45	538

Notes:

"EV" stands for electoral votes. State electoral votes provided in parentheses.

For Humphrey's strategy, *** indicates "too big to ignore"; ** "realistic possibility"; * "outside chance".

For Nixon's strategy, *** indicates "most critical"; ** New York included even though staff considered it "unwinnable"; * Tennessee added due to Agnew's presence on ticket.

Sources:

Chester, Lewis, Godfrey Hodgson, and Bruce Page. 1969. *An American Melodrama: The Presidential Campaign of 1968*. New York: Dell: see especially 795–796.)

Connell, Bill. 1968. "Memo from Bill Connell to Joe Napolitan," Hubert H. Humphrey Papers (9/9/68), Box 23 (C88F); Minnesota Historical Society Library.

Garment, Len, 1968. "Memo to Richard Nixon," Len Garment Papers (7/17/68), Box 71; Richard M. Nixon Presidential Birthplace and Library.

Haldeman, H.R. 1968. "Presidential Election Simulation," H.R. Haldeman Papers—White House Special Files (10/68), Box 36; Richard M. Nixon Presidential Birthplace and Library.

Phillips, Kevin. 1968. "Battleground States," Len Garment Papers (10/68), Box 85; Richard M. Nixon Presidential Birthplace and Library.

Wainstock, Dennis Dean. 1984. "The 1968 Presidential Campaign and Election." Ph.D. Dissertation, West Virginia University: see especially 435–436, 451–452.)

to win enough electoral votes in the southern states to deny either Nixon or Humphrey an Electoral College majority. This would presumably allow Wallace to extract policy concessions in exchange for his support. We can see that Wallace's involvement reduced the "playable" field in 1968 from 539 electoral votes to 493. Winning 270 electoral votes out of 493 required a 55% success rate.

From the Haldeman papers—which include strategic memos and election simulations—we know that Nixon's campaign considered 21 states worth 117 electoral votes as his base. They further identified 14 states worth 298 electoral votes as battleground states. Nixon therefore needed to win 153 electoral votes out of the 298 (52%) to win the election. His team identified five states worth 114 electoral votes as "most critical": Illinois, Michigan, Missouri, Ohio, and Pennsylvania. Interestingly, Nixon's campaign added New York to the list of battleground states even though his advisers did not think the state was winnable. Based on internal memos and documents, this was partly to satisfy key Republican party officials from New York, but also to force Humphrey to spend precious resources there defending Democratic "turf." They also identified Tennessee as a Democratic base state worth watching due to Agnew's presence on the ticket and Wallace's candidacy.

Strategic memos from Democratic consultants Bill Connell and others demonstrate that Humphrey's campaign knew they had their work cut out for them heading into the fall. They identified 13 states worth 194 electoral votes as their base. Note that this constitutes a much larger set of base Democratic states than in any of our previous campaigns (more even than Johnson in 1964). They further targeted 14 states worth 173 electoral votes as their battleground universe. Humphrey's strategy was thus to win 76 of the 173 electoral votes (44%) contained in this set of states.

This might appear an unrealistically sanguine assessment of the contest. After all, Humphrey trailed Nixon by double digits in national polls through September 1968; states in the Democratic base surely seemed to be in play. A comparison with Nixon's strategy reveals that several states considered "base Democratic" by Humphrey were Nixon "battlegrounds": Michigan, Missouri, New Jersey, New York, Pennsylvania, and Texas. But we think it instead reflects the assumption by the campaign that if Humphrey could not compete across a wide array of battleground states, he should target the most competitive and assume those most inclined to lean their way would ultimately do so.

This approach was facilitated by a greater reliance on past voting data as well as contemporaneous statewide polling information: by mid-September, Humphrey's internal polls signaled that he was making up ground most everywhere, but especially in states—and in regions within those states—that had gone Democratic in 1960 and 1964. In this sense, the Democratic campaign of 1968 was a harbinger of campaign styles to come. Within their battleground states, Humphrey's team identified Illinois as "too big to ignore," Alaska, California, North Carolina, and South Carolina as "outside chance" states, and Colorado, Maryland, Nevada, New Mexico, Ohio, Oregon, Washington, West Virginia, and Wisconsin as "realistic possibility" states.

On Election Day, Richard Nixon climbed all the way back, erasing the failures of 1960 and 1962, and winning the White House. The Nixon-Agnew ticket defeated the Humphrey-Muskie ticket by 0.7 percentage points, 44.4% to 43.7%, and by an electoral vote margin of 110 votes (301 to 191). Wallace faded badly, but still managed to win 13.5% of the national vote, as well as five states worth 45 electoral votes. Indeed, it is worth bearing in mind that Nixon did not win any states in the Deep South, and his electoral plan suggests these states were never key to his Electoral College strategy. The Nixon team appeared to understand that Wallace would siphon off enough support among southern conservatives to carry the swath of states across the Louisiana and Mississippi deltas.

It is also worth bearing in mind that the Democrats narrowed the race over the final six weeks (Boller, 2004; White, 1969). As is often the case with presidential campaigns, it is difficult to discern the reason for Humphrey's late surge. Clearly, Wallace's support cratered over the month of October, as he dropped from the low twenties to the mid-teens. When considering Humphrey's surge and Wallace's collapse, three factors are compelling. First, the Humphrey campaign targeted union members who were supporting Wallace. They almost certainly "came home" to the Democratic candidate. Second, Humphrey targeted Wallace on the issues of civil rights and "concentrated wealth," which Wallace had been using to appeal to lower status white voters. Third, Humphrey distanced himself from Johnson on the Vietnam War, calling for a bombing halt. On this last factor, Humphrey was aided by President Johnson's declaration of a bombing halt and a possible declaration of peace during the last weekend before the election.[29]

Humphrey also benefitted from a spot advertising campaign that relentlessly attacked Nixon as "untrustworthy." Sensing that voters had permanently soured on Johnson, Humphrey's team dispensed with defending the incumbent administration and instead sought to resurrect concerns about Nixon's ethics. The campaign produced several spots that were reminiscent in tone and style to Johnson's "Daisy" ad. For his part, Nixon relied on two brilliant young media consultants. Eugene Jones produced a series of visually arresting TV ad spots featuring the unrest and turmoil at home and abroad. Roger Ailes oversaw a remaking of Nixon's public image with carefully crafted public appearances and live interviews with citizen audiences. Both are detailed in Joe McGinnis's masterful *The Selling of the President 1968*. In the end, Humphrey's late charge fell just short. However, it was a remarkable comeback that provided a fittingly controversial and contentious end to one of the most eventful years ever in American politics.

President Richard Nixon headed into 1972 with significant tailwinds. After several shocks in the late 1960s and early 1970s, by 1972 the U.S. economy was growing at a robust rate of 6.4%, while prices remained stable, and unemployment dipped to 5.1% by the end of the year. The social unrest and political violence of the 1960s had ebbed. And while the conflict in Vietnam continued, in February of 1972 Nixon became the first American president to visit mainland China, which he used to pressure the Soviet Union into negotiations that led to the Anti-Ballistic Missile Treaty (and the subsequent Helsinki Accords, signed after he left office). But these triumphs came at some cost. Nixon had angered conservatives not only with his visit to China, but also by (briefly) imposing wage and price controls in 1970 and helping to pass the Clean Air Act, which established the Environmental Protection Agency. Liberals were angered by Nixon's continued prosecution of the Vietnam War, as well as by his support for (and use of) intrusive and aggressive law enforcement practices, including electronic surveillance of domestic protest groups. But Nixon's position heading into the re-election campaign was enviable, notwithstanding the grousing on the far right and the far left. Moreover, the Committee to Re-Elect the President (CREEP) was proving a fundraising and opposition research dynamo for the always wary Nixon.[30]

On the Democratic side, the usual suspects led the list of contenders seeking to unseat Nixon. Minnesota senator George McGovern, along with Hubert Humphrey, Edmund Muskie, and Eugene McCarthy all entered the Democratic fray. So did George Wallace. Washington senator Henry "Scoop" Jackson ran as representative of the hawkish wing of the Democratic Party. And New York representative Shirley Chisholm became the first African American women to seek a major party presidential nomination. Notably missing from this list is Massachusetts senator Edward "Ted" Kennedy. After the 1968 election, speculation immediately began about Kennedy's presidential ambitions. The younger brother of John and Bobby, Ted Kennedy had won election to the Senate from Massachusetts in 1962 and was elected majority party whip in 1971. But Kennedy's involvement in a car accident in Chappaquiddick in July 1969 that resulted in the death of Mary Jo Kopechne haunted his prospective candidacy (Matthews, 2011). Despite the power of his family name and his strength in the public polls both for the nomination and against Nixon, Kennedy refused to run and rejected subsequent efforts at the Democratic convention to include him on the ticket.[31]

With Kennedy out of the picture, the Democratic contest quickly narrowed to a fight among Muskie, Humphrey, Wallace, and McGovern. Muskie led in most of the polls and seemed the front-runner heading into the New Hampshire primary. But Muskie's campaign came undone amid allegations that he had written a derogatory letter about French-Canadians (the so-called Canuck letter), that his wife had an alcohol problem, and that she had used profane language during campaign events.[32] Things came to a head as Muskie responded to these issues outside the offices of the Manchester Union-Leader, an influential and conservative-leaning New Hampshire newspaper. Muskie offered an emotional defense, but the main reaction among those covering the appearance was that Muskie was "losing it" and that he had cried (Muskie and others claimed he had not cried; rather, snowflakes had melted on his face). Whatever the truth, the damage was done: support for Muskie plummeted and his campaign effectively ended (White, 1973).

Wallace, meanwhile, was dominating in the southern primaries (he won every county in the Florida primary) and running surprisingly well among dissatisfied and alienated Democrats in the northern states. But Wallace's run was ended by an assassin's bullet on May 15: he was paralyzed from the waist down and was confined to a wheelchair for the remainder of his life. Wallace subsequently won the Michigan and Maryland primaries but dropped out of the race in July.

That left McGovern, who had assiduously built a grass-roots campaign organization since announcing his candidacy nearly two years earlier. Drawing on support from liberal, anti-war Democrats, McGovern was targeting the primary elections that had become the dominant mechanism for selecting delegates, in large part due to the changes mandated by the party commission McGovern himself had chaired (Boller, 2004; Troy, 1996). With Kennedy out and Muskie marginalized, McGovern dominated the primaries. Humphrey attempted to galvanize opposition to McGovern, saying he could never appeal to Middle America. Other Democratic leaders concurred, with Missouri senator Thomas Eagleton commenting that McGovern was for "amnesty, abortion, and the legalization of pot" and as such stood no chance of winning (Saad, 2000). The subsequent tagline of "amnesty, abortion, and acid" dogged McGovern throughout the election, but the indifference of Democratic Party and elected officials was even more problematic. They opposed both McGovern and the system he had designed that marginalized them in the selection process. In the end, they were powerless to stop him from becoming the Democratic nominee for president.

They were far from powerless, however, when it came to the vice-presidential nominee. Opposition to McGovern's choice, the aforementioned

Eagleton, became the preferred way of expressing opposition to McGovern. Eagleton was eventually nominated, but three other candidates allowed their names to be placed into nomination and over 70 candidates won votes. After the convention, revelations emerged that Eagleton had undergone electroshock therapy to deal with his depression and had not disclosed this to McGovern. Despite saying that he backed Eagleton "1000 percent," McGovern asked that he withdraw from the ticket three days later (Troy, 1996; White, 1973). A special convention of the Democratic Party then nominated Sargent Shriver, former ambassador to France and former director of the Peace Corps, and brother-in-law to John, Robert, and Ted Kennedy.

Thus, McGovern entered the general election phase of the campaign as seriously damaged goods. Rather than unite his party and lift his poll numbers, McGovern's convention had re-opened party wounds and given him no bounce in the national polls (Saad 2000). In fact, a late August Gallup Poll showed Nixon ahead by a 60% to 22% margin.[33] An underrated consequence of the lack of support among Democratic officials is that the party refused to raise money or enlist the efforts of organized labor to help the ticket. Neither side harbored any illusions: this was Nixon's race to lose. As shown in Table 3.6, Nixon's campaign strategy—mainly drawn from the comprehensive papers of Jeb Magruder, who was political director of CREEP—reflected both his own strength as well as the changing coalitional realities sparked by the Democrats' newly problematic relationship with the White South. Nixon's team conceded only five states worth 35 electoral votes as the Democratic base. Conversely, they tabbed 24 states worth 163 states as the Republican base. Their battleground category encompassed 22 states worth 340 electoral votes, meaning they needed to carry only 31% of the battleground votes to win a majority in the Electoral College. Within their battleground states, they distinguished among eight "large, key" states (California, Illinois, Michigan, Missouri, New Jersey, Ohio, Texas and Wisconsin) worth 183 electoral votes, and six "small, key" states (Alaska, Delaware, Maryland, Oregon, Washington, and West Virginia) worth 37 electoral votes. If focused on these states, Nixon needed 49% of them to win. The campaign further targeted eight states as "major" or "southern" state opportunities and identified six of their base states as needing defense or maintenance. In totality, the Nixon plan seems a spot-on strategic appraisal of the 1972 electoral landscape.

McGovern's plan is laid out in the candidate's personal papers, which include memos from several key players, including Gary Hart, his campaign manager. This plan also reflects the reality of the race. The Democrats conceded 28 states and 207 electoral votes as "Republican base." By contrast, they saw McGovern's base as seven states and 45 electoral votes. That necessitated winning 225 of the 286 electoral votes available among the 16 battleground states. This 79% winning percentage needed is the highest we have seen in this era, though its pessimistic approach to the prospect of winning seems an appropriate reflection of the electoral realities in 1972. McGovern's campaign concedes the South, except for Texas, and counts instead on sweeping California, Illinois, Michigan, New York, Ohio, Pennsylvania, and Wisconsin. By attempting to "thread the needle," McGovern and his team wrote off states that had been critical to Democratic success since the end of the Civil War. Given the openly and defiantly progressive posture of their candidate, however, it is not obvious what their other options were.

In November, Nixon scored one of the greatest victories in modern American politics, winning 61% of the national vote and 520 electoral votes. Only Massachusetts and the District of Columbia went for the Democratic ticket. In the South, the Republican ticket won with almost 75% of the vote. As in 1964, the results showed what could happen when one major party was fractured while the other was focused and intent.

These results also show the cresting of certain trends that would by 1976 give rise to a substantively new era. The television advertising strategies in 1972 were modern in concept and increasingly recognizable in terms of execution. Nixon's ads were produced by the November Group, a virtual all-star team of advertising executives headed by Peter Dailey, who ran his own Los Angeles agency, Phil Joanou from Doyle Dane Bernbach, William Taylor from Ogilvy and Mather, and an advisory board of executives from many top agencies. They manifested a two-pronged strategy of showing Nixon as an effective world leader and attacking McGovern's liberalism. But the documentary style of the former, giving audiences a sense that they were watching Nixon "back-stage," was revolutionary. McGovern's ads were created by Charles Guggenheim, a documentary filmmaker who had worked on ads for Stevenson in 1956. Guggenheim used cinema-verité techniques—hand-held cameras and portable sound—to create a sense of casualness and spontaneity. Later, McGovern used a word crawl against a black backdrop in his attack ads against Nixon; while not enough to overcome the environmental factors that so favored Nixon, this stark imagery has been a staple of political ads ever since.

More broadly, the excesses in fundraising that permeated the 1972 contest, with slush funds and dirty tricks outfits, were directly targeted by federal campaign finance reform legislation that followed the election. The dominance of television as a communication medium and of polling as a means for crafting messages and developing strategy were significant factors in the 1972 Nixon

Table 3.6 1972 Presidential Campaign Plans

	McGOVERN			NIXON		
# of states	Base Democratic	Battleground/ Targets	Base Republican	Base Democratic	Battleground/ Targets	Base Republican
1	D.C. (3)	Alaska (3)	Alabama (9)	D.C. (3)	Alabama (9)**	Arizona (6)
2	Hawaii (4)	California (45)	Arizona (6)	Hawaii (4)	Alaska (3)***	Colorado (7)
3	Massachusetts (14)	Connecticut (8)	Arkansas (6)	Massachusetts (14)	Arkansas (6)**	Florida (17)*
4	Minnesota (10)	Delaware (3)	Colorado (7)	Minnesota (10)	California (45)****	Idaho (4)
5	Rhode Island (4)	Illinois (26)	Florida (17)	Rhode Island (4)	Connecticut (8)**	Indiana (13)
6	South Dakota (4)	Iowa (8)	Georgia (12)		Delaware (3)***	Iowa (8)
7	West Virginia (6)	Maryland (10)	Idaho (4)		Georgia (12)**	Kansas (7)
8		Michigan (21)	Indiana (13)		Illinois (26)****	Kentucky (9)
9		New Jersey (17)	Kansas (7)		Louisiana (10)**	Maine (4)
10		New York (41)	Kentucky (9)		Maryland (10)***	Montana (4)
11		Ohio (25)	Louisiana (10)		Michigan (21)****	Nebraska (5)
12		Oregon (6)	Maine (4)		Mississippi (7)**	Nevada (4)
13		Pennsylvania (27)	Mississippi (7)		Missouri (12)****	New Hampshire (4)
14		Texas (26)	Missouri (12)		New Jersey (17)****	New Mexico (4)
15		Washington (9)	Montana (4)		New York (41)**	North Carolina (13)*
16		Wisconsin (11)	Nebraska (5)		Ohio (25)****	North Dakota (3)
17			Nevada (4)		Oregon (6)***	Oklahoma (8)
18			New Hampshire (4)		Pennsylvania (27)**	South Carolina (8)*

19			New Mexico (4)			Texas (26)****	South Dakota (4)*	
20			North Carolina (13)			Washington (9)***	Tennessee (10)*	
21			North Dakota (3)			West Virginia (6)***	Utah (4)	
22			Oklahoma (8)			Wisconsin (11)****	Vermont (3)	
23			South Carolina (8)				Virginia (11)*	
24			Tennessee (10)				Wyoming (3)	
25			Utah (4)					
26			Vermont (3)					
27			Virginia (11)					
28			Wyoming (3)					
States	7	16	28	51	5	22	24	51
EVs	45	286	207	538	35	340	163	538

Notes:

"EV" stands for electoral votes. State electoral votes provided in parentheses.

For Nixon's strategy, **** indicates "large/key" states; *** "small/key" states; ** "major/southern opportunity" states; * "defensive/safe".

Sources:

Finkelstein, Arthur. 1972. "Memo from Arthur Finkelstein to Jeb Magruder," Files of Jeb Magruder (2/4/72), Box 19; Hoover Institution Library.

Haldeman, H. R. 1972. "National Election Media Plan," H.R. Haldeman Papers (n.d.), Box 338; Richard M. Nixon Birthplace and Presidential Library.

Magruder, Jeb. 1972. "Memo from Jeb Magruder to John Mitchell," Files of Jeb Magruder (3/27/72), Box 19; Hoover Institution Library.

McGovern, George. 1972. "Surveys and Analysis, 1971–73," George S. McGovern Papers (n.d.), Boxes 174–175;

Public Policy Papers, Department of Rare Books and Special Collections, Princeton University Library.

Moore, Jonathan and Janet Fraser (eds.). 1973. *Campaign for President: The Managers Look at '72*. Cambridge, MA: Ballinger Publishing Company.

White, Theodore. 1973. *The Making of the President, 1972*. New York: Atheneum.

landslide. The end of party control of the nominating system was also laid bare by McGovern's nomination victory in 1972. In this light, Nixon's downfall a mere twenty-one months after his historic victory signals the end of one era and the beginning of another.

How Good Were These Guys?

In the coming chapters, we consider the extent to which campaigns adhered to their plans when allocating television advertising and candidate appearances, as well as the effect those allocations had on election outcomes. However, having reviewed the proposed Electoral College plans for each of the major party campaigns across this initial era, it seems appropriate to offer some preliminary observations, especially given our larger research hypotheses. The first observation that jumps out from the documents and memos we have read is that the advisors running these campaigns were probably even more sophisticated than we had expected. We expected to characterize them as having "medium sophistication" relative to more recent campaigns, but their use of past election results (down to the county and township levels) and the introduction of polling information across the era might justify an even higher rating. They were about as sophisticated as the limitations of their available technologies let them be. Here, the Kennedy campaign is particularly worthy of notice. The work of pollster Lou Harris and the statistical modeling of the Simulmatics Corporation (headed by Edward L. Greenfield) are clear harbingers of the work of analytics and big data scientists in the presidential campaigns of today.[34] Consider the following description from a recent article in the *New Yorker*:

> Led by an M.I.T. political scientist named Ithiel de Sola Pool, the chairman of Simulmatics' research board, Greenfield's scientists compiled a set of "massive data" from election returns and public-opinion surveys going back to 1952, sorting voters into four hundred and eighty types, and issues into fifty-two clusters. Then they built what they sometimes called a voting-behavior machine, a computer simulation of the 1960 election, in which they could test scenarios on an endlessly customizable virtual population: you could ask it a question about any move a candidate might make and it would tell you how voters would respond, down to the tiniest segment of the electorate. (Lepore, 2020)

And Kennedy was not an outlier. Johnson and Nixon also relied heavily on polling data to inform both messaging and strategy. Our assumption was that data from previous elections would drive most strategic planning in campaigns from this era, but extensive and innovative use of polling data was more common than we had thought, at least after 1956.

The second observation relates to our expectations about execution. We have not yet considered whether the campaigns adhered to their plans closely or just generally, but the plans themselves appear to be directly geared toward informing resource allocation. There is, of course, variance across the campaigns. The Nixon campaigns, especially those of 1968 and 1972, seem to be drawn up with an explicit expectation of driving television advertising and candidate appearances. In each campaign, the designation of strategic categories carried with it an estimation of expected TV ad buys. With respect to candidate appearances, the expectations were less explicit, but strategic memoranda seem to assume the primacy of battleground states with respect to the candidates' time. As befits an era where the main communication modalities were still perceived to be national radio broadcasts rather than geographically focused spot ads, the Stevenson campaigns of 1952 and 1956 seem, by contrast, more loosely drawn and structured. There is, however, little indication that campaigns in this era were especially flexible: actionable information from polls did not seem to be expected during the fall, nor did plans appear to have been altered much as campaigns were underway.

The third observation concerns the possibility of campaign effects. This is an era in which the partisan allegiances forged during the New Deal began to shift. It is possible that presidential campaigns served to hasten this shift, with pro-Republican movement being stimulated by GOP spending and campaigning advantages. But it is even more likely, in our view, that these shifts occurred irrespective of campaigning differentials. In addition, four of the races during this era were landslides (however defined): Eisenhower in 1952 and 1956, Johnson in 1964, and Nixon in 1972. Campaign effects are possible in such elections but are less obviously critical to the outcomes. In contrast, the elections of 1960 and 1968 were extremely close. In 1960, the polls suggest small swings of a few points here and there. In this way, 1960 looks a great deal like more modern presidential elections, which are constrained by polarized politics and entrenched partisanship. However, in 1968 the polls suggested a large swing toward Humphrey and the Democrats. This election occurs to us as a most obvious choice for campaign effects: three candidates, a dynamic and fluid coalitional environment, and numerous divisive and salient issues. Did Humphrey successfully ignore the Southern states and regain the support of Northern Democrats and independents in 1968? Or did Nixon effectively target the "Silent Majority" throughout?

Given the level of sophistication of presidential campaigns in this most distant of eras under consideration, we may need to revise our expectations about strategic acumen upward even further as we consider the middle and most recent eras. But does increased strategic sophistication matter if the available resources for candidates and their campaigns are severely constrained? This question is uppermost in our minds as we turn to the middle era of modern presidential campaigns.

4
Zero-Sum Campaigning (1976–2000)

Fall-Out from Watergate

It is obvious to most observers that the Watergate scandal and the subsequent resignation of President Richard M. Nixon in 1974 was one of the most consequential events in American politics in the twentieth century. While the details and intricacies of the scandal have been meticulously chronicled and repeatedly told in both popular and scholarly literature, Watergate might be *underrated* as an event that shaped modern campaigns. Put simply, there is a direct line between Watergate and changes in federal campaign finance laws that fundamentally reshaped the playing field for the next few decades of presidential election campaigns.

Here's how it happened. As we saw in chapter 3, presidential campaigns during the 1950s and 1960s were strategically sophisticated and competitive. The rise of television advertising as a means of political communication increased the need to raise money. However, aside from a few broad laws restricting the use of public property for fundraising and limiting the ability of corporations and other outside groups to contribute directly to candidates, there were almost no limits on the acquisition and distribution of campaign funds. This meant raising funds was an important part of campaigning and substantial asymmetries in campaign war chests were common.

The culmination of this era was the 1972 presidential campaign, in which Republican incumbent Richard Nixon outspent Democrat George McGovern by a three-to-one margin ($380.0 million to $131.2 million, in 2020 dollars) (Alexander, 1976: Tables 7-1 and 7-4). The Nixon campaign's Committee to Re-Elect the President (CREEP) was, by all accounts, maniacal in its quest to accumulate money and obsessive in its desire to dig up dirt on opponents (Matthews, 2011; Thompson, 1973; White, 1973). Given Nixon's razor-thin loss in 1960 to John F. Kennedy by about 112,000 votes nationally, and his narrow victory in 1968 over Hubert Humphrey by about 500,000 votes nationally, this mentality is somewhat understandable. Nevertheless, it was this push to win by larger margins that drove the bizarre events of June 17, 1972. On that date, five individuals were caught breaking into the Watergate

Battleground. Daron R. Shaw, Scott L. Althaus, and Costas Panagopoulos, Oxford University Press.
 DOI: 10.1093/oso/9780197774366.003.0004

Hotel headquarters of the Democratic National Committee (DNC). The plot was planned by a group called "the plumbers," a rogue operation within the White House headed by G. Gordon Liddy, which had begun coordinating with the CREEP.[1] The group was apparently seeking incriminating information about Democratic candidates in the files of the DNC. After the arrest of the five burglars, the various investigations of the Watergate affair brought to light numerous campaign-finance abuses, including illegal contributions from corporations, other illicit cash donations, hidden funds controlled by the CREEP, and favors extended to donors in exchange for large contributions (Woodward and Bernstein, 1974).

Coupled with the Nixon campaign's massive overall spending advantage, these abuses propelled substantive amendments to the Federal Election Campaign Act (FECA) in 1974. The "new" FECA was but one of several important pieces of congressional legislation designed to reign in the increasingly "imperial" presidency. For present purposes, though, it is perhaps the most consequential, as it completely redefined the terms of presidential campaigns for the next generation.

What Is the FECA and Why Do We Care?

The amended FECA had five critical provisions with respect to the conduct of federal (U.S. House, Senate, and presidential) elections. First, it limited individual citizen contributions to candidate campaigns, imposing a hard cap of $1,000 on individual contributions to a single candidate campaign for federal office, per election cycle.[2] It also imposed limits on individual contributions to party committees ($5,000) and overall limits on how much an individual could spend on federal election candidates. Beyond individual contributors, the FECA also defined and recognized "multi-candidate committees" as legitimate players, limiting them to $5,000 per candidate committee, per campaign.[3] Second, it limited candidate campaign expenditures for a given election. However, the Supreme Court quickly struck down this provision as an unconstitutional limitation of free speech in *Buckley v. Valeo* (1976). Third, the FECA required candidate campaign committees to disclose contributions and expenditures, on a quarterly basis. Fourth, it established the Federal Election Commission (FEC) to oversee enforcement of the new law.

But it was a fifth provision that fundamentally structured the strategic landscape for all campaigns that followed: the FECA established a public finance system for presidential campaigns using federal dollars (accumulated through a voluntary "check-off" on tax forms) for funding. This system included "matching" public funds for primary elections, as well as complete funding for national conventions and the general election campaigns, provided candidates themselves met several eligibility criteria and agreed to certain restrictions.

While contribution limits and disclosure requirements are consequential to the conduct of presidential campaigns, we believe this public funding system most profoundly altered the strategic and competitive terrain beginning in 1976. In creating a real, breathing public finance system, the new law allowed candidates to mostly forego general election fundraising and simply take public funds for their campaigns. According to the FEC:

> Public funding for major party presidential nominees in the general election takes the form of a grant of $20 million plus the difference in the price index. To be eligible to receive public funds, the presidential nominee of a major party must agree to limit spending to the amount of the grant and may not accept private contributions for the campaign. Candidates may spend an additional $50,000 from their own personal funds, which does not count against the expenditure limit. In 1976, each major party nominee received $21.8 million. By 2008 (the last year a major party candidate chose to accept a general election grant), that amount had grown to $84.1 million. (The general election grant for 2024 is $123.5 million.)[4]

From 1976 through 2000, for seven presidential elections, every Republican and Democratic presidential candidate received a check from the U.S. Treasury Department the day after accepting their party's nomination. This was the total amount they had for the general election campaign, not counting "soft money" spending by the parties and outside interest groups.[5] The upside was that the campaigns could concentrate solely on persuading and mobilizing voters, rather than on raising funds. The downside was that they had limited money with which to accomplish these tasks, and no one had a resource advantage over their opposition. By design, the playing field was essentially leveled, and strategic acumen and execution—rather than fundraising skills—became paramount. Under the FECA, presidential campaigns no longer had an incentive (or an opportunity) to excessively raise funds to outpace their opponent.

This era did not last much past the turn of the century. As noted in the FEC quote, presidential campaigns began to turn down public money due to the ease of raising funds in the new era—an era marked by the internet and polarized politics, which combined to produce billion-dollar campaigns. But from 1976 to 2000, presidential elections were contests between campaigns that were roughly equal in terms of resources, motivation, and information. As such, the ability to out-do the opposition was constrained, and aggregate or "net" campaign effects were probably difficult to realize. Indeed, much of the "minimal effects" literature on presidential campaigns has its roots in analyses of these elections. Yet, as we discuss in this chapter, improved targeting and relatively less polarization than would appear in more recent years suggests that the ability to persuade individual voters may have been substantial.

Expectations in the Era of Zero-Sum Campaigns

So, in this era of publicly financed presidential campaigns, what are our expectations? With respect to strategy, having a well-defined, finite set of resources is important, but other developments matter here as well. Most notably, by the 1970s public opinion polling had matured to the point where national and statewide surveys were extensively employed in presidential campaigns. Perhaps more to the point, these surveys were used to develop, refine, and update strategic decisions on the part of the candidates. By the 1980s, focus groups—small collections of specific kinds of voters, who were interviewed in a casual group setting about their attitudes toward politics, policy preferences, opinions about the candidates, and receptiveness to campaign messages—supplemented polling information, a kind of qualitative supplement to quantitative data. Together, these tools allowed campaigns in this second era to go beyond the first era's reliance on previous election results as they plotted which voters to target with their precious resources. In short, we expect strategic sophistication to have been high in this era.

When it comes to the execution of campaign strategy and targeting of campaign activities, we expect to see improvements from the previous era. We expect resource allocations to hew even more closely to plans. Campaigns from 1952 through 1972 targeted their television advertising and candidate appearances at the media market level based on data from previous election cycles and, in later years, from current polling. But this approach is almost certain to have become more pronounced in the "zero-sum campaign" era as the quantity and quality of polling information improved, and the sophistication of market-level buys presumably increased as more detailed political and consumer data emerged for media markets. We also expect that the focus of these targeting strategies was undecided voters; again, as high-quality polling in general (and high-quality statewide polling in particular) became commonplace, persuading voters who were not locked into a partisan preference would seem to be the holy grail for presidential campaigns of the era. In addition, it seems that certain campaigns employed more creative ad buy strategies. For example, in 1992 the Clinton campaign bought local TV ad time on Monday for the following Wednesday through Tuesday. As a memo from the Bush campaign pointed out, this was "brilliant," as "it takes away our ability to use the weekend to study a traditional Thursday or Friday buy; it gives them the weekend to revise their plans if we buy traditionally; it gives them the weekend to incorporate the past week's polls into their buying strategy; it lets them ship copy to arrive 24 hours before air instead of 72 hours (Friday for Monday); it confuses our competitive analyses which look at data on a Monday to Sunday media week."[6]

The historical context of the second era leads us to depart from conventional wisdom and expect campaign effects to be potentially substantial in this period. Our reasoning is that voters were less partisan than they are today, and (as noted earlier) campaigns had an increasing ability to identify persuasive messages (through polling and focus groups) and deliver them to specific demographic groups (through television and radio). Nevertheless, there is a caveat. Any individual-level impact of campaigns was likely offsetting because both campaigns had strong incentives to target the same parts of the country due to the proliferation of available information and the structural equality of available funds. In addition, campaigns in this era tended to focus more on persuasion than mobilization, which (in hindsight) limited their ability to swing the vote in their favor. It would be the last years of this second era before academic research would finally end up confirming a basic fact that changing the minds of voters about anything they think is important or worthy of reflection is among the most difficult things that a campaign could ever attempt to do, and among the least likely things that a campaign could ever hope to accomplish on anything like the national scale and in the short span of time over which presidential election contests are measured.

As in chapter 3, we assess these expectations by pulling together and analyzing descriptive information on each of the presidential campaigns. Though we offer some basic statistical analyses, our focus here is on a qualitative consideration of the development of campaign plans, the execution of those plans, and the effectiveness of those plans from Carter-Ford to Bush-Gore.

Jimmy Who? The Carter-Ford Election

The Nixon presidency cast a long shadow over the first election of this zero-sum campaign era. Not only did the Watergate scandal generate substantive campaign finance reform, it also paved the way for an "outsider" candidate to emerge as the candidate of the challenger party. Georgia governor Jimmy

Carter, a born-again Christian from a southern state who promised "never to lie to the American people," stunned the political world by defeating an array of better-known contenders to win the Democratic nomination. Carter's personal piety and public-spirited rhetoric nicely fit the nation's zeitgeist after the fall of Nixon.

Carter faced off against incumbent President Gerald Ford, who, though never directly elected either as president or even vice-president—he was appointed after Spiro Agnew, Nixon's first-term vice-president, resigned in disgrace following a political corruption scandal—captured the Republican nomination after a long and contentious battle against former California governor Ronald Reagan. In fact, after Ford dominated the early primary season, Reagan reeled off a series of wins that narrowed the president's delegate advantage enough to create doubt about the outcome heading into the GOP convention in Kansas City (Boller, 2004; Garcia, 2012; Troy, 1996). Despite trailing in the delegate count, Reagan even named a vice-presidential candidate, Senator Richard Schweiker of Pennsylvania, in advance of the convention. Reagan's charge was too little and too late, however, and Ford headed into the fall campaign with the Nixon scandal and a splintered party weighing him down (Boller, 2004). In the end, the election was one of the closest in American history, and Carter prevailed with 290 electoral votes and 50.1% of the popular vote.

The strategy animating Carter's presidential campaign was primarily developed by Hamilton Jordan, who had led Carter's successful campaign for Georgia governor at the age of 26 in 1970. While serving as Carter's executive assistant, Jordan wrote a long memorandum that served as the basis for Carter's strategy, both to win the Democratic nomination and as the basis for the campaign's Electoral College strategy, although Jordan continued to tweak the particulars, usually based on input from pollster Pat Caddell and communications strategist Gerald Rafshoon (Anderson, 1994; Bird, 2012; Jordan, 2001).

As seen in Table 4.1, by our reckoning the Carter team counted 21 states worth 213 electoral votes as base or leaning Carter. Unlike Humphrey in 1968 or McGovern in 1972, Carter—a native of the South—counted on winning all or most of the southern states. Even though they were considered part of his base, Carter's campaign treated them as requiring particular attention, going as far as to divide them into three categories: (1) "likely to carry", (2) "contested" (Texas and Florida), and (3) "important" (Maryland and Missouri). On the other end of the spectrum, Carter's campaign categorized 15 states worth 74 electoral votes as base or leaning Ford. This left 15 battleground states worth 251 electoral votes, with Carter needing 57 (23%) to win the White House. Initially, Carter's campaign identified eight battleground states worth 215 electoral votes. They later added seven states and another 36 electoral votes in October as data indicated that Carter was within striking distance of Ford in those locales.

Ford's strategy had several architects, but the contours are revealed in memos from Robert Teeter (the campaign's pollster, and someone we will meet again as we proceed throughout this era), Jerry Jones (Ford's staff secretary and deputy assistant), and Michael Raoul-Duval (formerly Ford's domestic council director, who then worked directly under Ford's campaign manager, Dick Cheney). Generally, the Ford team saw a wide-open electoral map, with New England, Mid-Atlantic, Midwest, Rocky Mountain, and Pacific states populating the battleground category. Specifically, while they had only 15 states worth 83 electoral votes as Ford's base, in our reading of their strategy they had a whopping 25 states worth 368 electoral votes in the battleground category. Thus, a winning campaign required 183 electoral votes, or almost 50% of the total available votes from battleground states. Within the battleground category, they further distinguished among "have to win" states (11 states worth 150 votes), "traditionally swing" states (six states worth 113 votes), and "peripheral South" states (eight states worth 105 votes). Furthermore, they agreed with the Carter campaign that the states of the Deep South were base Carter states in this election, ceding Alabama, Arkansas, Georgia, Louisiana, Mississippi, and South Carolina.

An examination—and cursory comparison—of the plans reveals two important things. First, the Electoral College plans from 1976 were complex and sophisticated. In part, this is undoubtedly a function of a tricky election: a southern, white, born-again Christian running just as the white South seemed to be permanently slipping away from the Democratic Party over racial issues, opposed by an establishment Republican who had pardoned a disgraced Republican president. This produced more ambiguity than we saw in preceding elections. But in part it might also be a function of the principal campaign players. For those who study presidential campaigns, Jordan and Teeter are legends from a time before successful political consultants became rock stars. And their status is partly due to their prescience in appreciating and understanding the role of data in driving campaign decisions: from the campaign memos, we see how Jordan and Teeter used past election results and current polling trends to craft multi-tiered conceptualizations of states and where they fell in 1976.

Second, despite the apparent relative openness of the Ford campaign's strategy, the campaign plans demonstrate a fair degree of synergy. The base Ford states, for example, are mostly the same for both campaigns. There are

Table 4.1 1976 Presidential Campaign Plans

	CARTER			FORD		
# of states	Base Democratic	Battleground/ Targets	Base Republican	Base Democratic	Battleground/ Targets	Base Republican
1	Alabama (9)*	California (45)	Alaska (3)	Alabama (9)	Alaska (3)***	Arizona (6)
2	Arkansas (6)*	Connecticut (8)****	Arizona (6)	Arkansas (6)	California (45)***	Colorado (7)
3	D.C. (3)	Delaware (3)****	Colorado (7)	D.C. (3)	Connecticut (8)*	Idaho (4)
4	Florida (17)**	Illinois (26)	Idaho (4)	Georgia (12)	Delaware (3)***	Indiana (13)
5	Georgia (12)*	Indiana (13)	Kansas (7)	Hawaii (4)	Florida (17)**	Iowa (8)
6	*Hawaii (4)*	Iowa (8)****	Maine (4)	Louisiana (10)	Illinois (26)***	Kansas (7)
7	Kentucky (9)*	Michigan (21)	Nebraska (5)	Massachusetts (14)	Kentucky (9)**	Maine (4)
8	Louisiana (10)*	Montana (4)****	New Hampshire (4)	Minnesota (10)	Maryland (10)***	Nebraska (5)
9	Maryland (10)***	Nevada (3)****	New Mexico (4)	Mississippi (7)	Michigan (21)***	New Hampshire (4)
10	Massachusetts (14)	New Jersey (17)	North Dakota (3)	Rhode Island (4)	Missouri (12)**	North Dakota (3)
11	Minnesota (10)	New York (41)	Oklahoma (8)	South Carolina (8)	Montana (4)***	Oklahoma (8)
12	Mississippi (7)*	Ohio (25)	Utah (4)		Nevada (3)***	South Dakota (4)
13	Missouri (12)***	Oregon (6)****	Vermont (3)		New Jersey (17)*	Utah (4)
14	North Carolina (13)*	Pennsylvania (27)	Washington (9)		New Mexico (4)***	Vermont (3)
15	*Rhode Island (4)*	South Dakota (4)****	Wyoming (3)		New York (41)*	Wyoming (3)
16	South Carolina (8)*				North Carolina (13)**	
17	Tennessee (10)*				Ohio (25)***	
18	Texas (26)**				Oregon (6)***	
19	Virginia (12)*				Pennsylvania (27)*	

20	*West Virginia (6)*					Tennessee (10)**		
21	Wisconsin (11)					Texas (26)**		
22						Virginia (12)**		
23						Washington (9)*		
24						West Virginia (6)**		
25						Wisconsin (11)*		
States	21	15	15	51	11	25	15	51
EVs	213	251	74	538	87	368	83	538

Notes:

"EV" stands for electoral votes. State electoral votes provided in parentheses.

For Carter's strategy, states in italics were not mentioned in the Jordan memo, but were clearly regarded as Democratic states.

For Carter, **** indicates states added to battleground list late; *** "important border" states; ** "contested southern" states; * "likely to carry southern" states.

For Ford, *** indicates "have to win"; ** "peripheral south"; * "traditionally swing".

Sources:

DED. 1976. "Rank-Order of States by Republican Presidential Vote," DED Papers (n.d.), Box 1; Gerald R. Ford Presidential Library.

Downton, Dorothy. 1976. "The Campaign Strategy for President Ford," Dorothy E. Downton Papers (n.d.),

Box 1; Gerald R. Ford Presidential Library. (Downton was President Ford's personal secretary.)

Moore, Jonathan, and Janet Fraser (eds.). 1977. *Campaign for President: The Managers Look at 1976.*

Cambridge, MA: Ballinger Publishing Company.

Rashoon, Gerald. 1976. "Memo from Gerald Rashoon to the Carter-Mondale Re-Election Campaign," Hamilton Jordan's Campaign Files (5/5/80), Box 79: Jimmy Carter Presidential Library.

Schram, Martin. 1976. *Running for President 1976: The Carter Campaign.* New York: Stein and Day. (See especially pages 239–250).

Teeter, Robert, Jerry Jones, and Michael Raoul-Duval. 1976. "Memo and Report for William Casey from Robert Teeter, Jerry Jones, and Michael Raoul-Duval." Ed Meese Papers (4/2/80), Box 102; Ronald Reagan Presidential Library.

differences in exactly how southern and border southern states are classified, but these may reflect the necessary simplifying nature of the classifications we use. In other words, Carter's campaign viewed southern states as part of their base, but perhaps needing some attention and outreach, while Ford's viewed many of the border South states as battleground, but perhaps a bit of a stretch.

Despite the GOP's loss in 1976, there are many who believe that Ford's campaign was one of the most expert of all time. Faced with double-digit inflation, soaring unemployment, and long gas lines, hobbled by the unpopular decision to pardon Nixon, embarrassed by the challenge from Reagan, and opposed by a pious, newcomer candidate who seemed the antidote to the corruption of the previous administration, Ford rallied from an 18-point deficit in the July polls to a 2-point loss on Election Day. From our perspective, the Ford campaign's Electoral College plan was similarly praiseworthy. In particular, the targeting of the western states (where, Hawaii and Texas notwithstanding, they essentially ran the table on Election Day) was spot on. If there was a weakness to the plan, it was targeting the border South states: although Ford won Virginia, Carter ended up carrying every other state in this category.

Morning in America: The Reagan-Carter and Reagan-Mondale Elections

The Reagan campaigns of 1980 and (especially) 1984 are considered by many as exemplars of efficiency and effectiveness in what we are referring to as the zero-sum era. Like most myths, this one has some basis in fact. For instance, the 1980 Reagan campaign pioneered the "Issue of the Day" strategy that soon became commonplace in American campaigns (Germond and Witcover, 1981; Stacks, 1981). In addition, the 1984 Reagan campaign was remarkably adept at framing the election in a way that both favored their candidate and resonated with voters. But both these campaigns and the candidate they served were far from perfect. For while Reagan was an excellent candidate whose skills had been honed during his time in Hollywood and as a two-term governor of California, he was also viewed by many as dangerously unproven and aggressive on foreign policy issues (Germond and Witcover, 1981). Furthermore, he was prone to unscripted remarks that threw his campaigns off message. In late August 1980, for instance, he committed a string of unforced errors, the most famous of which was his claim that trees caused smog, which led to protestors at his rallies putting signs on nearby trees that read "stop me before I kill again!" (Boller, 2004). Of course, these two seemingly contradictory things can both be true. Indeed, the campaigns' belief in

Reagan's communication skills may have led to an overly aggressive schedule that contributed to these mistakes.

But we are getting ahead of ourselves. A systematic evaluation of these campaigns requires more information about all the relevant players as well as the political context. So let us begin with the 1980 campaign and Ronald Reagan's quest to become the first challenger to defeat an incumbent president seeking re-election since Franklin Roosevelt in 1932. After a slow start that included an upset loss at the hands of George H. W. Bush in the Iowa caucuses, Reagan seized control of the Republican nomination with a commanding win in the New Hampshire primary and never looked back (Germond and Witcover, 1981). His opponent was the incumbent president, Democrat Jimmy Carter, who faced a strong challenge for his own party's nomination from Massachusetts senator Edward Kennedy. It is impossible to put enough emphasis on how unusual Kennedy's campaign was. In fact, Kennedy's bid represented the last time an incumbent Democratic president faced any major opposition and the last time any incumbent president lost multiple states to an opponent. Kennedy's campaign was considered by many to be one of the main reasons Carter lost his re-election bid, although a struggling economy and the American hostage crisis in Iran also exacted a toll (Dickerson, 2017). Nevertheless, the general election campaign was an extremely close, back-and-forth race. Dissatisfaction with both candidates allowed independent candidate John Anderson—a moderate Republican senator from Illinois who had briefly challenged Reagan in the GOP primaries—to further disrupt the race by grabbing a small but consequential share of the vote in some states. In the last 10 days, however, the electoral dam broke, and Reagan seized control of the race. In the end, Reagan defeated Carter in a landslide, garnering 489 electoral votes and 50.8% of the vote (his margin over Carter was 9.7%).

A detailed Electoral College strategy for the Reagan campaign was circulated among key personnel by June 1980.[7] The basic elements of this strategy, including the nomenclature, were used throughout the remainder of the campaign: "A" states were "key targeted states: essential"; "B" states were "battleground states: important, but tougher wins"; "C" states were "important states: deserving additional attention." Within the A, B, and C categories, states were further classified as 1, 2, or 3, based on the recommended allocation of resources (1s getting the most, followed by 2s and then 3s). Changes in resource allocations were recommended in August and then again in October.[8] As seen in Table 4.2, we classify the A and B states as battleground, but not the C states. This means that Reagan's campaign had 17 battleground states worth 320 electoral votes. Given that they had 17 states worth 84 votes as Reagan's base, the campaign needed 186 of the 320 battleground electoral

Table 4.2 1980 Presidential Campaign Plans

	CARTER			REAGAN		
# of states	Base Democratic	Battleground/ Targets	Base Republican	Base Democratic	Battleground/ Targets	Base Republican
1	Alabama (9)*	Pennsylvania (27)	Alaska (3)	Alabama (9)	California (45)***	Alaska (3)
2	Arkansas (6)	California (45)**	Arizona (6)	Arkansas (6)	Colorado (7)*	Arizona (6)
3	D.C. (3)	Colorado (7)**	Idaho (4)	Connecticut (8)	Florida (17)**	Idaho (4)
4	Georgia (12)	Connecticut (8)**	Kansas (7)	D.C. (3)	Illinois (26)***	Indiana (13)
5	Hawaii (4)	Delaware (3)**	Nebraska (5)	Delaware (3)	Maine (4)*	Iowa (8)
6	Kentucky (9)*	Florida (17)	North Dakota (3)	Georgia (12)	Maryland (10)**	Kansas (7)
7	Maryland (10)*	Illinois (26)**	Utah (4)	Hawaii (4)	Michigan (21)***	Montana (4)
8	Massachusetts (14)*	Indiana (13)**	Wyoming (3)	Kentucky (9)	Missouri (12)**	Nebraska (5)
9	Minnesota (10)*	Iowa (8)**		Louisiana (10)	New Jersey (17)**	Nevada (3)
10	North Carolina (13)*	Louisiana (10)		Massachusetts (14)	New York (41)***	New Hampshire (4)
11	Rhode Island (4)	Maine (4)		Minnesota (10)	Ohio (25)***	New Mexico (4)
12	South Carolina (8)*	Michigan (21)		Mississippi (7)	Pennsylvania (27)***	North Dakota (3)
13	Tennessee (10)*	Mississippi (7)**		North Carolina (13)	Tennessee (10)**	Oregon (6)
14	West Virginia (6)	Missouri (12)		Oklahoma (8)	Texas (26)***	South Dakota (4)
15		Montana (4)**		Rhode Island (4)	Virginia (12)**	Utah (4)
16		Nevada (3)**		South Carolina (8)	Washington (9)*	Vermont (3)
17		New Hampshire (4)**		West Virginia (6)	Wisconsin (11)**	Wyoming (3)
18		New Jersey (17)**				
19		New Mexico (4)**				
20		New York (41)**				

21		Ohio (25)**						
22		Oklahoma (8)**						
23		Oregon (6)						
24		South Dakota (4)**						
25		Texas (26)						
26		Vermont (3)**						
27		Virginia (12)**						
28		Washington (9)						
29		Wisconsin (11)						
States	14	29	8	51	17	17	17	51
EVs	118	385	35	538	134	320	84	538

Notes:

"EV" stands for electoral votes. State electoral votes provided in parentheses.

For Carter's strategy, ** indicates "marginal Reagan" states; * "marginal Carter" states.

For Reagan's strategy, *** indicates "large" states; ** "medium" states; * "small" states.

Sources:

Caddell, Pat. 1980. "Campaign Strategy" Hamilton Jordan Papers--Campaign Files (5/26/80), Box 77; Jimmy Carter Presidential Library.

Dailey, Peter. 1980. "Campaign 80 Media Plan," Peter Dailey Papers (n.d.), Boxes 221–222; Ronald Reagan Presidential Library.

Drew, Elizabeth. 1981. *Portrait of an Election: The 1980 Presidential Campaign*, New York: Simon & Schuster: 388–409.

Jordan, Hamilton. 1980. "General Election Media Plan," Hamilton Jordan Papers—Campaign Files (7/15/80), Box 79; Jimmy Carter Presidential Library.

Meese, Ed. 1980. "Campaign 80 Marketing Plan," Ed Meese Papers (8/8/80), Box 101; Ronald Reagan Presidential Library.

Moore, Jonathan (ed.). 1981. *Campaign for President: 1980 in Retrospect. Institute of Politics*, Harvard University. Cambridge, MA: Ballinger Publishing.

Wirthlin, Richard. 1980. "Reagan for President, Campaign Plan," Richard Wirthlin Papers (6/29/80), Box 177; Ronald Reagan Presidential Library.

votes to win (58%). Perhaps learning from the Ford campaign, Reagan's team was judicious in targeting Southern states: only Florida, Texas, Tennessee, and Virginia made the cut. Reagan was also aided by his strength in the West: from the Missouri River to the Pacific coast, only Colorado and Washington appear on the battleground list.

As in 1976, Carter's electoral strategy was shaped by Hamilton Jordan, only this time with critical input from pollster Patrick Caddell (Moore, 1981). In some ways, Carter's campaign viewed the race as Ford's campaign had viewed the 1976 contest: exceptionally fluid, with many opportunities for pick-ups and many opportunities for losses. It is therefore somewhat difficult to fit their thinking neatly into our three-fold categories. However, from Table 4.2 we see that they had 14 states worth 118 electoral votes as Carter base states, and 29 states worth 385 votes as battleground states. Within the Carter base states, they acknowledged some weak points that might need shoring up (eight states worth 87 electoral votes). Within the battleground category, they further specified that 19 of the 29 states (worth 242 votes) were "marginal Reagan." Given that they had eight states worth 35 electoral votes as "base Reagan," this meant that Carter had to hold all the "marginal Carter" and win some of the "marginal Reagan" states to carry the day. Put simply, even though the national polls showed a tight race throughout the fall, Carter's team saw the path to victory as even more precarious given Reagan's edge in the big states of California, New York, Illinois, and New Jersey, as well as throughout the West and Southwest. This realism permeated Caddell's memos as Election Day neared and the path further narrowed.

Still, what do we make of the Carter strategy? The election of 1980 is one of the few elections of this era in which we see significant movement in the polls over the last two weeks. Considering this, it is difficult to evaluate the efficacy of the campaigns' plans, especially those of the Carter campaign. States that looked winnable were suddenly firmly in Reagan's column. And states that leaned toward Carter, and therefore received little attention in a presumably tight race, ended up tilting toward Reagan in the end. Still, as noted earlier, the signs were there, and no meaningful adjustments were made by the Carter team.

In contrast to 1980, the 1984 election was a landslide almost from the start, as a recovering U.S. economy propelled Reagan to re-election with 525 electoral votes and 58.8% of the vote. Reagan's victory was over Carter's former vice-president, Walter Mondale. Mondale had been a solid favorite to win the Democratic nomination but encountered surprisingly stiff competition from Colorado senator Gary Hart and from civil rights icon Reverend Jesse Jackson. The contest was, in the words of Mondale, "glacial," and the slog afforded the Reagan campaign additional latitude to develop themes and to frame the election in a way that would dominate the fall campaign (Germond and Witcover, 1985). Mondale chose U.S. Representative Geraldine Ferraro as his running mate—the first time a major party ticket featured a woman—to give his candidacy some historical heft. But the headwinds were too fierce. Even Reagan's disastrous first debate performance, in which he appeared old and confused at several points, failed to give Mondale more than a temporary boost of a point or two in the polls. In fact, perhaps the most memorable moment of the campaign was Reagan's damage-control quip in the second debate that he would not "exploit for political purposes the relative youth and inexperience of his opponent" (Boller, 2004; Germond and Witcover, 1985).

In post-election discussions, the Mondale team's general election campaign dilemma was laid bare. Should they ignore their base states—where Reagan's popularity had eradicated the Democratic edge—and focus exclusively on battleground states? Or should they shore up the candidate's standing in the base states and hope that this would elevate his national standing and make it easier to ultimately engage Reagan in the battlegrounds? The former strategy was an "all or nothing" approach, while the latter might help avoid a total blowout and perhaps save other Democratic candidates running on the ballot (Moore, 1986). Mondale's team, led by campaign manager Robert Beckel and acting at the explicit behest of the candidate, opted for the "all or nothing" approach, to the consternation of many Democratic operatives (Germond and Witcover, 1985; Moore, 1986).

Table 4.3 demonstrates the scope of Mondale's strategic task. Based on Democratic media ad buy reports, as well as discussions from post-election conferences, the Mondale team sorted states into four different tiers. There were 23 Tier 1 states, worth 351 electoral votes. These are clearly the battleground states. Tier 3 states encompassed six states, worth 37 electoral votes. We treat these as the Mondale base states. Carrying all the base states required Mondale to win 233 votes from the battleground states (66%). This extraordinary win percentage is undoubtedly the explanation for the Mondale campaign's designation of Tier 2 states. These are six states—some southern and some New England states—worth 58 electoral votes that leaned toward Reagan but might be movable. Finally, Tier 4 states appear to have been unassailably for Reagan. In contrast to 1976 and 1980, when the southern states were either contested or even conceded to Carter, by 1984 no southern states are considered base Mondale.

The Reagan campaign's plan is laid out in memos sent from strategic advisers and from the advertising team. Stunningly, the Reagan strategy assumed Reagan's base was 32 states worth 300 electoral votes. This advantageous starting point required a further distinction among "southern base" states, "western base" states, and "snow-belt base" states. They identified 10 states worth 142 electoral votes

Table 4.3 1984 Presidential Campaign Plans

	MONDALE			REAGAN		
# of states	Base Democratic	Battleground/ Targets	Base Republican	Base Democratic	Battleground/ Targets	Base Republican
1	D.C. (3)	Alabama (9)*	Alaska (3)	D.C. (3)	Connecticut (8)****	Alabama (9)**
2	Hawaii (4)	Arkansas (6)*	Arizona (7)	Delaware (3)	Illinois (24)****	Alaska (3)*
3	Maryland (10)	California (47)*	Colorado (8)	Maryland (10)	Iowa (8)****	Arizona (7)*
4	Minnesota (10)	Connecticut (8)*	Delaware (3)**	Massachusetts (13)	Maine (4)****	Arkansas (6)**
5	Rhode Island (4)	Georgia (12)*	Florida (21)**	Minnesota (10)	Michigan (20)****	California (47)*
6	West Virginia (6)	Illinois (24)*	Idaho (4)	New York (36)	Missouri (11)	Colorado (8)*
7		Iowa (8)*	Indiana (12)	Rhode Island (4)	New Jersey (16)****	Florida (21)**
8		Kentucky (9)*	Kansas (7)	West Virginia (6)	Ohio (23)	Georgia (12)**
9		Maine (4)*	Louisiana (10)**	Wisconsin (11)	Pennsylvania (25)	Hawaii (4)
10		Michigan (20)*	Massachusetts (13)**		Vermont (3)****	Idaho (4)*
11		Mississippi (7)*	Montana (4)			Indiana (12)***
12		Missouri (11)*	Nebraska (5)			Kansas (7)***
13		New Jersey (16)*	Nevada (4)			Kentucky (9)**
14		New Mexico (5)*	New Hampshire (4)			Louisiana (10)**
15		New York (36)*	North Dakota (3)			Mississippi (7)**
16		North Carolina (13)*	Oklahoma (8)			Montana (4)*
17		Ohio (23)*	South Carolina (8)**			Nebraska (5)***
18		Oregon (7)*	South Dakota (3)			Nevada (4)*
19		Pennsylvania (25)*	Utah (5)			New Hampshire (4)***
20		Tennessee (11)*	Vermont (3)**			New Mexico (5)*

21		Texas (29)*	Virginia (12)				North Carolina (13)**	
22		Washington (10)*	Wyoming (3)				North Dakota (3)***	
23		Wisconsin (11)*					Oklahoma (8)**	
24							Oregon (7)	
25							South Carolina (8)**	
26							South Dakota (3)***	
27							Tennessee (11)**	
28							Texas (29)**	
29							Utah (5)*	
30							Virginia (12)**	
31							Washington (10)	
32							Wyoming (3)*	
States	6	23	22	51	9	10	32	51
EVs	37	351	150	538	96	142	300	538

Notes:

"EV" stands for electoral votes. State electoral votes provided in parentheses.

For Mondale's strategy, *indicates "Tier 1 target" states; ** indicates "Tier 2 target" states (which lean towards Reagan). "Tier 3 target" states are Democratic base, and "Tier 4 no-target" states are Republican base states.

For Reagan's strategy, **** indicates "Ford 1976" states; *** "snow-belt base"; ** "southern-base" states; * "western-base" states.

Sources:

Deaver, Michael. 1984. "Campaign 1984," Michael Deaver Papers (n.d.), Box 67; Ronald Reagan Presidential Library.

Deaver, Michael. 1984. "1984 Campaign Advertising," Michael Deaver Papers (n.d.), Box 67; Ronald Reagan Presidential Library.

Germond, Jack, and Jules Witcover. 1985. *Wake Us When It's Over*, New York: MacMillan. (See especially references to Robert Beckell's 6/26/84 memo and Lee Atwater's 7/24/84 memo.)

Mondale, Walter F. 1980. "Media Buys-General," Walter F. Mondale Papers (8/18–10/23/84), Box 105: Minnesota Historical Society.

Moore, Jonathan (ed.). 1986. *Campaign for President: The Managers Look at '84*. Institute of Politics, Harvard University. Dover, MA: Auburn House Publishing.

as battleground states. To win re-election, Reagan only needed to carry his base states, which presumably meant that the less secure states in that category would have received attention (these are states we later classify as "lean Reagan"). Within the battleground states, Reagan's team distinguished states that Ford has carried in 1976 from the other targets. Finally, they considered nine states worth 96 electoral votes as base Mondale. Over the course of the campaign, even these states came into relief, although there does not appear to be any formal reclassification after October 1.

A few points merit attention. Reagan's list of battleground states is the smallest since Carter's in 1976 (10 states) and previews the tighter and more focused battles we see in more recent campaigns. Interestingly, a small set of battleground states made sense for Reagan, because he had a commanding lead in so many states that he could concentrate on the very few he needed to reach an Electoral College majority. Carter in 1976, however, ended up in a remarkably close election with Ford and could easily have been second-guessed for being too targeted had he not won enough electoral votes from his battleground universe.

We would again also observe that it is important to appreciate the strategic reality facing the Mondale campaign. Mondale had to contest states where he realistically had almost no chance of victory. However, this is not evidence that his campaign had a poor strategy. Rather, it is evidence that his campaign *was* strategic but had to choose from among several unlikely alternative paths to victory. For example, Mondale targeted Reagan's home state of California. It was extremely unlikely that Mondale could defeat the incumbent president in the Golden State in 1984. Nonetheless, Mondale needed to amass 270 electoral votes to win, and it was probably even more unlikely that he could take down Reagan in some combination of other states equaling California's 47 electoral votes. This is not to say that Mondale's electoral strategy in 1984 was good: most notably, the Democratic campaign seemed to overestimate the appeal of Mondale in southern states and to perhaps underestimate Reagan's potential weakness in the heretofore conservative New England states. Such an assessment, though, requires understanding the strategic context of the race and that the campaign's choices were made from among a set of unlikely alternatives.

Ideology versus Competence: The Bush-Dukakis Election

After serving as vice-president for eight years under Reagan, George H. W. Bush attempted to do something that no one had accomplished since Franklin

D. Roosevelt: win a third consecutive presidential term for the party. In fact, no sitting vice-president had won a third consecutive term for their party since Martin Van Buren succeeded two-termer Andrew Jackson in 1836. Moreover, Bush had substantial obstacles in his path. He was under congressional and media scrutiny for his role in the Iran-Contra Affair, a scandal that plagued the final two years of the Reagan administration. The economic recovery that began in 1983 had slowed a bit, taking with it some of the shine from the Reagan years. And Bush was perceived by some pundits and voters as relatively weak compared to the charismatic Reagan, giving rise to what was popularly referred to as "the wimp factor" (Brady, 1996; Cramer, 1993; Germond and Witcover, 1989). Several prominent Republicans opposed him for the nomination, including Kansas senator Robert Dole, New York representative Jack Kemp, and televangelist Pat Robertson. Although Bush won the Republican nomination comfortably, the fight was contentious, and he was down by double digits in the polls to the Democratic nominee, Massachusetts Governor Michael Dukakis, in late July after the Democratic Convention (Cramer, 1993; Germond and Witcover, 1989).

Bush, however, had several advantages heading into 1988. Most notably, his association with Reagan helped him with conservative Republicans. His prominence as Reagan's vice-president and the still-robust economy also helped him with independent voters. Finally, Bush proved to be a dogged and tenacious candidate, guided by an aggressive and disciplined campaign team (Boller, 2004; Cramer, 1993). Foremost among Bush's advisors was Lee Atwater, a South Carolina native who had served in both Reagan campaigns. As the Republicans convened in New Orleans in mid-August, Atwater and the Bush team were redefining their opposition as a far-left liberal who was out of touch with the concerns and preferences of ordinary Americans on issues such as crime and national defense (Brady, 1996; Fleegler, 2023; Germond and Witcover, 1989).[9] By early September, Bush had erased Dukakis's lead and pulled ahead in the race. On Election Day, Bush carried 426 electoral votes and won 53.4% of the popular vote.

In hindsight, some viewed the Dukakis campaign as a mishap. From our perspective, this appraisal seems overwrought. Dukakis had wrested control of the Democratic nomination from a deep and talented field of contenders, including Tennessee senator Al Gore, Delaware senator Joe Biden, Representative (and House Speaker) Richard Gephardt, and Reverend Jesse Jackson. His emphasis on the "Massachusetts Miracle" and administrative competence were seen by many at the time as effective appeals following eight years of conservative Republican rule (Cramer, 1993; Fleegler, 2023). The vitriol poured on the Dukakis campaign was at least in part a function of their

Table 4.4 1988 Presidential Campaign Plans

	DUKAKIS			BUSH		
# of states	Base **Democratic**	Battleground/ **Targets**	Base **Republican**	Base **Democratic**	Battleground/ **Targets**	Base **Republican**
1	D.C. (3)*	California (47)*	Alabama (9)	D.C. (3)	Arkansas (6)	Alabama (9)
2	Hawaii (4)*	Connecticut (8)*	Alaska (3)	Hawaii (4)	California (47)	Alaska (3)
3	Iowa (8)*	Illinois (24)*	Arizona (7)	Iowa (8)	Colorado (8)	Arizona (7)
4	Maryland (10)*	Michigan (20)*	Arkansas (6)***	Maryland (10)	Connecticut (8)	Delaware (3)
5	Massachusetts (13)*	Missouri (11)**	Colorado (8)**	Massachusetts (13)	Illinois (24)	Florida (21)
6	Minnesota (10)*	New York (36)*	Delaware (3)	Minnesota (10)	Kentucky (9)	Georgia (12)
7	Rhode Island (4)*	Ohio (23)*	Florida (21)	New York (36)	Maine (4)	Idaho (4)
8	West Virginia (6)*	Oregon (7)*	Georgia (12)***	Rhode Island (4)	Michigan (20)	Indiana (12)
9		Pennsylvania (25)*	Idaho (4)	West Virginia (6)	Missouri (11)	Kansas (7)
10		Texas (29)***	Indiana (12)		New Jersey (16)***	Louisiana (10)
11		Vermont (3)*	Kansas (7)		Ohio (23)***	Mississippi (7)
12		Washington (10)*	Kentucky (9)**		Oregon (7)	Montana (4)
13			Louisiana (10)***		Pennsylvania (25)	Nebraska (5)
14			Maine (4)		Washington (10)	Nevada (4)
15			Mississippi (7)		Wisconsin (11)	New Hampshire (4)
16			Montana (4)**			New Mexico (5)
17			Nebraska (5)			North Carolina (13)
18			Nevada (4)			North Dakota (3)
19			New Hampshire (4)			Oklahoma (8)
20			New Jersey (16)***			South Carolina (8)
21			New Mexico (5)**			South Dakota (3)
22			North Carolina (13)***			Tennessee (11)

23			North Dakota (3)**				Texas (29)	
24			Oklahoma (8)				Utah (5)	
25			South Carolina (8)				Vermont (3)	
26			South Dakota (3)**				Virginia (12)	
27			Tennessee (11)***				Wyoming (3)	
28			Utah (5)					
29			Virginia (12)					
30			Wisconsin (11)					
31			Wyoming (3)					
32								
States	8	12	31	51	9	15	27	51
EVs	58	243	237	538	94	229	215	538

Notes:

"EV" stands for electoral votes. State electoral votes provided in parentheses.

For Dukakis's strategy, *** indicates low priority targets among lean Bush states; ** high priority targets among lean Bush states; * "18-state strategy" states.

For Bush's strategy, *** indicates Lee Atwater's "fire-wall" states.

Sources:

Germond, Jack W., and Jules Witcover. 1989. *Whose Broad Stripes and Bright Stars*, New York: Warner Books. (See especially pages 448–449.)

Market Opinion Research. 1988. "Post-election Report Prepared for the Republican National Committee Assessing Television Advertising and Candidate Travel," Personal papers of Daron Shaw.

Runkel, David R. 1989. *Campaign for President: The Managers Look at '88*. Institute of Politics, Harvard University. Dover, MA: Auburn House Publishing.

Shaw, Daron R. 1999. "The Effect of TV Ads and Candidate Appearances on Statewide Presidential Votes, 1988–96," *American Political Science Review*, 93, (2), 345–362.

Taylor, Paul, and David S. Broder. 1988. "Dukakis Electoral Strategy Set," *Washington Post*, October 16, 1988.

Yellin Communications. 1988. "Media Buy Reports," Michael S. Dukakis Papers, courtesy of Ruth Rowley. (Rowley was personal assistant to Governor Dukakis.)

early success and big summer lead in the polls. Still, the perceived passivity of Dukakis in the face of Bush's relentless effort to define him as a liberal chafed Democrats for a long time. In fact, we see the cautionary lessons gleaned from the Dukakis campaign—do not let charges go unanswered, fight fire with fire—as critically important for understanding the logic and behavior of subsequent (and especially Democratic) campaigns (Fleegler, 2023).

The Dukakis electoral strategy was complex and extremely lean, even in the summer when things looked promising (Runkel, 1989). As seen in Table 4.4, it was also fluid; some states were considered both battlegrounds and leaning toward a candidate, and state classifications occasionally changed over time. Campaign manager Susan Estrich was nominally in charge of final decisions, but Dukakis and close advisor John Sasso (who returned to the campaign in September 1988, after having resigned under pressure in October 1987) were heavily involved. The initial plan identified eight states worth 58 electoral votes as base Dukakis, and 12 states worth 243 electoral votes as battlegrounds. Interestingly, some of the battleground states were seen as leaning toward Bush. Undoubtedly looking to hedge against this narrow path, the campaign also identified and targeted other states that leaned toward Bush: six lean Bush states worth 32 electoral votes were "high priority," and six lean Bush states worth 68 electoral votes were "low priority." By late October, the Dukakis campaign further narrowed its strategy, secretly adopting the "18-state strategy," which would have netted 261 electoral votes and allowed Dukakis to win with any other state or combination of states worth nine electoral votes (Runkel, 1989).

The Bush campaign's Electoral College strategy was, in contrast, relatively simple and unchanging. Atwater and company identified 27 states worth 215 electoral votes as base Bush and another 15 states worth 229 electoral votes as battlegrounds. This meant Bush needed only 29% of the available battleground electoral votes to triumph. Furthermore, Atwater identified New Jersey and Ohio as "firewall" states within the battleground category; regardless of the math, he did not believe Bush could lose so long as he carried those states. A major discrepancy between the campaigns was that the Bush side did not believe that Dukakis had a chance of successfully contesting any southern states, whereas the Dukakis team clung to the hope that they could pick off one or two from Dixie. Interestingly, the Bush campaign was much more pessimistic about New York than the Dukakis campaign (Runkel, 1989).

As hinted at earlier, 1988 has a contentious reputation among campaign scholars and practitioners. Some believe that Bush's comeback and victory was eminently predictable given the strength of the national economy and the relative popularity of the sitting president (e.g., Campbell, 1992). It was, they argue, only a matter of voters predisposed to support Bush finally "coming home." Others contend that the "passive" nature of the Dukakis campaign proved fatal to Democratic chances (e.g., Cramer, 1993). Our own view is somewhat mixed. The inevitability of a Bush victory seems overly deterministic, although the campaign was well positioned. In addition, the Dukakis campaign did commit several strategic blunders, in particular allowing Bush's campaign to define Dukakis and to reframe the election. With respect to developing an electoral plan, whatever "mistakes" were made seem to have been of a much lesser order. Indeed, the campaign's adoption of an "18-state strategy" in early October indicated a clear sense of strategic realism.

It's the Economy, Stupid: The Clinton-Bush and Clinton-Dole Elections

Despite Bush's resounding victory in 1988, a lingering question remained: whether the realignment of southern states in presidential election campaigns was complete. A serious economic recession in 1991 and the appearance of two southerners on the ticket in 1992 and 1996 revived Democratic fortunes, at least temporarily. Indeed, the broader suspicion that the Republicans had a "lock" on the Electoral College after winning five of the previous six elections—losing only in 1976 after Watergate—was exploded by the dominance of the Clinton campaigns.

Ironically, as 1992 approached it did not look to be a promising election for the Democrats. President Bush's job approval rating was over 70% after his successful prosecution of the 1991 Gulf War, and his re-election prospects seemed excellent (Germond and Witcover, 1993; Goldman, et al. 1994). Reading the tea leaves, many of the most formidable contenders who might have competed with Arkansas Governor Bill Clinton for the Democratic nomination disappeared by late 1991, as if by magic. Most obviously, New York Governor Mario Cuomo and Reverend Jesse Jackson dropped out, leaving the contest to Clinton along with a relatively undistinguished field, including Massachusetts senator Paul Tsongas, former Californian governor Jerry Brown, Iowa senator Tom Harkin, and Nebraska senator Bob Kerrey. Another fortuitous break (in political terms, anyway) was a lingering recession that by late 1991 had soured the mood of the country and dragged Bush's job approval ratings below 40%.

Despite his early good fortune, Clinton stumbled badly at the beginning of 1992. Allegations that he evaded the military draft, that he had protested the Vietnam War while in the Soviet Union, and (most significantly) of serial marital infidelity, dogged Clinton's campaign. But he managed to finish a strong second in the New Hampshire primary (allowing him to proclaim himself "the Comeback Kid"), and by early March he had taken command of the nomination contest.

With the Democratic nomination in hand, Clinton's team spent the late spring of 1992 doing polls and focus groups to better understand how badly their candidates had been damaged by his rough road. "The Manhattan Project," as it was known, discovered that Clinton was mis-perceived by voters as a child of privilege and as a Georgetown and Yale-educated elite, rather than someone who grew up poor, with no father, and who had worked his way through both college and law school. His campaign team—including lead strategist James Carville, chief strategist Paul Begala, communications director George Stephanopoulos, pollster Stanley Greenberg, and media consultant Mandy Grunwald—settled on a plan to re-introduce their candidate during May and June in a series of speeches and ads known collectively as "the Man from Hope" (Goldman et al., 1994).

Clinton's plan was complicated by the emergence of an independent candidate, Ross Perot, a billionaire from Dallas, Texas, who had founded the information and technology company Electronic Data Systems (EDS). Sharing the anxious mood of the country, Perot went on the popular CNN show *Larry King Live* on February 20, 1992, to issue a forceful critique of how both parties were mishandling the economy and not serving the American people. Perot then announced that he would run for president as an independent if his supporters could get his name on the ballot in all fifty states. Perot's candidacy picked up steam throughout the spring, and by April he had pulled even with Bush and Clinton in the polls.

Perot's impact on the race was complex. On the one hand, he hurt Clinton by garnering a substantial amount of news media attention and by giving voters who wanted a change someone else to consider. On the other hand, he hurt Bush by focusing relentlessly on the country's economic problems, highlighting the main weakness of the administration's record. Electoral strategies were significantly impacted by Perot's presence and particular appeal. Consider the two regions where Perot's support was greatest. In the New England states, Perot polled at about 30% and clearly took voters away from Clinton. In the Rocky Mountain states, Perot also polled at about 30% and clearly took voters from Bush. In both cases, Perot turned states that would otherwise have been strongly for one side or the other and made them competitive.

But just when it seemed like the United States might have the most serious independent candidacy since Teddy Roosevelt's in 1912, Perot's candidacy imploded. In late May, news media reports emerged of Perot's "paranoid" tactics while running EDS, which included loyalty oaths and surveillance. His campaign team—led by Republican consultant Ed Rollins and Democratic consultant Hamilton Jordan—began to squabble with each other and with the candidate. Rollins resigned on June 15, and Perot dropped out the next day. Perot later claimed that he dropped out because of a Bush campaign plot to ruin his daughter's wedding by releasing digitally altered photos. In the wake of Perot's withdrawal, Clinton's support skyrocketed. He went from the mid-twenties and third place in the polls to the mid-fifties and a double-digit lead over the incumbent Bush.

Meanwhile, Bush's formidable position in the fall of 1991 had deteriorated rapidly by early 1992, such that he had difficulty in the early primary contests, barely defeating populist conservative challenger and former Nixon speech writer Patrick Buchanan in the New Hampshire primary. Even though he eventually secured the nomination, Bush's team still faced a difficult strategic challenge: a fluid electoral map, a stagnant economy, low approval ratings, and two charismatic opponents making the claim for change after twelve years of Republican rule. The fluidity of the electoral map occupied the attention of the Bush campaign heading into the late summer, a campaign that lacked GOP stalwarts Lee Atwater (who had died of cancer in 1991) and James A. Baker III (who was serving as Bush's secretary of state). Baker reluctantly returned for the fall campaign as Bush's chief of staff, and he and pollster-turned campaign manager Robert Teeter had the final say with respect to identifying and targeting states. Numerous White House advisors—most notably Charlie Black and Richard Darman—also reviewed the campaign's plans (Royer, 1994).

As seen in Table 4.5, the Bush campaign saw 15 states worth 98 electoral votes as their base. Within their base, they recognized that 10 states worth 73 electoral votes were "potentially competitive." They further targeted 22 states worth 256 electoral votes as their battlegrounds. Thus, they needed 67% of the available battleground electoral votes to win re-election. Within their battleground states, Bush's campaign recognized they were in better shape in five states worth 72 electoral votes ("Level 1NC") but in a more precarious position in 15 states worth 159 electoral votes ("Level 1C"). Another two states—Iowa and Vermont—were judged to be "potentially competitive": Iowa was included as a battleground state, while Vermont was designated as part of Clinton's base ("Level 2").

For their part, the Clinton campaign used a five-fold categorization (Goldman et al., 1994; Royer, 1994). They classified 14 states worth 182 electoral votes as their base, which they referred to as "top end." They had 18 battleground states worth 194 electoral votes, including 12 "play very hard" states would ensure an Electoral College majority. They also identified 10 additional

Table 4.5 1992 Presidential Campaign Plans

	CLINTON			BUSH		
# of states	Base Democratic	Battleground/ Targets	Base Republican	Base Democratic	Battleground/ Targets	Base Republican
1	D.C. (3)	Colorado (8)**	Alabama (9)*	D.C. (3)	Colorado (8)***	Alabama (9)*
2	Arkansas (6)	Delaware (3)	Alaska (3)	Arkansas (6)	Connecticut (8)***	Alaska (3)*
3	California (54)	Georgia (13)**	Arizona (8)*	California (54)	Delaware (3)**	Arizona (8)
4	Connecticut (8)	Iowa (7)	Florida (25)*	Hawaii (4)	Florida (25)**	Idaho (4)
5	Hawaii (4)	Kentucky (8)**	Idaho (4)	Illinois (22)	Georgia (13)***	Indiana (12)*
6	Illinois (22)	Louisiana (9)**	Indiana (12)	Maryland (10)	Iowa (7)*	Kansas (6)*
7	Massachusetts (12)	Maine (4)**	Kansas (6)*	Massachusetts (12)	Kentucky (8)**	Mississippi (7)*
8	Minnesota (10)	Maryland (10)	Mississippi (7)	Minnesota (10)	Louisiana (9)***	Nebraska (5)
9	New York (33)	Michigan (18)**	Nebraska (5)	New York (33)	Maine (4)***	Nevada (4)*
10	Oregon (7)	Missouri (11)**	Nevada (4)*	Oregon (7)	Michigan (18)	North Dakota (3)*
11	Rhode Island (4)	Montana (3)**	New Hampshire (4)*	Rhode Island (4)	Missouri (11)***	Oklahoma (8)*
12	Vermont (3)	New Jersey (15)**	North Dakota (3)	Vermont (3)*	Montana (3)***	South Carolina (8)*
13	Washington (11)	New Mexico (5)**	Oklahoma (8)	Washington (11)	New Hampshire (4)**	Utah (5)
14	West Virginia (5)	North Carolina (14)**	South Carolina (8)*	West Virginia (5)	New Jersey (15)***	Virginia (13)*
15		Ohio (21)**	South Dakota (3)*		New Mexico (5)***	Wyoming (3)
16		Pennsylvania (23)	Texas (32)*		North Carolina (14)***	
17		Tennessee (11)	Utah (5)		Ohio (21)***	
18		Wisconsin (11)*	Virginia (13)		Pennsylvania (23)***	
19			Wyoming (3)		South Dakota (3)***	

20						Tennessee (11)***		
21						Texas (32)**		
22						Wisconsin (11)***		
States	14	18	19	51	14	22	15	51
EVs	182	194	162	538	184	256	98	538

Notes:

"EV" stands for electoral votes. State electoral votes provided in parentheses.

For Clinton's strategy, ** indicates "play very hard" states; * "watch hard" states. (Clinton classified states as "top end," "play hard," "play very hard," "watch hard," and "big challenge.")

For Bush's strategy, *** indicates "Level 1C (competitive)"; ** "Level 1NC (not competitive)"; * "Level 2 (potentially competitive)."

Sources:

Goldman, Peter, Thomas DeFrank, Mark Miller, Andrew Murr, and Tom Mathews. 1993. *Quest for the Presidency, 1992*. College Station: Texas A&M Press. (See especially page 505).

November Company. 1992. "Media Buy Plan Memos," Personal papers of Daron Shaw.

Royer, Charles T. (ed.). 1994. *Campaign for President: The Managers Look at 1992*. New York: Puritan Press.

Shaw, Daron R. 1999. "The Effect of TV Ads and Candidate Appearances on Statewide Presidential Votes, 198896," *American Political Science Review* 93 (2), 345–362.

Witcover, Jules. 1992. "Clinton Campaign Credits Success to Early Start, Careful Targeting of States," *Baltimore Sun*, November 5.

"watch hard" states worth 110 electoral votes, where their polling numbers suggested a win was possible. Given the unpredictable presence of Perot in the race and Clinton's apparent strength in southern states (states that had seemed lost to the Democrats only four years earlier), the plan emphasized flexibility and multiple paths to 270 electoral votes. It isn't just Clinton's campaign, either: Bush's 22 battleground states—the most since Mondale in 1984—and complex targeting plan corroborates the observation that 1992 was a volatile campaign.

Taken together, the Bush and Clinton plans reveal an electorate in transition. The previous movement of the South from the Democratic base to the Republican base pauses in the Clinton elections. Conversely, Republican bastions in New England either turn completely to the Democrats (Vermont) or drift toward battleground status (New Hampshire). Similar movement can be seen on the Pacific coast and in the Rocky Mountains. Washington, Oregon, and (especially) California begin their march to the left and away from the GOP, while Colorado, New Mexico, and even Montana become swing states. The one constant is that a handful of states in the upper Midwest and Mid-Atlantic—Wisconsin, Michigan, Ohio, Pennsylvania—remained critical to winning coalitions.

As if the electoral map wasn't complicated enough, the 1992 general election campaign got more complicated still when Perot re-entered the campaign on October 2, just five weeks before Election Day. During those crucial five weeks, Perot spent approximately $100 million on television advertisements, including thirty-minute "infomercials" on the major networks in the days before the election (Goldman et al., 1994). Perhaps most importantly, he participated in all three presidential debates, while his running-mate, Admiral James Stockdale, participated in the vice-presidential debate. Perot's standing in the polls when he re-entered was a dismal 3%. But his personality and message were undeniably powerful, and by late October Perot not only was polling in the low twenties but was threatening to win states such as Maine and Utah outright. His late momentum stalled following a piece on the CBS news show *60 Minutes*, in which Perot offered a somewhat unconvincing story about why he had dropped out of the race in June.

In the end, Clinton defeated Bush, 43% to 38%, with Perot taking 19% of the vote but failing to carry even a single state. Clinton's Electoral College victory was much more decisive, as he carried 370 electoral votes to 168 for Bush. The election marked the end of the Reagan-Bush era and was the first decisive win for a Democratic ticket since Johnson's landslide over Goldwater in 1964. How much credit does the Clinton campaign deserve for strategic acumen, given the sour mood of the electorate toward the incumbent administration? It is difficult to say. Political scientists point to economic models of the presidential election, which indicate that Clinton's victory (as well as its magnitude) was predictable. Pundits and practitioners point to the campaign's ability to guide a "flawed" candidate to the White House, winning despite allegations of marital infidelity, drug usage, and draft dodging (Germond and Witcover, 1993; Goldman et al., 1994). From our perspective, the Clinton campaign deserves credit for a flexible electoral strategy, targeting states that became competitive as events unfolded and conditions shifted, and refusing to divert its attention from its main goals.

Who did Perot hurt, Clinton or Bush? The data suggest that Clinton's win would have been even more decisive had Perot not siphoned off the "time for a change"/"reform" vote (Stone and Rappoport, 2007). In this sense, Perot "hurt" Clinton. But Fred Steeper, Bush's pollster, makes a critical point: "Perot spent almost a full year telling voters how terrible the economy was and how inept Bush had been as an economic steward. That had a powerful negative impact on the president's re-election prospects."[10] We acknowledge both perspectives but point again to the state-by-state data, which indicate that the question of impact is highly dependent on where one focuses. In the New England and Mid-Atlantic states, Perot undoubtedly hurt Clinton. But in the Rocky Mountain and Western states, Perot almost certainly hurt Bush.

By 1996, it was clear that Bill Clinton was an electoral roller coaster ride. Following his 1992 victory, his signature spending bill was changed by Congress into a deficit reduction package, mostly because members were spooked by the electoral resonance of Ross Perot's warnings about the federal budget deficit. His healthcare package, designed largely by a committee headed by First Lady Hillary Clinton, was declared "dead on arrival" by the House of Representatives. He suffered a crushing defeat in the 1994 midterm elections, as the Democrats lost 54 seats in the House and the Republicans won a majority for the first time since 1952 (Drew, 1995). But Clinton did not sit idly by and watch his presidency go up in flames. Rather, he began a systematic strategy of "triangulation" that positioned himself closer to the center of the political spectrum. Besides championing a series of popular "moderate" policies—such as increased funding for the police and welfare reform—he spent hundreds of millions of dollars on television advertisements in battleground media markets. The campaign, pursued throughout 1995, was designed to promote his accomplishments and bolster his ratings in states critical to his re-election. The plan was largely the brainchild of Dick Morris, a political consultant who had helped Clinton regain the governorship of Arkansas after Clinton's humiliating defeat in his initial re-election bid. Morris, a Republican, was distrusted by some members of Clinton's political team, and the significance of his "triangulation" positioning and early spending patterns was a matter of considerable dispute as Clinton's numbers rebounded and his re-election prospects rounded into shape (Thomas et al., 1997; Woodward, 2007).[11]

Clinton faced Senator Robert Dole, majority leader of the Senate and former vice-presidential candidate, in the next election. Dole claimed the Republican nomination by besting millionaire Steve Forbes, commentator Pat Buchanan, and senators Lamar Alexander, Phil Gramm, and Richard Lugar, among others. Dole spent all his available funds to beat back the challenge of Forbes, who had used his considerable fortune to fund his campaign. That left Dole with no money from May through late July, while Clinton used his primary money (he faced no Democratic opposition) to promote his own accomplishments and to paint his Republican opponents as old and out of touch (Thomas et al., 1997; Woodward, 2007). This becomes a theme in presidential re-election campaigns, especially Bush's in 2004 and Obama's in 2012: the incumbent president enjoys a massive spending advantage over an opponent who has spent all their money to win a competitive primary contest. Because images of the incumbent are mostly fixed by this point, they use this financial advantage to define their opponent negatively. Dole certainly felt the burden of this dynamic in 1996.

In addition to his Republican opponent, Clinton also faced another challenge from Ross Perot. This time, however, Perot was not running as an independent candidate. Rather, he was running as the head of the newly formed Reform Party. Perot's candidacy no longer had the novelty that it had in 1992, and his primary issue—the federal budget deficit—was less resonant given the growing economy and the deficit reduction legislation of 1993. Still, Perot was a wildcard whose impact in specific states caused concern for both Clinton and Dole (Institute of Politics, Harvard University, 1997).

Whether the result of strategic acumen or the economic upturn driven by some combination of the tech revolution and the "dot.com" boom, Clinton appeared to hold a commanding lead heading into the fall campaign. His team featured some holdovers from 1992, including senior advisor Stephanopoulos, media advisor Grunwald, and pollster Greenberg, as well as campaign manager Peter Knight and the aforementioned Morris.[12] As detailed in Table 4.6, the Clinton campaign classified 18 states worth 213 electoral votes as their base. This base included traditional swing states, such as Washington and Oregon, and New York and Wisconsin. Within their base, Clinton's team further marked seven states worth 120 electoral votes as "weak" or "lean" base. They also targeted 16 battleground states worth 197 electoral votes. They needed only 29% of the battlegrounds to retain the White House. Among their battleground states, four states worth 56 electoral votes were categorized as "lean Clinton." These plus the base totaled 269 electoral votes. Clinton's campaign marked 17 states worth 128 electoral votes as Dole's base but tagged seven of these states worth 79 electoral votes as "weak" or "lean" Dole.

Dole's team was led by campaign manager Scott Reed and included (among others) pollster Tony Fabrizio and media advisor Alex Castellanos. The precise provenance of Dole's Electoral College strategy is difficult to pin down, although the classification of states seems relatively straightforward based on internal memos and communications.[13] They started with a base of 15 states worth 132 electoral votes. Their battleground states included 19 states worth 265 electoral votes. Dole therefore needed 52% of his electoral vote targets to amass a winning coalition. Given his polling numbers, this looks to have been an expansive list; indeed, Dole's battleground states included eight "lean" Clinton states worth 139 electoral votes. The list is also expanded by the inclusion of seven states worth 54 electoral votes that were thought to lean toward Dole. In addition to current polling information, to round out their list Dole's team apparently targeted southern states as well as states with a history of voting Republican.

Despite the best efforts of the Dole and Perot campaigns, Clinton never relinquished control of the race. His strength was manifest across the board, including southern and western states that had seemed unattainable during the 1980s. He carried 31 states plus D.C. that were together worth 379 electoral votes. He did not receive a majority of the popular vote, however: he won 49% of the vote, to 41% for Dole and 8% for Perot. Did Dole ever have a chance? More relevant for this study, did his campaign make the most of their chances? It is difficult to see where Dole had much of an opportunity to improve his chances for victory. But the decision to contest California remains the most controversial: the cost of television advertising in the Golden State means that a serious campaign there significantly limits the resources a campaign has for other states. The Dole campaign's logic was intriguing in this regard: they thought a single campaign to "flip" California and its 54 electoral votes would be easier thematically and organizationally than executing several statewide campaigns in other states totaling a comparable number of votes. Given what we know now about partisan trends in California, this seems like a dubious gambit. But the success of Republican statewide candidates as recently as two years earlier (in 1994) made it seem less head-scratching at the time.

From a broader strategic perspective, several questions emerged after Clinton's successful re-election campaign. Was the Republican "lock" on the Electoral College picked? In particular, what should future presidential campaigns make of the swath of states stretching south from the Canadian

Table 4.6 1996 Presidential Campaign Plans

	CLINTON			DOLE		
# of states	Base Democratic	Battleground/ Targets	Base Republican	Base Democratic	Battleground/ Targets	Base Republican
1	Arkansas (6)	Arizona (8)	Alabama (9)	Arkansas (6)	Arizona (8)**	Alabama (9)
2	California (54)**	Colorado (8)	Alaska (3)	Connecticut (8)	California (54)	Alaska (3)
3	Connecticut (8)**	Florida (25)	Idaho (4)	D.C. (3)	Colorado (8)**	Idaho (4)
4	D.C. (3)	Georgia (13)	Indiana (12)*	Delaware (3)	Florida (25)*	Indiana (12)
5	Delaware (3)	Kentucky (8)	Kansas (6)	Hawaii (4)	Georgia (13)**	Kansas (6)
6	Hawaii (4)	Louisiana (9)	Mississippi (7)	Iowa (7)	Illinois (22)*	Mississippi (7)
7	Illinois (22)**	Maine (4)**	Montana (3)*	Maine (4)	Kentucky (8)**	Nebraska (5)
8	Iowa (7)**	Michigan (18)**	Nebraska (5)	Maryland (10)	Louisiana (9)	North Carolina (14)
9	Maryland (10)	Missouri (11)**	New Hampshire (4)	Massachusetts (12)	Michigan (18)*	North Dakota (3)
10	Massachusetts (12)	Nevada (4)	North Dakota (3)	Minnesota (10)	Missouri (11)*	Oklahoma (8)
11	Minnesota (10)	New Jersey (15)	Oklahoma (8)*	New York (33)	Montana (3)**	South Carolina (8)
12	New York (33)	New Mexico (5)	South Carolina (8)*	Oregon (7)	Nevada (4)	Texas (32)
13	Oregon (7)**	North Carolina (14)	South Dakota (3)*	Rhode Island (4)	New Hampshire (4)*	Utah (5)
14	Rhode Island (4)	Ohio (21)	Texas (32)*	Vermont (3)	New Jersey (15)*	Virginia (13)
15	Vermont (3)	Pennsylvania (23)**	Utah (5)	Washington (11)	New Mexico (5)	Wyoming (3)
16	Washington (11)**	Tennessee (11)	Virginia (13)*	West Virginia (5)	Ohio (21)*	
17	West Virginia (5)		Wyoming (3)	Wisconsin (11)	Pennsylvania (23)*	
18	Wisconsin (11)**				South Dakota (3)**	

19						Tennessee (11)**		
States	18	16	17	51	17	19	15	51
EVs	213	197	128	538	141	265	132	538

Notes:

"EV" stands for electoral votes. State electoral votes provided in parentheses.

For Clinton's strategy, ** indicates "leaning Clinton"; * "leaning Dole". Clinton spent over $500,000 during the 1995 "stealth campaign" in California, Florida, Illinois, Michigan, Missouri, Ohio, Pennsylvania, and Tennessee. He spent less than $500,000 in Connecticut, Iowa, Oregon, Washington, West Virginia, Wisconsin, Colorado, Georgia, Kentucky, Louisiana, Maine, Nevada, New Mexico, North Carolina, Indiana, South Dakota, and Texas.

For Dole's strategy, ** indicates "leaning Dole"; * "leaning Clinton". Scott Reed, Dole's campaign manager, offered additional detail about the initial strategy, but there are problems with his account (as conveyed to Woodward). Reed claimed that Dole's strategy initially assumed he would carry all of the southern states plus states that voted Republican in 7 of the last 8 elections. But, there is no evidence that Dole ever targeted Arkansas Furthermore, the 12 southern states together yield 138 electoral votes (not the quoted "73"); and only 10 (not the quoted "12") non-southern states voted 7 times for the GOP candidate between 1964 and 1992. These combine for 52, not 165, electoral votes.

Sources:

Institute of Politics, John F. Kennedy School of Government, Harvard University. 1997. *Campaign for President: The Managers Look at '96*. Hollis, NH: Hollis Publishing.

Competitive Media. 1996. "Clinton-Gore Ad Buys," Personal papers of Daron Shaw (2/13/96-11/3/96).

Competitive Media. 1996. "Dole-Kemp Ad Buys," Personal papers of Daron Shaw (2/13/96-11/3/96).

Shaw, Daron R. 1999. "The Effect of TV Ads and Candidate Appearances on Statewide Presidential Votes, 1988–96," *American Political Science Review* 93 (2), 345–362.

Time. 1996. "Clinton's Stealth Campaign," April 22.

Woodward, Bob. 1996. *The Choice: How Bill Clinton Won*. New York: Simon & Schuster. (See especially page 420).

Rockies to the southern border and then east toward the Atlantic Ocean (the so-called "Republican L")? Were they really battleground states? Or was their receptiveness to a Democratic candidate an aberrant combination of Clinton's charismatic appeal and a booming economy?

Lockboxes and Strategery: The Bush-Gore Election of 2000

The question of the nature of the Electoral College map was squarely at issue in the 2000 campaign. The election was the first "open" contest since 1988, with no incumbent seeking re-election. Instead, Vice-President Al Gore easily defeated New Jersey senator Bill Bradley for the nomination and set his sights on a third straight Democratic general election triumph. On the Republican side, Texas governor George W. Bush, son of the former president, cleared a large field of potential contenders and then defeated Arizona senator John McCain to win the nomination. The presence of two major party candidates with southern credentials, and the absence of either an incumbent or independent candidate Ross Perot, created an opportunity to gauge the underlying competitiveness of the states. The result was a pedestrian campaign and an unfathomably close election.

The Bush campaign was led by senior strategist Karl Rove, along with advisors Matthew Dowd, Karen Hughes, and Joe Allbaugh (Shaw, 2006; Stevens, 2001). Although Bush had exploded on the scene after winning the governorship in 1994 by upsetting popular Democratic incumbent Ann Richards, and then steamrolling to re-election in 1998, he had developed a reputation as a "lightweight" with the media early in the 2000 campaign (Boller, 2004). This reputation proved sticky as the primaries wore on and was a consistent thorn in the side of the Bush team (Institute of Politics, Harvard University, 2002; Jamieson and Waldman, 2001). From a practical perspective, it forced the campaign to focus on establishing Bush's gravitas through his advisory team and a series of policy rollouts (Rove, 2010). After eight years of Clinton-Gore, the American public was open to Bush's candidacy and slightly less interested in this narrative than were the media.

Bush's ability to fight back against this narrative was facilitated by his relatively robust financial situation. In a move that foreshadowed a new era in campaign spending, Bush decided to forego public financing for the primary elections. This was because his campaign judged (correctly) that he could significantly exceed the total amount provided by the federal funding system and that he did not want to be overwhelmed by a self-financed candidate like millionaire conservative Steve Forbes (as Bob Dole had been in 1996). Bush's war chest allowed him to defeat McCain and still have the funds to advertise—albeit modestly—in the spring of 2000.

By Memorial Day weekend, Bush had managed to gain a five-point advantage in the national polls, which he maintained until the conventions. During this time, Bush's team settled on an aggressive electoral strategy, targeting Democratic bastions such as West Virginia and the Clinton-Gore home states of Arkansas and Tennessee, as well as traditional battlegrounds. For the most part, Bush assumed that southern and western mountain states would revert to Republican form following their flirtation with Clinton (Shaw, 2006).

From Table 4.7, we see that Bush's campaign saw their base as comprised by 16 states worth 124 electoral votes. Their battlegrounds were 25 states worth a total of 280 electoral votes. Within this category, Bush's team further identified Florida and Maine as nominal "home" states that were nevertheless vulnerable, while—as already noted—Arkansas and Tennessee were "road" states that were nevertheless winnable. Also included in the high priority target list were traditional Midwest battlegrounds (Illinois, Michigan, Wisconsin, and Ohio), as well as wavering border south (Kentucky, Missouri, and North Carolina) and Rocky Mountain states (Nevada, Colorado, and New Mexico). Contrary to news media reports, the campaign never targeted California despite its tempting 54 electoral votes.[14] Bush needed to carry 47% of the electoral votes in the battleground states to win back the White House for the GOP.

The Gore campaign, meanwhile, was led by manager Donna Brazille and senior advisor Tony Coehlo, although the electoral strategy was heavily influenced by strategist Tad Devine, pollster Stanley Greenberg, and media guru Bill Knapp (Jamieson and Waldman, 2001; Institute of Politics, Harvard University 2002). Like the Bush team, the Gore team saw the race as exceptionally close. As Democratic pollster Paul Maslin put it, "This race is shaping up to be more like Kennedy-Nixon than anything else, mostly because of the closeness but also because of the dynamics of an incumbent hanging on with the country in pretty good shape but against a tough challenger" (Berke, 2000). The closeness of the race reflected the complexity of Gore's political situation. On the one hand, Gore benefited from the popularity of Bill Clinton, whose job approval ratings remained high. On the other hand, Gore was dragged down by the incumbent's scandals. President Clinton had been impeached by the House of Representatives in December 1998 for "lying under oath" and "obstruction of justice," both of which related to the president's attempts to hide a sexual relationship with Monica Lewinsky, a White House intern, from independent counsel Ken Starr's investigation of the Whitewater Land deal.

Table 4.7 2000 Presidential Campaign Plans

	GORE			BUSH		
# of states	Base Democratic	Battleground/ Targets	Base Republican	Base Democratic	Battleground/ Targets	Base Republican
1	California (54)**	Arizona (8)	Alabama (9)	California (54)	Arkansas (6)*	Alabama (9)
2	Connecticut (8)	Arkansas (6)*	Alaska (3)	Connecticut (8)	Arizona (8)*	Alaska (3)
3	D.C. (3)	Delaware (3)*	Colorado (8)	D.C. (3)	Colorado (8)*	Idaho (4)
4	Hawaii (4)	Florida (25)**	Georgia (13)	Delaware (3)	Florida (25)	Indiana (12)
5	Maryland (10)	Illinois (22)**	Idaho (4)	Hawaii (4)	Georgia (13)*	Kansas (6)
6	Massachusetts (12)	Iowa (7)*	Indiana (12)	Maryland (10)	Illinois (22)*	Mississippi (7)
7	New Jersey (15)	Kentucky (8)	Kansas (6)	Massachusetts (12)	Iowa (7)*	Montana (3)
8	New York (33)**	Louisiana (9)	Mississippi (7)	New York (33)	Kentucky (8)*	Nebraska (5)
9	Rhode Island (4)	Maine (4)*	Montana (3)	Rhode Island (4)	Louisiana (9)*	North Dakota (3)
10	Vermont (3)	Michigan (18)**	Nebraska (5)	Vermont (3)	Maine (4)	Oklahoma (8)
11		Minnesota (10)*	North Carolina (14)		Michigan (18)*	South Carolina (8)
12		Missouri (11)	North Dakota (3)		Minnesota (10)	South Dakota (3)
13		Nevada (4)	Oklahoma (8)		Missouri (11)*	Texas (32)
14		New Hampshire (4)*	South Carolina (8)		Nevada (4)*	Utah (5)
15		New Mexico (5)	South Dakota (3)		New Hampshire (4)	Virginia (13)
16		Ohio (21)	Texas (32)		New Jersey (15)*	Wyoming (3)
17		Oregon (7)*	Utah (5)		New Mexico (5)*	
18		Pennsylvania (23)**	Virginia (13)		North Carolina (14)*	
19		Tennessee (11)*	Wyoming (3)		Ohio (21)*	

20		Washington (11)*				Oregon (7)*		
21		West Virginia (5)				Pennsylvania (23)*		
22		Wisconsin (11)*				Tennessee (11)*		
23						Washington (11)*		
24						West Virginia (5)		
25						Wisconsin (11)*		
States	10	22	19	51	10	25	16	51
EVs	146	233	159	538	134	280	124	538

Notes:

"EV" stands for electoral votes. State electoral votes provided in parentheses.

For Gore's strategy, ** indicates "highest priority" states; *"high priority" states.

For Bush's strategy, * indicates "high priority" states.

Sources:

Institute of Politics, Harvard Kennedy School. 2001. *Campaign for President: The Managers Look at 2000*. New York: Hollis Publishing.

Jamieson, Kathleen and Paul Waldman. 2001. *Electing the President, 2000*. Philadelphia: University of Pennsylvania Press. (See especially comments by Stanley Greenberg, Tad Devine, and Bill Knapp from the "Annenberg Conference on the Presidential Campaign of 2000," held February 10, 2001, at the University of Pennsylvania.)

Shaw, Daron R. 2006. *The Race to 270: The Electoral College and the Strategies of 2000 and 2004*. Chicago: University of Chicago Press.

Voters still liked Clinton and his policies but had grown tired of his personal failings and equivocations, and Gore bore the brunt of their weariness.[15] The task for the campaign was threading the needle between running as his own man, while taking credit for the accomplishments of the Administration.

Table 4.7 shows the Gore campaign viewed the Electoral College situation similarly to the Bush campaign. They saw 10 states worth 146 electoral votes as Gore's base. They had 22 states worth 233 electoral votes in the battleground category, including (contrary to popular perception) Tennessee and West Virginia. Tennessee, however, was classified as a "high" (not "highest") priority battleground state, whereas West Virginia was added to the list relatively late and was not viewed as a priority within the battleground universe at all.

In the lore of presidential campaigns, Gore's team has received a substantial amount of opprobrium for "blowing" the 2000 election. Considering the complexity of feelings toward Clinton in 2000, it is our view that this censure is unwarranted. But more germane to the present analysis, criticism of Gore's Electoral College strategy is off target. Given the losses of Tennessee and West Virginia and given the closeness of the ultimate electoral vote count, some of this criticism makes sense. But after a quick glance at the Gore campaign plan in Table 4.7, one cannot help but be struck by how realistic their approach was in 2000. They needed to win 55% of the electoral votes available in their battleground category—a manageable percentage in a tough, close contest. They did not identify any southern or Rocky Mountain states as a "highest" or "high" priority, except Arkansas, Florida, and Tennessee. The correct assessment of Florida's competitiveness is praiseworthy, given that many strategists and pundits had put it in the Bush column since the state had been trending Republican and that Jeb Bush, the candidate's brother, was the sitting governor. Of the 14 "highest" and "high" priority battleground states, Gore delivered 11. This is an astonishing haul in such a close election. In fact, Gore's razor thin loss in Florida obscures the fact that the Gore campaign eked out victories of 6,765 votes in Oregon, 5,708 in Wisconsin, 4,144 in Iowa, and 366 in New Mexico. If the Bush campaign was aggressive, the Gore campaign was ruthlessly strict in its targeting strategy. And it almost worked.

The 2000 presidential election saw George W. Bush prevail with 30 states worth 271 electoral votes to 20 states (plus D.C.) and 266 electoral votes for Al Gore. Gore won the popular vote, 48.4% to 47.9% for Bush. The proximate reason for Bush's victory was his controversial win in Florida, where the vote count was contested legally due to ballot irregularities in a handful of counties.[16] It has been said that 2000 was a boring campaign followed by an incredible election. From a strategic perspective, our view is that the campaigns were fascinating. The electoral map that emerges from the 2000 election persists for the next three elections: Republican dominance in the South and Plains states, with Democratic dominance on the coasts and in the upper Midwest. It wasn't until Donald Trump's shocking 2016 victories in Wisconsin, Michigan, and Pennsylvania that the map, and the attendant strategic calculus, would shift again.

Conclusion

In pulling together detailed information on the Electoral College strategies for seven presidential campaigns from 1976 through 2000, several points merit attention. First, it is obvious that every campaign developed a classification plan for all 50 states (plus D.C.) for purposes of winning 270 electoral votes. Each of these strategies was detailed, with four to five categories being the norm. Somewhat distinct from the earlier era, past votes were still important markers but more recent election trends (including those of the most recent midterm election) and polling data were preeminent in driving the categorizations. While we might hope that the interests of all citizens would be considered by a national campaign, no one was targeting everyone anymore.

Second, we see that media consultants and pollsters became major players in developing and refining strategy during this period. This continued a trend from the previous era, particularly in the Kennedy and Johnson campaigns, but it accelerated dramatically during the zero-sum era. Pollsters such as Patrick Caddell, Robert Teeter, Richard Wirthlin, and Stan Greenberg, and media consultants such as Gerald Rafshoon, Roger Ailes, Robert Squier, Mandy Grunwald, and Alex Castellanos were all critical in the formulation of Electoral College strategy.

Third, electoral strategies were typically broad enough and relied on such refined data analyses that classification shifts were rare. Rather, states within the battleground category receive more or less emphasis (and, presumably, more or fewer resources). This was true even for campaigns that seemed to understand how dire their situation was, such as Carter in 1980, Dukakis in 1988, and Dole in 1996.

Fourth, the classification and targeting of states was supplemented by even more granular targeting *within* important states. It was during this era that the heavy allocation of financial resources in specific broadcast and cable television markets—the latter of which are often much smaller geographically—caused campaigns to rely more heavily than in the past on county-level voting data to develop target areas within states. Typically during this period, campaign analysts would estimate the number of persuadable voters within a television market (usually by calculating the difference between the highest and lowest vote percentage received by one party across a series of previous elections) and then divide by the cost of reaching those voters via advertising: this is the basis for a "cost per persuadable voter" measure, which facilitates a comparison of efficiency across markets.

As with the information in chapter 3, what we offer here constitutes an attempt to paint a more systematic picture of emerging trends in presidential campaign strategy; a picture that allows us to notice consistent tendencies in plans while also noting evolving differences over time. In doing this, we are laying the groundwork for a more detailed consideration of our broader hypotheses concerning the execution of strategy and the magnitude of campaign effects that will occupy chapters 7 and 8. But to do this, we must first complete our review of the three eras by examining strategies across the five most recent elections, in which campaigns were confronted by a vastly different financial and partisan environment than the one that had prevailed during the zero-sum era.

5

Micro-Targeted Campaigning (2004–2020)

Online and on Point

By the time the 2004 presidential election rolled around, campaigns had to contend with two seismic shifts in the social and political backdrops against which presidential races played out. First and foremost, emerging technology, in particular the growth and proliferation of the Internet and social media, revolutionized the ways campaigns communicated with voters and created unprecedented opportunities for direct and interactive contact with citizens. Digital media enabled campaigns to communicate, organize, and mobilize nearly instantaneously and to raise enormous sums of money with speed and ease.

In tandem with these developments, major changes in the federal campaign finance arena also uprooted the fundraising landscape. In March 2002, President George W. Bush signed into law the Bipartisan Campaign Reform Act (BCRA), also known as the McCain-Feingold Act after its chief sponsors in the U.S. Senate, John McCain (R-Arizona) and Russ Feingold (D-Wisconsin). BCRA represented the most sweeping set of federal campaign finance reforms in over three decades. Most notably, it eliminated so-called "soft money" amassed by national party organizations and spent without limit for "party-building" activities so nebulously defined that these funds inevitably found their way indirectly into presidential (and other) campaigns. The act also raised individual contribution limits (pegged to inflation) and prohibited "electioneering communications" by corporations and unions. Some of these provisions—including campaign spending prohibitions on corporations and other entities—were later struck down by the 2010 U.S. Supreme Court decision in *Citizens United v. FEC*. But others (like the ban on soft money) survived, eventually revitalizing the electioneering role of so-called 527 organizations (named after the IRS code that established such political organizations) and paving the way for the creation of super PACs, following the 2010 U.S. Supreme Court ruling in *SpeechNow.org v. FEC*. These independent, expenditure-only committees can raise unlimited sums of

Battleground. Daron R. Shaw, Scott L. Althaus, and Costas Panagopoulos, Oxford University Press.
 DOI: 10.1093/oso/9780197774366.003.0005

money from individuals and groups—including corporations and unions—and spend without constraint to promote or oppose political candidates if they do not coordinate with campaigns directly. Super PACs have become increasingly important players in presidential campaigns, routinely outpacing fundraising and spending by candidates themselves.

Technological and computing developments starting in the early part of the twenty-first century also transformed the ability of campaigns to refine their targeting strategies down to the level of individual voters. This marked the beginning of a new era involving data analytics and micro-targeted campaigns. The availability of large-scale databases of voter demographics joined to vote history records and to commercial information about voters' social, political, and consumer habits enabled political campaigns to leverage novel statistical techniques never used before in the history of American politics. These techniques allowed campaigns to develop sophisticated models to project which issues individual voters cared about, what their policy positions were, how easily (or not) they could be targeted for mobilization, persuasion, fundraising, and volunteering, and just about anything else that campaigns cared about. In fact, it was not unusual for candidates to know more about individual voters than voters knew about candidates. Campaigns could then use this information to hone their strategies and direct their efforts toward receptive audiences. Micro-targeting promised campaigns unprecedented efficiencies in resource allocation and impact. Although the strategic considerations dictated by the constitutional framework of the Electoral College kept the focus of presidential campaigns on entire states as the sites where the contest would be won or lost, campaign investments in micro-targeting techniques combined with an increasingly complex media ecosystem changed everything with respect to how presidential campaigns classified and targeted specific voters, affording operatives unparalleled opportunities to target individual voters with precision within the borders of priority states.

Over the course of the five presidential campaigns we discuss in this chapter, one other major shift that occurred deserves noting. Partisan polarization intensified and calcified, pushing voters and elites toward ideological extremes, and shrinking the numbers of both moderate voters and politicians (Abramowitz, 2010). Changes in the media environment over this period, especially the resurgence of partisan news outlets (notably, the right-leaning Fox News) as well as the growing popularity of social media, partly fueled (or at least coincided with) these developments (Prior, 2007). As more voters became more firmly rooted in their partisan and ideological camps, impervious to persuasion and typically supporting their respective party nominees for president by wide margins, campaigns' incentives shifted from winning hearts and minds within the shrinking pool of potentially "persuadable" or swing voters (which had been the main messaging priority in the second era) to mobilizing likely supporters with proverbial "red meat" messaging that was mainly aimed at rousing co-partisans to get out and vote. By 2004, the "battle of the bases" approach to presidential campaigning was in full swing (Panagopoulos, 2021): for the foreseeable future, presidential contests would be decided not by which side offered the most persuasive message to undecided voters, but by which side could out-mobilize its own likely supporters, voters who needed little to no persuasion at all. Going forward, it would be a battle of energizing the already decided more than of convincing the ambivalent. In many ways, this was simply turning back the clock to an earlier period of American history: mobilization strategies were already highly refined and effective methods for winning the presidency as early as 1828 (Kernell, 2000) and had been the primary means by which presidential campaigns were contested from at least the middle of the 1800s until well past the early 1900s (McGerr, 1988; Schudson, 1998).

Expectations in the Era of Micro-Targeted Campaigns

In this latest era, we expect presidential campaigns to be more precisely and strategically targeted than in the earlier two. The contests are invariably close (the largest margin in the popular vote is Barack Obama's eight-point victory over John McCain in 2008) and partisans are extremely unlikely to defect to the other party's candidate. Therefore, states that lean Republican or lean Democratic are often unmovable. Furthermore, the information available to the campaigns, in the form of polls and statistical models based on voter files, is voluminous and detailed. Thus, campaigns should be more likely than in the past to focus on small set of battleground states.

With respect to execution, we are of two minds. On the one hand, the tighter targeting plans and relatively smaller set of targets raises the stakes for any one battleground state. This suggests little deviation when it comes to allocating resources. On the other hand, the proliferation of contributions might allow candidates to spend money—if not time—in states that would have been prohibitively costly in the second era. We tend to think it more likely that plans are more rigorously adhered to in this most recent era, although we remain far from certain about this.

It seems to us that the targeting goals and tactics of this micro-targeting era depart from those of the preceding two. With the continued proliferation of polling information and the development of statistical models of individual preferences based on registered voter files, campaigns move from targeting aggregations of voters to targeting individual voters. To be clear, old-fashioned macro-targeting still drives the identification of states and markets where the candidates will campaign. But in this third era, decisions about which voters will be targeted with which specific messages are more likely to come from micro-targeting models than from geographic targeting at the county or media market level, the latter of which relies on prior voting trends (Hersh, 2015). Moreover, the polarized politics of the 2000s make identifying and mobilizing partisans the sine qua non of presidential elections (Panagopoulos, 2021). Within the confines of targeted states and markets, this means that voters ignored in previous eras—for example, Republican-leaning voters in liberal Madison, Wisconsin, or Democratic-leaning voters in conservative Asheville, North Carolina—are more likely to be targeted for outreach in the most recent era.

Finally, we think it likely that campaign effects are modest and predictable in recent elections. Tighter, more focused targeting might not persuade many voters in a polarized era, but perhaps more voters are reached and mobilized on behalf of a particular candidate. Similarly, errant outreach—targeting the wrong voters with the wrong messages—seems relatively less likely than in previous eras.

Wartime Re-election: The Bush-Kerry Election

Less than a year following the contentious conclusion of the 2000 presidential election, the terrorist attacks of September 11, 2001, set the stage for the election that followed. In the immediate aftermath of the attacks, President Bush's popularity skyrocketed, with his approval rating reaching an all-time high of 90% by late September 2001, according to Gallup, and surpassing the record held by his father, President George H. W. Bush, during the Gulf War in Kuwait in the early 1990s. In October 2002, Congress voted to authorize President Bush to launch military hostilities in Iraq as part of its post-9/11 war on terror and to preclude Iraq from using or acquiring weapons of mass destruction (WMDs) that could threaten the United States and its allies. The Bush administration claimed it possessed evidence that Iraq was a harbor for terrorists and that it was on the verge of developing WMDs. Based on these alarming claims, it led a coalition of allies in invading Iraq in March 2003. The initial phase of the invasion, designed as a full-scale "shock and awe" campaign, quickly toppled the authoritarian regime of Saddam Hussein, leading Bush to declare victory aboard the aircraft carrier USS *Abraham Lincoln* on

May 1, 2003, against the backdrop of a banner emblazoned with "Mission Accomplished."

By spring 2004, however, it had become clear the mission was perhaps not quite accomplished. No WMDs had been found, and civil war as well as a lengthy insurgency against coalition forces had intensified in Iraq. The American public had become wary of troop escalations, growing U.S. casualties, and an ongoing occupation in Iraq with no end in sight. Just as the 2004 presidential election was heating up, Bush's approval ratings dropped significantly, often registering below 50%. Nevertheless, Bush faced virtually no opposition for the GOP nomination, and, although he did not campaign during the primary phase of the contest, on March 10, 2004, he clinched the requisite number of delegates required to be the 2004 standard-bearer.

The path to the Democratic nomination was bumpier. Al Gore opted out, leaving the Democratic field wide open. Little-known Vermont governor Howard Dean managed to achieve early frontrunner status in a crowded field, largely by doubling down on innovative uses of social media and the Internet to organize supporters and to raise unprecedented sums of money. By 2004, three-in-four Americans had access to the Internet and the number of Americans online had surged past 200 million for the first time (Panagopoulos, 2009: 127). Nearly one-in-five registered voters reported the Internet was their primary source of information about the presidential election in 2004, up from 3% in 1996 and 11% in 2000 (Rainie, Cornfield and Horrigan, 2005). Dean strategists Joe Trippi (national campaign manager), Larry Biddle (director of grassroots fundraising), and Zephyr Teachout (director of Internet organizing) jointly pioneered "networked campaigning" and innovations facilitated by new media to bring together a national, grassroots coalition of supporters. This novel approach allowed them to raise about $50 million, more than any other Democratic presidential candidate had previously raised, largely in small donations averaging less than $80 made over the Internet (Medvic, 2011).

Dean's Internet-fueled fundraising prowess was especially significant because campaigns could not rely on soft money in the post-BCRA era. This eventually enabled Dean to forgo federal matching funds (and the restrictions that go along with them), the first Democrat to do so since the program was established in 1974. The campaign also leveraged online blogging and Meetup, a social media platform founded in 2002, to organize and connect its supporters across the country to each other, boasting at its peak 143,000 Meetup users spread over 600 locations nationally (Sifry, 2011). Although the Dean campaign imploded after a lackluster third-place finish in the Iowa caucuses (and the infamous "Dean scream" that ensued, where the candidate uttered an inappropriately primal howl at a boisterous campaign rally that quickly sunk whatever had been left of his candidacy), the cat was out of the bag in terms of harnessing the power of the Internet for grassroots organizing and fundraising. Massachusetts senator John Kerry, who ultimately clinched the Democratic nomination for president in 2004 with former rival North Carolina senator John Edwards on the ticket as his running mate, capitalized on the shift, reportedly raising $82 million using the Internet during the 2004 election cycle (dwarfing Bush's $13 million online take in the same cycle). Kerry also opted out of the public funding program (as had Bush for the primaries in both 2000 and 2004), which effectively collapsed the program for future campaigns since the incentives to participate had deteriorated (Panagopoulos and Bergan, 2009). This was an important development since it meant campaigns would no longer play out on the financially level playing fields that the second era's public funding system was designed to ensure.

The Internet featured prominently in both major party general election campaigns in 2004, with the Republican National Committee boasting an email database of 6 million voters and the Democrats 2.5 million (Malbin, 2006). One study counted more than 900 different email communications sent from the two major party campaigns or the national parties in the final six months of the campaign alone (Graf et al., 2006). Heavy reliance on social media and the Internet became an enduring feature of each of the presidential campaigns that followed.

The 2004 general election between Bush and Kerry focused largely on the Iraq War, the top issue for voters in the race. Kerry criticized Bush for mismanaging the conflict, while Bush cast Kerry as a "flip-flopper," pointing out that Kerry had initially voted for the force authorization resolution even though he now claimed to oppose the war. Kerry, a prominent Vietnam War veteran who had been awarded multiple combat medals including three Purple Hearts as well as the Silver Star and the Bronze Star for heroism, was also put on the defensive when a series of harsh ads were released alleging the candidate willfully distorted his war record and was unfit to serve. The ads were broadcast widely, including in several swing states, and received considerable media attention. This episode is notable because the ad campaign was created and financed by a 527 organization, Swift Boat Veterans for Truth. Despite its controversial allegations—inspiring use of the pejorative term "swift boating" to describe unfair or inaccurate political attacks—many believed the ad caused the Kerry campaign irreparable damage.

Led once again by chief strategist Karl Rove, the Bush campaign relied extensively on micro-targeting and campaign analytics in 2004. Bush operatives leveraged insights from tests conducted in 2000 and 2002, and strategists doubled down on micro-targeting and predictive modeling approaches (Panagopoulos, 2021; Rove, 2010). By 2004 the technology had advanced, and large-scale collections of voter information compiled since 2000 could be used to improve statistical models. Republicans had also ramped up efforts to build sophisticated databases of voters, and their Voter Vault program—first developed in the 1990s but not used until 2002—contained about 168 million entries in 2004 (Tynan, 2004). Democrats had also learned lessons since 2000. Determined to catch up to the GOP, Democrats worked to close the micro-targeting gap in 2004, but technological glitches ultimately compromised their efforts (Panagopoulos, 2021).

In terms of Electoral College strategy, Table 5.1 demonstrates that the Bush campaign believed its base had expanded considerably since 2000, especially in the South and West. The campaign counted 24 states totaling 206 electoral votes in its base (or at least leaning toward Bush), having moved eight states (Arizona, Arkansas, Colorado, Georgia, Kentucky, Louisiana, North Carolina, and Tennessee) into its base classification since the previous cycle. In 2004 the Bush team essentially conceded two prior battleground states to Kerry (Illinois and New Jersey) along with 10 other states totaling 168 electoral votes, which left 15 states with 164 electoral votes that the Bush campaign viewed as competitive. To win, the Bush campaign needed to capture 39% of the electoral votes in these competitive states.

For its part, we know from post-election interviews and conferences that Kerry's team relegated 26 states worth 222 electoral votes to Bush off the bat, expecting Missouri and West Virginia to end up in the GOP column on Election Day, in addition to states the Bush campaign included in its base. It counted 13 states comprising 178 electoral votes in the Democratic base, expecting to clinch at least three of Maine's four electoral votes and to best Bush in Washington (11 electoral votes). Accordingly, Kerry planned to do battle in 12 states with 138 electoral votes, notably conceding every southern state to the GOP in 2004 except for Florida. Ultimately, it would need to capture more than two in three of the available electoral votes in the battleground states to emerge victorious. Clearly, the Kerry team expected Bush had an advantage in the contest, which is not unusual even for an unpopular incumbent seeking reelection.

On Election Day, Bush prevailed, sweeping the former Confederacy and the Mountain states, flipping Iowa and New Mexico to the GOP, and clinching victory in Ohio, to carry 31 states and a total of 286 electoral votes. Unlike in 2000, Bush carried Florida decisively (by a 5-percentage point margin) and won the popular vote: the first (and only) time a Republican contender has done so since 1988. From the Kerry team's perspective, losing Ohio was the

Table 5.1 2004 Presidential Campaign Plans

	KERRY			BUSH		
# of states	Base Democratic	Battleground/ Targets	Base Republican	Base Democratic	Battleground/ Targets	Base Republican
1	D.C. (3)	Florida (27)	Alabama (9)	California (55)	Florida (27)	Alabama (9)
2	California (55)	Hawaii (4)*	Alaska (3)	Connecticut (7)	Iowa (7)	Alaska (3)
3	Connecticut (7)	Iowa (7)	Arizona (10)**	D.C. (3)	Maine (4)	Arizona (10)**
4	Delaware (3)	Maine CD2 (1)	Arkansas (6)**	Delaware (3)	Michigan (17)	Arkansas (6)**
5	Illinois (21)	Michigan (17)*	Colorado (9)**	Hawaii (4)	Minnesota (10)	Colorado (9)**
6	Maine (2)	Minnesota (10)	Georgia (15)	Illinois (21)	Missouri (11)	Georgia (15)
7	Maine CD1 (1)	Nevada (5)	Idaho (4)	Maryland (10)	Nevada (5)	Idaho (4)
8	Maryland (10)	New Hampshire (4)*	Indiana (11)	Massachusetts (12)	New Hampshire (4)	Indiana (11)
9	Massachusetts (12)	New Mexico (5)	Kansas (6)	New Jersey (15)	New Mexico (5)	Kansas (6)
10	New Jersey (15)	Ohio (20)	Kentucky (8)	New York (31)	Ohio (20)	Kentucky (8)
11	New York (31)	Oregon (7)*	Louisiana (9)**	Rhode Island (4)	Oregon (7)	Louisiana (9)
12	Rhode Island (4)	Pennsylvania (21)	Mississippi (6)	Vermont (3)	Pennsylvania (21)	Mississippi (6)
13	Vermont (3)	Wisconsin (10)	Missouri (11)**		Washington (11)	Montana (3)
14	Washington (11)		Montana (3)		West Virginia (5)	Nebraska (5)
15			Nebraska (5)		Wisconsin (10)	North Carolina (15)
16			North Carolina (15)**			North Dakota (3)
17			North Dakota (3)			Oklahoma (7)
18			Oklahoma (7)			South Carolina (8)
19			South Carolina (8)			South Dakota (3)
20			South Dakota (3)			Tennessee (11)

21			Tennessee (11)				Texas (34)	
22			Texas (34)				Utah (5)	
23			Utah (5)				Virginia (13)**	
24			Virginia (13)**				Wyoming (3)	
25			West Virginia (5)**					
26			Wyoming (3)					
States	13	12	26	51	12	15	24	51
EVs	178	138	222	538	168	164	206	538

Notes:

"EV" stands for electoral votes. State electoral votes provided in parentheses.

For Kerry's strategy, ** indicates "leaning Kerry" states; * "leaning Bush" states.

For Bush's strategy, ** indicates "leaning Bush" states.

Sources:

Institute of Politics, John F. Kennedy School of Government, Harvard University. 2006. *Campaign for President: The Managers Look at 2004*. Lanham, MD: Rowman and Littlefield.

Jamieson, Kathleen Hall. 2006. *Electing the President 2004: The Insiders' View*. Philadelphia: University of Pennsylvania Press. (See especially comments by Mark Mellman, Matthew Dowd, and Karl Rove at the Annenberg Conference on the Presidential Campaign of 2004, held December 3, 2004, at the University of Pennsylvania.)

Shaw, Daron R. 2006. *The Race to 270: The Electoral College and the Strategies of 2000 and 2004*. Chicago: University of Chicago Press.

key blow, a defeat made even more bitter by the closeness of the contest (Bush won by roughly 118,000 out of 5.6 million votes cast) and the fact that the Kerry campaign allegedly had $14 million in unspent campaign funds, a topic we will return to later.[1]

Voting Hope: The Obama-McCain and Obama-Romney Elections

The 2008 presidential election nomination contest was wide open on both sides of the aisle. President George W. Bush's popularity had steadily eroded during his second term, dropping to about a 30% job approval rating as the campaign heated up, as frustration with the unpopular Iraq War, Bush's mishandling of Hurricane Katrina in 2005, and the concerns about national economy mounted. Bush was, of course, constitutionally prevented from seeking a third term, but his vice-president, Dick Cheney, decided not to seek the GOP nomination, making it the first time since 1928 that neither the incumbent president nor vice-president sought their party's nomination for the presidency. Several high-profile Republicans tossed their hats into the ring, including former New York city mayor Rudy Giuliani, Arizona senator John McCain, former Massachusetts governor Mitt Romney, former Tennessee senator Fred Thompson, Arkansas governor Mike Huckabee, and Texas representative Ron Paul. Polls throughout 2007 consistently found Giuliani to be at the head of the pack, yet it would be John McCain, overcoming a disappointing fourth place in the Iowa caucuses, who would come back to win the New Hampshire primary and ultimately prevail on March 4, 2008.

The nomination battle on the Democratic side was especially spirited. The contest attracted a wide field of candidates that included former first lady and New York senator Hillary Clinton, 2004 vice-presidential candidate and former North Carolina senator John Edwards, Illinois senator Barack Obama, New Mexico governor Bill Richardson, Indiana senator Evan Bayh, Delaware senator Joe Biden, Connecticut senator Chris Dodd, former Alaska senator Mike Gravel, former Iowa governor Tom Vilsack, and Ohio representative Dennis Kucinich. In a sign of just how prominently the Internet had penetrated political campaigns in only a few short years, both early frontrunner Clinton and relative newcomer Obama announced their candidacies via online videos and featured the Internet and social media prominently in their campaigns. Clinton and Obama both also proved to be voracious fundraisers, and both rejected public money in the primaries. An astonishingly strong fundraising sprint by Obama in the fourth quarter of 2007 and the first quarter of 2008 helped to catapult his candidacy to the forefront, and he eventually bested Clinton in the Iowa caucuses. Clinton rebounded to win the New Hampshire primary, but the race between the two sitting senators remained exceedingly close for the duration. One key area of policy differentiation between the two was the war in Iraq that Clinton, like several other presidential contenders, had voted to authorize. Obama claimed he would have opposed authorization if he been serving in the Senate at the time of the vote (he was elected after the fact). After a grueling 17-month long campaign, Obama eventually emerged victorious to secure the nomination on June 3, 2008.

Many analysts believed Clinton's vote to authorize the Iraq War and her refusal to disavow it cost her the nomination, but others attributed Obama's victory to his effective use of social media and the Internet, and especially to Facebook, which had exploded onto the scene in 2006. According to the Campaign Finance Institute, Obama was able to raise about $320 million during the primary period in 2008 (and over $750 million in total over the entire cycle), in large part from online donors who contributed small amounts under $200.[2] Obama doubled down on these tactics in the general election, becoming the first presidential candidate since 1974 to opt out of the public funding system in both the primary and general election stages. In the end, general election spending was rather lopsided, with Obama outspending his GOP opponent—who accepted public funds and the strings attached to them—by a nearly four to one margin. Obama's team, led by campaign manager David Plouffe, also invested heavily in sophisticated targeting and analytics techniques, tapping experts like Steve Hildebrand and Ken Strasma to exploit big data for its micro-targeting operations.

McCain's team was initially led by Rick Davis, who served as campaign manager for Robert Dole in 1996 and John McCain in 2000. But McCain's persistent weakness in the polls caused a staff shake-up in early July 2008 that led to Steve Schmidt taking command. Pollster Bill McInturff, veteran GOP consultant Charlie Black, and McCain's former Senate chief of staff Mark Salter were also notable members of the team. Just prior to the Republican nominating convention, McCain injected some enthusiasm into his candidacy by choosing Alaska governor Sarah Palin as his running mate, the first woman ever to be picked as a vice-presidential contender by a Republican nominee. But before long, several gaffes caused Palin's appeal to implode, much as the economy did starting in mid-September 2008.

Table 5.2 provides a glimpse into the electoral strategies of both teams. At the Annenberg Conference on the 2008 presidential campaign, Bill McInturff (for the Republicans) and David Plouffe (for the Democrats) provided detailed accounts of the campaigns' respective Electoral College strategies. Interestingly,

Table 5.2 2008 Presidential Campaign Plans

	OBAMA			McCAIN		
# of states	Base Democratic	Battleground/ Targets	Base Republican	Base Democratic	Battleground/ Targets	Base Republican
1	California (55)	Alaska (3)	Alabama (9)	California (55)	Colorado (9)	Alabama (9)
2	Connecticut (7)	Colorado (9)	Arizona (10)*	Connecticut (7)	Florida (27)	Alaska (3)**
3	D.C. (3)	Florida (27)	Arkansas (6)	D.C. (3)	Indiana (11)	Arizona (10)
4	Delaware (3)	Georgia (15)*	Idaho (4)	Delaware (3)	Iowa (7)	Arkansas (6)
5	Hawaii (4)	Indiana (11)	Kansas (6)	Hawaii (4)	Michigan (17)	Georgia (15)**
6	Illinois (21)	Iowa (7)	Kentucky (8)	Illinois (21)	Missouri (11)	Idaho (4)
7	Maine (4)	Michigan (17)	Louisiana (9)	Maine (4)*	Montana (3)	Kansas (6)
8	Maryland (10)	Missouri (11)	Mississippi (6)	Maryland (10)	Nevada (5)	Kentucky (8)
9	Massachusetts (12)	Montana (3)	Nebraska (5)	Massachusetts (12)	New Hampshire (4)	Louisiana (9)
10	Minnesota (10)	Nevada (5)	Oklahoma (7)	Minnesota (10)*	New Mexico (5)	Mississippi (6)
11	New Jersey (15)	New Hampshire (4)	South Carolina (8)	New Jersey (15)	North Carolina (15)	Nebraska (5)
12	New York (31)	New Mexico (5)	South Dakota (3)	New York (31)	Ohio (20)	North Dakota (3)***
13	Oregon (7)	North Carolina (15)	Tennessee (11)	Oregon (7)*	Pennsylvania (21)	Oklahoma (7)
14	Rhode Island (4)	North Dakota (3)*	Texas (34)	Rhode Island (4)	Virginia (13)	South Carolina (8)
15	Vermont (3)	Ohio (20)	Utah (5)	Vermont (3)	Wisconsin (10)	South Dakota (3)
16	Washington (11)	Pennsylvania (21)	West Virginia (5)	Washington (11)*	Tennessee (11)	

17		Virginia (13)	Wyoming (3)			Texas (34)		
18		Wisconsin (10)					Utah (5)	
19							West Virginia (5)	
20							Wyoming (3)	
States	16	18	17	51	16	15	20	51
EVs	200	199	139	538	200	178	160	538

Notes:

"EV" stands for electoral votes. State electoral votes provided in parentheses.

For Obama's strategy, * indicates "lower priority." Arizona was added-along with Georgia and North Dakota, which were added back-in late October, 2008.

For McCain's strategy, *** indicates "moved from battleground, 9/23/08"; **"moved from battleground, 9/3/08"; *"moved from battleground, 7/26/08."

Sources:

Institute of Politics, John F. Kennedy School of Government, Harvard University. 2009. *Campaign for President: The Managers Look at 2008*. Lanham, MD: Rowman and Littlefield.

Jamieson, Kathleen Hall. 2009. *Electing the President 2008: The Insiders' View*. Philadelphia: University of Pennsylvania Press. (See especially comments by David Plouffe (chapter 2) and Bill McInturff (chapter 5) at the "Annenberg Conference on the Presidential Campaign of 2008," held December 5, 2008, at the University of Pennsylvania.)

after the McCain team moved Maine, Minnesota, Oregon, and Washington into the Obama column, both campaigns came to believe the Democratic base was comprised of the identical set of 16 states totaling 200 electoral votes. The Obama campaign counted 18 states with 199 electoral votes as battlegrounds (three of these—Arizona, Georgia, and North Dakota—were reclassified as "lower priority" battlegrounds in late October 2008), conceding 17 states with 139 electoral votes to McCain. Democrats would need to capture 35% of the electoral votes in states deemed battlegrounds to win. The McCain campaign, believing it had made gains in Alaska, Georgia, and North Dakota, moved these states (and their 21 electoral votes) from battlegrounds into its base category in September 2008, resulting in a total of 20 states (160 electoral votes) it considered its base. The GOP expected to duke it out with Democrats primarily in 15 states with 178 electoral votes viewed as battlegrounds, implying McCain would need to capture nearly 62% of the available battleground electoral votes to triumph.

In the first-ever contest between two sitting senators, voters in 2008 decisively endorsed Democrat Barack Obama over his Republican opponent John McCain. Obama captured 52.9% of the popular vote and carried 28 states plus the District of Columbia as well as Nebraska's second congressional district to garner 365 electoral votes, while McCain received 45.7% of the popular vote and 173 electoral votes from victories in 22 states. Turnout in the historic election that produced the first African American president of the United States was 61.6% of the eligible electorate, the highest since 1968 (McDonald, 2008). Obama managed to crack the "Republican L"—the band of red-leaning states stretching south from the Canadian Rockies to the Mexican border and then east to the Atlantic Ocean—by carrying Colorado, Nevada, New Mexico, North Carolina, and Virginia. But while there were some geographic similarities between Obama's victory and Clinton's in 1992 and 1996, the coalitions were distinct. Clinton's moderate "New Democrats" were eclipsed by Obama's younger, more racially diverse, and more progressive supporters.

Despite steady (if slow) economic growth following the collapse of the financial sector in 2008 and 2009 and the enactment of landmark healthcare reform in the Affordable Care Act in March 2010, Democrats suffered a "shellacking" in the 2010 midterms, losing 63 seats—and the majority—in the House of Representatives as well as six seats in the Senate. Nevertheless, President Obama faced only token opposition for the 2012 Democratic nomination. By contrast, the Republican nomination was fiercely contested by a number of high-profile candidates including former Massachusetts governor Mitt Romney, former House speaker Newt Gingrich, former Pennsylvania senator Rick Santorum, former Utah governor Jon Huntsman, former

Minnesota governor Tim Pawlenty, businessman Herman Cain, and several others. After a few tumultuous months in which rival candidates rose and fell from frontrunner status, Romney surged to the head of the pack following the Super Tuesday contests and eventually secured enough delegates to clinch the nomination after the Texas primary on May 29, 2012.

The big story of the 2012 election was big money. Total spending soared past $2 billion, shattering previous records. For the first time, both major-party contenders rejected public funding in both the primary and general election stages. Obama raised and spent over $700 million (including about $234 million from small donors), considerably more than Romney (who raised and spent about $450 million), but pro-Romney super PACs made up the difference, spending over $400 million to boost his candidacy, compared to the $113 million that pro-Obama groups spent.

One legacy of the groundbreaking 2008 Obama for America campaign remained central to Obama's 2012 re-election campaign: coupling big data and micro-targeting techniques with principles and practices of community organizing (McKenna, Han, and Bird, 2014). Obama assembled a cutting-edge team of data scientists, developers, and digital advertising experts that included Chief Innovation and Integration Officer Michael Slaby, Chief Analytics Officer Dan Wagner, Battleground States Analytics Director Elan Kriegel, and many others working in The Cave—as Obama's 2012 data war room at the Chicago headquarters was nicknamed—to ensure every key strategic decision was informed by data (Goldmacher, 2016). Jeremy Bird, Obama's National Field Director in 2012, noted, "[w]e didn't make a single decision about battleground state strategy without first talking with Elan [Kriegel] about his numbers" (Goldmacher, 2016). Carol Davidsen, who ran the Obama television ad "Optimizer" project, explained that the campaign worked with Rentrak, a data company, to track television viewership for target groups of voters on over 60 channels every 15 minutes every day (Beckett, 2012).[3] Although the Republican analytics operation at Romney headquarters in Boston was less robust, Romney also invested in big data approaches in 2012, hiring experts like Zac Moffatt as digital director in-house, while outsourcing much of the campaign's analytics needs to external vendors (Issenberg, 2012).[4] As one analysis put it, the Romney team appeared in 2012 to have had accepted, "the David and Goliath dynamic between Boston and Chicago where analytics are concerned" (Issenberg, 2012).

As we have alluded to in our previous reviews, being the incumbent president is a double-edged sword. On the one hand, a president accrues critics with every policy decision and legislative accomplishment, and sentiments toward the incumbent that calcify are difficult to improve. On the other hand, presidents most often do not face appreciable opposition when seeking the nomination and are therefore free to raise money and level their political guns on the other party's nominee long before the general election campaign ever gets started. Bill Clinton and George W. Bush had proven formidable in this regard in 1996 and 2004, respectively, and Barack Obama was equally adroit in 2012. Overall, polls during spring 2012 and into the summer showed that support for Obama remained stable (relative to support for Romney) until mid-August when it began to climb steadily for about a month before dipping downward until the final 10 days or so of the campaign, when support strengthened anew (Panagopoulos, 2013; Panagopoulos and Farrer, 2014). Poll support ebbed and flowed as events including the conventions, presidential debates, and Hurricane Sandy left lasting imprints on voter preferences over the course of the election cycle (Panagopoulos, 2013), but most reputable, national polls showed a tight race between the two contenders (Panagopoulos and Farrer, 2014).

Against this backdrop, Table 5.3 displays the electoral strategies of each campaign. The Obama team, led by 2008 veterans David Axelrod, Jim Messina, and David Plouffe, conceded 22 states (with 180 electoral votes) to the Republican base and counted 17 states with 207 electoral votes in its base. After new data coming in from the field in October 2012 suggested Pennsylvania, Indiana, and Minnesota were competitive, Democrats designated these states along with nine others totaling 151 electoral votes as battlegrounds. An Obama victory would require 42% of these electoral votes. Romney's electoral strategy, crafted by campaign manager Matt Rhoades, pollster Neil Newhouse, and long-time GOP consultant Ed Gillespie, ultimately mirrored Obama's quite closely, with just a single exception. While the Obama team considered it had a lock on Michigan, Romney's came to believe that the Wolverine State—where he was born and raised and where his father George Romney had been elected governor—was competitive. In late October 2012 Romney's team reclassified it, alongside Pennsylvania and Minnesota, as a battleground. Accordingly, the GOP campaign counted 13 states with 167 electoral votes as battlegrounds. Romney's team viewed the same set of 22 states (with 180 electoral votes) in its base, meaning it would need to win more than half (54%) of the available battleground electoral votes to defeat Obama.

On Election Day, the Democratic incumbent Barack Obama triumphed over his Republican challenger by 332–206 in the Electoral College and by 51–47% in the popular vote. Turnout among eligible voters was 58.2%, a slight but noticeable decline from the 61.6% participation rate in 2008.[5] Obama secured a second term with fewer electoral votes and fewer popular votes than he had accrued in the historic 2008 election cycle but became only the third

Democrat to win a majority of the popular vote more than once. Most polls conducted prior to the November 6 election predicted such a result, with most surveys in battleground states showing a lead for Obama. Still, the Romney team believed that they were poised to win based on their polling data and their confidence in a mobile-optimized web application (dubbed ORCA) that the campaign would use as a critical component of their micro-targeted get-out-the vote effort.[6] ORCA was inspired by the 2008 Obama campaign's Houdini system, which enabled precinct-level poll watchers to report data to a national campaign hotline.[7] Reports from Romney personnel at polling stations were used to report vote totals in real time and to identify locations where GOP support was underperforming so that mobilization resources could be rapidly targeted by the campaign. Unfortunately for the Republicans, their polling proved inaccurate, and ORCA suffered catastrophic failures on Election Day, crashing several times, making it extremely difficult for volunteers to upload data.

Making America Great Again? The Trump-Clinton and Trump-Biden Elections

As the Obama era approached its end, the 2016 election cycle held many surprises in store. On the Democratic side, the heir-apparent for the nomination and former secretary of state Hillary Clinton ended up in a closer-than-expected battle with independent Vermont senator Bernie Sanders for the nod. Clinton ultimately prevailed in the Iowa caucuses—by the closest margin in the history of the first-in-the-nation contests, but widespread grassroots support for Sanders, fueled in large part by his strong social media presence, threatened Clinton's frontrunner status for much of the primary season as the two rivals traded state wins through early June. Clinton eventually claimed enough support to clinch the nomination on June 7, 2016, and, after adding Virginia senator Tim Kaine to the ticket, went on to officially become the first female major-party nominee for president at the Democratic National Convention held in Philadelphia July 25–28, 2016.

The Republican nomination battle was even more surprising to many observers. In a crowded field of seventeen contenders that initially included Texas senator Ted Cruz, Florida senator Marco Rubio, Ohio governor John Kasich, among others, it was New York businessman, television personality, and political neophyte Donald Trump who prevailed, with a bombastic campaign rooted in right-wing populism and nationalist themes that promised to "Make America Great Again" by deriding political correctness; building a wall

Table 5.3 2012 Presidential Campaign Plans

	OBAMA			ROMNEY		
# of states	Base Democratic	Battleground/ Targets	Base Republican	Base Democratic	Battleground/ Targets	Base Republican
1	California (55)	Colorado (9)****	Alabama (9)	California (55)	Colorado (9)*	Alabama (9)
2	Connecticut (7)	Florida (29)***	Alaska (3)	Connecticut (7)	Florida (29)**	Alaska (3)
3	D.C. (3)	Indiana (11)	Arizona (11)	D.C. (3)	Indiana (11)***	Arizona (11)
4	Delaware (3)	Iowa (6)*	Arkansas (6)	Delaware (3)	Iowa (6)*	Arkansas (6)
5	Hawaii (4)	Minnesota (10)	Georgia (16)	Hawaii (4)	Michigan (16)	Georgia (16)
6	Illinois (20)	Nevada (6)****	Idaho (4)	Illinois (20)	Minnesota (10)	Idaho (4)
7	Maine (4)	New Hampshire (4)	Kansas (6)	Maine (4)	Nevada (6)*	Kansas (6)
8	Maryland (10)	North Carolina (15)**	Kentucky (8)	Maryland (10)	New Hampshire (4)*	Kentucky (8)
9	Massachusetts (11)	Ohio (18)*	Louisiana (8)	Massachusetts (11)	North Carolina (15)***	Louisiana (8)
10	Michigan (16)	Pennsylvania (20)	Mississippi (6)	New Jersey (14)	Ohio (18)**	Mississippi (8)
11	New Jersey (14)	Virginia (13)**	Missouri (10)	New Mexico (5)*	Pennsylvania (20)	Missouri (10)
12	New Mexico (5)****	Wisconsin (10)	Montana (3)	New York (29)	Virginia (13)***	Montana (3)
13	New York (29)		Nebraska (5)	Oregon (7)	Wisconsin (10)*	Nebraska (5)
14	Oregon (7)		North Dakota (3)	Rhode Island (4)		North Dakota (3)
15	Rhode Island (4)		Oklahoma (7)	Vermont (3)		Oklahoma (7)
16	Vermont (3)		South Carolina (9)	Washington (12)		South Carolina (9)
17	Washington (12)		South Dakota (3)			South Dakota (3)
18			Tennessee (11)			Tennessee (11)

19			Texas (38)				Texas (38)	
20			Utah (6)				Utah (6)	
21			West Virginia (5)				West Virginia (5)	
22			Wyoming (3)				Wyoming (3)	
States	17	12	22	51	16	13	22	51
EVs	207	151	180	538	191	167	180	538

Notes:

"EV" stands for electoral votes. State electoral votes provided in parentheses.

For Obama's strategy, **** indicates "western path"; *** "Florida path"; ** "southern path"; * "Midwest path." Pennsylvania, Indiana, and Minnesota were added in October based on data from the field.

For Romney's strategy, ***indicates "Three" states; ** "Two" states; * "One" state (as part of the 3-2-1 strategy). Pennsylvania, Michigan, Minnesota added October 20, 2012.

Sources:

Institute of Politics, John F. Kennedy School of Government, Harvard University. 2013. *Campaign for President: The Managers Look at 2012*. Lanham, MD: Rowman and Littlefield.

Jamieson, Kathleen Hall. 2013. *Electing the President 2012: The Insiders' View*. Philadelphia: University of Pennsylvania Press. (See especially comments by David Axelrod, Joel Benenson, Neil Newhouse, and Stuart Stevens at the "Annenberg Conference on the Presidential Campaign of 2012," held December 6, 2012.)

Messina, Jim. 2012. "Obama 2012 Strategy Briefing," YouTube.com presentations on April 25, 2011, December 29, 2011, May 16, 2012.

along the southern border to curb illegal immigration; as well as dismantling the Iran nuclear deal, Obamacare, and free-trade agreements like NAFTA. In a nod to conservatives concerned about the authenticity of Trump's ideological convictions, the presumptive nominee announced (on Twitter) that he had tapped former Indiana governor Mike Pence as his running mate.

In the general election race, which pitted two New Yorkers against each other, Clinton was perceived widely as the odds-on favorite to win. Most polls projected an almost-certain Clinton victory, and the prominent poll aggregators estimating the likelihood of a Clinton win ranged from 71% (*FiveThirtyEight*) to 98% (*HuffPost*).[8] In a contentious and exceedingly negative campaign, Clinton touted her experience on the campaign trail and warned that Trump lacked the "temperament" to be president, at one point referring to half of Trump supporters as a "basket of deplorables" comprised of bigots and extremists. She also accused Trump of misogyny following the release of an *Access Hollywood* video tape recording that featured him making lewd comments about women in 2005. For his part, Trump hammered Clinton's ethics, alleging that she had improperly used a personal email server during her tenure as secretary of state that potentially compromised classified information. This issue led to investigations by Congress and the FBI as well as chants of "lock her up" at the GOP convention. Although her legal culpability was never firmly established, late-breaking news in October 2016 that the FBI was "reopening" the investigation after discovering new evidence in the matter complicated Clinton's attempt to close the deal with voters who found her personally unlikable.

Table 5.4 displays the Electoral College strategies for the Clinton and Trump campaigns. Although John Podesta was the campaign chair for Clinton, campaign manager Robby Mook, communications director Jenn Palmieri, political director Amanda Renteria, and pollster Joel Benenson were the primary architects of the Electoral College strategy. The Clinton team had assessed that 21 states with 249 electoral votes comprised its base. This formulation was based loosely on the notion of a "blue wall," denoting 18 states plus the District of Columbia that had voted Democratic in presidential elections since 1992. Included in the Clinton base were five states—Colorado, Maine, Michigan, Virginia, and Wisconsin—deemed to "lean" Democrat, but not solidly so. The Clinton camp believed Trump's based was comprised of 24 states (with 196 electoral votes) but assessed that five of these states—Arizona, Georgia, Iowa, Texas, and Utah—only "leaned" toward the GOP and could be worth targeting. That left an historically small number of six states (with 93 electoral votes) plus one district in Nebraska as battlegrounds, and Clinton would need to capture about 23% of these electoral votes to win. Of course, if the Clinton campaign's calculations were accurate, a win in Florida alone, or victories in some combination of the toss-up states that met or exceeded 21 electoral votes, would be sufficient to elect the first female president of the United States.

The Trump campaign went through several shake-ups, but by August Steve Bannon assumed control as chief executive officer, with Kellyanne Conway serving as senior advisor and Brad Parscale managing data and voter targeting. Trump's team assessment was that it had a stronghold on 23 states with 191 electoral votes, but it viewed twice as many states as the Clinton campaign—12, totaling 150 electoral votes—as competitive. Interestingly, the GOP battleground included all five states that the Clinton team believed only "leaned" in its direction plus Iowa, which Democrats categorized as part of the GOP base despite assessing that the Hawkeye state only "leaned" toward Trump. These calculations imply Trump needed more than half (53%) of the available battleground electoral votes to topple the Clinton machine.

As in 2012, analytics—and data-driven approaches—featured prominently in the 2016 presidential race, especially on the Democratic side of the aisle. Taking a page from the Obama campaigns, the Clinton team invested heavily in a robust, sophisticated analytics and targeting operation based mainly in its Brooklyn, New York, headquarters. Mook and Podesta relied heavily on director of analytics, Elan Kriegel. "Overlooking downtown Brooklyn in two directions, Kriegel's skyline view is the backdrop for what is on the windows themselves: erasable marker scribblings reminiscent of [the film] *A Beautiful Mind* that amount to some of the earliest drafts of the computer algorithms that underlie nearly all of the Clinton campaign's most important strategic decisions" (Goldmacher, 2016).[9]

Kriegel's team of more than sixty mathematicians and analysts—described invariably as both "the central nervous system for the campaign" and its "invisible guiding hand" (Goldmacher, 2016)—crunched volumes of data to inform nearly every important choice made by the "data-driven" campaign. The efforts paid off in the primary, in which modeling techniques for identifying likely supporters at the individual level helped Clinton to surge past Sanders, but also in fundraising. Although Clinton did not raise as much as Obama had in previous cycles, analytics helped her campaign to raise and spend almost $564 million (an additional $206 million was spent by outside groups supporting Clinton), which allowed her to outspending her GOP opponent significantly (Trump raised and spent $333 million, and groups spent another $100 million to promote his candidacy).[10]

Trump initially eschewed the value of campaign analytics, calling them "overrated," and invested little in data-driven approaches during the GOP

Table 5.4 2016 Presidential Campaign Plans

	CLINTON			TRUMP		
# of states	Base Democratic	Battleground/ Targets	Base Republican	Base Democratic	Battleground/ Targets	Base Republican
1	California (55)	Florida (29)	Alabama (9)	California (55)	Colorado (9)	Alabama (9)
2	Colorado (9)*	Nebraska (1)	Alaska (3)	Connecticut (7)	Florida (29)	Alaska (3)
3	Connecticut (7)	Nevada (6)	Arizona (11)**	D.C. (3)	Iowa (6)	Arizona (11)*
4	D.C. (3)	New Hampshire (4)	Arkansas (6)	Delaware (3)	Maine (4)	Arkansas (6)
5	Delaware (3)	North Carolina (15)	Georgia (16)**	Hawaii (4)	Michigan (16)	Georgia (16)
6	Hawaii (4)	Ohio (18)	Idaho (4)	Illinois (20)	Nevada (6)	Idaho (4)
7	Illinois (20)	Pennsylvania (20)	Indiana (11)	Maryland (10)	New Hampshire (4)	Indiana (11)
8	Maine (4)*		Iowa (6)**	Massachusetts (11)	North Carolina (15)	Kansas (6)
9	Maryland (10)		Kansas (6)	Minnesota (10)*	Ohio (18)	Kentucky (8)
10	Massachusetts (11)		Kentucky (8)	New Jersey (14)	Pennsylvania (20)	Louisiana (8)
11	Michigan (16)*		Louisiana (8)	New Mexico (5)*	Virginia (13)	Mississippi (6)
12	Minnesota (10)		Mississippi (6)	New York (29)	Wisconsin (10)	Missouri (10)
13	New Jersey (14)		Missouri (10)	Oregon (7)		Montana (3)
14	New Mexico (5)		Montana (3)	Rhode Island (4)		Nebraska (5)
15	New York (29)		Nebraska (4)	Vermont (3)		North Dakota (3)
16	Oregon (7)		North Dakota (3)	Washington (12)		Oklahoma (7)
17	Rhode Island (4)		Oklahoma (7)			South Carolina (9)
18	Vermont (3)		South Carolina (9)			South Dakota (3)
19	Virginia (13)*		South Dakota (3)			Tennessee (11)

20	Washington (12)		Tennessee (11)				Texas (38)	
21	Wisconsin (10)*		Texas (38)**				Utah (6)	
22			Utah (6)**				West Virginia (5)	
23			West Virginia (5)				Wyoming (3)	
24			Wyoming (3)					
States	21	6	24	51	16	12	23	51
EVs	249	93	196	538	197	150	191	538

Notes:

"EV" stands for electoral votes. State electoral votes provided in parentheses.

For Clinton's strategy, * indicates leaning Clinton states, ** indicates leaning Trump states worth targeting. Initial targeting was loosely based on the "Blue Wall" notion: that the base consisted of the 18 states (+ D.C.) that had gone Democratic in every election since 1992.

For Trump's strategy, * indicates states that were part of the "fourteen state strategy." Virginia was dropped from the strategy in late Sept./early Oct. Minnesota was added in very late October.

Sources:

Brownstein, Ronald. 2016. "Is Donald Trump Out-Flanking Hillary Clinton?" *The Atlantic*, November 2.

Conway, Kelly Ann. 2016. "Memo," Email to supporters (10/21/16), confirmed in personal correspondence.

Debenedetti, Gabriel. 2016. "They Always Wanted Trump," *Politico*, November 7.

Institute of Politics, John F. Kennedy School of Government, Harvard University. 2017. *Campaign for President: The Managers Look at 2016*. Lanham, MD: Rowman and Littlefield. (See especially comments made by Robby Mook, Joel Benenson, Kelly Anne Conway, Tony Fabrizio, and Brad Parscale at "Campaign Insiders," Dec. 1–2, 2016 conference at Harvard University's School of Public Policy.)

primary. Operatives confessed they struggled to get Trump to buy into the value of data and to abandon his skepticism of data-driven techniques. With Trump choosing to stump in "far-afield" states like Mississippi, Texas, and Washington, Republicans had to implore the campaign to incorporate "some data inputs" into choices as fundamental as the candidate's schedule (Goldmacher, 2016). The campaign eventually hired Parscale (who later served as Trump's re-election campaign manager in 2020) as digital director to head up its analytics efforts and retained Cambridge Analytica—later criticized for its questionable acquisition of Facebook data on millions of Americans and possible connections to Russia—to exploit analytics techniques to design target audiences for digital ads and fundraising appeals, model turnout, buy $5 million in television ads, and even to "determine where Trump should travel to best drum up support" (Rosenberg, Confessore, and Cadwalladr, 2018).[11]

As the votes were tabulated on Election Day, it became clear that Donald Trump would become the forty-fifth president of the United States. Trump's win shocked many observers, even though most polls throughout the election cycle foreshadowed a close race. In the end, Clinton did win the national popular vote, earning 48.2% to Trump's 46.1% (and exceeding Trump by nearly three million votes), but the Electoral College victory went to Donald Trump, who managed to secure victories not only in Florida and North Carolina, but also in key states situated in the Midwest and Rust Belt regions. Wisconsin, for example, voted Republican for president for the first time since 1984, and Pennsylvania and Michigan went red for the first time since 1988. In fact, the 2016 presidential vote in all but a handful of states shifted in a Republican direction compared to 2012.

As the 2020 presidential election loomed, a global pandemic and the economic dislocation it caused eclipsed everything else. Despite a first term laden with chaos and controversy, including unsubstantiated allegations of collusion with Russians in the 2016 election, an impeachment (and acquittal) over claims that President Trump threatened to withhold foreign aid support from Ukraine unless it promised to investigate Hunter Biden (son of the former vice-president and a leading Democratic rival, Joe Biden), a controversial COVID-19 response, and record low popularity in polls, Trump maintained an iron grip on Republican voters and faced virtually no opposition for the GOP nomination.

By contrast, a total of 29 major candidates declared for the Democratic nomination—more than in any presidential primary in any political party since the system of modern primaries began in 1972. These included 2016 runner-up Vermont senator Bernie Sanders; Obama vice-president Joe Biden; sitting and former senators including Michael Bennet (Colorado), Cory Booker (New Jersey), Amy Klobuchar (Minnesota), Kamala Harris (California),

Kirsten Gillibrand (New York), Mike Gravel (Alaska, served 1969–1981), and Elizabeth Warren (Massachusetts); several governors, U.S. representatives, and mayors, including Michael Bloomberg and Bill DiBlasio (New York city) as well as Pete Buttigieg (South Bend, Indiana); and businesspeople like entrepreneur Andrew Yang and hedge fund manager Tom Steyer. Following desultory showings in Iowa, New Hampshire, and Nevada, a Biden triumph in the South Carolina primary highlighted his appeal with a broad and diverse electorate, and his main rivals Buttigieg and Klobuchar quickly dropped out and endorsed the former vice-president. Biden's momentum continued through Super Tuesday, and he soon wrapped up the nomination. Biden picked California Senator Kamala Harris as his running mate, the first African American and Asian American woman to assume the role.

The general election race featuring two septuagenarians turned mainly on issues relating to pandemic response and recovery, which, by that point, had become increasingly politicized. A Biden victory appeared likely throughout the election year as the Democratic nominee routinely out-performed Trump in head-to-head matchups. In fact, Biden trailed Trump in only two (of 229) national surveys conducted between January 2020 through Election Day (Panagopoulos, 2021). With signs of a potential loss on the horizon, Trump consistently planted seeds of doubt about the integrity of the election, alleging that fraud could be rampant (but only if he lost) and questioning, among other things, the reliability of mail-in and absentee voting that had been expanded in light of COVID-19.

With the presidential public funding system essentially defunct, 2020 was also the most expensive election cycle to date, with total spending exceeding $5.7 billion, according to the Center for Responsive Politics. The Biden campaign was the first to raise more than $1 billion from donors, while Trump raised $774 million, mostly from small donors contributing $200 or less (Evers-Hillstrom, 2021).[12]

Table 5.5 presents the Electoral College strategies of the two 2020 campaigns. Relying heavily on Brad Parscale and chief strategist Michael Glassner, the Trump re-election team once again counted 23 states (with 187 electoral votes) in its base, but these reflected some adjustments compared to 2016. The Trump campaign moved Arizona and Georgia and one district in Nebraska to the battleground category and believed it had a lock on Ohio and Iowa in 2020. In total, 12 states with 139 electoral votes, including one district in Maine and one in Nebraska, made up what Trump considered to be the battleground, with 18 states (212 electoral votes) comprising the Biden base. The GOP would need to capture 60% of the electoral votes in swing states to win if its base held as expected. It also formulated a number of victory scenarios,

Table 5.5 2020 Presidential Campaign Plans

	BIDEN			TRUMP		
# of states	Base Democratic	Battleground/ Targets	Base Republican	Base Democratic	Battleground/ Targets	Base Republican
1	California (55)	Arizona (11)**	Alabama (9)	California (55)	Arizona (11)**	Alabama (9)
2	Colorado (9)	Florida (29)**	Alaska (3)	Colorado (9)	Florida (29)**	Alaska (3)
3	Connecticut (7)	Georgia (16)*	Arkansas (6)	Connecticut (7)	Georgia (16)	Arkansas (6)
4	D.C. (3)	Maine CD2 (1)	Idaho (4)	D.C. (3)	Maine CD2 (1)	Idaho (4)
5	Delaware (3)	Michigan (16)**	Indiana (11)	Delaware (3)	Michigan (16)**	Indiana (11)
6	Hawaii (4)	Nebraska CD2 (1)	Iowa (6)*	Hawaii (4)	Minnesota (10)*	Iowa (6)
7	Illinois (20)	North Carolina (15)**	Kansas (6)	Illinois (20)	Nebraska CD2 (1)	Kansas (6)
8	Maine (3)	Pennsylvania (20)**	Kentucky (8)	Maine (3)	Nevada (6)*	Kentucky (8)
9	Maryland (10)	Wisconsin (10)**	Louisiana (8)	Maryland (10)	New Hampshire (4)*	Louisiana (8)
10	Massachusetts (11)		Mississippi (6)	Massachusetts (11)	North Carolina (15)	Mississippi (6)
11	Minnesota (10)*		Missouri (10)	New Jersey (14)	Pennsylvania (20)**	Missouri (10)
12	Nevada (6)		Montana (3)	New Mexico (5)	Wisconsin (10)**	Montana (3)
13	New Hampshire (4)		Nebraska (4)	New York (29)		Nebraska (4)
14	New Jersey (14)		North Dakota (3)	Oregon (7)		North Dakota (3)
15	New Mexico (5)		Ohio (18)*	Rhode Island (4)		Ohio (18)
16	New York (29)		Oklahoma (7)	Vermont (3)		Oklahoma (7)
17	Oregon (7)		South Carolina (9)	Virginia (13)		South Carolina (9)
18	Rhode Island (4)		South Dakota (3)	Washington (12)		South Dakota (3)

19	Vermont (3)		Tennessee (11)				Tennessee (11)	
20	Virginia (13)		Texas (38)*				Texas (38)	
21	Washington (12)		Utah (6)				Utah (6)	
22			West Virginia (5)				West Virginia (5)	
23			Wyoming (3)				Wyoming (3)	
States	21	9	23	51	18	12	23	51
EVs	232	119	187	538	212	139	187	538

Notes:

For Biden's strategy, ** indicates "tier 1 priority"; * "tier 2 priority" states. Among the tier 2 states, only Georgia was considered a battleground. The assumption of the campaign was that the most likely victory scenarios—in order—were (1) victories in Michigan, Pennsylvania, and Wisconsin, (the so-called "Rust Belt spike"); (2) victories in Arizona, Georgia, and North Carolina (the so-called "Sun Belt spike"); or (3) victory in Florida plus almost any other battleground state.

For Trump's strategy, ** indicates "tier 1 priority" states; * "tier 2 priority" states. The "Landslide scenario" encompasses victory in all battleground states; the "Southwest strength scenario" encompasses victory in Arizona and Nevada, but losses in the Rust Belt states of Minnesota, Wisconsin, Pennsylvania, and Michigan; the "Blue Wall collapse scenario" encompasses a loss in Florida but wins in Wisconsin, Pennsylvania, and Michigan (and Ohio).

Sources:

Bill Stepien, Trump Campaign Briefing, September 7, 2020 (https://www.washingtontimes.com/news/2020/sep/8/trump-campaign-officials-show-multiple-pathways-vi/)

Mike Donilon (chief strategist), Jennifer O'Malley Dillon (campaign manager), Kate Bedingfield (deputy campaign manager), Biden Campaign Briefing, September 5, 2020 (https://www.nytimes.com/2020/09/05/us/politics/Joe-Biden-2020.html)

Institute of Politics, John F. Kennedy School of Government, Harvard University. 2022. *Campaign for President: The Managers Look at 2020*. Lanham, MD: Rowman and Littlefield.

See also Allen, Jonathan, and Amy Parnes. 2021. *Lucky: How Joe Biden Barely Won the Presidency*. New York: Crown Publishing. (Especially pages 363–365, 383–384.)

the most optimistic of which was the "landslide scenario"—a sweep of the swing states. The "Southwest strength" scenario assumed wins in Arizona and Nevada to offset "Rust Belt" losses in Minnesota, Wisconsin, Pennsylvania, and Michigan. Still another victory possibility was the "Blue Wall collapse" scenario comprised of wins in Wisconsin, Pennsylvania, and Michigan (along with Ohio) to counterbalance a Florida loss.

Interestingly, the Biden campaign compiled an identical list of 23 states and districts with 187 electoral votes as the GOP base, but believed it had a shot in "tier 2 priority" states Iowa, Ohio, and Texas. Led by campaign manager Jennifer O'Malley Dillon and senior consultant Anita Dun, the Democratic team counted 21 states with 232 electoral votes in the Democratic base but designated one of these—Minnesota (10 electoral votes)—as a "tier 2 priority" state. That left 119 electoral votes across nine states (including a single vote in each of both Maine and Nebraska) as the battlegrounds, and Biden would need 32% of these electoral votes to deny Trump the White House for a second term. For its part, the Biden campaign had a number of scenarios that could get Democrats past the post; it judged the most likely victory scenario was the "Rust Belt spike" (wins in Pennsylvania, Michigan, and Wisconsin), followed by the "Sun Belt spike" (wins in Arizona, Georgia, and North Carolina). Still another victory scenario was a win in Florida with just about any other battleground state win (see Institute of Politics, 2021; also Allen and Parnes, 2021).

Biden was ultimately victorious in 2020, making Trump the tenth U.S. president to be denied a second term. The Democrat defeated the incumbent president by a margin of 51.3% to 46.8% in the national popular vote, securing 306 electoral votes, compared to 232 for Trump. Democratic wins in the key Rust Belt states of Michigan, Pennsylvania, and Wisconsin—where Clinton was essentially denied the White House four years earlier—along with more surprising victories in states like Georgia and Arizona, which had not voted for a Democratic presidential candidate since 1992 and 1996 respectively, were crucial to Biden's success. (Biden also won Nebraska's second congressional district, boosting his electoral count by an additional vote.)

Conclusion

Presidential campaigns in the twenty-first century adapted to significant changes in the social and political landscape. In the campaign finance domain, regulatory changes ushered in by passage of the BCRA and the court rulings that followed—especially the landmark ruling in *Citizens United v. FEC*—coupled with total collapse of the system of public funding in presidential races that had been in place for three decades changed both the nature of fundraising as well as campaigns' ability to exert control over independent spending by outside groups in support or opposition to their candidacies.

The growth of the Internet and social media also transformed campaigns' communications and fundraising capacities, enabling direct and near-immediate contact and rapid response and allowing campaigns to bypass traditional media filters and information gatekeepers. Technological advancements facilitated the big-data revolution, helping campaigns to hone their micro-targeting abilities and to leverage data analytics to refine their targeting strategies with considerable accuracy and precision.

Notwithstanding the promise these developments held in store for presidential campaigns, many expectations failed to materialize. For one, election victories were not dictated by financial advantages. John Kerry in 2004 and John McCain in 2008 managed to clinch their parties' nominations despite lagging other contenders in terms of fundraising and campaign spending, and Hillary Clinton failed to win the 2016 general election despite her significant financial edge over Trump (nearly two to one in terms of total spending). Campaigns from this period offered a second lesson as well: data is not destiny. Howard Dean, for example, failed to win the 2004 nomination even though his campaign revolutionized how the Internet and social media could be used to attract donors and supporters. Similarly, Clinton's path to the presidency in 2016 was foiled despite an unrivaled analytics operation. In the end, these developments are essentially tools, and there are often unintended—or unexpected—consequences of using them. For example, scholars often find voters are impervious, resistant to, or even repulsed by highly targeted and personalized campaign appeals, resulting in backlash (Panagopoulos, 2021). Campaigns from this era serve as a useful reminder that despite the several advantages brought about by micro-targeting and digital media, election contexts and outcomes remain exceedingly complex and, often, just as unpredictable as they were back in 1952.

6 Tracking Electoral Strategy Over Time

Are Campaigns Smarter Today?

In the first two chapters of this book, we made the case that presidential campaigns have varied over the course of recent American history. Much like politics itself, campaigns are dynamic and those of us who seek to better understand the electoral process in the United States should consider the nature and scope of this dynamism. The last three chapters offered a review of the historical record for each of three distinct eras of presidential campaigning. More than simply revisiting some particulars from those campaigns, we sought to integrate more detailed information about the campaigns' electoral strategies into the narrative. In doing this, we aimed at providing both original data on Electoral College strategies and context for understanding why those strategies made sense for a given time and party.

We now pivot to a more systematic analysis of the data we have collected to assess how the Electoral College strategies of presidential campaigns have affected the allocation of valuable campaign resources across states and the impact of those resource allocations on the national vote. The following chapters rely on these data to assess not only the strategies and their effects, but also how these have (and have not) changed over the course of sixty-eight years, eighteen elections, and three distinct campaign eras. Our conclusions are informed by detailed empirical analyses of the data we have collected. But we try to keep the statistics simple and understandable, and when we need to enlist a slightly higher degree of statistical difficulty, we strive to render these analyses in a plain-spoken and easily interpretable manner.

It may strike some as odd that we would put so much stock in television advertising and candidate appearances as our measures of campaigning because the dominant modes of candidate outreach seem to be shifting. During the pandemic election of 2020, for example, the presidential and vice-presidential candidates seemed to do less travelling than they had in previous elections. For while we saw many text messages, television and radio advertisements, billboards, lawn signs, and bumper stickers, we did not see much of the principals or their volunteers. Democratic candidate Joe Biden spent days on end isolated—with his family and advisors—in his Delaware

Battleground. Daron R. Shaw, Scott L. Althaus, and Costas Panagopoulos, Oxford University Press.
 DOI: 10.1093/oso/9780197774366.003.0006

home. Republican candidate Donald Trump, while more visible than Biden, held far fewer events than he had in 2016. But candidate appearances, along with television advertisements, remain among the most pervasive and visible manifestations of presidential campaigns. They have been consequential for strategists throughout this time period, and it is likely that they will continue to be relevant markers moving forward.

We would also observe that while the "reduced" campaign of 2020 was surely a function of the caution necessitated by a global pandemic, it also reinforces a basic fact of American presidential campaigns: they do not target everybody. Reality dictates that an individual candidate could not personally reach out to millions of eligible voters in 2020 any easier than they could in 1952. But how do candidates decide who gets attention and who does not? If democracies are supposed to follow the logic of "one person, one vote," the Electoral College system in the United States appears to give disproportionate influence to voters who live in battleground states. As noted in previous chapters, political science studies have provided interesting and important theoretical perspectives on how strategic actors behave under these rules, while campaign narratives have provided some details on the strategies of specific candidates. We argue that leveraging these two important sources increases our ability to theorize, and that systematically adding data on allocations of advertising and candidate appearances to these sources creates a myriad of opportunities to bolster our knowledge of presidential campaigning.

This chapter focuses on two simple questions: what do Electoral College strategies look like, and have their essential features changed over time? This requires us to identify the factors that drive campaigns to designate states as battlegrounds. To answer this, we reconstruct and analyze the strategies of the 36 major-party U.S. presidential campaigns from 1952 to 2020. Based on the data presented in chapters 3, 4, and 5, we know that each of these presidential campaigns had a macro-targeting plan, often based on the expected probability of carrying particular states as well as the respective value of those states to a winning coalition. The evidence also suggests that campaign strategies *might* have become more sophisticated over time, mostly due to better (and timelier) information about dynamic changes in candidate standing after the campaign was underway. Presumably, this could reduce the number of battleground states in more recent years along with whatever bias there might possibly have been if campaigns in earlier eras were more likely to target more populous states. Whatever tendencies or trends these analyses turn up will be critical for gauging the representational "biases" of the Electoral College system (see Edwards, 2005).

How to Think about Electoral College Strategies

In chapter 2, we reviewed the extant literature with an eye toward developing plausible expectations about how presidential campaigns approach their primary task of winning an Electoral College majority. Most political scientists have emphasized that candidates and their campaigns should be treated as rational actors, operating with limited resources and attempting to maximize the probability of obtaining a winning coalition of 270 electoral votes (Mann and Shapley, 1960; Longley and Dana, 1984, 1992; Smith and Squire, 1987; Wright, 2009). Some studies have emphasized that this suggests a slight bias in favor of larger states (Longley and Braun, 1972; Longley and Dana, 1984, 1992; Longley and Pierce, 1999; Smith and Squire, 1987). Other more recent studies assume that the order in which states "commit" matters, as does the size of the state's contribution to the winning coalition (Wright, 2009). If a large state is known to be part of the winning coalition early on, it will not be an important target. Neither will competitive states be important if those states do not supply a large enough share of electoral votes to be required in a winning coalition.

Based on this research, we think it likely that campaigns throughout our time period will have focused on states that are pivotal to their "minimum" winning coalitions. Put simply, states that are most likely to get the candidate to 270 electoral votes should be the ones that are targeted by the campaign. Journalists and practitioners have used the notion of "pivot" (or "tipping point") states over the years and in recent elections they have offered independent assessments of the statistical likelihood that specific states will put a candidate "over the top."[1] Note, however, that while this theoretical perspective predicts that certain states are more likely to be targeted than others, it does not necessarily lead to specific predictions about *how* campaigns conceptualize individual states.

In chapter 2, we introduced the notion that campaigns rank-order states based on their likelihood of voting for their candidate and that states around the 270 electoral vote mark are likely to be distinguished as "battleground" states. In chapters 3, 4, and 5, our investigation of campaign records showed that campaigns sort states into distinct categories: battleground, base support, and base opposition. In this chapter, and in subsequent analyses, we go further. Across the range of elections from 1952 to 2020, we will leverage the tendency for campaigns to also classify states as leaning a particular way but not firmly committed to a candidate. Some campaigns explicitly identify them as "leaning" Republican or Democratic, while other campaigns include them in the battleground category with some sort of note or caveat. As we will soon demonstrate, it turns out that these more nuanced categories play important roles in presidential campaigns for attracting particular forms of campaign attention (and resource allocations).

To illustrate how this matters in a particular campaign, consider the 1980 Electoral College plans of the Reagan and Carter campaigns. As related in chapter 4, Carter's campaign marked states in the targeting plan as "marginal Carter" states ("lean Democratic") and "marginal Reagan" states ("lean Republican"). Reagan's campaign did not use a comparable nomenclature, but in their strategic memos assessing Carter's likely coalition, they distinguished between "base Democratic" states and potential-but-not-quite-yet "battleground" states: Connecticut, Delaware, Mississippi, North Carolina, and Oklahoma all fell into this "lean Democratic" category.

This 1980 example suggests the value of developing a scale that allows us to capture both the direction and likelihood of the partisan vote. To do so, we now revisit the methodology previously articulated in chapter 2. Rather than use a three-fold categorization—one that would require us to make difficult judgments about how to classify "leaning" states—we will rely on an enhanced version of this scale encompassing five categories: Republican Base (+2), Republican Lean (+1), Battleground (0), Democratic Lean (−1), and Democratic Base (−2). Beyond our own interpretation of past electoral strategies, we relied on input and advice from several former presidential campaign consultants in opting for the five-fold categorization.[2] As noted in chapter 2, to code each campaign's strategy, two different researchers classified the states using the five-category scale just described. The resultant inter-coder reliability score, measured by Cohen's kappa coefficient, is an acceptable 0.82.[3] Differences in coding were then discussed and resolved by consensus. Depending upon the analytic task at hand, we might also jettison the partisan direction of categories, recoding −2 or +2 states as 0 (safe), −1 and +1 as 1 (lean) and 0 as 2 (battleground).

By systematically ordering these data on presidential campaign strategies, we can begin the process of assessing the significance of different factors and trends. Based on our adaptation of "pivot state" theory—and our understanding of over-time tendencies—we have a few specific (and testable) hypotheses.

First, we expect that recent campaigns will be more strategically sophisticated than earlier campaigns. Not only is information about voter preferences available more often, at a more granular level of detail, and for more states than it used to be, but the American media audience has become more highly segmented over time with increasing abilities for campaigns to communicate not only through traditional radio and television broadcasts structured at the level of media markets, but starting in the 1980s, through city-level cable systems and by the first decade of the 2000s, through a variety of digital channels ranging from email and text messages to personalized banner ads on internet sites and even billboard ads embedded in popular online gaming environments.[4] Yet we freely admit that "more strategically sophisticated" is a broad expectation that will (mostly) be assessed subjectively. Strategic sophistication is, after all, somewhat in the eye of the beholder. However, the data we have collected do allow us to note *the number and the range of states* targeted by campaigns of different eras, and to examine the factors that drive classification for clues about strategic complexity and sophistication.

It should be noted that one ticklish aspect of strategic sophistication is dynamism. It is reasonable to assume that more sophisticated strategies will include options for updating the classification of individual states as the campaign progresses, especially when extant circumstances shift or when new or better information becomes available. It is therefore tempting to hypothesize that more recent presidential campaign strategies will be more likely to change—that is, to move states from one category to another—than those in earlier years. We think this is possible but depends greatly on whether new information suggests that the political reality has changed in some appreciable way.

Second, we do *not* expect that more populous states are more likely in general to be classified as battlegrounds. The idea that "bigger" states garner more attention is an oft-cited bias attributed to the Electoral College. It has been buttressed by research suggesting that such states contribute more to a 270-vote majority than states with fewer electoral votes and are (by virtue of accounting for more electoral votes) more likely to be "pivotal." We are skeptical of this bias, though, based on recent theoretical and empirical work on presidential campaign strategies (see Shaw, 2006 and Stromberg, 2008). Our expectation is particularly strong in more recent elections, as campaigns now have better information on voter behavior and may be more willing to forego more populous (and therefore more expensive) states if enough medium and small states can be targeted as replacements.

Third, we *do* expect that close, competitive states are more likely to be classified as battlegrounds. In particular, states that were competitive in the last election are likely to be viewed as battlegrounds in the current election. This expectation draws on the fact that national elections (especially recent ones) have been close and statewide results do not vary much from one election to the next. Therefore, a state that is decided by a few points in one election is likely to be designated as a battleground in the next go-around. As noted earlier, however, contemporary presidential campaigns have polling and voter file information that allows them to discern the occurrence of inter-election shifts in political attitudes.[5] This creates some ambivalence in our over-time expectations concerning the influence of past competitiveness on presidential campaign strategy: although recent election outcomes have looked similar to each other, campaigns from these years also possessed more and better information about whatever changes in statewide voter preferences might have occurred since last time around. In short, we expect past competitiveness to predict battleground status in the current election but are unsure whether this correlation has changed over time.

Fourth and finally, we expect there to be some differences between Republican and Democratic campaign plans in each election. Why? Consider what would happen if both campaigns had the exact same rank order of states by expected partisan vote for a given election. If the campaigns were perfectly strategic, both would mainly focus on the one state that falls on their 270 electoral vote marker. Beyond that single state, the Republican campaign would have some states that contribute to its coalition, whereas the Democratic campaign would have some other states that contribute to its coalition. But these would not be the same states. In other words, coalitional differences dictate that Democratic and Republican campaigns do not see the election identically. Furthermore, given that information about how states are likely to vote is both imperfect and dynamic, campaigns want some leeway in their coalition to hedge against uncertainty. But different campaigns may want more (or less) leeway based on how they assess that uncertainty. This might lead one campaign to judge a state as "in play" while the other campaign concludes it is not. Finally, campaigns might have the same rank order of states but different estimates of how well they are doing overall. For example, in 2012 the Obama and Romney campaigns focused on roughly the same set of battleground states, but the Obama team (correctly) thought they were up across the board whereas the Romney campaign (incorrectly) thought their own campaign was ahead in most. If Romney's team had the same information as the Obama team concerning the current state of play, the GOP might have expanded the map to include additional lean-Democratic states.

Analyzing Electoral College Strategies

Before turning to the data, we think it is important to reassert that our initial review of internal memos from the campaigns, along with insider and journalistic accounts, suggest that Electoral College strategies have *always* been multi-faceted and sophisticated. One cannot help but be impressed by the efforts of, for example, the Eisenhower, Kennedy, and Johnson campaigns; compared to the data enjoyed by modern campaigns they were flying relatively blind, but their creative use of historical election results and trends to inform their own macro-targeting priorities is impressive. We still expect some temporal variance in the extent of this sophistication, but we are hardly moving from the medieval to the enlightenment era of presidential campaigning.

Given this apparent strategic sophistication over the totality of the time series, it may be surprising that prior chapters suggested Electoral College strategies were mostly fixed. This is not to say that states were never added to (or subtracted from) the battleground category over the course of the campaign. Rather, the data indicate that such changes were typically confined to a single state, or two at most, and typically reflected the desperation of one side and the dominance of the other. For example, the Dukakis campaign "sharpened" its focus to an "eighteen-state strategy" in 1988 after the disastrous second presidential debate and the realization that they had little chance of winning most of the states on their battleground list.

It may also be surprising that more recent campaigns are not necessarily more dynamic. The main reason is that the last six presidential elections—from 2000 through 2020—were close throughout, such that the essential contours of these most recent races were consistently stable. In other words, recent presidential elections have been marked by close, polarized electorates, which were well-understood by the campaigns due to extensive high-quality polling and data analytics. This produces a relatively static strategic environment in recent years. The exception to this finding proves the rule: in 2008, Democrat Barack Obama held a lead of roughly six points over Republican John McCain for most of the spring and summer, but the economic collapse in late September shifted the race further toward the Democrat and caused three additional states (Arizona, Georgia, and North Dakota) to be moved into the "lean/battleground" category.

That said, strategic adjustments do appear slightly more likely in very recent years. For instance, consider how the interplay between data and strategy affected views toward Pennsylvania in 2012. Both the Obama and Romney campaigns categorized Pennsylvania as a "lean Democratic" state, just outside the battleground category. But polling and analyses of early vote data in late October from Florida and Ohio suggested that Romney could not count on winning either of those two crucial states. Thus, the Romney campaign elevated Pennsylvania (along with Michigan and Minnesota) onto its "battleground" list because they had become the more relatively attainable targets. The Obama campaign did not respond in kind, although they did shift some resources into Pennsylvania. Similar shifts occurred in late October 2016 when the Trump campaign dropped Virginia and added Minnesota and in mid-September 2020 when the Trump campaign moved Georgia to its battleground list.

These observations about strategic sophistication and dynamism aside, a simple descriptive representation of the underlying data is in order given (1) their uniqueness and (2) normative interest in the possibility that the Electoral College may produce systematic distortions in attention from presidential candidates and campaigns (see Edwards, 2005). Figure 6.1 shows that across eighteen presidential elections, some states stand out as consistent battlegrounds. Perhaps most notably, Pennsylvania has been classified as a battleground state 18 times by the Republicans and 17 times by the Democrats. For Ohio, it is 17 by each side. For Michigan, it is 17 and 15, respectively. For Wisconsin, it is 15 and 17. For Florida, it is 15 and 14. We do see differences in the aggregate by party. Most notably, Arizona has been a battleground state in nine Democratic campaigns, but only four Republican campaigns; Oregon has been a battleground 11 times for the Democrats, but only six times for the Republicans; Illinois has been a battleground 13 times for the Democrats, but only nine times for the Republicans. Still, there is symmetry in the parties' strategic classifications. Moreover, while the political landscape of the United States has changed dramatically over the years, some states remain perennial battlegrounds.

But why? What factors drive campaigns to designate a state as a battleground? More specifically, how much do electoral votes and/or past competitiveness matter? To test these ideas empirically, we specify and estimate

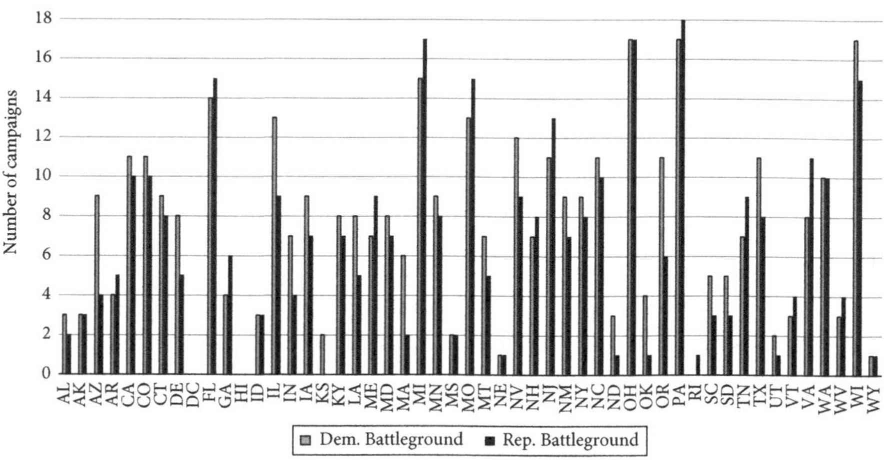

Figure 6.1 Frequency of Battleground Status, 1952–2020

a model predicting Electoral College strategy (0 = base state, 1 = lean state, 2 = battleground) with two predictor variables: number of electoral votes in the state and closeness of the state in the previous election. For the former, we simply use the number of electoral votes in each state for each election year. For past competitiveness, we operationalize closeness in the previous election using presidential vote totals (1 = margin of 20 points or greater, 2 = margin of 10–19.9 points, 3 = margin of 5–9.9 points, 4 = margin of 0–4.9 points). The logic is that small shifts in the vote margin, especially as results move further away from 50–50, are relatively less likely to affect battleground categorization (and, as we explore in chapter 7, models of resource allocation) in the subsequent presidential campaign. We also include over-time interactions with the "electoral votes" and "closeness" variables to examine if the importance of these variables has changed in campaign strategy over time.

What Predicts Battleground Status?

We use the five-category strategic classification models described earlier in this chapter to generate predicted probabilities of battleground categorization as a final illustration of the changing influence of competitiveness and electoral votes on campaign strategy over time (for brevity, we do not present predicted probabilities of "lean" and "safe" ordinal categories). Readers interested in the details of this regression analysis can find them in the appendix to this chapter. Here, our focus is merely to present the main findings of interest.

Figure 6.2 displays graphically how varying closeness of the previous election (where higher values of "closeness" indicate a closer election) changes the probability of battleground categorization for both Democrats and Republicans. For each party, we plot three predicted probability curves, one for each election in each era (we randomly selected 1952, 1980, and 2012) to show that the relationship between closeness and battleground status grows stronger in recent elections. These figures present the probability that a given state will be classified as a battleground (along the Y-axis, with higher values indicating greater probabilities, where 0.4 means a 40% probability of being classified as a battleground) as a function of the state's closeness in the two-party vote from the previous presidential election (along the X-axis, with higher values representing increasing levels of closeness so that 1 represents the widest margin of 20 points or greater while 4 represents the closest margin of between 0 and 5 points).

Figures 6.2a and 6.2b show very similar patterns across parties: electoral closeness used to be at best a minor factor in predicting battleground status,

(a) Republican Campaigns

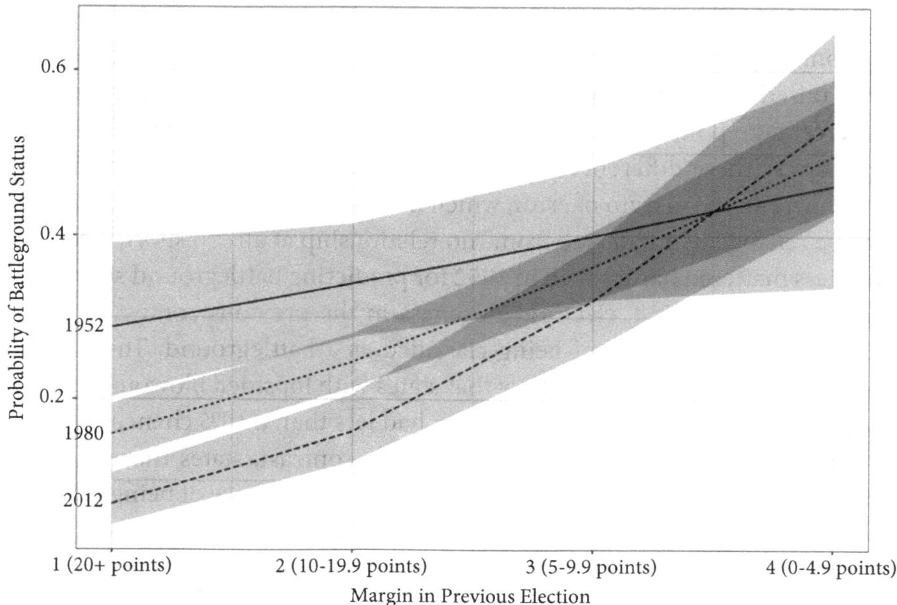

(b) Democratic Campaigns

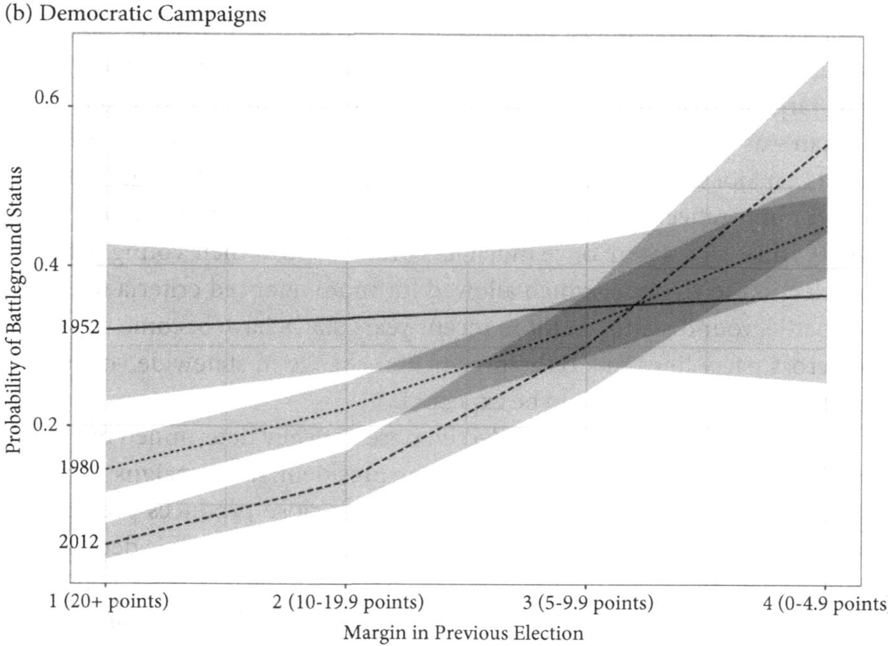

Figure 6.2 How Closeness of the Previous Election Predicts Battleground Status by Party
Note: For details on the regression model, see chapter appendix.

but has become a strong predictor in more recent years. In 1952, battleground status had little to do with the closeness of the two-party vote in the previous election: varying the closeness measure from "not at all close" to "extremely close" raised the probability of being selected as a battleground by only around 15 percentage points for Republicans and perhaps 2 percentage points for Democrats. These differences across levels of closeness are small enough to remain within the margin of error, which means even this apparent difference can't be reliably distinguished from "no relationship at all." In short, electoral closeness mattered hardly at all in 1952 for predicting battleground status.

By 2012, in contrast, electoral closeness in the previous contest strongly predicts a state's chances of being classified as a battleground. The dashed lines in Figures 6.2a and 6.2b show that states with lopsided blowouts for one party or another in the previous election had less than a 10% chance of being selected as battlegrounds for both parties. In contrast, states that were decided by 5 percentage points or less had about a 55% chance of being selected as battlegrounds by both parties. Even though campaign strategists in 1952 were paying extremely close attention to prior election results at the state and county levels, because this was the primary source of predictive information they had about state-level vote intentions, the closeness of the previous race was, at best, only a minor factor in deciding which states would be most aggressively contested. By 2012, in contrast, despite the abundance of micro-targeting data that should allow more nuanced finessing of voter behavior than was ever possible before, both parties were using statewide election totals as a major factor for determining battleground status. In large part, this change simply reflects the changing variability in the electoral map from 1952 to 2020: while states were once much less predictable in their voting patterns from election to election, which allowed for more nuanced criteria to determine battleground status, in more recent years states have become so polarized across party lines that only incremental change in statewide vote totals from election to election could be expected.

In an era in which presidential elections are typically determined by razor-thin margins, the increasing tendency for presidential campaigns to focus their attention on states with a history of being close produces predictable results: tight elections within the battleground states. This fact is depicted in Figure 6.3, where we see that the Republican share of the two-party vote in all battleground states since 1992 ranges between a low of 47% (1996) and a high of 52% (2004). By contrast, prior to 1992 the GOP's share of the two-party vote in all battleground states was as high as 63% (1972) and as low as 41% (1964).

Are campaigns missing an opportunity to "move" voters in less historically competitive states? Possibly. But modern campaigns rely on more than just

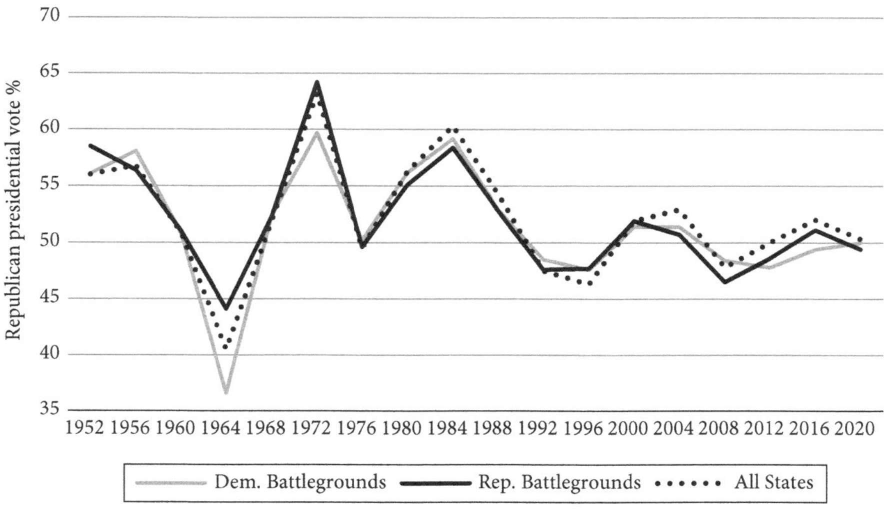

Figure 6.3 Republican Share of the Major-Party Vote for President by Battleground Status
Note: Data points represent the average Republican share of the two-party presidential vote in states by the strategic categories of each party.

past election results; they have contemporaneous survey data and updated registered voter files that ought to serve as an early warning system when statewide electorates are on the move. Some think that states like Minnesota and Texas might become battlegrounds before we see significant signs of competitiveness in any prior presidential election result (Rakich, 2020; Rogers, 2016). This is more than just intuition, as demographic shifts in states might well alter partisan voting patterns as much (or more) than campaign outreach. Still, one cannot help feeling that there is a bit of a self-fulfilling prophecy at play: presidential campaigns target the same states from election to election and ensure their competitiveness, while ignoring other potential targets and thereby guaranteeing their stasis.

Using the same methodology as Figure 6.2, Figure 6.4 shows how varying a state's electoral vote count changes the predicted probability of battleground status for Democrats and Republicans. Again, we plot results for the same three distinct election years (1952, 1980, and 2012) to illustrate how the effect of this variable grows weaker over time. In this figure, the Y-axis is the predicted probability that a state would be classified as a battleground, and the X-axis is the state's number of Electoral College votes. Since a state's Electoral College votes are the number of U.S. senators (every state has two) plus the number of U.S. representatives (every state has at least one, with the number going up in more populous states), the X-axis also offers a rough measure of the size of a state's population. Figure 6.4a shows these plots for Republican

(a) Republican Campaigns

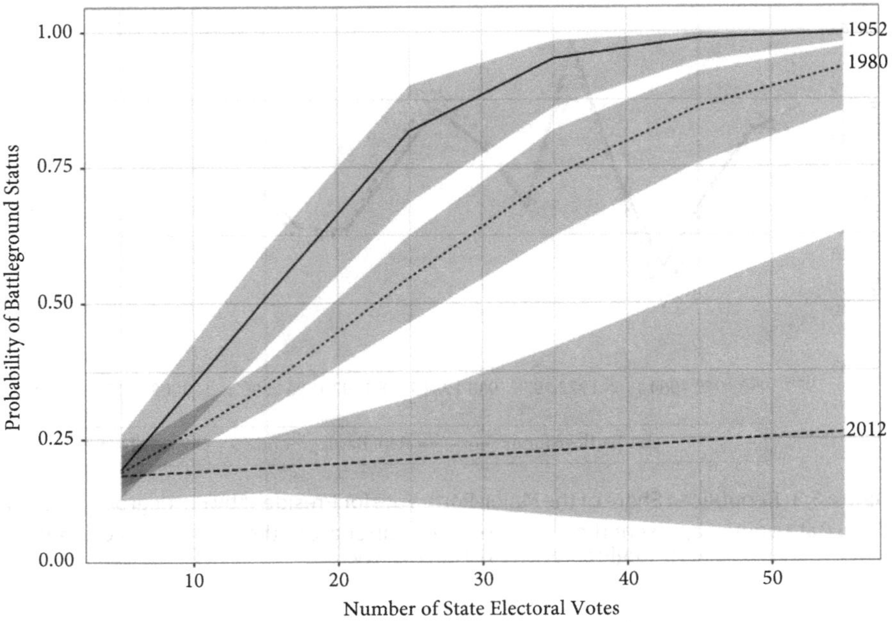

(b) Democratic Campaigns

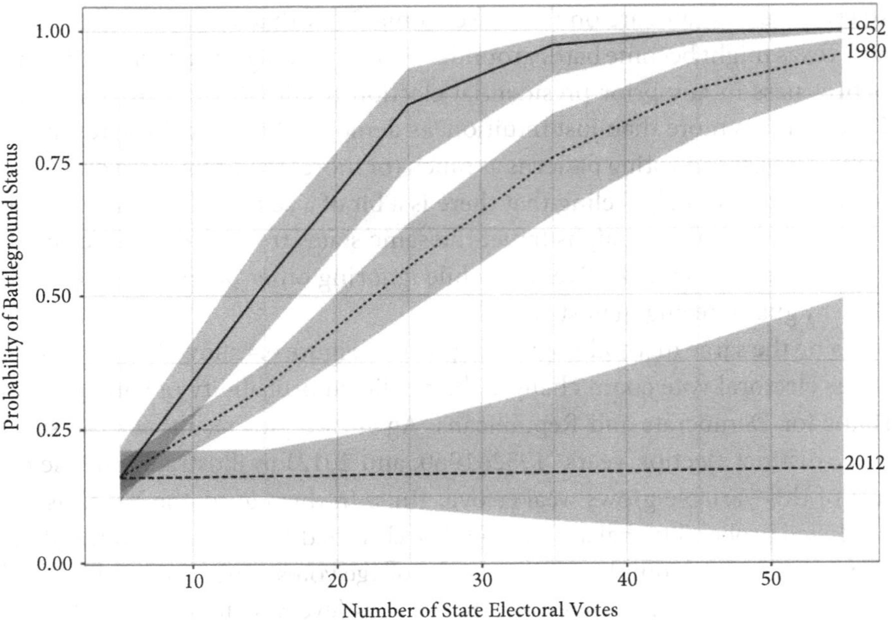

Figure 6.4 How the Number of Electoral College Votes Predicts Battleground Status by Party
Note: For details on the regression model, see chapter appendix.

campaigns while Figure 6.4b shows the relationships for Democrats, but since the plots are nearly identical for both parties, we will discuss them together.

Back in 1952, a state's Electoral Vote count was an extremely important predictor of battleground status for both Democratic and Republican campaigns. The smallest states with just three Electoral College votes had a roughly one in five chance of being selected as a battleground, while the largest states with 35 or more Electoral College votes were almost guaranteed to be designated as battlegrounds by both parties. But by 2012, the figure shows a complete reversal at the high end of the spectrum: by this period, the largest states had at most a 5% larger chance than the smallest states of being chosen as a battleground, and for neither Democrats nor Republicans could this very small chance be reliably distinguished from zero. In short, while the number of Electoral College votes was almost a perfect predictor in 1952 of a state's chance of being selected as a battleground, by 2012 it was no longer a factor at all. This was one thing on which the parties could both agree given increasingly polarized electorates.

These results square with the simple time-series plot in Figure 6.5. Averaging across decades from the 1950s to the 1980s, the percentage of states classified as battlegrounds with fifteen or more electoral votes never dipped below 70%. From the 1990s on, however, the percentage of these "big" states classified as battlegrounds never rose above 41%. Put plainly, after the

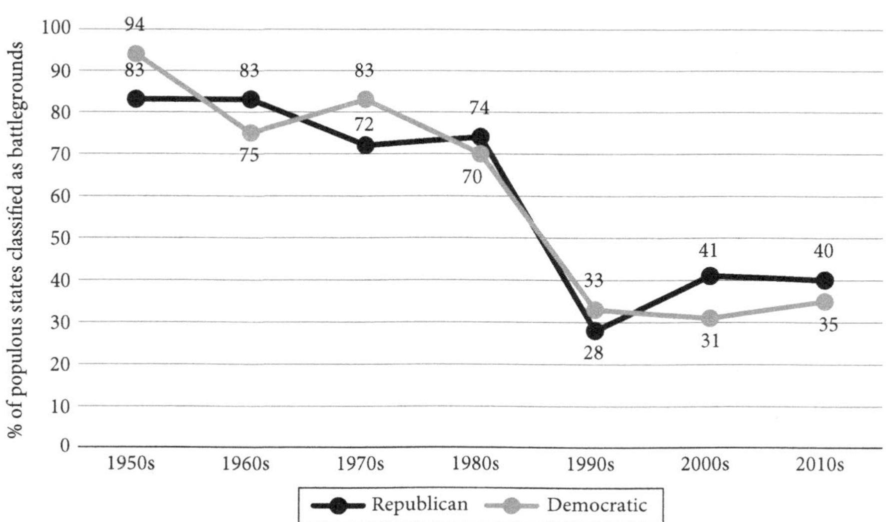

Figure 6.5 Percent of States with Fifteen or more Electoral Votes Classified as Battlegrounds

Note: Data points represent the percentage of large states considered battleground by the respective campaigns. "Large" is defined as fifteen or more electoral votes.

1980s states with larger electoral vote totals were no longer considered automatic targets by presidential campaigns. To be sure, this reflects a host of idiosyncratic, state-by-state stories of political change. California, New Jersey, Illinois, and New York moved decidedly to the left politically; Texas moved to the right with similar swiftness. At the same time, relatively smaller states such as Colorado, Iowa, Nevada, New Hampshire, and Virginia have become more competitive, presenting inviting targets and (perhaps) increased strategic flexibility. But this development may also reflect better data from these smaller states in recent elections, such that campaigns feel more comfortable replacing larger states (that strongly lean one way) with innovative combinations of smaller states.

The question of whether campaigns have gotten more strategic is a tougher nut to crack. In Table 6.1, we see that the percentage of states classified as "battlegrounds" moved around across the three eras. For elections from 1952 to 1972, the first two data columns show that both parties sorted about 40% of states into this category, on average. If one prefers the percent of total electoral votes in the battleground state category—which accounts for the possibility that many states could contain few votes (or vice-versa)—the second pair of data columns show the average is closer to 60% in the first era.

In the second era, Democratic candidates are more expansive in their designation of battlegrounds, while the Republicans are narrower in focus relative to the first era. The Democrats, on average, categorize 52% of states and 64% of electoral votes as battleground. The Republicans, on average, drop to 38% of states and 49% of votes. Based on these data, it is tempting to conclude that the Republicans were more focused and perhaps more strategic, both compared to the earlier era and to their contemporaneous Democratic counterparts. However, this neglects the fact that the Republicans won four of the seven elections during this era, including three by landslide margins. Put another way, due to the circumstances of their elections the Carter, Mondale,

Table 6.1 The Percentage of States and Total Electoral College Votes Selected as Battleground States by Presidential Election Era

	States Classified as Battlegrounds (%)		Total Electoral Votes Classified as Battlegrounds (%)	
	by Democrats	by Republicans	by Democrats	by Republicans
1952–1972	41	43	59	63
1976–2000	52	38	64	49
2004–2020	27	29	32	33

and Dukakis campaigns might have *needed* to target a wide range of states that in an ordinary year would have been safely Democratic. In contrast, the Republicans could afford to be more focused.

In the third era, both parties become much more selective in their identification of battleground states despite the dramatic increase in campaign funds noted in chapter 5. Democrats and Republicans both designate roughly 28% of states on average as battlegrounds in this most recent era, amounting to roughly 33% of available electoral votes. One is tempted to conclude that the tighter and more concentrated classifications in the third era reflect both the greater availability of data on partisan vote choice in the states as well as a drop in its year-to-year variance. However, if one calculates the average deviation in the Republican share of the two-party vote across the states by era, it is not the case that this average deviation has decreased over time. In fact, variance in partisan vote choice has slightly increased: from a standard deviation of 11.2 in the period 1952–1972, to 10.1 in 1976–2000, to 11.8 in 2004–2020. Put simply, whatever else polarized politics has done, it has not made presidential voting in the states more stable, at least when we assess those trends at the level of entire eras. Thus, we are left with more precise targeting opportunities as the more probable explanation for observable patterns in the data.

Discussion

The data reported here confirm the long-standing assumption that presidential election strategies are strongly conditioned by the Electoral College system. Examining an array of original strategic documents and insider accounts spanning 68 years and 18 elections, we show that sophisticated campaign strategies have long guided U.S. presidential elections and that these strategies appear to be evolving over time to become even more refined and sophisticated. The same data that give rise to these basic facts about Electoral College strategies also shed light on several important empirical and normative questions. States such as Pennsylvania, Michigan, Ohio, and Florida have been consistently targeted by presidential campaigns for special attention in the lion's share of contests since the early 1950s. Yet, more populous states are not necessarily more likely to be categorized as battlegrounds by the campaigns, at least not in recent elections. In addition, states that were more competitive in the last election are increasingly likely to be classified as battlegrounds in the current election. Put another way, states that were *not* competitive in the last election are more likely to be ignored in the subsequent election, a fact Democrats were only too aware of after 2016.

In terms of how well today's more geographically focused campaigns address the interests of all citizens equally, the results are mixed. Previous studies clearly demonstrate that battleground states get the lion's share of attention in presidential campaigns (Shaw, 2006), and the current study finds the number of battlegrounds is decreasing. But these classifications are not entirely static over time. Some formerly safe states—Virginia, North Carolina, and Colorado—have become battlegrounds. And some currently safe states will undoubtedly become battlegrounds as demographic shifts continue. Moreover, there is little evidence supporting the concern that campaigns disproportionately target and spend resources in more populous states.[6] This was true in the past, but not any more. Finally, even if a smaller number of battlegrounds is being targeted, because the media market structure in the United States is poorly aligned with state boundaries, it is still the case that messaging from highly targeted campaigns will spill over to adjacent states in ways that expose large numbers of citizens in non-targeted states to intense presidential campaign activity (Althaus, Nardulli, and Shaw, 2002).

To be clear, no one seriously doubts that *some features* of the Electoral College map drive the strategic thinking of presidential campaign *in some way*. This chapter for the first time has revealed how and why macro-targeting considerations in the Electoral College are translated into strategic plans for winning presidential elections. We have also identified for the first time how those considerations have evolved since 1952. But whether the Electoral College system also drives the strategic allocations of those scarce campaign resources that presumably move voters is another question. The famous quip attributed to Prussian Field Marshal Helmuth von Moltke that "no plan survives first contact with the enemy" might hold true for presidential campaigns as well as it does for military operations. Perhaps these carefully drawn campaign strategies are simply tossed to the four winds as soon as the polling numbers start rolling in, so that what the campaigns actually do during the election season has little resemblance to what they intended. It is to this possibility that we turn in chapter 7.

Chapter 6 Appendix

This appendix details some additional findings from a regression analysis exploring the factors that predict battleground status for Democratic and Republican campaigns. Broadly speaking, the data demonstrate that the competitiveness of the last presidential election in the state has become more predictive of battleground status over time, whereas a state's total number of electoral votes is decidedly less predictive over time.

Table A6.1 presents ordered logit results predicting the battleground categorization variable for Democrats and Republicans, respectively. The models pool all states and all election years, though we include the interaction terms "Electoral Votes × Election Year" and "Closeness × Election Year" to approximate over-time trends. The "Election Year" variable ranges from 1 (1952) to 69 (2020). In the Democratic model, closeness of the previous election is not significant on its own—only the closeness/election year interaction term is significant. The positive interaction term suggests that a smaller margin of victory in the previous election becomes more predictive of battleground status over time during the period of our study.

These results provide qualified support for the expectation that margin of victory in the previous election matters for battleground classification for Democrats, but these data suggest that it is more influential for campaign strategies in recent elections.[7]

The Democratic model also suggests that a state's number of electoral votes has a positive, significant main effect, but its interaction with election year has a negative coefficient. The positive main effect suggests that (in the early years of our data) as a state's number of electoral votes increases, Democrats are more likely to characterize that state as a battleground than "lean" or "safe." However, we need to add the interaction coefficient, multiplied by the

Table A6.1 Predicting Battleground Status

	Democrats		Republicans	
	Coeff.	S.E.	Coeff.	S.E.
Closeness of State in Last Election	0.050	0.133	0.239*	0.136
Electoral Votes	0.176***	0.024	0.148***	0.023
Election Year	−0.023	0.011	−0.014	0.011
Electoral Votes × Election Year	−0.003***	0.001	−0.002***	0.001
Closeness × Election Year	0.017***	0.004	0.011***	0.004
Intercept:				
Safe|Lean	1.642***	0.405	2.130***	0.415
Lean|Battleground	2.634***	0.413	2.693***	0.420
AIC	1,441.374		1,326.170	
Observations	911		911	

Note: Ordered logit regression. *p<0.1; **p<0.05; ***p<0.01. The total number of observations is 911, as Alaska and Hawaii are states in advance of the 1960 election, while D.C. gains electoral votes in advance of the 1964 election.

election year, to the main effect to calculate the total effect of electoral votes in a given election (since the main effect should be interpreted as the effect of electoral votes when election year = 0). The negative interaction coefficient on the Electoral Votes × Election Year variable suggests that increasing the number of a state's electoral votes has become less predictive of battleground status over time. The overall effect of electoral votes in battleground status remains positive by 2020, for example, but only barely, and it is not significantly distinct from a zero effect. These findings provide some support for the expectation that at some point in time there was a strategic bias in favor of larger states. However, the story presented by these results aligns much more closely with research suggesting that the high costs of advertising in populous states may, in recent cases, counterbalance the advantages of picking up a large number of electoral votes (Shaw, 2006).

For the Republicans, we see that closeness has a positive main effect and a positive coefficient on the interaction term. This means that we should expect closer previous elections to increase the probability of battleground status for Republicans and for that effect to get larger over time. These results again provide support for the expectation that margin of victory in the previous election matters for battleground classification. Perhaps more interestingly, this importance has increased over time. Indeed, the tendency for recent presidential campaigns to focus their attention on previously competitive states, in an era in which the overall election results are typically determined by razor-thin margins, produces predictable results: very close elections within the battleground states.

As in the Democratic model, the Electoral Votes × Election Year coefficient indicates that the influence of electoral votes on Republican strategic categorizations has decreased over time, such that by 2020 it is barely positive and is effectively zero. Thus, the relationship between population and battleground states exists mostly for the early years in the time series. The decreased prominence of larger states in the stratagems of recent campaigns is truly striking. From 1952 to 1988, Democratic and Republican campaigns classified populous states (fifteen electoral votes or more) as battlegrounds 82% of the time (87% for Democrats, 77% for Republicans); from 1992 to 2020, the percentage shrinks to 35% (33% for Democrats, 36% for Republicans).

7
Tracking the Allocation of Resources Over Time

How Disciplined Are Presidential Campaigns?

At the Republican National Convention in 1960, Richard Nixon promised a national audience that he would take his campaign to every state in the union. This was not an impromptu, overzealous gaffe. Rather, it was a planned and important part of his speech: "I've been asked by my friends in the press, 'where are you going to concentrate? What states are you going to visit?' And this is my answer. In this campaign we are going to take no states for granted and we aren't going to concede any states to the opposition . . . I pledge to you that I, personally, will carry this campaign into every one of the 50 states between now and November 8th."[1]

This pledge made some sense in light of Nixon's Electoral College strategy presented in chapter 3. The Republican campaign had sixteen states in its "battleground" category, along with another in its "base" category that was considered worth targeting (Indiana). States such as Alaska and Hawaii were new to the process, and their political leanings were not established. Even some of the more reliable base states had swung Republican in the 1952 and 1956 Eisenhower elections but would swing Democratic in Johnson's 1964 landslide victory.

Unfortunately for Nixon, however, his aggressive schedule proved problematic. First, he injured his left knee while exiting a limousine during a campaign swing through North Carolina in the late summer, which resulted in septic arthritis. Ultimately, the infection caused him to be hospitalized and lose about ten days on the trail.[2] Second, while frenetically trying to fulfill his pledge and pull ahead in his tight battle with John F. Kennedy, Nixon campaigned so aggressively upon his return to the trail that he came down with a bad cold and fever. He lost weight and appeared thin and haggard during subsequent campaign appearances as well as the first presidential debate. Third, Nixon had committed to appearances that later came to seem strategically dubious as Election Day neared given the state of the race. As

Battleground. Daron R. Shaw, Scott L. Althaus, and Costas Panagopoulos, Oxford University Press.
 DOI: 10.1093/oso/9780197774366.003.0007

Theodore White put it: "Nixon was cramped by his public (50-state) pledge—so on the last weekend of the campaign, as Kennedy barnstormed through populous Illinois, New Jersey, New York and New England, Nixon found himself committed to fly all the way north to Alaska, which offered only three electoral votes" (White, 1961).

The consequences of Nixon's appearance strategy are difficult to assess. There is some reason to believe that the diffuse focus cost the Republicans dearly. As Rhodes Cook points out: "Nixon lost most of the other closely contested states with much larger electoral vote payoffs, including Illinois, Michigan, Missouri, New Jersey, Pennsylvania and Texas. All were states where a late effort by Nixon might have made a difference. Instead, he lost decisively to Kennedy in the electoral vote, 303 to 219 (with 15 votes for Southern-based unpledged electors), to go along with an extremely narrow 49.7%-to-49.5% loss in the popular vote" (Cook, 2012).

Because of this, Nixon's 1960 campaign has become a cautionary tale about the need to carefully marshal and allocate resources in a presidential election contest. But was Nixon's campaign using a less sophisticated methodology from a bygone era? Or was this simply an unfortunate miscalculation that causes us to mistakenly underrate the strategic intelligence of the practitioners of yore? And what about presidential campaigns today? Do campaigns in the more recent eras feature more tightly bunched appearances and television ad buys in a handful of states? Or has the proliferation of campaign funds and communication modes in contemporary elections led to a wider but still carefully targeted dispersion of these classic resources?

While few would question the strategic acumen of campaign professionals in earlier eras, some openly posit that the modern presidential campaign and its attendant strategic approach has evolved (e.g., Stevens, 2001; Plouffe, 2009). For example, in the 2020 campaign between August 31 and September 29 (the day of the first presidential debate), Democratic candidate Joe Biden made only ten public campaign appearances. His running mate, Kamala Harris, made only eight. Of course, the COVID-19 pandemic greatly affected the willingness of candidates to hit the trail. And it is well known that Biden's campaign was happy to embrace a scaled back campaign because (1) it reinforced how seriously he took the pandemic as a public policy issue, and (2) it limited the likelihood that he would say or do something embarrassing on the hustings. Still, the campaign's happy pivot to relying on digital outreach while the candidate spent most of the summer and fall in the basement of his Wilmington, Delaware, home is perhaps instructive.

In this chapter, we examine how closely campaigns have hewed to their Electoral College strategies when dispensing candidate visits and TV ad dollars. A central premise of this project is that presidential campaigns allocate most of their time and money to locations that are considered critical to their Electoral College plans. We assume they are both strategic and disciplined. This premise has important consequences for democratic representation and public policies. If campaigns seek to win over voters in certain locations, these voters are likely to receive more attention and perhaps more favorable policy commitments from the candidates. Simple enough. But how accurate is this simple premise? And is it more or less accurate across different eras of presidential campaigns?

We expect that campaigns across our time frame have been disciplined in their allocation of both candidate appearances and television advertisements. In the wholesale campaigning era (1952–1972) we expect that this discipline will be somewhat obscured by the fact that many states were considered battlegrounds—resources would therefore have been sprinkled across a relatively wider array of targets than in recent years. In the zero-sum campaigning era (1976–2000) we expect that this discipline was at its highest. The number of battleground states shrank due to better information about their partisan tendencies, as well as increased partisan polarization toward the end of this period. Equally important, money and time were limited in these elections due to changes in election laws and the parties' nomination processes. In the most recent micro-targeted campaigning era (2004–2020) the number of targeted states contracts even further but money proliferates and travel becomes easier. At the same time, potential substitutes for in-person appearances, such as video-conferencing and televised town halls, reduce the intense pressure for on-site visits from candidates.

Ads and Appearances as Measures of the Campaign

An attentive reader might recall our discussion in chapter 1 on the difficulty of defining and measuring the presidential campaign. Some scholars have treated the campaign as a "residual variance category": that is, one estimates the power of "objective," "non-campaign" factors on the vote—like the state of the economy or presidential approval—and whatever is left over is attributed to the campaign (see, for example, Gelman and King, 1993). Other research has attempted to measure the impact of major campaign events on voters, such as conventions and debates (see, for example, Holbrook, 1996 and Campbell, 2000). Still other research has isolated the effect of specific campaign outreach on the short-term preferences of voters (see, for example, Shaw 1999, 2006).

In contrast to those approaches, we focus on the deployment and Election Day effects of two high-profile elements of modern presidential campaigning: television spot advertisements and candidate appearances. We concede that these two elements are not the totality of campaigning; they are, however, important commitments and definitive markers of who and what the campaigns think is important. We suspect few would doubt that these have been fundamental to contemporary presidential campaign strategies and electioneering—still, it is worth spelling out why we think they are appropriate for gauging the totality of campaign outreach and how we measure them across the time series.

Although radio advertising occupied 51% of campaign broadcast expenditures in the general election season of 1952 compared to 49% for television, by 1956 the balance had already tilted to 72% of campaign broadcast expenditures for television and just 28% for radio (Heard, 1962: 356).[3] From 1960 onward, television advertising has been by far the most important mode by which presidential candidates reach out to voters and attempt to sway them to turn out to vote and to cast their ballots in desired ways (West, 2018; Ansolabehere and Iyengar, 1995; Shaw, 2006; Freedman, Franz, and Goldstein, 2004). Over this period roughly two-thirds of campaign spending has been allocated to TV ads, and this tendency shows no signs of abating even as alternative, cheaper forms of communication arise (see, for example, Herbert Alexander's [1992] work on presidential campaign finance over time). Moreover, television advertising is hardly the blunt instrument that some have assumed it to be, especially back in the early days of commercial advertising. While national TV advertisements have existed throughout our time span, so have spot ads, which allow candidates to buy commercials on local TV stations and thereby target specific geographical audiences at specific times during a given day.[4] Our records indicate that these spot buys have consistently been a major part of presidential campaign outreach. Indeed, finding and systematically recording spot buy data—most often aggregated to the state-level—was one of the more significant data-gathering efforts of this project.

For this project, we have identified spot television buy estimates aggregated to the level of individual states for every general election presidential campaign from 1952 to 2020 except for 1960, where we have ad count and time duration data at the state level but not dollar buy amounts.[5] In addition, we also have detailed spot buy estimates for every media market in the country covering general election presidential campaigns for 1956, 1972, and the full series from 1988 to 2020. These data come from a variety of sources. In 1956 and 1972 they come from Federal Communication Commission (FCC) records, which also form the basis of confirming state-level ad buys in 1952 using an ahead-of-its time doctoral dissertation written shortly after that election year (Merrill, 1954).[6] For 1952, 1964, 1968, and 1976 through 2004, we rely on accounts from the campaigns themselves (Stevenson, the DNC, and Eisenhower in 1952; Johnson in 1964; Humphrey and Nixon in 1968; Carter and Ford in 1976; Reagan in 1980 and 1984; Bush and Dukakis in 1988; Bush in 1992; Dole in 1996; Bush in 2000 and 2004).[7] For 2008 and 2012, we utilize data from the Campaign Media Analysis Group (CMAG) and Kantar Media. For 2016 and 2020, we rely on data from Advertising Analytics. For several years, we also have estimates from Herbert Alexander's books (covering the years 1960–1992, beginning with *Financing the 1960 Election*), which we use as a cross-check.[8]

For analytical purposes, we define the general election as beginning in the last week in August (most often, after the national conventions have concluded) and running through Election Day. Because our focus is assessing the adherence of the campaigns themselves to their Electoral College plans, as well as the attendant effects of this outreach, we do not include associated spending by the national party committees or outside interest groups (more on this shortly). We will occasionally comment on the level of spending on national (or other "non-spot") buys, as this spending elevates the total amount of television advertising that reaches voters in an election across all states, especially in the earlier years, and sometimes in a lopsided partisan manner.

As hinted at earlier, spot buys are typically purchased through a local television station (say, the NBC affiliate in Albuquerque) for a specific show (say, *The Today Show*) or a specific day part (say, late night). These buys allow campaigns to reach a more targeted audience at a lower relative cost than could be had for a broader buy.[9] Based on our conversations with media experts from recent political campaigns, on average, local stations have 6–7 minutes of advertising time every half hour, with roughly 1–2 minutes reserved for local spot buys.[10] Given that we are examining the dispensation of resources across multiple elections, it is important to account for the increased value of everything—including the cost of advertising—over time. Otherwise, more recent elections will dominate the analysis by virtue of the massive spending by contemporary campaigns.

To facilitate these comparisons, we transform each campaign's total spot buy spending in each state into constant 2020 dollars. One might reasonably ask why not use the number of advertisements aired or a measure of audience reach, such as gross rating points? It is our view that advertisements aired is an imperfect estimate of how much advertising voters are seeing.[11] A campaign could air many advertisements on a low-rated station during a lonely day part or it could air fewer advertisements on a high-rated station during a popular day part. Because the latter buy might reach many more voters than the former, simple counts of ads aired provide at best a fuzzy metric for measuring potential exposure to campaign messaging. Total ad buy costs, however, represent a superior indicator of audience reach because ad costs are mostly a function of the size of the audience exposed to them, plus additional premiums for reaching more desirable audience segments like younger women (Webster, Lichty, and Phalen, 2005).[12]

Gross rating points (GRPs or "points") are also an improvement over simple counts of ads aired when assessing audience reach. GRPs represent the number of ads aired on a given station during a given time slot multiplied by the percentage of a market's available audience that normally tunes in to that station at that time (Webster, Lichty, and Phalen, 2005). Because they are calculated without reference to the number of persons living in a media market, GRPs provide a measure of audience reach that is directly comparable across differently sized markets (Shaw, 1999, 2006). Unfortunately, GRPs suffer from their own form of ambiguity, because the same numerical value can represent very different patterns of exposure: 100 GRPs could mean that 10% of a market's audience is exposed to an ad 10 times, ($10 \times 10 = 100$ GRPs) or it could mean that 100% of a market's audience is exposed only once ($100 \times 1 = 100$ GRPs). These are qualitatively different kinds of audience reach. It is also the case that presidential campaigns have only recently (and inconsistently) adopted this metric to measure television advertising. Because of these limitations with ads aired and GRPs as possible measures of audience reach, we opt for ad spending, adjusted for inflation.

If television advertising is the hallmark of contemporary election efforts, candidate appearances are perhaps the canonical example of presidential campaigns historically. Of course, presidential candidates have not always personally and publicly campaigned for the office. In the early days of the republic, candidates declined to tour the country and give public speeches because it was considered unseemly (arrogant, even) to personally seek this highest of offices. But as time passed, things changed. For example, while Andrew Jackson mostly stayed at home in Tennessee and allowed others to campaign on his behalf in 1828, as president he claimed a national mandate from the people. This mentality gradually seeped into the consciousness of some candidates in subsequent elections. From our reading of the record, the first candidate to actively advocate in public for his own election was William Henry Harrison, who gave multiple speeches during a three-week tour in June 1840 and a month-long tour in September of that year (Troy, 1996). Subsequent candidates generally refrained from such tactics, however, relying instead on friends and surrogates to carry their political water. The modal approach was to stay at home and receive visitors, occasionally offering a carefully vetted set of remarks. This approach gradually changed and was thoroughly rejected by candidates such as William Jennings Bryan in 1896, 1900, 1904, and 1908 as well as by Theodore Roosevelt in 1904 and 1912. By the mid-twentieth century, whatever reticence that previously restrained personal campaign appearances was long gone. Truman's innovative whistlestop tour described in chapter 3 was an exception, of course, but his heavy schedule of public appearances would soon become the rule rather than the exception. From 1952 through 2016, on any given day in September or October the presidential and vice-presidential candidates would each visit two or three locations to deliver their stump speeches to voters.

The logic of the candidate personally appealing to voters is simple but merits a brief review. First, campaigns assume that voters are more likely to support someone with whom they are familiar. Second, campaigns assume that voters are favorably impressed when the candidate takes the time to visit their community. Third, campaigns assume that an appearance is likely to generate local news media coverage and that this local coverage is likely to be relatively more positive than that offered by national news outlets. Local news reporters, in particular, are thought to be less jaded than the national press and grateful to have the opportunity to cover a candidate's visit for local residents. Voters who tune into local news or read the local newspaper are therefore assumed to be more likely to encounter positive coverage of the candidate because of these visits, which may pay off at the ballot box. Taken as a whole, all of this means campaigns believe that appearances by presidential and vice-presidential candidates can increase votes in specific locations and that the sum of these efforts can help deliver key states. Where candidates show up matters for generating positive campaign attention, and not just state by state, but market by market, which means targeting county by county.

We rely on scheduling data from the campaigns themselves to recreate calendars for each of the elections under scrutiny. These records are consistently available from the relevant libraries and archives. For example, the Kennedy campaign archive from 1960 includes records of his own appearances as well as records from the Democratic National Committee detailing the schedule of Stevenson campaigns in 1952 and 1956. Nixon's and Humphrey's campaigns kept similarly meticulous records of candidate visits in 1968. Meanwhile, detailed travel records are available for re-election bids (Eisenhower-Nixon in 1956, Johnson-Humphrey in 1964, Nixon-Agnew in 1972, Ford-Dole in 1976, Carter-Mondale in 1980, Reagan-Bush in 1984, H. W. Bush-Quayle in 1992, Clinton-Gore in 1996, W. Bush-Cheney in 2004, Obama-Biden in 2012, and Trump-Pence in 2020) through the White House records of the president's (and vice-president's) schedule. Because campaign schedules sometimes change at the last minute, we took the additional step of confirming scheduled appearances by looking up contemporaneous newspaper reports of where the candidates were appearing day by day over the course of the fall campaigns. On days when news accounts of candidate appearances deviated from the locations mentioned in internal campaign schedules, we recorded the visits mentioned in news accounts. Historical records from the *Chicago Tribune* and the *New York Times* were especially thorough and useful in this regard.

We record appearances at the county (or comparable) level and then aggregate to the state level.[13] Note that we treat each appearance in which the candidate stops and interacts with voters as a distinct visit to that locale. Thus, a candidate could make several appearances in the same state on a given date. At a theoretical level, we are therefore assuming each appearance has distinct and independent value. At a practical level, the total number of appearances can exceed the number of days in the campaign. We do not treat private fundraising appearances as public appearances, even though these occasionally draw local media mention.

We are not claiming that spot buys and candidate appearances are the sum total of presidential campaign activity. Rather, we believe these are important markers of how the campaigns are sizing up the race: if they spend scarce money and time trying to win voters in a specific place, presumably they put greater value on doing well in that place relative to other possible locations for campaign attention. Campaign practitioners often say that the most precious resources in an election are time and money—at their core, our data measure how campaigns allocated these resources in ways that are historically valid across the full span of election years from 1952 to 2020. Perhaps in the future other measures of human and digital outreach might supplant the ones we use. But for now, ads and visits remain the best indicators of how the players viewed the game and, perhaps, how well they played according to their plans.

Television Spot Ad Spending across the Eras

Earlier, we specified exactly what we mean when we refer to "TV ad spending" by presidential campaigns. Above all, it is important to reiterate that we are considering only spending on television spot buys in local markets by the candidates' general election campaigns. We are not looking at primary election spending. Nor are we examining national ad spending, which was occasionally considerable, especially in the early years of the time series, but does not reflect strategic priorities. We are also not considering spending by the political parties—national, state, and local—or interest groups that support one side or the other. Party spending was considerable (and perhaps consequential) in the 1990s, when soft money expenditures exploded and the national parties purchased millions of dollars of local TV ads on behalf of their presidential candidates (see Shaw, 2006).[14] But this spending did not usually off-set or reverse candidate spending advantages, and it dissipated dramatically after the passage of BCRA in 2002, which effectively outlawed soft money spending by the parties. Ironically, in the wake of BCRA and the subsequent legal rulings in *McConnell v. FEC* (2003) and *Citizens United* (2010), soft money flowed to interest groups, which were not allowed to legally coordinate with the campaigns but nonetheless managed to raise and spend hundreds of millions of dollars during election campaigns in the 2010s and 2020s.[15] Still, despite the proliferation of interest group spending, the proportion of expenditures coming from these sources has barely increased since 2010. Instead, expenditures by the campaigns themselves are still the dominant source of money in elections.[16] The upshot is that while we are admittedly looking at only one source of TV spot buy spending in presidential campaigns, it is far and away the dominant one. Moreover, we see no reason to think that our estimates of spending differentials are biased in any meaningful way that would affect our conclusions.

With that said, when all such data are pulled together, the first notable observation is that far more campaign money was spent on localized television messaging in recent years relative to the earlier years in our period of interest. Figure 7.1 shows the growth in average general election television spot buy spending per state by candidate campaigns in 2020 dollars. In this figure and all the analyses that follow, by "television spot buy spending per state" we specifically mean the total amount of money spent on spot buys by a campaign over the course of the entire general election season divided by the total number of states in the union for that election year. The famous Eisenhower Answers America commercials from 1952 were entirely spot ads shown in just twelve states,[17] and since television time was cheap in those early years, neither campaign had to put a sizeable war chest into spot buys for television. This is why 1952 spot ad spending on television appears hardly different from zero: the entire buys for both campaigns were so targeted and heavily concentrated that the average state did indeed receive almost no advertising dollars for television. Per-state television spot spending remained fairly restrained until 1980, when money going into state-specific spot buys jumped more than threefold from 1976 levels. It has been on an upward rise ever since. Notable in Figure 7.1 are years in which one party substantially outspent the other in state-specific

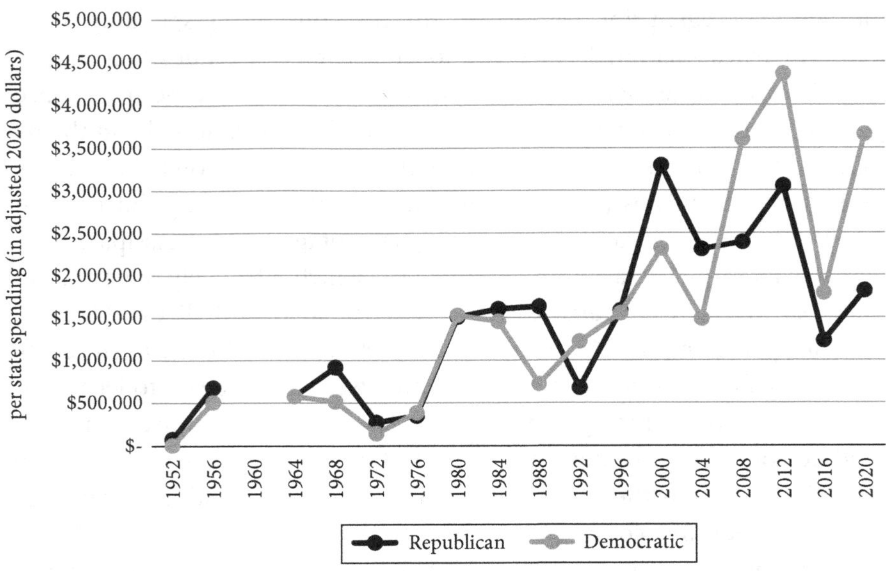

Figure 7.1 Average Television Spot Buy Spending per State by Year in 2020 dollars, 1952–2020

television buys, with substantial Republican advantages in 1968, 1988, 2000, and 2004, but sizable Democratic advantages from 2008 to 2020. We will return to these "outlier" years in chapter 8 to see if we can find evidence that these unbalanced spending patterns made any detectable difference on Election Day.

It is important to keep these dramatically rising per-state spending levels in mind as we turn to later figures in this section, which will compare percentages of advertising dollars spent by the campaigns across various categories. The percentages shown in these figures are good indicators of strategic emphasis by the campaigns, but they will mask what is shown so clearly in Figure 7.1: in constant 2020 dollars, Republican per-state television spending in 2012 was 4.5 times higher than in 1956, while Democrats in 2012 spent 8.6 times more on per-state spot advertising than they did in 1956.

Figure 7.2 shows the mean percentage across all elections of spot buy money allocated by the Republican and Democratic presidential campaigns in each of their Electoral College categories across the full set of 18 elections. As expected, the lion's share of spot buy money is spent on battleground states: between 1952 and 2020, Democratic campaigns spent an average of 52% of their spot buy budgets on battleground states so designated in their plans, while Republicans put an average of 56% of spot dollar outlays into their battleground states. By comparison, neither party spent more than 5% of their spot buy budgets in base states on average. It is in the leaning states where things get interesting: over the

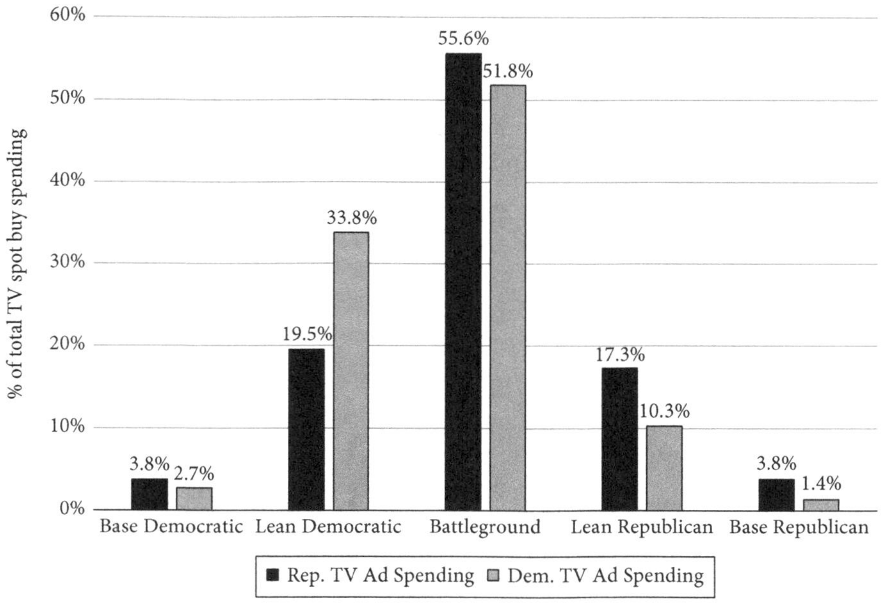

Figure 7.2 Television Spot Buy Spending by Strategic Categories

period 1952–2020, lean Democratic states received consistently more spot buy spending (20% from Republicans, 34% from Democrats) than lean Republican states (17% from Republicans, 10% from Democrats).

This imbalance in strategic emphasis is even more glaring if we look at dollars spent, because the percentages mask between-party spending differentials noted in Figure 7.1. In constant 2020 dollars, the average Democratic battleground state received $4.6 million of that campaign's spot television ad spending between 1952 and 2020, while the average Republican battleground state received $4.0 million. In contrast, each state on the Democrats' own lean Democratic list received an average of $3.0 million in spot advertising, compared to just $0.9 million for states categorized by Democrats as lean Republican. Republican spending in the lean categories was more evenhanded: states that Republicans considered lean Democratic received an average of $1.4 million each in spot buys, while those on their lean Republican list received an average of $1.2 million. Among the states considered base Democratic or base Republican, neither party put more than $0.3 million per state into spot buys. So, while their respective battleground states were consistently lavished with the majority of spot buy spending by both parties while their respective base states were consistently ignored, both parties (but especially the Democrats) put more advertising emphasis into marginal Democratic states than into states tipping Republican.

Before making too much of these differences, we should examine these same patterns over our different eras. Looking first at Republican campaigns, we see in Figure 7.3a that patterns have changed over time. From 1952 to 1972, Republican candidates spent an average of 57% of their spot buy money in their set of battleground states and 24% in lean Democratic states. They spent

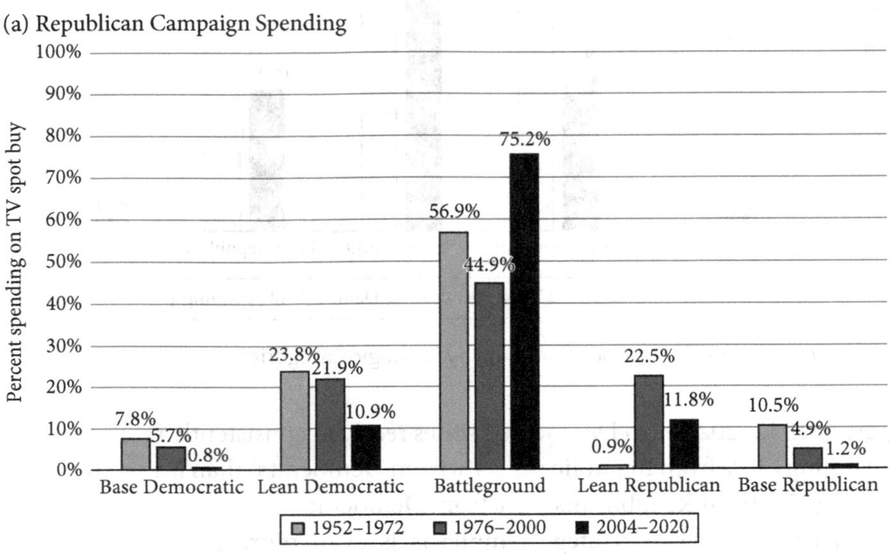

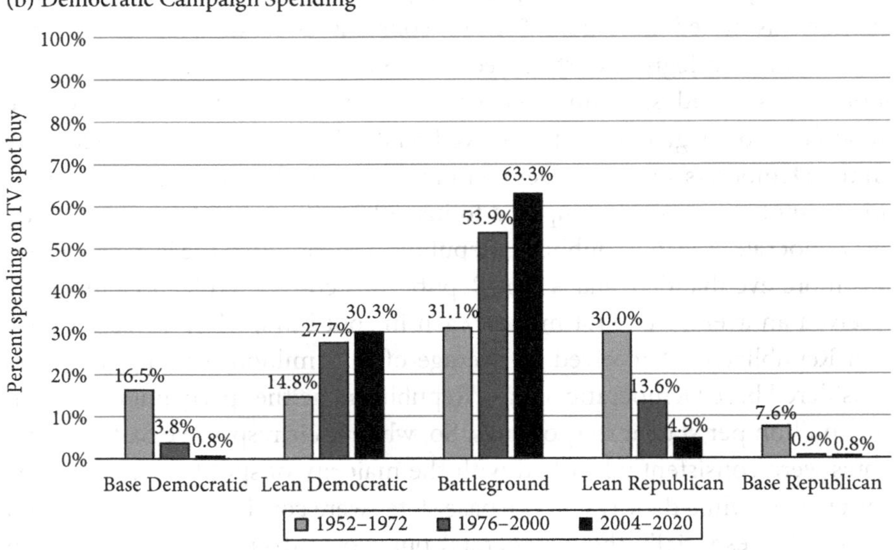

Figure 7.3 Television Spot Buy Spending by Strategic Categories

almost nothing in lean Republican and less than 11% in each of the two base state categories. From 1976 to 2000, Republican candidates spent an average of just 45% of their spot budget in battlegrounds and 22% in lean Democratic states. There was a noticeable increase in average spending in lean Republican states, however, from 1% in the early era to 23% of spot money in the middle era. Base states on both sides during 1976–2000 received even less ad emphasis from Republicans than they had gotten in the earlier era. In contrast, from 2004 to 2020 spending in the battleground states skyrocketed up to 75% of spot ad spending among Republican candidates, while spending in the lean Democratic and lean Republican states was only half the level seen in the previous era. In this most recent era, Republican candidates almost completely ignored the base states. In short, Republican campaigns in the 1976–2000 era were spreading their advertising money across a broader range of states than they did in the earlier and later eras. This pattern deviated substantially from the heavy focus on battleground spending in the 1952–1972 era and in the 2004–2020 era, with the most recent period seeing the most extreme contraction of Republican ad spending into battleground states. This suggests that the extra money Republicans amassed in the most recent era is almost exclusively targeted toward a tighter set of battleground states.

On the Democratic side, Figure 7.3b shows a different over-time progression but a similar narrowing of emphasis in the most recent era. From 1952 to 1972 Democratic spot ad spending was generously distributed across the five categories: only 31% of spot ad money flowed to battleground states, with 30% targeting lean Republican states and another 8% targeting base Republican states along with nearly one fifth of the average ad budget targeting base Democratic states. In this early era, Democratic campaigns targeted lean Democratic states with only slightly more ad spending than base Republican states. This changed dramatically in the 1976–2000 era, when Democrats consolidated 54% of their television spot buy spending into their set of battleground states, pushed 28% of their spending into lean Democratic states, and reduced spending to 14% in lean Republican states while leaving little for base states on either side. From 2004 to 2020, the growing focus on battlegrounds is even more obvious for Democratic campaigns. On average, Democratic candidates spent 63% of their ad budgets in battleground states during this most recent era and another 30% in lean Democratic states, leaving just 5% for lean Republican states and next to nothing for base states.

The comparison between Republicans and Democrats over time is intriguing, but the percentage changes tell only part of the story. The most striking fact is that the Democrats have—at the level of the candidate, at least—been more proficient than the Republicans at increasing their available funds in the contemporary era. Between 2004 and 2020, while Republican campaigns have spent an average of $9.2 million (in 2020 dollars) on spot buys per battleground state, the Democrats have averaged $14.5 million per battleground. So, while the distribution of Democratic spot buy spending—and especially the concentration on lean Democratic states compared to lean Republican states—is an important finding, it is difficult to assess without noting the more general point that Democratic campaigns have simply had more money to spend in the most recent era. It is also worth noting that this edge is not just a function of Barack Obama's fundraising prowess: Hillary Clinton and Joe Biden enjoyed similarly significant fundraising advantages over Donald Trump.[18]

With respect to Electoral College strategies, the allocation patterns suggest that TV ad spending is not perfectly predicted by the campaigns' plans. Although base states get next to nothing when it comes to spot buys—except during the first era, which suggests either that these early campaigns were somewhat less strategic or that they had less ability to narrowly target than their more recent counterparts with respect to resource allocation—lean states do receive some advertising. The intensity of this advertising varies over time and by party.

It is notable that states leaning Democratic receive proportionally more spot buy advertising in the two most recent eras than states leaning Republican, especially so by Democratic campaigns. This may suggest that Democratic candidates were more likely to be defending their turf. Or perhaps states that tilt Democratic were perceived to be less predictable in their voting tendencies. Or maybe Democratic campaigns had more money or more inclination to invest in states that seemed safe but whose loss could spell disaster. Or it could be that TV ads simply cost more in lean Democratic states than in their safer counterparts. Whatever the explanation, the pattern of ad spending in the lean states indicates that this second-tier category is an important one for the campaigns. It also indicates that (1) campaigns acknowledge uncertainty by targeting states beyond the high-end battleground states, and that (2) campaigns distinguish between and among targeted states even within these broad strategic categories.

Candidate Visits across the Eras

While money for ad spending surged in presidential campaigns over the past seven decades, and especially since the 2000 election, the time available for candidate visits has remained a constant since 1952. Some might quibble with that assertion, as travel is somewhat quicker and easier now than it was in the middle of the twentieth century. But for the most part, presidential and vice-presidential candidates remain circumscribed and limited in their ability to directly visit and address audiences of voters. On this matter, variance in the number of campaign appearances seems less a matter of faster airplanes than of the will and endurance of the candidates. Thus, patterns of visits would appear to be excellent indicators of where campaigns think the race will be decided.

Figure 7.4 shows three distinct patterns over time, patterns that only somewhat correspond with our eras. From 1952 to 1964, presidential and vice-presidential candidates made many public appearances over the course of the general election campaign. At the high end, Dwight Eisenhower logged over 250 appearances in 1952 and John Kennedy topped our list with 289 in 1960. At the low end for the Republicans is Eisenhower's re-election bid when the incumbent president made just 41 public appearances during the 1956 general election campaign. For the Democrats, 2020 marked the historic low as a worldwide pandemic limited Joe Biden to 51 public appearances. The higher numbers of visits in the earlier years largely reflects the continued prevalence of train trips as a staple of presidential campaigns. This once-common

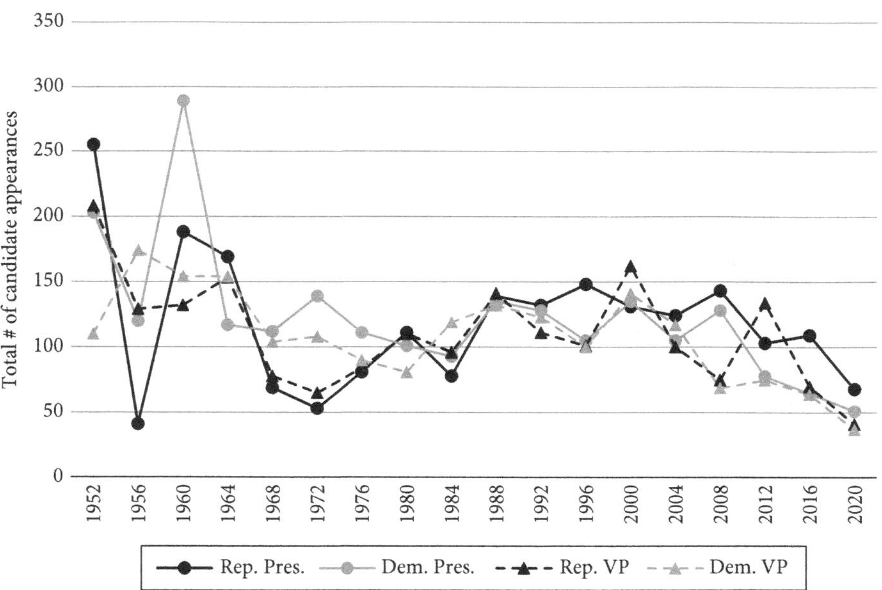

Figure 7.4 Total Number of Presidential (Pres.) and Vice-Presidential (VP) Candidate Appearances in the General Election Campaign, 1952–2020

"whistlestop strategy" made it easy to log many appearances in a concentrated geographic area over a short time period. For example, during October 28–30, 1960, Kennedy made short speeches or offered public comments in 20 distinct locations over three days while touring Pennsylvania by rail and car.

Beginning in 1968, however, the number of general election appearances decreases and then stabilizes at around 120 appearances per candidate through the 2000 election. This seems to be a function of the decline of train tours in favor of airplanes and automobiles, which leaves time for fewer appearances during a given swing through a state relative to the whistlestop era. Finally, from 2004 through 2020, we see a further decline in candidate appearances, with the average number of visits per candidate settling in at around 80 or so. This reflects a downward trend that bottomed out in the pandemic election year of 2020, which saw the candidates struggle to log 50 appearances on the general election trail. Beyond the personal and public health concerns accompanying 2020's worldwide pandemic, there seems to have been a general tendency to take more "days off," presumably to raise money, communicate with voters via digital modes, and rest.

Figure 7.5 show the average percentage of total appearances during the general election campaign by Republican and Democratic candidates between 1952 and 2020 for states clustered in their respective strategic categories. This distribution of public appearances among Republican campaigns is summarized in Figure 7.5a. The combined set of Republican battleground states received an average 39% of Republican presidential candidate visits and 34% of vice-presidential visits, while the set of lean Democratic states in Republican lists collectively received 28% of presidential and 29% of vice-presidential candidate visits and lean Republican states received 19% and 22%, respectively. Base states, in turn, were not totally ignored: the set of base Democratic states collectively received 8% of appearances from the Republican presidential candidate and base Republican states received about 5% of them.

On the opposite side of the ledger, Figure 7.5b shows that between 1952 and 2020 Democratic campaigns clustered a relatively higher proportion of candidate visits into the set of states marked as Democratic battlegrounds, which collectively received an average 49% of presidential and 45% of vice-presidential appearances. Relative to the Republicans, Democratic campaigns put proportionally fewer candidate appearances into states they classified as lean Republican (which collectively received 14% of both presidential and vice-presidential candidate appearances) and as lean Democratic states (targeted with an average of 22% of presidential appearances and 23% of vice-presidential candidate appearances).

(a) Republican Campaign Appearances

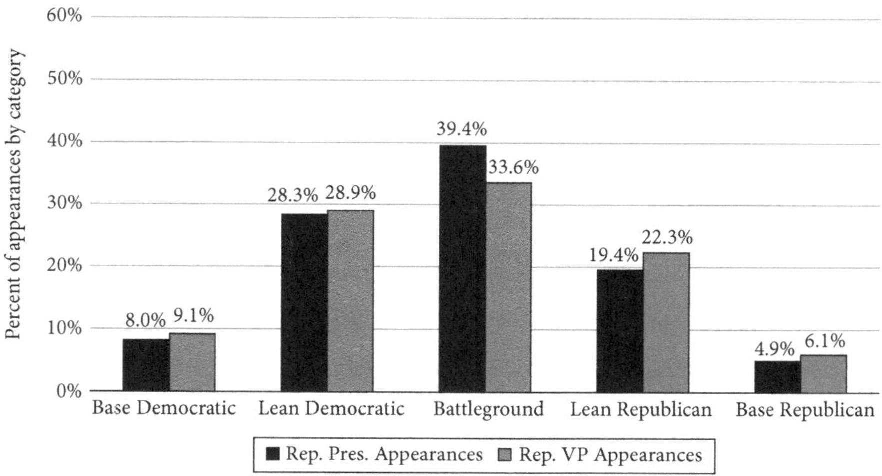

(b) Democratic Campaign Appearances

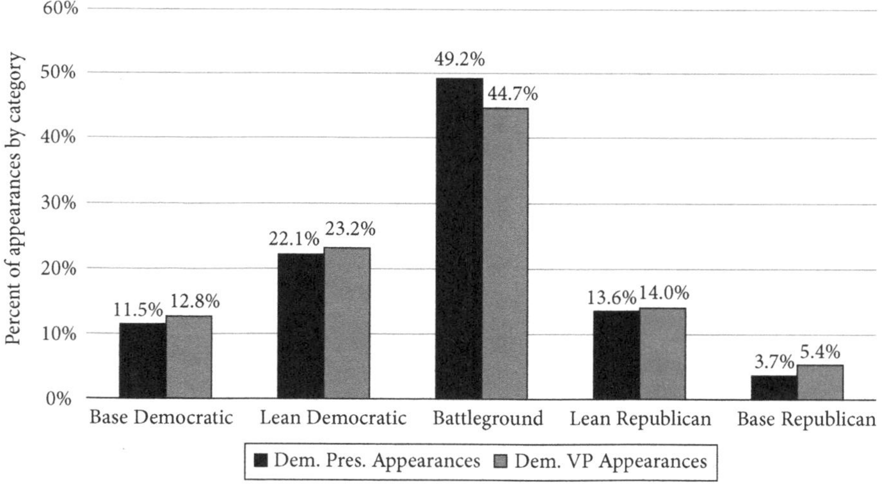

Figure 7.5 Candidate Appearances by Strategic Categories, 1952–2020

Overall, what we see in Figure 7.5 is that candidate appearances over the 1952–2020 period were consistently concentrated in the battleground states, which again demonstrates that strategic focus and professionalism in presidential campaigns is no recent development. Yet these "candidate time" resources were not exclusively lavished on battleground voters. Campaigns frequently sent their candidates to speak to voters in states that leaned toward one party or another. As with spot advertising on television, we see a distinct emphasis in candidate visits by both parties toward targeting the lean

Democratic states more heavily than the lean Republican states in their respective lists. Moreover, they even made a small set of stops in their own base states as well as those of their opponents.

These general tendencies obscure a distinctive evolution in the targeting of candidate appearances over the three eras that is revealed in Figure 7.6. Among the Republican campaigns shown in Figure 7.6a, the 1952–1972 era

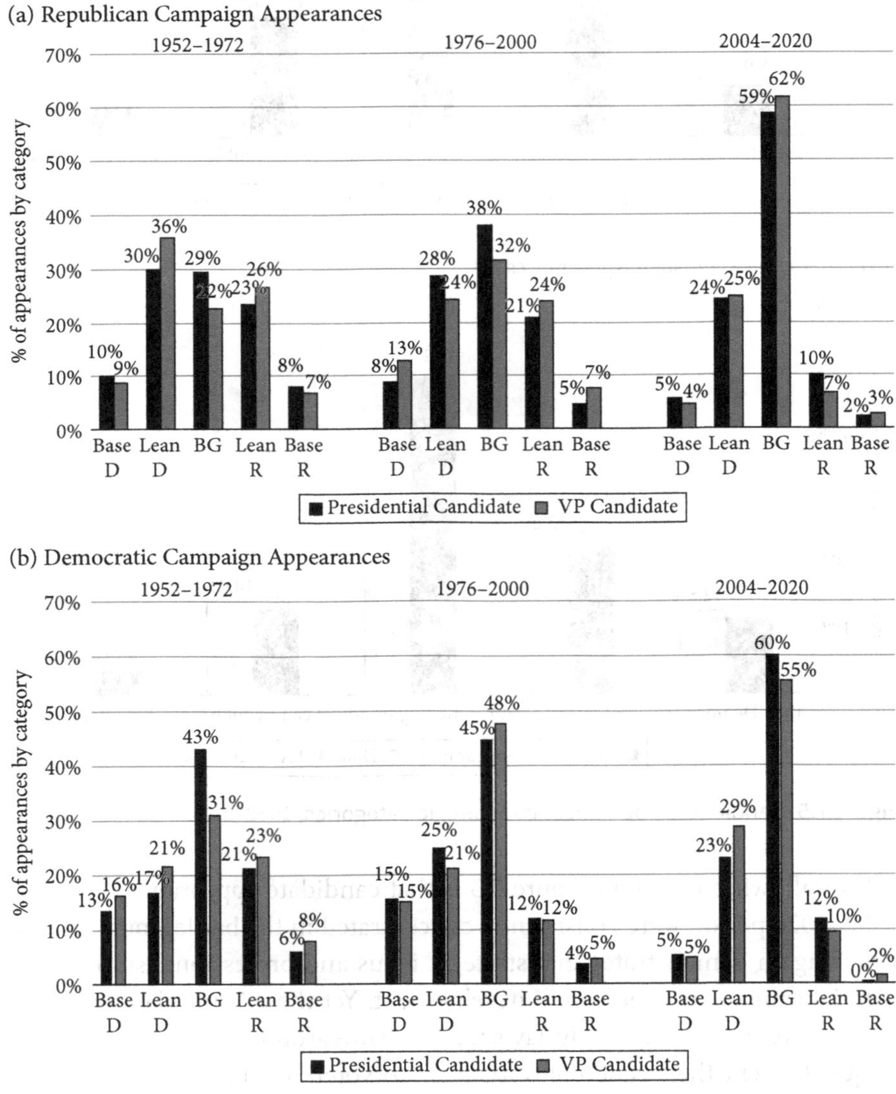

Figure 7.6 Candidate Appearances within Strategic Categories by Campaign Era

had a relatively broad distribution of candidate appearances across the five strategic categories on Republican lists, with battleground states drawing a combined total of just 29% of presidential and 22% of vice-presidential candidate appearances. This relatively broad distribution among the five strategic categories in this first era—where even base Democratic states got on average 10% of Republican presidential candidate visits—evolved to a more bell-curve distribution in the 1976–2000 era with battleground states on Republican lists attracting 38% of the party's presidential and 32% of vice-presidential candidate visits. The most significant transformation of this pattern occurred in the third era: from 2004 to 2020, fully 59% of Republican presidential candidate appearances and 62% of vice-presidential candidate visits were clustered in the set of Republican battleground states. During this most recent period, the second highest concentration of Republican candidate visits went to their set of lean Democratic states, with much the same weight as seen in the second era. But for Republican campaigners, the increased visits to battleground states came at the expense of lean Republican states, which saw relatively few appearances by Republican candidates in this third era. Mirroring the trend in Republican spot advertising, in this most recent era a decreasing number of Republican candidate appearances have become increasingly concentrated into a smaller number of battleground states.

The record of Democratic candidate appearances by era shown in Figure 7.6b has also changed over time, though in a different way than for the Republicans. In contrast to the Republican tendency to broadly distribute candidate appearances across strategic categories in the first era from 1952 to 1972, Democratic candidate visits in this same period were already concentrated in battleground states: on average, 43% of presidential and 31% of vice-presidential campaign appearances went to the set of Democratic battleground states. Outside the battleground states, Democratic appearances were more broadly distributed, as with the Republican pattern. But unlike the Republicans, in the 1976–2000 era Democratic campaigns became even more heavily invested in visiting their list of battleground states at the expense of leaning states, with 45% of presidential candidate visits targeting the set of battlegrounds, 25% targeting the campaigns' lists of lean Democratic states, and 12% targeting the set of lean Republican states. This increasing focus on battleground visits became even more extreme in the 2004–2020 era, when 60% of presidential and 55% of vice-presidential appearances by Democratic candidates went to the campaigns' lists of battleground states. And unlike the earlier or middle eras, by this third era the strategic targeting of candidate appearances was nearly identical for both parties. The only difference is that for Democrats, this was merely a continuation of a longer-term trend that emphasized battleground visits, while for Republicans this pattern represented a sharper break with the tendencies of both previous eras.

Looking across the party distributions, Figure 7.6 reveals one additional insight. It would make a certain strategic sense if the campaigns deployed presidential and vice-presidential candidates differentially during the campaign, sending the top-of-ticket presidential candidates to woo swing voters in the battleground and lean states while reserving vice-presidential appearances to engage the party's core supporters in its base and lean states. Such a logic would envision the use of these different types of candidate visits to compensate for one another, using the vice-presidential candidate to cater to the base in ways that free up the presidential candidate for battleground work. But this is not what we see: across Electoral College categories and across eras, Figure 7.6 shows that both Democrats and Republicans tended to allocate presidential and vice-presidential candidate appearances in roughly the same ways. Although a small number of exceptions to this tendency can be seen—Democrats moving vice-presidential appearances into less competitive states during the first era and Republicans doing the same in the second era—these exceptions involve relatively small differences in visit allocations. We see instead that both parties seem to be using presidential and vice-presidential campaign appearances in complementary rather than compensatory ways. The notion that campaigns will deploy vice-presidential candidates to stoke the base, so that presidential candidates can be reserved for moving swing voters in competitive states, receives little support in these data.

Discussion

Several key findings emerge from these data. First, we confirm our assumption that Republican and Democratic presidential campaigns across our time series have disproportionately allocated their key resources in those states considered most essential to winning an Electoral College majority. This is, of course, unsurprising. But confirmatory analyses are important as we add to our understanding of these election campaigns.

Second, we also confirm the dynamic nature of "disproportionality" over time. While concentrated in strategically important states, resource allocation in the first era was more balanced, with some spot buys and candidate appearances in leaning and even base states. Lean Democratic states were particularly likely to draw visits (and, to a lesser degree, spot buys) from Republican candidates. Presumably, these reflect the breadth of states targeted by GOP candidates in this era, and perhaps a more aggressive approach toward the Democrat's electoral coalition.

In the second era, the primacy of the battleground states for resource allocation strengthens; spot advertising and candidate visits increase in those states while they decrease (relatively) in base states. The lean states continue to be an important part of allocation patterns, however, and we continue to see relatively aggressive targeting of resources by both Republicans and Democrats toward lean Democratic states. The tighter concentration of spot buy allocation patterns supports our hypothesis that campaign finance limits imposed after 1972 further reduced strategic incentives to spend in non-essential states. Furthermore, Republican activity in lean Democratic states may reflect the strategic positions of the Reagan and G. H. W. Bush campaigns: from 1980 to 1988, the Republicans were flying high and engaged actively in states that had traditionally leaned slightly to the left; in 1992, GOP fortunes had ebbed, but Bush's only chance was to roll the dice in states that the campaign conceded were leaning toward Bill Clinton.

In the third and most recent era, there is a spike in the amount of available spot buy money along with a diminishing number of candidate appearances relative to earlier periods. Furthermore, ad money and candidate visits are overwhelmingly allocated in battleground states. This is consistent with our hypothesis that spending would skyrocket after the 2000 election due to the rejection of public funds by presidential candidates and the proliferation of campaign money fueled by innovative online, small donor fundraising. Beyond this general trend, there is also a discernible drop in the allocation of both TV advertising and candidate visits to lean Republican states. Resource allocation in the lean Democratic states, by contrast, is largely unchanged from the second era. Indeed, TV spot buy spending by Democratic campaigns ticks upward.

This last tendency is somewhat unexpected. One will recall that we were more ambivalent about whether twenty-first century campaigns would allocate spot buy funds exclusively into the most critical states. On the one hand, the development of voter lists and big data analyses suggested even narrower allocation patterns, as did a more polarized political environment that appears to limit variation in statewide voting so that only a handful of states are truly competitive. On the other hand, having $500 million to spend rather than $75 million for the general election campaign creates opportunities to take chances in states that might otherwise be written off.

So, what is going on? It seems likely that states such as Michigan, Pennsylvania, and Wisconsin, which had been battleground states for much of the second era, shifted into lean Democratic territory by the third era.

Moreover, the Democrats became more likely to win in the remaining battleground states, such as Colorado, Florida, Nevada, New Hampshire, and Virginia. This created incentives for the Republicans to expand the map and for Democrats to shore up their hold on these states, which Hillary Clinton's 2016 campaign referred to as the Blue Wall. But why didn't Republican spot buy spending match that of the Democrats in these lean Democratic states? First, these states are dominated by expensive media markets (Denver, Miami, and Las Vegas), some of which waste money because they include voters outside the target states (Washington, DC, and Boston). Second, the data reveal that GOP spending in these states *has* increased significantly, but only in 2016 and 2020. This reflects both the new strategic reality as well as Donald Trump's greater appeal to lower-socioeconomic status white voters in these upper Midwest states.

Of course, the tendency of presidential campaigns to develop and adhere to strategic plans when allocating scarce campaign resources represents a key part of our story. The nature of these plans and the efficacy of their execution has heretofore been the stuff of legend. We find that these plans are grounded in a strategic and contextual reality that lends itself to systematic classification and study. It remains to be seen, however, whether these plans have had discernible effects on state-level voting that are large enough to influence national election outcomes. This is the crucial question that occupies our attention in chapter 8.

8
Putting It All Together: Resource Allocation and Vote Outcomes

The 2020 presidential election in the United States was the most expensive in history—by a lot: all told, spending topped $5.7 billion from all sources, more than double that of the 2016 cycle, when $2.4 billion was spent. The major-party contenders themselves spent over $1.8 billion in 2020. Biden—the first candidate to ever raise over $1 billion from donors—bested Trump's spending total of $778 million.[1] In the 2016 cycle, more than one million television ads were aired in the presidential race alone (Fowler, Ridout, and Franz, 2016). Even during a global pandemic, both candidates and their running mates crisscrossed the country in search of votes. This pattern—raise, spend, stump—is the touchstone of contemporary presidential campaigns in the United States. It is the routine that dozens of presidential hopefuls have followed for decades (Panagopoulos, 2017).

Given this standard paradigm, it is perhaps surprising that so many observers and analysts have questioned whether all this massive effort matters for anything on Election Day. To what extent—if any—does presidential campaign activity materially affect voters' ballot choices? As noted in chapter 2, the nature of this relationship has been the subject of considerable scholarly debate, including some important recent research (see, for example, Holbrook, 1996, 2002; Gordon and Hartmann, 2013; Shaw, 2006; Sides and Vavreck, 2013; Sides, Tesler, and Vavreck, 2018; Sides, Tausanovitch, and Vavreck, 2022; Huber and Arceneaux, 2007; Kenski, Hardy, and Jamieson, 2010; Hill, Lo, Vavreck and Zaller, 2013; Johnston, Hagen, and Jamieson, 2004; Coppock, Hill, and Vavreck, 2020; Fowler, Franz, and Ridout, 2016; Goldstein and Ridout, 2004; Kalla and Broockman, 2018; Ridout and Franz, 2011; Krasno and Greeen, 2008; McGhee and Sides, 2005; Spenkuch and Toniatti, 2018; Sides, Vavreck, and Warshaw, 2022; Devine, 2023). Despite voluminous scholarship, the topic is far from settled, and the effectiveness of campaign tactics *writ large* remains in question. Most studies suggest campaigns "matter," at least a little, by nudging votes on Election Day a few percentage points at most.

Battleground. Daron R. Shaw, Scott L. Althaus, and Costas Panagopoulos, Oxford University Press.
 DOI: 10.1093/oso/9780197774366.003.0008

We conclude this book by weighing in on the question of whether (and how much) campaigns matter given the novel data about campaign activity over nearly seven decades that we have amassed. To this end, we hope the analyses in this chapter both complement and extend extant research on this topic, offering insight into change and continuity across eras. As a preview we note that, overall, our findings often coincide with what recent academic studies have posited. Yet our novel data allow us to explore nuances in campaign effects over longer spans of time than previous studies have considered, and this allows us to conjecture about some compelling variation across time that previous studies have never explored. So, let's jump in.

In chapter 7 we demonstrated that campaigns have mostly hewed to their strategic plans when allocating campaign resources in presidential campaigns. There are, to be sure, some intriguing differences in these patterns over eras with important consequences for where and how widespread the attention of political campaigners is concentrated, some of which we predicted but some of which we did not. In terms of the relationship between campaigning and presidential election votes, based not only on previous studies but also on our own sense of contemporary presidential elections it is worth reiterating that we expect presidential campaign effects to most likely be (1) modest yet potentially consequential overall and (2) variable across eras.

When Closeness Is the Rule, Small Effects Matter

In considering the question of campaign impact, as well as the expectation of "modest yet potentially consequential effects," it is important to underscore how remarkably competitive American presidential elections have been over our time frame. Consider how a few small shifts in critical states could have changed the course of history in these keenly contested elections:[2]

- In 1960, 4,429 votes shifting from Kennedy to Nixon in Illinois (0.09%), along with 4,990 in Missouri (0.26%) and 11,046 in New Jersey (0.40%) would have inaugurated President Nixon in 1961 and left Dallas's Daley Plaza as just another small park in a very large city.
- In 1968, a change of mind among 548 voters in Alaska (1.32%), 5,123 in Missouri (0.57%), and 15,316 in New Jersey (1.07%) would have put President Humphrey in the reception line to welcome returning astronaut Neil Armstrong from the moon.
- In 1976, just 5,558 voters choosing Ford rather than Carter in Ohio (0.14%) and another 17,623 last minute changes in Wisconsin (0.84%)

would have left President Ford to manage the Camp David Accords between the Israelis and the Palestinians, if the gathering had ever happened at all.

- In 2000, a shift of 269 votes from Bush to Gore in Florida (0.00026%) would have left President Gore to deal with the 9/11 attacks.
- In 2004, a shift of 59,300 votes from Bush to Kerry in Ohio (1.05%) would have put a Vietnam War hero in the White House to address the escalating insurgency in Iraq.
- In 2012, a shift of 37,155 votes in Florida (0.44%), 19,822 votes in New Hampshire (2.79%), 83,136 in Ohio (1.49%), and 74,649 in Virginia (1.94%) would have left Barack Obama as a one-term president.
- In 2016, if just 5,352 Michigan voters (0.11%) had cast ballots for Clinton rather than Trump, along with 22,142 others in Pennsylvania (0.36%) and 11,374 in Wisconsin (0.38%), Hillary Clinton would have been inaugurated as the country's first female president.
- In 2020, a shift of 5,229 votes from Biden to Trump in Arizona (0.15%), along with 5,890 in Georgia (0.12%), 16,798 in Nevada (1.20%), and 10,341 in Wisconsin (0.31%) would have spared the country from the coup attempt that was part of the January 6, 2021, assault on the U.S. Capitol.

Put another way, shifts of fewer than sixty thousand votes nationwide in just the right states would have changed the Electoral College results in seven of the eighteen elections from 1952 to 2020. If we expand the range to encompass shifts of roughly three hundred thousand votes, the number increases to half (nine of eighteen) of presidential elections over the period of our study. Even conceding that these shifts are hypothetical and geographically concentrated, it is striking evidence that even smallish campaign effects in the right states can change the course of presidential history.

The huge significance of relatively modest shifts in the presidential vote is particularly intriguing given that precisely these sorts of effects are suggested by recent analyses of television advertising (Broockman and Kalla, 2022; Coppock, Hill, and Vavreck, 2020; Fowler, Ridout, and Franz, 2016; Gerber et al. 2011; Gordon and Hartmann, 2013; Huber and Arceneaux, 2007; Ridout and Franz, 2011; Sides, Vavreck, and Warshaw, 2022) and candidate appearances (Chen and Reeves, 2010; Devine, 2018 and 2023; McClurg and Holbrook, 2009; Shaw, 2006; Snyder and Yusaf, 2020; Stromberg, 2008; Wolak, 2006). It is with this context in mind that we engage with the question: *does presidential campaigning matter?* Our distinctive contribution to the voluminous literature estimating and assessing the precise impact of these activities is an important one: unlike any previous study of which we are aware, the analysis in this chapter isolates campaign effects across the entirety of modern presidential elections, which allows us to capture over-time variation and trends in the ways that television advertising and candidate appearances matter for Election Day vote totals. This unique vantage point will clarify for the first time whether campaigns have gotten better (or worse) at moving hearts and minds over a seven-decade period, during which the technologies available for targeting and reaching individual voters have advanced, through multiple generations, in sophistication, diversity, and customizability.

A Simple Look at Campaign Ad and Candidate Appearance Effects

With this as our backdrop, our analysis focuses on perhaps the most historically consistent and publicly visible manifestations of modern presidential campaigning: we gauge the extent to which television spot advertising spending as well as presidential and vice-presidential candidate appearances move vote totals on Election Day. To measure effects, we must estimate what Election Day totals might have looked like if there was no campaigning at all. As a statistical exercise, gauging an expected baseline vote from which over- or under-achieving can be measured is worthy of its own chapter in a book like this. We experimented with several potential measures before settling on a simple yet empirically and theoretically plausible one: we take the Republican candidate's share of the two-party vote in a state (or media market) and subtract it from a weighted average of the Republican vote over the past three elections, where voting in the previous election counts a bit more than voting from two elections back, and so on to three elections back.[3] This weighted average provides a powerful baseline predictor of voting in the current election (accounting for over 70% of variance in state-level Election Day results), such that deviation from this average is a reliable measure change induced by election- or campaign-specific factors.

With our dependent variable in place, the question at hand is how closely a state's deviation from longer-term tendencies in the presidential vote is associated with the local intensity of television advertising and candidate appearances in the current election. As described in chapter 7, we utilize the campaign's spending on locally targeted advertising from the end of August until Election Day. The total dollar figures in each election are translated into 2020 dollar equivalents. Excepting 1960, we have these TV spot buy data for every campaign in every general election from 1952 through 2020. Likewise, candidate appearances are defined as the total number of public appearances—excluding fundraising events—in a state from the end of August until Election Day. A candidate can make multiple appearances in the same state on a given day. We have these data for every presidential and vice-presidential candidate for every election from 1952 through 2020.

In gauging effects, our approach should provide a lower end estimate of campaign impact. This conservatism reflects several important choices, including the following:

- *Our unit of analysis is the state.* This is appropriate because presidential elections are decided by amassing electoral votes, and those votes are mostly decided by statewide election outcomes. However, at the risk of stating the obvious, states are big. They are so big that campaign effects in one part of a state might be lost or offset by counter-effects in other parts. Thus, later in this chapter we offer analyses of the effects of TV advertising and candidate appearances at the level of the media market, where one might more accurately assess whether geographically focused allocations in campaign resources reliably persuade or mobilize voters in favor of the campaign's ticket.
- *Our measure of effects encompasses (but does not distinguish between) persuasion and mobilization.* That is, the difference in a state's vote in the current election compared to its weighted average from the state's last three races is a function of *both* the asymmetric mobilization of voters as well as the asymmetric persuasion of voters on behalf of one candidate. If the campaigns are getting something from their spending and activities, then television advertising and candidate appearances should be shown to mobilize and/or persuade voters in a state. But it is possible that persuasion could favor one side and mobilization the other, such that effects cancel each other out. While our approach remains agnostic about the potential mechanism that may give rise to any campaign effects we detect, there remains considerable scholarly debate about the extent to which vote shifts are attributable to mobilization or persuasion. Some scholars argue, for example, that the primary mechanism for ad effects is likely persuasion rather than mobilization of partisans (e.g., Sides, Vavreck, and Warshaw, 2022). Similarly, Krasno and Green (2008) find that television advertising in the closing days of the 2000 presidential campaign exerted negligible effects on turnout. In an examination of presidential races between 2008 and 2020, Devine (2023) also found that campaign visits did not tend to affect voting behavior, but when they did, most often it was by persuading undecided voters. By contrast, other

analysts are dubious about the persuasive capacity of campaign activity (e.g., Kalla and Broockman, 2018 and Broockman and Kalla, 2022). Still others have shown that modern presidential campaigns can significantly affect turnout, altering the size and composition of the voting population (e.g., Enos and Fowler, 2018). Our admittedly blunt approach to measuring campaign effects cannot adjudicate between these perspectives. Thus, we view questions about the underlying mechanisms for campaign effects to be very much open when making sense of our findings.

- *The only effects we consider are those that directly influence the vote.* We do not assess other possible effects that could also be important factors shaping election outcomes. For instance, we do not measure whether the allocation of these campaign resources improves the images of candidates or alters issue agendas among people in a state. We neglect the messages conveyed in ads, as well as what candidates say in their stump speeches. Nor do we measure whether these outreach efforts encourage financial contributions to the campaign or mobilize volunteers. We also ignore other forms of campaigning, such as mail, phones, door-to-door contact, or digital outreach. Only if the effects of these other influences were perfectly correlated with our measures of ad dollars and candidate visits would our approach reliably detect them.
- *We do not consider activities in the spring and summer of a presidential election year.* In the earlier years of our study, little general election activity occurred before the parties' national conventions. This changed, however, by the second era such that significant television spot buy ads and many candidate appearances happened before the traditional Labor Day kick-off to the general election campaign. In choosing to standardize our time frame, we do not consider these "early" campaign effects.
- *We do not consider campaign effects that decay before Election Day.* Recent research (see, for example, Gerber et al. 2011 and Hill et al. 2013) indicates that television ad effects exist but tend to be short-lived, decaying after a period of several days. The importance of these ephemeral effects is debatable, but because we focus only on shifts in the vote, we consider only durable effects or those that occur so late that they do not have time to decay before the election.
- *We do not consider how campaign activity from past elections might have shaped our measure of expected vote in the current election.* In previous chapters, we demonstrate that states tend to be regarded as battlegrounds for multiple consecutive elections. Considering this, a state that receives substantial campaign attention in one election—which might persuade and mobilize many voters—is relatively likely to be targeted in the next

election. But campaign effects in one election probably reduce the likelihood and magnitude of unique and substantial effects in the next election and this is something for which we do not account.

A Simple Look at TV Ad Spending and Candidate Appearance Effects

We begin with a simplified look at the data to gain a broad overview of campaign activity effects (and why estimating this impact with any precision is so difficult). Later in the chapter we consider more compelling (but also more complicated) ways of estimating what size bang campaigns get for their resource bucks.

Our starting point is shown in Table 8.1, where we estimate the average Republican vote shift at the state level—defined as the difference between the Republican share of the two-party vote in the current election minus the weighted average of the Republican share from the past three elections—that is associated with two types of states: those where Republicans have outspent Democrats on television in the current election ("Republican Advantage" states) and those where Democrats have outspent Republicans on television ("Democratic Advantage" states). Table 8.1 contains no fancy statistics, but simply reports average Republican percentage-point vote shifts within each category of state across the entire time series (the "All Years" column) as well as separately for each of our three eras. Positive numbers in this table indicate

Table 8.1 Shift in Average State-Level Republican Presidential Voting by Relative Television Advertising Advantages

	All Years		1952–1972		1976–2000		2004–2020	
	Vote Shift	% of Total	Vote Shift	% of Total	Vote Shift	% of Total	Vote Shift	% of Total
Balance of State-Level Spot Ad Spending								
Republican Advantage	1.83	54%	4.68	64%	−0.60	54%	0.14	37%
Democratic Advantage	−1.36	46%	3.66	36%	−5.18	46%	−0.88	63%
Average All States	0.69	100%	4.01	100%	−1.78	100%	0.36	100%

Notes: Vote shift cell entries are the average state-level difference between the Republican share of the two-party vote in an election and the weighted average from the previous three presidential elections. We omit states where there is no TV spending advantage; percent of total reflects only states where such an advantage exists.

that the Republican candidate "over-achieved" in the current election of interest by performing better than the state's historical Republican average from the previous three elections, while negative numbers (indicating a lower Republican vote percentage in the current election relative to the state's recent historical average) indicate that the Democratic candidate over-achieved. More consequentially, the row entries allow us to observe candidate performance (compared to historical expectations) by campaign advantages. Does having more advertising on the air in a state produce reliable electoral benefits for a campaign?

In Table 8.1, the "Vote Shift" column shows whether Republicans did better (positive values) or worse (negative values) in each election relative to a state's weighted historical average Republican vote, while the "% of Total" column shows the percentage of states in each of the two campaign advantage categories. States with precisely equal levels of ad spending (including those with no ad spending at all from either campaign) are omitted from this table. In the "Republican Advantage" row we see that across all elections, Republicans had an edge in television spending for 54% of the state-years in our dataset where one of the parties outspent the other, and that Republican candidates did 1.83 points better than expected in those states where they spent more on spot advertising buys than the Democratic candidates. In the "Democratic Advantage" row we see that Democrats held a spending advantage on television in 46% of our state-years, and that Democratic candidates did about 1.36 points better than expected in those states where they spent more on television spot buys than their opponents. So far, so good—this looks like about what most observers would expect: smallish Election Day bumps favoring the campaign that spent more on television. Looking at the "Average All States" row shows that across all state-years the Republicans averaged a small 0.7 point increase, so the GOP tended to do a bit better than the previous election in nearly every year from 1952 to 2020.

These patterns persist when we examine the data era by era, but in ways that require us to consider larger historical changes taking place in the electoral landscape nationwide. In the 1952–1972 era the "Average All States" row shows that Republicans tended to over-perform their expected historical vote by about 4.01 points per election in every state. This reflects the start and the end of this era, which opened with consecutive Eisenhower victories that undid a Democratic lock on the presidency that had been in place since 1932, and that closed with a pair of Nixon victories after two terms of Democratic incumbents, most notably the landslide Nixon sweep of 1972. Relative to later eras, this whipsaw of party control meant that statewide voting patterns were relatively less predictable during the 1952–1972 period, and outcomes were more in flux relative to more recent elections. Against this backdrop, Table 8.1 shows that Republicans did particularly well in this first era when they had a spot buy spending advantage (+4.68 percentage point shift relative to historical Republican voting patterns). While Republicans did relatively less well in places where Democrats outspent them on television during this era (just a + 3.66 point Republican shift in such states), they were still outperforming recent historical averages even in those places.

With this historical backstory in place, we are now able to observe that even in this early era, the Election Day impact of television ad spending was relatively small. This can be seen by comparing the vote shift when one party has an edge to the "Average All States" vote shift, which shows that the net effect of a television spot buy advantage in this era is only about 0.5 percentage point in the direction of the party that is outspending the other. Yet because Republicans had a spot buy spending advantage in more than half of the statewide contests across this era (54% of state-years between 1952 and 1972, relative to 46% of statewide contests where Democrats had the edge) these smallish state-level net effects of television spending cumulated into a distinctive Electoral College advantage favoring Republicans in this first era.

Moving next to the 1976–2000 era, Table 8.1 shows a systematic change in the nationwide electoral landscape in favor of the Democrats. Across this second era, the "Average All States" row shows that Democrats do slightly better—by about 1.78 percentage points in a typical state during this period—than their historical state-level voting patterns would have suggested. But in contrast to the first era, the performance of candidates is significantly affected by winning or losing the ad spending wars: in states where Democrats enjoyed a television spot buy advantage, they over-performed by 5.18 points over weighted historical averages. When the Republicans had the advertising edge, they held the Democratic over-performance back to just 0.60 points on average, which degraded but did not eliminate the nationwide Democratic momentum in these states.

The "% of Total" column for this second era shows an additional change relative to earlier elections: Democratic tickets reduced the Republican advantage in TV spot buy spending across the states from 28 percentage points in the first era (that is, 64% of state-years with a Republican advantage minus 36% of state-years with a Democratic advantage is a 28 point difference) to just 8 points in the second era. Although the GOP candidates still outspent their Democratic counterparts in 54% of statewide contests in this era, the Democrats won the air wars in 46% of state-years during this second era relative to just 36% in the first era. In other words, even though Democrats lost four of seven elections in this second era, Democratic candidates all but neutralized the Republicans' television spot buy edge in the states and saw larger Election Day vote shifts from these advantages than did the Republicans. The television contest had turned in this second era, and increasingly the benefits were accruing to Democrats more than to Republicans.

In the third era from 2004 to 2020, Table 8.1 shows that the Democrats continued building upon the television spending trend we saw in the previous era: they outspent the Republicans in 63% of statewide contests with a spending advantage to one side or the other, while the GOP retained the edge in just 37%. As might be expected in this polarized era, the "Average All States" row shows that the mean state-level vote shift was only 0.36 percentage points (favoring the Republicans), reflecting the limited opportunities for persuading voters away from established tendencies in this fully sorted and highly antagonistic partisan environment. Despite this challenging electoral landscape, in states where the Democrats held the television spending advantage, they did 0.88 points better than expected. For some reason, GOP candidates weren't as fortunate: in this third era, a Republican ad spending advantage shifted vote totals toward the GOP by only 0.14 of a percentage point on average.

This last (Republican) result seems somewhat strange: the pro-Republican vote shift was smaller in states where the GOP held a TV spending edge than it was across all states, leading one to infer that Republicans did especially well in states with no campaigning (or where TV ad spending was even). It seems to us that this is because the Republicans were aggressively targeting states critical to their winning coalition, but that voters in these states were harder to convert or mobilize. Thus, the overall pro-Republican drift across the third era was concentrated in states that were decidedly partisan (one way or the other). This, rather than poor messaging or TV ad content, seems a more plausible explanation for this subset of patterns in Table 8.1.

Table 8.2 offers the same simple analysis but focuses on numbers of presidential and vice-presidential candidate appearances. For presidential appearances, the main finding is like that for spot advertising differentials: when comparing average state-level Election Day swings by the relative frequency of presidential candidate appearances in a state, the effects are typically small and in the expected direction. For example, across all elections and all states we see that when Democrats have a presidential appearance advantage, the vote shift favors them by 0.21 points over weighted historical averages for a state, and when Republicans have the advantage, the vote shift favors them by 0.47 points. Again, the direction of these effects is

Table 8.2 Shift in Average State-Level Republican Presidential Voting by Relative Candidate Appearance Advantages

	All Years		1952–1972		1976–2000		2004–2020	
	Vote Shift	% of Total	Vote Shift	% of Total	Vote Shift	% of Total	Vote Shift	% of Total
Balance of State-Level Presidential Candidate Visits								
Republican Advantage	0.47	48%	3.94	39%	−2.20	45%	0.24	71%
Democratic Advantage	−0.21	52%	3.67	61%	−3.93	55%	−1.40	29%
Balance of State-Level Vice Presidential Candidate Visits								
Republican Advantage	0.00	51%	2.56	42%	−1.62	55%	−0.24	60%
Democratic Advantage	0.56	49%	3.87	58%	−3.18	45%	0.45	40%
Average All States	0.69	100%	4.01	100%	−1.78	100%	0.36	100%

Notes: Vote shift cell entries are the average state-level difference between the Republican share of the two-party vote in an election and the weighted average from the previous three presidential elections. We omit states where there is no candidate appearance advantage; percent of total reflects only states where such an advantage exists.

entirely consistent with the usual expectations, even if the average magnitude of effects is rather small in this very blunt way of sizing up results.

The general pattern is maintained over time, although there is interesting variation through the eras. In the era from 1952 through 1972, Republicans exceed their expected vote share by 3.94 points when they have a presidential candidate visit edge, compared to only 3.67 points when the Democrats have the edge. From 1976 through 2000, the Republicans under-achieve by 2.20 points when they have the advantage, but by 3.93 points when the Democrats have the edge. From 2004 through 2020, the Republicans over-achieve by 0.24 points when they have the edge, but they under-achieve by 1.40 points when the Democrats have the edge.

Overall, there were more states where the Democratic presidential candidates had a numerical appearance advantage than vice-versa (52% to 48%). As with television advertising, this masks considerable variation across eras. From 1952 through 1972, Democratic presidential candidates enjoyed the appearance edge 61% of the time, whereas Republicans only held the advantage 39% of the time. From 1976 through 2000, the Democrats won the visit contest in 55% of the states, compared to 45% for the Republicans. But from 2004 through 2020, the GOP's candidates owned the lead in appearances 71% of the time, while the Democrats carried the advantage 29% of the time.

While we had expectations about the nature and magnitude of vote effects for TV spot buys and presidential candidate visits based on theory and previous empirical work, we were less certain about the potential impact of vice-presidential visits. Our assumption that vice-presidential candidate appearances are targeted at battleground and "lean" states was validated in chapter 7, however the tendency was less pronounced than for presidential candidate visits. Moreover, it is unclear whether these appearances drive local news coverage the way presidential appearances are likely to, thus complicating what sort of effect we are likely to see on the vote. For example, Shaw (2006) shows that vice-presidential appearances in the 2000 and 2004 election campaigns were a decidedly mixed bag, with Republican vice-presidential candidate Dick Cheney counter-mobilizing as many Democrats as mobilizing Republicans. The data indicate that our ambivalence was warranted: the lower set of rows in Table 8.2 suggest that the pro-Republican vote-shift is *greater* when the Democratic candidate out-visited the Republican (+0.56 points) compared to when the Republican had the edge (+0.00 points).

This counter-intuitive finding cannot be dismissed as a fluke of a bygone time. With one exception across the three eras, having one's vice-presidential candidate out-visit the other side's candidate is associated with relatively worse vote performance. From 1952 through 1972, the Republicans do 2.56 points better than the historical vote average when their vice-presidential candidate has an appearance advantage, but they do 3.87 points better when the Democratic vice-presidential candidate has an advantage. This is also the case in the third era, as from 2004 through 2020 a Republican vice-presidential appearance edge is associated with Democratic over-achievement by 0.24 points, whereas a Democratic vice-presidential edge is associated with Republican over-achievement by 0.45 points. Only in the second era, 1976–2000, is the correlation in the expected direction, as a Democratic vice-presidential candidate appearance advantage sees a 3.18 improvement over that expected by the Democratic ticket, while the improvement is only 1.62 point when the Republican vice-presidential has the advantage.

While we did not expect vice-presidential appearance advantages to produce substantial shifts in the vote, we must admit that we do not have an obvious explanation for why the effect seems to flow in the opposite direction than one would expect. It is tempting to expand on our earlier observation that vice-presidential candidates may not be deployed in quite the same way as presidential candidates and that they may be asked to visit states that are strategically important but with electorates that are relatively less receptive. This was the case with Cheney in 2000 and 2004 and seems to have been true for third era vice-presidential candidates such as John Edwards (D), Paul Ryan (R), and Tim Kaine (D). However, as with the findings for TV spot buy and presidential candidate appearances, we will refrain from additional speculation about effects until we confirm their existence with more demanding statistical analyses.

Setting aside the question of whether it helped or not, there was also variation across eras with respect to which party's vice-presidential candidates were more active in the most states. Although the Republican vice-presidential candidates maintained a slight edge across the entirety of our time frame (51% of statewide advantages to 49%), Democratic vice-presidential candidates had the edge from 1952 through 1972 (58% to 42%) whereas Republican vice-presidential candidates held the advantage from 1976 through 2000 (55% to 45%) as well from 2004 through 2020 (60% to 40%).

Taken as a whole, the results of this initial pass at the data mostly conform to our expectations. When looking at TV spot buy advertising or presidential candidate appearances, we see that out-campaigning the opposition is associated with small but consistent improvements in the vote compared to recent elections. This predictable pattern does not emerge from the data on vice-presidential appearances. The next step is to specify and estimate statistical models that allow us to gauge these effects more precisely and convincingly.

A Slightly More Complex Look at TV Ad and Candidate Appearance Effects

As we have already suggested, there are important limits to what one can reasonably infer from the preceding analyses. Comparing differences in means across simplified dichotomous distinctions (Republican versus Democratic campaign advantages) fails to account for the magnitude of campaigning differences, either in television spot buy spending or candidate appearances. Furthermore, this simple approach cannot control for alternative explanations in ways that give us confidence that what we are seeing is a true effect of campaign activities rather than of the decision to target some states over others. We therefore turn our attention to multivariate statistical models, which afford a more powerful and insightful assessment of the relationship between campaigning and presidential votes.

The Statewide Impact of Republican and Democratic Activities

Once again, our dependent variable is the vote shift measure defined earlier. To estimate the effects of television spot buy advertising, we take the natural log of the Republican and Democratic campaign spending measures.[4] This decision is based on the theoretical expectation that spending will have a steep positive effect on the vote which gradually diminishes beyond a certain level and then quickly falls to zero (Freedman, Franz, and Goldstein, 2004; Shaw, 2006; Sides, Vavreck, and Warshaw, 2022). This is widely known as a logarithmic or "ceiling effect," which assumes that increasing TV ad spending from $0 to $1 million will produce a greater impact than increasing it from $100 million to $101 million.

To estimate the effects of presidential and vice-presidential candidate appearances, we use a simple count variable. Given that candidates rarely make more than a dozen or so appearances in each state, there is little theoretical or empirical reason to employ a statistical transformation of this measure. We do, however, keep presidential and vice-presidential appearances separate (at least initially), as we are interested in ascertaining whether presidential candidate appearances might have different effects compared to vice-presidential appearances.

Two other sets of variables are included in our models for both substantive and methodological reasons. First, our statistical models include the number of electoral votes in a state. We wish to account for the possibility that it may be more difficult to induce vote shifts in states with larger populations because campaigns would have to persuade larger numbers of voters in big states to produce the same percentage shift from historical averages that one might find in small states. Controlling for electoral votes is also important because for at least part of the period considered here larger states were more likely to be targeted by both campaigns in the first place, which would make it harder for one campaign to gain much of an advantage in larger states. Second, we allow each election to have its own unique effects on voters apart from ad and visit differentials by including dummy variables for the different elections (typically setting 2020 as our base category). By including these fixed effects in our models, we are assuming that each election has the potential to produce a unique and independent effect on presidential voters that needs to be controlled for in our estimations.[5] For estimation purposes, we rely on ordinary least squares regressions. In what follows, we describe and interpret the results of these statistical models.

We can interpret the results of statistical models that use our full set of campaign variables to predict shifts from the expected statewide presidential vote percentages across all elections in our time series, as well as by elections within our three different eras (full model results are presented in Table 8.1A in the technical appendix at the end of the chapter). Because the coefficients are based on logarithmic transformations of TV ad spending numbers, we can provide more intuitive estimations of these effects by calculating the impact of moving from zero spending on TV spot buys in a state to $100,000 in 2020 dollars. For the overall time series, increasing Republican TV ad spending by this amount produces a 0.30 point pro-Republican improvement over the expected vote, while for the Democrats it produces a 0.09 point pro-Democratic improvement. Although the effects are in the expected direction, neither register as statistically significant. Nor are they substantively impressive, even acknowledging the potential significance of small vote shifts in many elections.

The overall impact masks interesting variation by era, however. In the initial era, 1952–1972, the estimated effects of Republican and Democratic TV spot buy spending are negative. For the Republicans, going from $0 to $100,000 in a state increases the Democratic share of the vote by 0.88 points compared to expected, whereas for the Democrats it increases the Republican share of the vote by 1.85 points compared to expected. This counter-intuitive tendency in the early days of television reverses in later eras. From 1976 through 2000, a $0 to $100,000 increase in Republican TV ad spending is associated with a 0.31 point improvement over expected; for the Democrats, it is associated with a 0.35 point improvement over expected. From 2004 through 2020, the improvement over expected induced by such a shift in TV spot buy ad spending is 0.46 points for the Republicans and 0.31 points for the Democrats.[6] We hasten to observe that estimated effects are not quite significant at conventional statistical levels but are consistent with extant scholarship (e.g., Broockman and Kalla, 2022; Franz, et al., 2008; Gordon and Hartman, 2013; Shaw, 2006).

For presidential candidate appearances, the broad contours of the story are similar though with a few interesting twists. The statistical models indicate that one additional public appearance by the Democratic nominee in a state increases the Democratic vote compared to expected by 0.19 points. This effect is statistically significant. For the Republican nominees, the effect is barely negative but is much smaller and is not statistically significant: an additional appearance decreases the GOP's vote over expected by about 0.02 points.[7] As with the TV ad spending estimates, however, we find that the first era stands out. In this instance, the Democrats seem to have been the beneficiaries. For presidential candidate appearances, the data from 1952 through 1972 show that an additional Democratic appearance increased the Democratic vote by 0.32 points relative to the expected vote. On the other side of the aisle, each additional Republican candidate appearance increased their opponents' support by 0.29 points relative to the expected vote. Neither effect registers as statistically significant, but both findings are notable.

The Republican appearance impact is particularly notable because the estimated effect of Republican TV spot buy spending was also correlated with pro-Democratic vote shifts. We are left with the question of why more vigorous GOP campaigning in 1952–1972 seems to have been associated with the Republicans doing less well than expected at the ballot box. One possibility is that the findings are statistical noise. While we cannot dismiss this possibility, it seems more likely than not that the Republicans did not receive much benefit from their campaign activities in this early era. Another possibility is that there was a general movement toward the Republicans across the states during these elections, such that they consistently overachieved compared to historically based averages. Certainly, the Republicans did well in 1952, 1956, 1968, and 1972. More importantly for present purposes, this pro-GOP movement might have been attenuated in states with substantial campaigning because it was there that the Democrats were able to mobilize some appreciable portion of their New Deal coalition and remain competitive.[8] Thus, macro-forces were the dominant influence on vote shifts, and campaigning—especially Democratic campaigning—was mostly effective at re-animating traditional, long-standing partisan allegiances.

In the 1976–2000 era, more conventional effects reassert themselves, as an additional appearance by a Republican presidential candidate improves the GOP vote in a state over the expected average by 0.12 points. On the other side, an extra visit by a Democratic candidate boosted that party's vote from the expected average by 0.28 points. This effect remains in the expected direction but is slightly smaller in the 2004–2020 era. The impact of an extra Republican presidential candidate appearance is to boost the vote by 0.07 points above what one would otherwise expect; an extra visit by the Democratic candidate boosts the vote by 0.17 points. In the crudest terms, in elections from 1976 through 2020 a presidential candidate would need to make a swing through a state with four to five public appearances to raise their vote over expected by an additional percentage point. As we expected, the sledding appears to have gotten tougher in more recent elections, presumably due to entrenched preferences associated with partisan polarization.

Before exploring different statistical models later in this chapter, we should also observe that state population size (measured by electoral votes) does not appear to have been associated with any systematic or consistent effect on vote shifts in these models, either overall or within any of the three eras. The closest we have to a statistically significant effect is for 2004–2020, where more populous states tended to see more pro-Democratic vote shifts than expected. More specifically, for every 10 additional electoral votes associated with a state, the Democrats would do better than historical expectations by 0.34 points. This may simply reflect increased Democratic dominance in states such as California, New York, and Illinois. The vote shift effects associated with specific elections are also statistically significant and in the anticipated direction for our election year dummy variables. For example, 1964 has an estimated pro-Democratic shift of 11.73 points while 1972 has an estimated pro-Republican shift of 15.93 points. These fixed effects increase our confidence that our estimated campaign effects are real and unbiased.

The Statewide Impact of Differential Activities

Teasing out the singular and independent effects of campaign efforts by each party is intriguing, but it presents some conceptual and methodological issues. Most obviously, if one side campaigns heavily, but their efforts are offset by even heavier campaigning by the other side, we might mistakenly conclude that campaigning does not matter when in fact campaigning produces large effects that offset one another. It is therefore useful to estimate statistical models assessing the differential impact of campaign efforts.

Using the difference between the Republican share of the two-party vote in the current election and the weighted historical average as our dependent variable, we estimate the impact of the TV spot buy ad spending differential (logged), as well as the presidential candidate appearance differential and (for the first time) the vice-presidential candidate appearance differential. We also keep the electoral vote and fixed effect terms, and again rely on a least squares estimator. The full models are presented in Table 8.2A of this chapter's appendix.

The data show that spot TV advertising differentials are positively correlated with shifts in the expected presidential vote. Overall, if we increase TV spot buy ad spending from even levels for both campaigns to +$100,000 favoring one side, there is a 0.16 point increase in the two-party share of the vote compared to the weighted historical average. While positively signed, the relationship never reaches conventional levels of statistical significance. One reason for this is that the relationship between differential TV ad spending and vote shifts is negative (though statistically insignificant) in the first era. This is expected given the previous analyses. In contrast, there is a consistent, albeit small, positive effect in the second and third eras. For example, from 1976 through 2000 a +$100,000 increase in the TV ad spending differential is associated with a 0.33 point increase in the vote favoring the campaign with a spending advantage compared to the average. From 2004 through 2020, the effect is a 0.38 point increase.

Presidential appearance differentials also produce a statistically significant and positive statewide effect. Overall, adding a single visit to your appearance advantage produces a 0.92 point improvement over the two-party share of the weighted historical average vote in a state. This impact is even greater in the first era—from 1952 through 1972, a one appearance gain in the presidential campaign appearance differential leads to a 1.26 point statewide improvement for the advantaged campaign. From 1976 through 2000, the improvement is 0.66 points, while from 2004 through 2020 it is 0.69 points. Each of these estimated effects are statistically significant at conventional levels.

Unlike for TV ad spending and presidential candidate appearances, the expected positive impact does not occur for vice-presidential appearances. As suggested by the earlier bivariate analysis of vice-presidential visit effects, here the models show that having an edge with respect to vice-presidential appearances is not associated with more positive statewide vote shifts. While the negative tendency is modest and statistically insignificant, we cannot help but be struck by the fact that it holds overall and across each of our three eras. The impact of adding a single vice-presidential candidate appearance to the overall statewide differential appears to reduce the party's share of the vote compared to the weighted average vote by about −0.15 points. The effects from eras 1, 2, and 3 are −0.38, −0.08, and −0.19 points, respectively. So, while this finding could be a statistical anomaly, it is also worth considering that there is something puzzling about the impact of vice-presidential candidate visits to critical electoral locales. It's not clear whether they might ultimately hurt the ticket for some reason, or whether vice-presidents merely get sent to places where voters are unfriendly and unlikely to be moved in the first place.

In these statistical models, the effect of state population—captured through the electoral vote variable—is mostly significant and negative. That is, states with more electoral votes are likely to see relatively lower Republican vote totals, all other factors held constant. This effect is insignificant in the 1952–1972 era but becomes statistically significant in each of the two eras capturing elections from 1976 through 2020. As in previous models, the election year variables are almost all statistically significant.

All told, the data suggest that campaign advantages likely produce a modest but potentially consequential improvement in the campaign's vote share compared to historical expectations. This is consistent with our expectations and corroborates other recent research on the topic. There are important nuances to the overall story, though. For starters, these effects exclude vice-presidential appearances, which seem to have produced a wide range of results and are, overall, negative and statistically insignificant. More importantly, these effects were more sizable and less predictable in the first era of campaigning. Prior to 1976, TV spot buy ad effects on vote shifts were both highly variable and (often) counterproductive for the campaign that aired them. In contrast, presidential candidate appearances were powerfully and consistently correlated with positive shifts in the party's share of the vote. Since 1976, however, TV spot buy advertising and presidential candidate appearance effects have become smaller and more predictable. Even the unexpected negative vice-presidential appearance effects are significantly smaller since 1976.

This over time variation could reflect differences in the strategic dispensation of campaign resources. It may be that these "early" campaigns allocated TV spot buys and candidate appearances in places and at times and with messages that had less reliable or consistently positive impact than in later eras. Thinking about TV ad spending, it is probably worth remembering that national television ad buys were commonplace during the first era, with the Republicans outspending the Democrats nationwide and at the state level in most of these contests. This national-level spending (which is not accounted for in our models) could distort the estimated impact of local TV spending differentials in the first era. The apparently distinctive effects prior to 1976 could also reflect differences in the electorate's consumption of electoral politics and presidential campaigns during this initial era. Perhaps voters in the 1950s and 1960s were not used to getting (or taking seriously) information conveyed by political ads on television or by news coverage of campaign visits. Or maybe these ad buys were not sufficiently large in the early days to produce detectable positive movement. Or maybe the messages in these early ads were every bit as corny to historical voters as they seem to viewers today.

As we hinted at earlier, if we further expand our perspective to include party system shifts, it seems conceivable that differences in the reactions of voters across eras might also reflect features of the American electorate at different points in time. In the 1950s and 1960s, the New Deal coalition was realigning (Petrocik, 1981; Phillips, 1969; Sundquist, 1983). The issues of race and social order caused White Southerners to move away from the Democratic Party toward the Republican Party, while racial and ethnic minorities joined liberal Northerners in shifting from the Republicans to the Democrats. It is therefore possible that voters were already changing from their historical patterns in a way that was difficult for campaigns to magnify or diminish. We wish our data would allow us to tease these different possibilities apart, but unfortunately we are left merely to ponder what our statistical models cannot reveal.

A More Granular Look at TV Ad and Candidate Appearance Effects

One possibility alluded to earlier is that looking for impact at the level of entire states might be the wrong way to properly observe campaign effects. Presidential campaigns tend to target highly populated and geographically large states like California, Florida, Ohio, Pennsylvania, and Texas using multiple region-specific campaigns rather than a single campaign with even saturation across the whole state. Thus, a Republican campaign might produce localized effects (say, in the conservative Florida Panhandle) that are offset by localized effects produced by a Democratic campaign elsewhere (say, in the liberal enclave of Orlando). The obvious solution is to collect and analyze data at the level of the media market.

The Media Market Impact of Differential Activities

Media markets are groups of counties that share a common set of broadcast media stations. Not only are media markets smaller and more numerous than states, but both television advertising and news coverage of candidate appearances are aired at the level of the media market, making this an appropriate level of measurement.[9]

The difficulty is obtaining complete data on television spending and candidate appearances, as well as the presidential vote, at the level of media markets. We were nonetheless able to collect such data for the presidential elections from 1988 through 2020.[10] As with the statewide data, the media market data comes from both campaign sources (Bush and Dukakis for 1988, Bush for 1992, Dole for 1996, Bush for 2000 and 2004) as well as outside media tracking organizations such as Kantar's Campaign Media Analysis Group (CMAG) and Advertising Analytics' Media Monitor for more recent elections.[11] To estimate campaign effects based on these market-level data, we use a statistical modeling strategy similar to the one we used for the state-level data. The dependent variable is the difference between the Republican share of the two-party vote in each election minus a weighted historical average.[12] Television spending for each campaign is calculated in 2020 dollar equivalents, and then logged to account for diminishing returns from higher spending levels ("ceiling effects"). Candidate appearances are again measured using a simple count variable. We also include a variable to control for the number of votes in the media market, which captures the possibility that the ability to change the distribution of market-level votes is influenced by market size, as well as election year variables such that fixed effects are accounted for in our models.[13] Finally, we employ a least squares estimator.

While statistical models including separate variables for Republican and Democratic activities are often instructive, here we are more interested in corroborating the general findings from the statewide analyses; we therefore focus on the impact of differential campaign efforts, which seems to us the most accurate and compelling way to judge the impact of the candidates' electioneering. Table 8.3A in the chapter appendix presents the estimated effects of differential partisan presidential campaign efforts at the media market level both overall (1988–2020), as well as by era (1988–2000 and 2004–2020).

The media market vote share models indicate that TV spot buy spending advantages produced a positive—though still modest—vote shift. Moving from parity in TV spot buy spending to a +$100,000 advantage increased vote share compared to the weighted historical average by 0.56 points in the direction of the advantaged campaign. This easily reaches conventional levels of statistical significance. Interestingly, this effect was markedly greater in the second era, 1988–2000, when such an increase in the spot buy differential produced a shift 1.03 points above the average. From 2004 through 2020, the impact at this more granular level fades to statistical insignificance.

As for candidate appearances, at the media market level an extra appearance by a presidential candidate improves the vote shift by about 0.18 percentage points favoring the candidate. This impact is always in the same direction, although it is slightly higher in the second era (+0.25 points) then in the third (+0.11 points). As for vice-presidential candidate appearances, the puzzle of negative effects washes away with the more localized data of the media markets. Overall, increasing the visit differential by a single vice-presidential appearance increases vote share for the candidate's campaign by 0.16 points compared to the historical average, with the second era producing an effect of +0.17 points and the third an effect of +0.10 points. The impact on the campaign of adding an additional vice-presidential candidate visit is always positive and it is always in the direction of helping the candidate's party.

The size of media markets matters as well. The total votes in the media market are associated with pro-Democratic vote shifts compared to historical averages. For every increase of 1 million voters in a market, the vote shift compared to historical average moves toward the Democrats by 0.93 points overall (1.15 points pro-Democratic in the second era and 0.89 points pro-Democratic in the third era). This effect is statistically significant at conventional levels. Again, more populous markets (e.g., New York City, Los Angeles, Chicago, Philadelphia, etc.) tend to be highly urbanized areas that are more likely to already be moving in a pro-Democratic direction over the course of these elections, even controlling for the weighted historical average vote. In addition, the variables for specific election years are mostly significant and in the expected directions.

One might ask whether the estimated effects are potentially artifacts driven by states (or by media markets) that were never targeted by the campaigns. Our analysis includes states or media markets where neither campaign did anything, and potentially this could bias the results.[14] With the states as the unit of analysis, we found only nominal differences when focusing on battleground states or states that lean toward a candidate. Furthermore, excluding uncompetitive, non-battleground states caused some statistical issues—mostly associated with having many fewer cases—that convinced us that this was not worth it. However, with 210 media markets—compared to 50 states plus D.C.—we might gain additional insight by examining effects only in media markets that fall within targeted states. These statistical models that exclude non-contested states are therefore presented in Table 8.4A in the chapter appendix for the interested reader.

Interestingly, if we look only at media markets in battleground states from 1988 through 2020, we estimate that television spot buy advantages are slightly greater overall (compared to our estimates using all media markets), mostly because of the increased impact associated with these efforts in the second era (1988–2000). Overall, if a campaign increased its TV spot buy advertising differential from $0 to +$100,000, the estimated improvement in vote share compared to the weighted historical average is 1.03 points. But this varies considerably across eras: from 1988 through 2000 a similar increase produces a 1.40 point improvement, while from 2004 through 2020 the estimated improvement is only 0.09 points.

These percentage point estimates might seem small, until we translate them into actual numbers of votes on Election Day. If we use the overall effect estimates for Atlanta, Georgia, in 2020, a shift of 1.03 points in a media market with 3,488,410 votes corresponds to moving 35,931 votes from one side to the other. In Detroit, Michigan, it would correspond to moving 28,171 votes. In Miami, Florida, 22,592. In Milwaukee, Wisconsin, 13,495. In Philadelphia, Pennsylvania, 45,996. In Phoenix, Arizona, 28,014. In other words, the estimated impact of one campaign spending a bit more on television ads than the other is undeniably important even when the percentage point impact seems modest at best. While seemingly small in magnitude, advertising effects of this size—when registered in the right states—are easily large enough to have determined the Electoral College winner in 2020.

The estimated effects associated with presidential candidate appearances are positive but slightly smaller when based on only the battleground media markets. Adding one extra appearance in a media market to the differential improves the candidate's vote share compared to the weighted historical average by +0.07 points; the increase is +0.13 points from 1988 through 2000 and +0.04 points from 2004 through 2020. The steep decline in local appearance effects in recent elections is also manifest in the media market data for vice-presidential candidates. The overall vote improvement compared to the weighted historical average for an additional net appearance is +0.24 points; the increase is +0.42 for 1988–2000, and a near-zero −0.03 for 2004–2020.

We thus see little support for the idea that localized appearances by presidential or vice-presidential candidates move the needle very much at the level of media markets, at least in recent elections. Indeed, these numbers suggest candidate appearances in local markets may be eliciting an entirely different reaction now—among voters and perhaps also the local news media (a point we return to later)—than in previous eras.

Discussion

Data from the level of entire states and from smaller media markets tell a similar story with respect to the impact of television ad spending and candidate appearances. Both show modest but positive effects on expected vote share. However, the devil is in the details. The effects associated with the first era of presidential campaigns (1952–1972) suggest that campaigns were not terribly effective, as they struggled to properly target and utilize television advertising. Spot buy advantages did not consistently produce more votes in specific locales, perhaps because in this first era national television advertising was still an important factor. Candidate appearances during these elections also failed to positively move voters. Both results are at least somewhat surprising given the relatively high percentage of persuadable individuals during this period of partisan realignment. Indeed, the television advertising advantages that accrued to Republican campaigns did not seem to add to the expected pro-Republican vote shift. And while the Democrats managed to match the Republicans' activity on the campaign trail, they appear to have been even less effective than Republicans at moving the electorate.[15] As we move to the second era, candidate appearances more consistently have a positive effect, while television advertising advantages—which are more evenly distributed between the parties—become much more predictive of positive vote shifts. In the third era, candidate appearances have a positive yet slightly diminished impact, while television advantages produce approximately the same effect on vote shifts as they had in the second era, even as voters polarize, and persuasion becomes more elusive.

When considering the question of candidate visit effects, it is worth pointing out that one major assumption behind candidates travelling and making speeches in front of local audiences is that local news media will provide favorable coverage of these events. This assumption seems rooted in a compelling logic: local news reporters are more likely than the national press to be favorably inclined toward candidates who take the time to visit their cities or towns. Certainly, they are less likely than reporters from the *New York Times* or the *Wall Street Journal* to author critical articles about a candidate's struggling campaign or low poll standing. But it is unclear whether positive local press coverage was *ever* guaranteed just because the candidate decided to pay a visit. Moreover, even if candidates might have (despite our findings here) elicited positive coverage with their visits in the good old days, local news media increasingly take their cues from their national counterparts (Patterson, 1994) and local newspapers are now dominated by wire service stories provided by Reuters, Bloomberg, and Associated Press (Bennett, 2016). Then there is what we might call counter-mobilization. When a candidate comes to visit, partisans notice and are often mobilized by the appearance. But partisans on the other side may also notice and be mobilized in opposition. This was something the George W. Bush campaign found when analyzing the movements of vice-presidential candidate Dick Cheney (Shaw, 2006). All this is to say that we are not surprised by data showing that candidate appearances might be less likely than ever to produce the positive net impact on local vote totals that campaigners expect.

As for television spot buy spending, the modest changes in Election Day voting associated with differential ad spending by the campaigns should not obscure the fact that Democratic candidates have become increasingly competitive on this front over time. In the early elections of our time series, they were notably outspent by the Republican campaigns. This pro-GOP edge decreased in the second era and reversed in the most recent one.

It is important to again acknowledge that this finding is based only on data from the campaigns' own spending, and therefore does not account for party spending or the spending of outside interest groups on TV advertising (the latter of which is particularly interesting and relevant in the wake of the *Citizens United* and *FEC v McConnell* court decisions). In the second era, for example, the Republican National Committee tended to outspend the Democratic National Committee by a lot, which partially offset Democratic gains at the candidate level (see FEC data for 1976–2000). In elections from 2004 through 2020, the pro-Republican advantage in party and interest group spending has been reduced, and in some cases, eliminated. The Republican National Committee has tended to out-raise and outspend the DNC but left-leaning interest groups—in the form of Super PACs—have almost caught up with their Republican counterparts. Given the sizable ad spending differentials that favored Democratic presidential candidates in 2008, 2012, 2016, and 2020, the Democrats have enjoyed a clear financial edge in recent election cycles. Of course, not all this money is spent on television ads, let alone spot buys. But it is still a major shift in the competitive environment.

So, what can we say in summary about campaign effects brought about by effective execution of a well-crafted Electoral College strategy? Two things at least.

First, campaign effects might be smallish on average, moving perhaps a fraction of a percentage of Election Day votes, but when paired with a well-constructed Electoral College strategy, our analysis shows that even smallish effects in the right states can be potentially decisive for Election Day victory.

This insight suggests that a campaign's macro-targeting strategy might matter as much as—and perhaps even more than—its micro-targeting tactics.

Second, while the available technologies for finding and engaging individual voters have improved by leaps and bounds over the past seventy years, and while the varieties of information stored about every potential voter in the country far exceed what campaigners in 1952 could ever have imagined, we see only trace evidence that presidential campaigns today are appreciably better at moving voters than the campaigns of the 1950s. At the same time, the impact of campaign effects has become more consistently predictable over time, with campaign activities consistently moving Election Day votes in the intended directions in recent campaigns compared to those of the more distant past. We sense that some of this historical evolution in campaign effects may reflect the growing awareness among campaigners that persuading ambivalent voters is much harder than mobilizing your own likely supporters. But our data unfortunately cannot shed much light on this possibility.

We can say with confidence that the growing degree of party polarization and partisan animosity that has taken root in the United States over the past seven decades must certainly have diminished the possibility for shifting large numbers of votes based on campaign activities alone. In this light, it is remarkable that recent campaigns have still been able to generate the consistent (even if smallish) effects that our analysis demonstrates. It might be harder to move voters today than in the 1950s, but this chapter shows that campaigns still matter for winning the presidency.

Chapter 8 Appendix

Table 8.1A Statistical Models Estimating the Effects of Statewide Campaigning on the Presidential Vote

Dep var = Republican share of the two-party vote – the (weighted) average Republican share of the two-party vote	OVERALL	1952–1972	1976–2000	2004–2020
Log of Republican TV Spot Buy Spending (in millions)	0.059 (0.049)	−0.176 (0.241)	0.062 (0.050)	0.092 (0.062)
Log of Democratic TV Spot Buy Spending (in millions)	−0.017 (0.048)	0.370 (0.220)	−0.070 (0.050)	−0.062 (0.057)
Republican presidential candidate appearances	−0.018 (0.079)	−0.291 (0.190)	0.119 (0.113)	0.072 (0.097)
Democratic presidential candidate appearances	−0.190 (0.089)	−0.316 (0.234)	−0.281 (0.135)	−0.174 (0.109)
Electoral Votes	−0.004 (0.026)	0.111 (0.105)	−0.006 (0.036)	−0.034 (0.022)
1952	13.792*** (1.207)	—	—	—
1956	6.615*** (1.204)	9.765** (3.077)	—	—
1964	−11.729*** (1.186)	−27.266*** (2.936)	—	—
1968	4.678*** (1.192)	−11.068*** (2.926)	—	—
1972	15.930*** (1.173)	0.229 (2.542)	—	—
1976	−5.279*** (1.148)	—	—	—
1980	2.744** (1.147)	—	7.781*** (0.953)	—
1984	4.915*** (1.149)	—	10.032*** (0.949)	—
1988	−2.097* (1.147)	—	3.034*** (0.948)	—
1992	−8.627*** (1.154)	—	−3.575*** (0.954)	—
1996	−5.416*** (1.148)	—	−0.288 (0.955)	—
2000	4.111*** (1.151)	—	9.134*** (0.958)	—
2004	4.025*** (1.152)	—	—	3.799*** (0.647)

(continued)

Table 8.1A Continued

Dep var = Republican share of the two-party vote – the (weighted) average Republican share of the two-party vote	OVERALL	1952–1972	1976–2000	2004–2020
2008	−3.073**	—	—	−3.221
	(1.152)			(0.640)
2012	0.265	—	—	0.120
	(1.150)			(0.640)
2016	2.429*	—	—	2.321***
	(1.143)			(0.629)
Constant	−0.202	13.506	−5.019	0.177
	(0.873)	(1.515)	(0.796)	(0.537)
Standard Error	5.762	8.528	4.754	3.152
Adjusted R-Square	0.586	0.559	0.520	0.367
N	853	241	356	254

Notes: ***P<.001; **P<.01, *P<.05 one-tailed. All equations use a least squares estimator. Standard errors of the coefficients are provided in parentheses.

Table 8.2A Statistical Models Estimating the Effects of Differential Statewide Campaigning on the Presidential Vote

Dep var = Republican share of the two-party vote – the (weighted) average Republican share of the two-party vote	OVERALL	1952–1972	1976–2000	2004–2020
TV spot buy spending differential (log R spending – log D spending)	0.031	−0.245	0.065	0.075
	(0.044)	(0.200)	(0.044)	(0.055)
Presidential candidate appearance differential (R–D)	0.917***	1.258*	0.659*	0.685*
	(0.283)	(0.762)	(0.350)	(0.336)
Vice-presidential candidate appearance differential (R–D)	−0.150	−0.383	−0.080	−0.191
	(0.265)	(0.704)	(0.330)	(0.304)
Electoral Votes	−0.046*	−0.046	−0.040*	−0.048*
	(0.021)	(0.063)	(0.028)	(0.021)
1952	12.950***	—	—	—
	(1.157)			
1956	7.093***	−5.508**	—	—
	(1.176)	(1.858)		

Table 8.2A Continued

Dep var = Republican share of the two-party vote – the (weighted) average Republican share of the two-party vote	OVERALL	1952–1972	1976–2000	2004–2020
1964	−11.747	−24.392***	—	—
	(1.160)	(1.767)		
1968	5.062***	−7.225***	—	—
	(1.171)	(1.830)		
1972	16.252***	3.823*	—	—
	(1.160)	(1.816)		
1976	−4.969***	—	—	—
	(1.148)			
1980	2.666*	—	7.672***	—
	(1.143)		(0.955)	
1984	5.094***	—	10.030***	—
	(1.148)		(0.948)	
1988	−2.088*	—	2.907**	—
	(1.144)		(0.955)	
1992	−8.630***	—	−3.689***	—
	(1.152)		(0.952)	
1996	−5.486***	—	−0.0384	—
	(1.140)		(0.955)	
2000	3.973***	—	8.931***	—
	(1.143)		(0.951)	
2004	3.773***	—	—	3.644***
	(1.146)			(0.641)
2008	−3.261***	—	—	−3.296***
	(1.139)			(0.624)
2012	0.202	—	—	0.131
	(1.142)			(0.630)
2016	2.290*	—	—	2.277***
	(1.139)			(0.622)
Constant	0.120	12.791	−4.947	0.260
	(0.842)	(1.461)	(0.739)	(0.495)
Standard Error	5.749	8.561	4.757	3.136
Adjusted R-Square	0.588	0.556	0.519	0.373
N	853	241	356	254

Notes: ***P<.001; **P<.01, *P<.05 one-tailed. All equations use a least squares estimator. Standard errors of the coefficients are provided in parentheses.

Table 8.3A Statistical Models Estimating the Effects of Differential Media Market Campaigning on the Presidential Vote, 1988–2020

Dep Var = R share of two-party vote in current election compared to weighted average	Overall	1988–2000	2004–2020
TV spot buy spending differential (R logged–D logged)	0.111***	0.205***	−0.054
	(0.028)	(0.047)	(0.030)
Presidential appearance differential (R–D)	0.183*	0.250	0.107*
	(0.109)	(0.241)	(0.088)
Vice presidential appearance differential (R–D)	0.155*	0.174	0.104
	(0.091)	(0.155)	(0.091)
Incumbent president (−1=Dem, 0=open, +1=Rep)	—	—	2.505***
			(0.168)
Total votes (in millions)	−0.929***	−1.147***	−0.893***
	(0.139)	(0.330)	(0.109)
1992	13.068***	−13.124***	—
	(0.447)	(0.584)	
1996	−1.052**	−1.016*	—
	(0.446)	(0.583)	
2004	1.459***	—	—
	(0.447)		
2008	−7.978***	—	−7.029***
	(0.447)		(0.290)
2012	−3.637***	—	—
	(0.449)		
2016	−0.004	—	1.023***
	(0.448)		(0.290)
2020	−2.176***	—	−3.990***
	(0.449)		(0.341)
Constant	5.617	5.758	4.655
	(0.266)	(0.372)	(0.182)
Standard Error	5.225	6.820	3.389
Adjusted R-Square	0.430	0.408	0.501
N	1,853	823	1,029

Notes: *P<.05, **P<.01, ***P<.001, one-tailed. The weighted average is 2 × the R share of the two-party vote in the previous election +1 × the R share of the two-party vote in the election before that ÷ 3. The dependent variable is thus interpreted here as a percentage, such that a coefficient of 0.050 means that a unit increase in the explanatory variable would produce an "over-achievement" of 0.05% in the vote.

Table 8.4A Statistical Models Estimating the Effects of Differential Media Market Campaigning on the Presidential Vote (Battleground States Only)

Dep Var = Rep share of two-party vote in current election compared to weighted average	Overall	1988–2000	2004–2020
TV spot buy spending differential (R logged–D logged)	0.205*** (0.042)	0.279*** (0.062)	0.018 (0.045)
Presidential appearance differential (R–D)	0.068 (0.125)	0.131 (0.261)	0.036 (0.094)
Vice presidential appearance differential (R–D)	0.235* (0.102)	0.417** (0.167)	−0.030 (0.095)
Incumbent president (−1=Dem, 0=open, +1=Rep)	—	—	2.145*** (0.247)
Total votes (in millions)	−1.079*** (0.238)	−0.961* (0.417)	1.360*** (0.206)
2020	−2.298** (0.789)	—	−3.267*** (0.553)
2016	1.364* (0.682)	—	2.887*** (0.431)
2012	−3.862*** (0.683)	—	—
2008	8.828*** (0.629)	—	−7.709*** (0.412)
2004	0.846 (0.665)	—	—
2000	—	—	—
1996	−2.234*** (0.611)	−2.504*** (0.760)	—
1992	−13.191 (0.577)	−13.202 (0.712)	—
Constant	5.833 (0.368)	5.819 (0.478)	4.774 (0.286)
Standard Error	5.157	6.351	3.112
Adjusted R-Square	0.498	0.460	0.64
N	852	459	392

Notes: *P<.05, **P<.01, ***P<.001, one-tailed. Standard errors of the coefficients are provided in parentheses. The weighted average is 2 × the R share of the two-party vote in the previous election +1 × the R share of the two-party vote in the election before that ÷ 3. The dependent variable is thus interpreted here as a percentage, such that a coefficient of 0.050 means that a unit increase in the explanatory variable would produce an "over-achievement" of 0.05% in the vote.

9 The Past, the Present, and the Future of Presidential Campaigns

In many ways, presidential campaigns have changed dramatically since the 1950s. Candidates and their allies have had to adapt to ever-changing social and political contexts. In this book, we argue that the most fundamental shifts over the past seven decades or so have occurred across three distinct eras that transformed the backdrop against which presidential campaigns unfold. Changing landscapes have included evolving campaign finance regimes as well as the advent and proliferation of mass communications technologies, most notably television and, later, the Internet and digital media. Sociopolitical developments like intensifying partisanship and the growing partisan polarization over this period have also affected political campaign strategies. Other factors that contributed to transforming how campaigns operate in the modern era include growing campaign professionalization, refinements of and accessibility to polling and survey research methods, and, eventually, micro-targeting, big data, and analytics capabilities (Panagopoulos, 2017). With each of these developments—and many others—presidential campaigns have struggled to keep pace with the shifts and to leverage their potential opportunities while at the same time avoiding the inevitable pitfalls and challenges these changes presented. This creates a natural tempo where each successive contest produces new refinements and novel learning opportunities as it confronts an ever-changing landscape of electoral contestation. Campaigning at the presidential level has never been easy, or routine.

In other ways, however, the path to the White House has been remarkably stable. Despite the steady stream of momentous change we describe, the basic institutional (and constitutional) infrastructure and processes governing presidential selection in the United States have remained essentially unchanged. Candidates still need to be first nominated by their respective parties and then to amass at least 270 electoral votes to win the presidency. The constitutional scheme that assigns electoral votes to states based on the size of the population and state-based systems of winner-take-all allocations of electoral

Battleground. Daron R. Shaw, Scott L. Althaus, and Costas Panagopoulos, Oxford University Press.
 DOI: 10.1093/oso/9780197774366.003.0009

votes in each state (apart from Maine and Nebraska) still reign supreme in dictating electoral strategies. Moreover, despite changing circumstances over time, campaign resources (like time and money) remain finite, so presidential campaigns must be strategic in deploying these scarce resources to maximize impact and prospects for victory.

In this volume, we have documented both continuity and change in electoral strategies for president in the modern era. Even as the Electoral College setup creates incentives for presidential campaigns to prioritize certain states—namely, competitive or battleground states in which the outcome is not a foregone conclusion—our analyses have revealed evolution in strategic choices over time. For example, we found that presidential campaigns increasingly (and especially in the most recent era) direct resources and attention to a shrinking subset of battleground states. This implies that majorities of Americans residing in less competitive states may increasingly be overlooked by presidential campaigns, except insofar as indirect exposure to campaign activities may reach them. This possibility has important consequences for democracy as both preference formation (Panagopoulos, 2009) and turnout (Bergan et al., 2005) are more pronounced among voters in battleground states compared to their counterparts in less competitive environments. While we might wish that the attention of every voter was taken equally seriously by the campaigns, it is important to remember that doing so is a nearly certain path to electoral defeat unless your opponent also takes this higher road. Winning the election is what opens the door to serving the public, so winning must come first. And to win the White House, the battleground is king.

Despite this truism, even today presidential campaigning remains as much art as science. The most seasoned operatives using the most advanced technologies still fall prey to flawed expectations and unwise choices. For example, when the Kerry campaign folded in 2004 its bank account still contained $17 million unspent out of the $74.6 million in general election public funds that Senator Kerry had received as the Democratic nominee (Shaw, 2006). As Shaw (2006: 149) noted, spending an extra three million over the last two weeks in Iowa and New Mexico could have flipped those states, and an extra $10 million would have produced a virtual tie in Ohio. A similar case could be made about the Bush campaign in 2000, which during early October expended substantial resources in California of all places, one of the most solid of the Democratic base states. There were reasons for doing so, but redirecting those efforts to Florida, Wisconsin, Iowa, Oregon, or New Mexico would have provided more bang for the bucks (Shaw, 2006).[1] In 2016, critics contend that Hillary Clinton took for granted Democratic strongholds in the industrial Midwest—the so-called blue wall—in her historic but failed campaign. It was the first time a Democratic presidential candidate had lost in Wisconsin since 1984, and critics often assert that her failure to visit the Badger State during the fall campaign cost her a victory there. Even as scholarly analyses debunk this claim (Devine, 2018), Clinton herself conceded in her memoir that Wisconsin was "the one place where we were caught by surprise" (Clinton, 2017), because internal data consistently suggested the Democratic ticket was not in danger. We may never know what would have happened if different decisions were made in 2016. And that is true about any presidential race. Hindsight may be 20/20, but presidential campaigns cannot be replayed with different choices, and we may never know if some decisions—whether good or bad—might have been sufficient to alter the outcomes.

Our book has focused almost exclusively on electoral strategy and on the strategic allocation of resources in presidential campaigns. We view this as the most fundamental set of decisions presidential campaigns can make. But we concede that other decisions and strategic choices are also crucial. We have little to say about strategic priorities that presidential campaigns face. For example, we do not grapple with the sorts of ideological or policy positions that presidential campaigns adopt, even though prior studies have clearly shown that both the kinds of messages that campaigns emphasize (Vavreck, 2009) and how they do so (Hillygus and Shields, 2008) affect the chances of winning. Our analyses also do not focus much on the temporal dimensions of strategic deployment of resources, even though we concede that the timing of candidate spending and visits can shift preferences and influence election outcomes (Gerber et al., 2011; Shaw, 1999). Campaign effects can also be more pronounced at the outset, but decay quickly (Gerber et al., 2011; Hill et al., 2013). Furthermore, our study does not contend with how effectively or efficiently presidential campaigns allocated resources, nor do we examine the audience characteristics or receptivity, nor the tone, nature or content of the appeals deployed. Strategic choices about how and when presidential campaigns spend time and money can be as important (maybe even more important at times) as where these resources are spent. Although we do not diminish the influence of these decisions, we remain agnostic about the relative impact of these strategic choices. All we wish to say is that electoral strategy in presidential campaigns—which guides strategic deployment of resources to certain states over others—matters too. And as we have shown throughout this book, electoral strategy can matter more—perhaps far more—than some campaign outsiders have previously recognized.

The 2024 Election and Beyond

As we approach the 2024 presidential election cycle and beyond, what insights can our findings offer about what electoral strategies might look like down the road? We should start by stipulating that any such speculation assumes two things: that campaign resources will remain scarce and that the basic Electoral College framework currently in place remains intact. We realize, of course, that abolishing the Electoral College in favor of the national popular vote has been a popular enterprise among reformers since the founding of the republic. We also recognize that initiatives like the National Popular Vote Interstate Compact—an agreement among states to award their votes to the winner of the national popular vote regardless of how their respective states vote—has attracted, as of 2023, support from 16 states and the District of Columbia constituting 205 electoral votes (which amounts to 76% of the 270 needed to give the compact legal force). So, while it is conceivable that efforts to abolish (or circumvent) the Electoral College will eventually bear fruit, we view these currently as long shots facing uphill practical, political, and constitutional battles. As a result, presidential campaign strategies in 2024 and beyond will continue to reflect Electoral College priorities for the foreseeable future.

That said, the electoral math will look slightly different in 2024 and 2028 if only because of the reapportionment put in place after the completion of the 2020 decennial census. As Ed Gilgore put it, "[t]he map never stops changing" (Kilgore, 2023). Population shifts resulted in electoral vote (and congressional seat) changes in thirteen states following the 2020 census, and this is this map that will govern the 2024 and 2028 presidential races. Texas was the big winner, gaining two electoral votes (after gaining four electoral votes in the 2010 census). Colorado, Florida, Montana, North Carolina, and Oregon each gained one electoral vote, while shrinking populations caused California, Illinois, Michigan, New York, Ohio, Pennsylvania, and West Virginia to each lose one electoral vote after the 2020 census.

In 2020, Biden garnered 306 electoral votes to best Trump (232 electoral votes). If the 2020 race were to be replayed using the 2024 map, Biden's electoral vote count would drop by six (to 300) and Trump would gain six votes (238). Among the seven states that lost a seat in the 2020 reapportionment, Biden won in five (California, Illinois, Michigan, New York, and Pennsylvania), while Trump won in Ohio and West Virginia. This implies a net gain of three electoral votes to Trump. Trump also won Texas in 2020, adding another two electoral votes to his tally. In the five other states that gained seats in the 2020 reapportionment, Biden won in two (Colorado and Oregon) while Trump bested him in three (Montana, North Carolina, and Florida), amounting to a net gain of another electoral vote to Trump in these states, for a total net gain of six electoral votes due to reapportionment alone. Of course, Biden would still win the election, but his electoral advantage would shrink.

Reapportionment can reshape the electoral map, but there are other ways in which the map can shift. Demographic changes, mobility, and fluctuating political preferences can also shake things up. Democrats have been hopeful that demographic momentum would push Texas, a reliably Republican state, in a blue direction, for example. While the Lone Star state has not shed its ruby-red tinge quite yet, it is worth noting that Trump won the popular vote in Texas by only six percentage points in 2020, compared to nine in 2016. The slight blue drift in Texas may be compromised by a particularly intriguing, recent political-demographic development: Latinos seem to be much less reliably Democratic over the past two election cycles. This movement can easily be overstated, as Latinos remain more Democratic than Republican in their partisan predispositions. But the "emerging Democratic majority" thesis depends heavily on a 2:1 Democratic tilt among this segment of the electorate that may be a thing of the past (Judis and Teixeira, 2004). States with burgeoning Latino populations, such as Texas, Arizona, Florida, and Nevada, may be wildcards moving forward. Whether certain groups realign or not, we expect that some states will still be more important than others because these will represent the places where the campaign will be fought and where resources will be strategically allocated.

Which states will be decisive in 2024 and 2028? At a minimum, we expect that at least six states will be critical in the next few election cycles. Georgia ended up as the closest battleground state in 2020. Biden's razor-thin 0.2 percentage point victory over Trump in 2020—after Trump won the state by 5.2 percentage points in 2016—almost guarantees the Peach state will be a key battleground in 2024. Similarly, the margin of Biden's victory in Arizona in 2020 was 0.3 percentage points; Trump won it by 3.6 percentage points in 2016. The Grand Canyon state is almost certainly in play for 2024. North Carolina, decided in Trump's favor by 1.3 percentage points in 2020, is also up for grabs in 2024, and it is difficult to imagine a winning GOP coalition that excludes North Carolina at this stage. In the Rust Belt, the three blue wall states shifted (in unison, as they have since 1992) from red to blue in 2020, but it is worth noting that the margins in these states were still quite close. Michigan, perhaps the biggest reach for Republicans, was decided by 2.8 percentage points in 2020 (in Biden's favor, after Trump won it by 0.2 percentage points in 2016), but the margins in both Wisconsin and Pennsylvania remained quite narrow (0.6 and 1.2 percentage points, respectively, in Biden's favor, both from

0.7 percentage points in Trump's favor in 2016). Among these, Wisconsin may be the best bet for Republicans in 2024: it was the only state won by Biden that elected a Republican (incumbent Ron Johnson) to the U.S. Senate in the 2022 midterms. But all three of these blue wall states could be potentially decisive components of a winning strategy in 2024. Nevada (Biden won by 2.4 percentage points in 2020) has moved to the left in recent cycles, while Florida (Trump won by 3.4 percentage points in 2020) has moved to the right, but both could be on target lists in 2024 and perhaps beyond. A more expansive list of "in play" states could include Minnesota, New Hampshire, Ohio, Iowa, Maine, and Texas, which were each decided by less than 10 percentage points in 2020. Of course, whether the 2020 outcomes reflect ephemeral shifts due to peculiar circumstances (e.g., Trump, COVID-19) or enduring patterns remains in question. Based on the analyses in this book, however, and as of this writing, we expect this is where the lion's share of campaign spending and visits will be concentrated in 2024. And what happens in 2024 will, to a great extent, shape what the constellation of competitive states will be in 2028 and so on, noting that the electoral map in 2032 and for the two successive presidential elections that follow will be governed by the reapportionment implemented after the 2030 census is completed.

Closing Thoughts

This book represents an ambitious undertaking: collecting, documenting, and analyzing detailed and novel information about presidential campaign electoral strategies since 1952. The voluminous data we compiled affords observers the most comprehensive, under-the-hood glimpse ever assembled about actual presidential campaigns' game plans. We have strived to extract some useful insights into how presidential campaigns devise and implement campaign strategies and to examine the impact of these decisions on voting outcomes. As much as we hope this study makes a valuable contribution, we are mindful that we have only scratched the surface in terms of analyzing how presidential campaigns operate and unfold.

Along these lines, we think it is important to note several limitations that are certainly part of the larger picture of presidential campaign strategy. For instance, our study essentially bypasses questions about the role special interests and allied groups play in shaping presidential election outcomes. We recognize these players represent essential actors in presidential selection, often outpacing candidate spending and other activities with independent activities that are, theoretically anyway, uncoordinated with candidates' efforts.

In practice, these groups' activities often overlap quite closely with candidates' choices (Panagopoulos, 2006), so a more complete analysis might incorporate some material along these lines. We also focus almost exclusively on the general election contests, even though this book's historical chapters showed how primary politics and nomination races may help shape general election strategies and influence outcomes. Our analyses are also restricted to spot television and campaign visit data, although we realize that candidates spend enormous sums on other activities, including get-out-the-vote efforts and advertising spending in other media. We acknowledge these limitations, as well as others we have described earlier in this volume, to emphasize the complexity of presidential campaign strategy and implementation.

In the end, no single volume may ever be able to fully capture the nuance of these quadrennial events. It was certainly not our aim to do so. Our goal was primarily to put some meat on the bones of what we can glean about presidential campaign strategy by undertaking a systematic study of the information available from actual presidential campaigns in the modern era. A full understanding of what happened in presidential elections would be incomplete, at best, without some sense of the strategic calculations and choices candidates' campaigns made during these cycles. We hope the light we have shed on this topic has not only brought these campaigns to life in fresh ways, but also shown how the sophisticated nature of presidential campaign strategy in recent years is not without precedent: earlier campaigns were developing extremely sophisticated strategies and tactics to pursue them long before micro-targeting and digital media were ever even the stuff of dreams. In many ways, our analysis has shown just how much harder it is to produce reliable Election Day effects today than it used to be in mid-twentieth century contests with relatively less complicated communication ecosystems. At the least, we hope that the book has fostered an appreciation for how strategic decisions about resource allocation in presidential campaigns can shape the direction of public policy, life, and society in the United States and—given the outsized role that the U.S. president has played over this period—can even influence the broader contours of history across the modern world.

APPENDIX

Strategy Categorization, Candidate Appearances, and Ad Spending by State, 1952–2020

State	1952								1956							
	Rep. E.C. Strategy	Dem. E.C. Strategy	Rep. Pres. Visits	Dem. Pres. Visits	Rep. VP Visits	Dem. VP Visits	Rep. Spot Buy Spending (2020$)	Dem. Spot Buy Spending (2020$)	Rep. E.C. Strategy	Dem. E.C. Strategy	Rep. Pres. Visits	Dem. Pres. Visits	Rep. VP Visits	Dem. VP Visits	Rep. Spot Buy Spending (2020$)	Dem. Spot Buy Spending (2020$)
Alabama	−2	−2	1	0	0	2	$—	$—	−2	−2	0	0	0	0	$22,627	$109,893
Alaska	—	—	0	0	0	0	$—	$—	—	—	0	0	0	0	$72,475	$30,851
Arizona	−2	0	2	2	0	1	$28,294	$5,733	2	0	1	1	1	2	$241,648	$562,316
Arkansas	−2	−2	1	0	0	1	$—	$—	−2	−2	0	0	0	0	$39,579	$141,930
California	1	0	11	20	23	10	$—	$42,152	0	0	2	10	20	10	$1,835,110	$1,728,668
Colorado	2	2	0	2	3	3	$79,216	$—	2	1	1	1	2	1	$305,846	$217,657
Connecticut	0	0	7	15	2	0	$56,587	$5,420	0	0	0	2	5	1	$1,226,396	$641,474
Delaware	0	2	1	1	1	1	$30,559	$—	0	0	0	0	1	2	$150,899	$94,746
D.C.	—	—	2	0	1	3	$—	$—	—	—	9	2	5	5	$252,201	$87,235
Florida	−2	−2	1	2	0	4	$—	$—	0	1	2	2	1	6	$576,069	$736,692
Georgia	−2	−2	0	0	0	2	$—	$—	−2	−2	0	0	0	0	$85,955	$339,782
Hawaii	—	—	0	0	0	0	$—	$—	—	—	0	0	0	0	$1,059	$13,291
Iowa	2	2	12	3	6	3	$—	$—	2	2	5	0	1	5	$390,123	$453,462
Idaho	2	2	0	0	0	0	$—	$—	2	1	0	1	1	1	$66,853	$60,548
Illinois	2	0	16	19	13	5	$656,367	$38,900	0	0	1	10	9	15	$2,204,830	$2,198,872
Indiana	1	2	8	6	8	0	$—	$—	2	0	0	2	4	0	$1,472,607	$962,835
Kansas	2	2	0	0	0	1	$—	$—	2	2	0	1	1	2	$556,746	$492,610
Kentucky	0	0	3	4	0	0	$—	$7,598	0	0	2	2	1	4	$591,468	$619,141
Louisiana	−2	−2	1	1	0	3	$—	$—	−2	−2	0	1	0	0	$263,330	$254,487
Maine	1	2	0	0	11	0	$—	$—	2	2	0	0	0	0	$172,445	$121,107
Maryland	0	2	6	3	6	1	$—	$—	0	1	0	2	2	4	$599,524	$471,672
Massachusetts	0	0	12	13	8	0	$254,622	$15,812	0	0	1	8	3	5	$1,717,140	$1,021,548
Michigan	0	0	11	13	14	0	$413,064	$31,770	0	0	0	9	12	7	$3,689,270	$1,494,888
Minnesota	0	0	9	3	7	3	$—	$8,370	0	0	3	1	2	21	$776,879	$722,593

Mississippi	−2	−2	0	0	0	0	$—	$—	−2	−2	0	0	0	0	$32,110	$47,709
Missouri	0	0	11	3	6	4	$—	$22,473	0	−1	0	2	1	5	$467,057	$579,740
Montana	0	0	6	1	1	2	$—	$6,504	2	0	0	1	1	1	$309,539	$248,676
Nebraska	1	2	5	0	1	7	$—	$—	2	2	0	0	1	2	$64,681	$72,161
Nevada	0	0	0	0	2	0	$8,487	$2,481	2	0	0	0	2	1	$141,468	$103,505
New Hampshire	2	2	2	0	0	0	$—	$—	2	2	0	0	1	1	$107,481	$22,952
New Jersey	0	0	7	6	11	0	$—	$1,856	0	1	0	10	1	6	$262,260	$123,226
New Mexico	−2	−2	1	1	0	3	$15,275	$—	0	0	0	1	0	4	$254,057	$379,234
New York	0	0	43	28	14	14	$1,459,857	$71,295	0	0	2	16	9	10	$2,504,078	$2,358,225
North Carolina	−2	−2	2	0	0	1	$—	$—	−2	−2	0	0	0	0	$133,852	$142,108
North Dakota	1	2	3	0	0	0	$—	$—	2	0	0	0	1	2	$219,839	$202,142
Ohio	0	0	14	16	14	5	$—	$39,984	0	0	1	7	12	14	$3,406,764	$1,144,742
Oklahoma	2	−2	2	1	3	3	$—	$—	0	−1	0	4	1	4	$326,711	$251,540
Oregon	2	2	4	2	8	2	$—	$—	2	0	3	1	2	4	$855,690	$761,920
Pennsylvania	0	0	8	15	14	6	$548,858	$34,407	0	0	5	15	14	10	$2,965,471	$2,391,049
Rhode Island	−2	−2	1	2	1	0	$—	$—	0	−2	0	2	1	1	$180,334	$305,175
South Carolina	−2	−2	1	0	0	1	$—	$—	−2	−2	0	0	0	0	$16,050	$99,749
South Dakota	2	2	1	0	0	1	$—	$—	2	2	0	0	1	2	$244,312	$219,168
Tennessee	−2	−2	2	1	2	2	$—	$—	0	−1	0	0	1	2	$332,019	$158,535
Texas	−2	0	6	5	8	3	$311,210	$42,777	0	0	0	0	4	6	$1,224,225	$526,504
Utah	0	0	1	1	2	1	$—	$4,180	2	0	0	0	1	1	$326,061	$131,534
Vermont	1	2	0	0	0	0	$—	$—	2	2	0	0	0	0	$81,329	$48,936
Virginia	−2	−2	5	4	4	1	$—	$—	0	−1	1	2	0	0	$243,557	$157,046
Washington	0	0	10	3	1	0	$—	$11,466	0	0	2	1	2	3	$684,011	$736,828
West Virginia	0	−2	8	1	2	7	$—	$—	−2	−2	0	2	1	2	$646,688	$590,241
Wisconsin	0	0	6	4	7	0	$—	$10,069	2	1	0	1	1	1	$1,085,201	$385,298
Wyoming	0	2	2	2	4	4	$5,088	$2,481	2	0	0	0	0	1	$78,696	$45,684

(*continued*)

State	1960								1964							
	Rep. E.C. Strategy	Dem. E.C. Strategy	Rep. Pres. Visits	Dem. Pres. Visits	Rep. VP Visits	Dem. VP Visits	Rep. Spot Buy Spending (2020$)	Dem. Spot Buy Spending (2020$)	Rep. E.C. Strategy	Dem. E.C. Strategy	Rep. Pres. Visits	Dem. Pres. Visits	Rep. VP Visits	Dem. VP Visits	Rep. Spot Buy Spending (2020$)	Dem. Spot Buy Spending (2020$)
Alabama	—	—	0	0	0	6	—	—	0	2	1	0	0	0	$124,954	$559,375
Alaska	2	2	1	2	0	0	—	—	−2	−2	0	0	0	0	$58,940	$87,241
Arizona	2	2	1	2	0	2	—	—	2	2	10	1	1	1	$306,490	$203,949
Arkansas	−2	−2	1	1	0	0	—	—	0	2	0	0	0	2	$117,881	$222,285
California	1	0	16	30	8	7	—	—	0	0	14	8	14	15	$3,048,677	$1,417,618
Colorado	0	0	1	1	0	0	—	—	2	2	1	1	2	2	$530,463	$367,751
Connecticut	2	0	4	4	5	2	—	—	0	−2	0	1	5	1	$436,705	$413,617
Delaware	−2	−2	1	1	0	2	—	—	−2	−2	1	2	1	0	$9,185	$—
D.C.	—	—	7	4	5	6	—	—	−2	−2	7	12	10	11	$—	$—
Florida	0	1	4	4	2	11	—	—	0	0	0	9	4	4	$1,253,252	$1,084,360
Georgia	−2	−2	0	3	0	1	—	—	0	2	3	3	2	4	$628,371	$442,951
Hawaii	−2	−2	0	0	0	0	—	—	−2	−2	0	0	0	0	$17,682	$129,367
Iowa	0	0	7	3	0	0	—	—	−2	−2	5	1	5	4	$240,063	$655,007
Idaho	2	2	1	1	0	0	—	—	2	2	1	1	2	1	$25,934	$177,897
Illinois	0	0	19	40	8	5	—	—	0	0	17	5	6	7	$2,095,850	$1,026,439
Indiana	2	2	3	8	2	5	—	—	2	0	8	4	8	6	$313,125	$418,811
Kansas	2	0	2	1	0	1	—	—	2	2	2	1	2	2	$337,048	$364,711
Kentucky	2	1	1	6	0	3	—	—	2	−2	2	2	0	3	$707,285	$352,721
Louisiana	−2	−1	1	0	0	1	—	—	0	2	2	1	2	0	$709,758	$685,401
Maine	2	2	1	4	1	0	—	—	0	−2	1	1	2	1	$288,075	$218,052
Maryland	0	0	1	4	4	3	—	—	0	0	2	3	0	1	$584,689	$495,746
Massachusetts	−2	−1	1	5	6	1	—	—	−2	0	1	1	0	2	$252,265	$—
Michigan	0	0	12	17	2	0	—	—	−2	0	1	2	1	7	$200,400	$1,422,758
Minnesota	−2	0	3	4	2	2	—	—	−2	0	1	0	3	5	$112,725	$—
Mississippi	−2	—	1	0	0	4	—	—	0	2	0	0	0	0	$84,335	$359,693

Missouri	−2	0	4	8	1	4	—	—	−2	0	3	2	3	3	$1,067,865	$1,253,302
Montana	2	2	1	1	0	1	—	—	2	2	1	2	2	1	$93,520	$231,704
Nebraska	2	2	1	0	0	2	—	—	2	2	1	2	3	0	$436,981	$354,090
Nevada	2	2	0	0	0	1	—	—	−2	−2	2	1	2	1	$65,548	$119,347
New Hampshire	2	2	1	2	1	0	—	—	0	−2	1	1	1	1	$70,975	$53,440
New Jersey	0	0	9	11	6	3	—	—	0	0	4	3	5	6	$758,790	$795,137
New Mexico	2	2	1	1	0	5	—	—	−2	−2	1	2	3	1	$94,355	$138,785
New York	−1	0	19	28	36	6	—	—	0	0	4	7	18	10	$1,218,357	$1,317,318
North Carolina	−2	−1	1	5	2	8	—	—	0	2	3	1	6	1	$206,291	$933,806
North Dakota	2	0	1	1	0	0	—	—	2	2	1	0	1	2	$69,305	$208,625
Ohio	0	0	18	22	8	4	—	—	0	0	18	3	4	8	$1,566,911	$810,296
Oklahoma	2	1	1	1	0	2	—	—	2	2	1	3	3	2	$202,905	$477,077
Oregon	0	1	1	3	2	0	—	—	−2	−2	3	1	3	2	$431,027	$431,202
Pennsylvania	−1	0	19	30	18	6	—	—	0	0	15	6	9	10	$2,503,430	$2,247,962
Rhode Island	−2	−2	0	1	0	0	—	—	−2	−2	0	1	2	0	$417,492	$381,411
South Carolina	−2	−2	1	1	0	9	—	—	0	2	2	1	0	0	$517,024	$430,317
South Dakota	2	0	1	2	0	1	—	—	2	2	1	0	3	5	$78,980	$214,712
Tennessee	2	1	2	4	1	4	—	—	0	−2	5	3	1	3	$1,401,957	$829,965
Texas	0	0	4	11	4	26	—	—	0	0	14	10	4	4	$4,173,330	$4,397,462
Utah	2	2	1	1	0	1	—	—	2	2	1	1	2	1	$82,517	$155,477
Vermont	2	2	1	0	0	0	—	—	0	−2	1	1	1	1	$88,411	$125,726
Virginia	0	1	3	2	1	7	—	—	0	2	0	2	0	1	$64,834	$552,102
Washington	0	0	2	2	2	1	—	—	−2	−2	2	2	1	3	$462,122	$619,127
West Virginia	−2	0	2	1	1	1	—	—	−2	−2	1	1	0	2	$91,947	$486,797
Wisconsin	0	0	4	4	4	0	—	—	0	0	3	1	5	6	$530,463	$504,332
Wyoming	2	2	1	2	0	0	—	—	2	2	1	1	1	1	$117,881	$142,426

(continued)

	1968								1972							
State	Rep. E.C. Strategy	Dem. E.C. Strategy	Rep. Pres. Visits	Dem. Pres. Visits	Rep. VP Visits	Dem. VP Visits	Rep. Spot Buy Spending (2020$)	Dem. Spot Buy Spending (2020$)	Rep. E.C. Strategy	Dem. E.C. Strategy	Rep. Pres. Visits	Dem. Pres. Visits	Rep. VP Visits	Dem. VP Visits	Rep. Spot Buy Spending (2020$)	Dem. Spot Buy Spending (2020$)
Alabama	—	—	0	0	0	0	$64,728	$26,040	−1	2	0	0	2	0	$43,027	$53,500
Alaska	2	1	0	0	1	0	$32,364	$8,184	0	0	0	0	0	0	$36,942	$17,765
Arizona	2	2	0	0	0	0	$174,096	$182,280	2	2	0	0	0	1	$6,407	$619
Arkansas	—	—	0	0	0	2	$52,824	$64,728	−1	2	0	1	0	1	$103,763	$111,474
California	0	1	8	14	7	6	$6,688,560	$3,623,280	0	0	7	12	5	6	$2,568,794	$1,761,315
Colorado	2	0	1	1	0	2	$260,400	$256,680	2	2	0	3	1	1	$—	$—
Connecticut	−2	−2	1	4	0	2	$465,000	$83,328	−1	0	0	0	1	4	$373,337	$12,529
Delaware	−2	−2	0	1	0	0	$5,952	$5,952	0	0	0	0	1	1	$—	$—
D.C.	−2	−2	6	6	6	6	$—	$—	−2	−2	14	4	7	4	$294,830	$12,071
Florida	0	2	4	1	2	2	$3,013,200	$1,331,760	1	2	0	0	1	1	$59,152	$18,353
Georgia	—	—	1	0	0	0	$416,640	$146,568	−1	2	1	0	2	0	$4,110	$104,017
Hawaii	−2	−2	0	0	2	0	$98,208	$33,480	−2	−2	1	0	0	0	$50,250	$53,985
Iowa	2	2	0	0	1	1	$178,560	$200,880	2	0	0	4	1	3	$114,707	$123,231
Idaho	2	2	1	5	0	0	$81,840	$17,112	2	2	0	0	1	0	$223	$619
Illinois	0	0	1	1	2	5	$5,022,000	$2,339,880	0	0	1	12	4	9	$1,096,292	$615,639
Indiana	2	2	1	0	0	2	$1,740,960	$736,560	2	2	0	0	1	4	$7,465	$16,051
Kansas	2	2	0	0	0	2	$139,128	$89,280	2	2	0	1	0	0	$4,383	$483
Kentucky	2	2	0	1	1	1	$171,120	$90,024	2	2	0	1	2	0	$131,575	$17,431
Louisiana	—	—	1	1	0	0	$156,240	$74,400	−1	2	0	0	1	0	$25,670	$27,578
Maine	−2	−2	0	0	0	8	$130,200	$2,009	2	2	0	1	0	1	$37,716	$40,518
Maryland	−2	0	0	2	14	2	$260,400	$272,304	0	0	4	1	2	1	$376,748	$79,789
Massachusetts	−2	−2	1	2	1	5	$156,240	$—	−2	−2	0	2	0	5	$351,233	$193,821
Michigan	0	−2	3	5	2	2	$884,616	$578,832	0	0	1	8	2	5	$660,912	$479,279
Minnesota	−2	−2	1	6	2	1	$13,764	$—	−2	−2	0	4	1	1	$340,431	$149,204
Mississippi	—	—	0	0	0	0	$93,000	$15,624	−1	2	0	0	1	0	$3,695	$3,970

Missouri	0	−2	2	5	4	3	$833,280	$407,712	0	2	0	3	2	2	$364,529	$189,853
Montana	2	2	0	0	1	0	$111,600	$8,184	2	2	0	1	1	1	$33,853	$36,369
Nebraska	2	2	0	0	0	0	$305,040	$182,280	2	2	0	0	1	0	$9,799	$10,527
Nevada	2	0	0	1	1	1	$147,312	$23,808	2	2	0	0	1	1	$21,176	$22,750
New Hampshire	2	2	0	0	0	0	$55,800	$8,184	2	2	0	0	1	1	$526	$565
New Jersey	0	−2	2	4	1	4	$604,872	$420,360	0	0	0	6	0	11	$50,968	$8,666
New Mexico	2	0	0	1	1	0	$99,696	$34,224	2	2	1	2	1	0	$51,191	$54,996
New York	0	−2	9	16	4	7	$8,347,680	$6,033,840	−1	0	5	20	5	8	$1,973,799	$1,283,237
North Carolina	0	1	2	1	1	0	$177,816	$32,736	1	2	1	0	2	0	$4,890	$7,125
North Dakota	2	2	0	0	0	0	$81,840	$17,112	2	2	0	0	0	0	$8,530	$1,052
Ohio	0	0	5	10	4	4	$5,341,920	$2,521,416	0	0	5	11	1	7	$1,312,119	$316,953
Oklahoma	2	2	1	0	0	3	$206,832	$20,088	2	2	1	0	0	0	$2,835	$3,046
Oregon	2	0	0	1	1	1	$334,800	$288,672	0	0	0	2	0	1	$194,966	$90,813
Pennsylvania	0	−2	4	8	4	15	$5,996,640	$2,648,640	−1	0	3	16	1	10	$1,042,359	$764,019
Rhode Island	−2	−2	0	0	0	0	$156,240	$107,136	−2	−2	1	0	0	0	$129,000	$23,163
South Carolina	0	1	0	0	1	0	$205,344	$159,960	1	2	0	1	1	1	$2,191	$2,354
South Dakota	2	2	0	3	0	0	$128,712	$34,745	1	−2	0	2	1	1	$130,231	$10,851
Tennessee	−1	2	2	1	2	2	$495,504	$398,040	1	2	0	0	2	0	$8,790	$7,242
Texas	0	−2	7	9	4	6	$1,674,000	$1,629,360	0	0	5	9	3	10	$803,778	$227,458
Utah	2	2	1	1	0	2	$33,480	$11,606	2	2	0	0	1	0	$7,614	$8,180
Vermont	2	2	0	0	0	1	$8,928	$18,079	2	2	0	0	0	0	$—	$—
Virginia	0	2	2	0	2	2	$72,912	$139,128	1	2	1	0	2	0	$7,142	$2,216
Washington	2	0	1	1	1	1	$286,440	$255,192	0	0	0	6	0	1	$157,876	$78,372
West Virginia	−2	0	0	0	2	1	$158,472	$98,952	0	−2	1	3	1	3	$140,383	$85,434
Wisconsin	0	0	1	0	3	1	$580,320	$534,192	0	0	0	3	1	2	$458,729	$220,859
Wyoming	2	2	0	0	0	1	$9,300	$2,418	2	2	0	0	1	0	$—	$—

(*continued*)

	1976								1980							
State	Rep. E.C. Strategy	Dem. E.C. Strategy	Rep. Pres. Visits	Dem. Pres. Visits	Rep. VP Visits	Dem. VP Visits	Rep. Spot Buy Spending (2020$)	Dem. Spot Buy Spending (2020$)	Rep. E.C. Strategy	Dem. E.C. Strategy	Rep. Pres. Visits	Dem. Pres. Visits	Rep. VP Visits	Dem. VP Visits	Rep. Spot Buy Spending (2020$)	Dem. Spot Buy Spending (2020$)
Alabama	−2	−2	1	1	2	0	$218,855	$296,587	−2	−1	1	1	0	0	$—	$—
Alaska	0	2	0	0	0	0	$—	$—	2	2	0	0	0	0	$—	$—
Arizona	2	2	0	1	0	0	$10,465	$2,120	2	2	0	0	0	0	$—	$—
Arkansas	−2	−2	0	1	2	0	$—	$58,872	−2	−2	1	1	0	1	$—	$—
California	0	0	11	11	5	7	$2,477,475	$2,709,593	0	1	11	4	3	6	$9,084,184	$8,478,000
Colorado	2	2	0	1	0	2	$—	$129,457	0	1	1	0	0	0	$1,023,477	$—
Connecticut	0	1	0	2	1	2	$245,700	$179,202	−2	1	1	2	6	0	$34,62,144	$—
Delaware	0	1	0	0	0	0	$658,840	$355,583	−2	1	0	0	1	0	$—	$3,736,600
D.C.	−2	−2	5	3	2	2	$—	$—	−2	−2	3	13	9	9	$—	$—
Florida	−1	−1	2	4	4	2	$618,345	$1,330,051	0	0	7	5	6	5	$5,121,652	$6,075,900
Georgia	−2	−2	0	4	0	1	$—	$—	−2	−2	0	3	0	0	$—	$—
Hawaii	−2	−2	0	0	0	0	$42,315	$45,177	−2	−2	0	0	0	0	$—	$—
Iowa	2	0	0	0	4	5	$—	$211,930	2	1	1	0	2	2	$698,096	$—
Idaho	2	2	11	8	0	0	$—	$—	2	2	1	0	0	0	$—	$—
Illinois	0	0	1	4	6	6	$1,264,900	$1,154,745	0	0	13	7	7	14	$4,498,018	$4,066,300
Indiana	2	1	2	0	1	3	$303,485	$371,808	2	1	1	0	1	0	$1,213,296	$—
Kansas	2	2	0	0	2	2	$—	$44,476	2	2	0	0	0	0	$—	$—
Kentucky	−1	−2	1	0	1	0	$120,575	$123,842	−2	−1	1	0	0	1	$1,770,678	$2,119,500
Louisiana	−2	−2	2	1	2	0	$52,525	$86,181	−2	0	4	1	3	0	$778,596	$1,130,400
Maine	2	2	0	2	1	1	$—	$71,908	0	0	0	0	1	0	$244,720	$—
Maryland	0	−1	0	2	1	0	$07,125	$55,096	0	−1	1	1	1	0	$—	$1,428,700
Massachusetts	−2	−2	0	1	2	0	$—	$387,433	−2	−1	0	1	0	0	$—	$2,260,800
Michigan	0	0	1	4	1	4	$1,565,200	$—	0	0	8	6	8	5	$3,132,899	$2,581,080
Minnesota	−2	−2	0	1	0	4	$—	$—	−2	−1	0	0	1	3	$—	$—
Mississippi	−2	−2	4	1	1	0	$98,280	$87,060	−2	1	1	1	1	0	$687,792	$—

Missouri	−1	−1	2	4	4	4	$593,320	$513,308	0	0	3	5	1	1	$2,024,978	$2,896,650
Montana	0	1	0	1	0	1	$18,200	$24,811	2	1	0	0	0	0	$—	$—
Nebraska	2	2	0	0	1	1	$—	$—	2	2	0	0	0	0	$—	$—
Nevada	0	1	0	0	0	1	$67,795	$—	2	1	0	0	0	0	$—	$—
New Hampshire	2	2	0	0	1	3	$—	$—	2	1	0	0	1	0	$—	$—
New Jersey	0	0	3	3	1	2	$—	$—	0	1	6	4	3	1	$4,443,600	$—
New Mexico	0	2	0	1	0	1	$51,415	$70,147	2	1	0	0	1	0	$—	$—
New York	0	0	11	8	6	10	$2,787,785	$3,124,203	0	1	3	8	4	7	$9,433,071	$9,891,000
North Carolina	−1	−2	1	1	2	0	$227,500	$350,905	−2	−1	0	2	0	0	$—	$2,458,620
North Dakota	2	2	0	1	1	0	$43,680	$—	2	2	0	0	0	0	$—	$—
Ohio	0	0	5	8	6	11	$1,181,635	$1,618,408	0	1	10	6	10	5	$3,884,206	$3,815,100
Oklahoma	2	2	1	2	1	0	$148,330	$168,910	−2	1	0	0	0	0	$—	$—
Oregon	0	1	1	1	0	1	$279,825	$165,356	2	0	2	2	2	1	$1,029,756	$1,036,200
Pennsylvania	0	0	9	9	5	7	$1,501,045	$1,843,223	0	0	9	6	10	5	$11,097,730	$11,445,300
Rhode Island	−2	−2	0	0	1	0	$165,620	$69,319	−2	−2	0	0	0	1	$—	$685,776
South Carolina	−2	−2	1	2	1	0	$203,840	$214,287	−2	−1	2	4	4	0	$1,243,242	$1,342,350
South Dakota	2	1	0	1	1	0	$30,940	$24,215	2	1	1	0	0	1	$—	$—
Tennessee	−1	−2	0	1	0	0	$245,245	$423,710	0	−1	2	4	1	0	$1,312,311	$1,692,774
Texas	−1	−1	3	8	6	0	$1,004,185	$1,778,932	0	0	9	9	14	2	$6,274,814	$7,065,000
Utah	2	2	0	1	1	0	$—	$—	2	2	0	0	0	0	$—	$—
Vermont	2	2	0	0	2	0	$—	$27,983	2	1	0	0	2	0	$—	$—
Virginia	−1	−2	0	4	3	1	$251,160	$269,246	0	1	2	0	3	0	$1,290,576	$1,190,000
Washington	0	2	1	0	0	2	$378,560	$128,501	0	0	1	2	1	6	$1,481,844	$—
West Virginia	−1	−2	1	0	0	0	$—	$110,497	−2	−2	0	1	0	0	$—	$401,292
Wisconsin	0	−2	1	3	3	4	$307,125	$368,791	0	0	5	2	3	5	$1,663, 935	$2,119,500
Wyoming	2	2	0	0	0	0	$—	$—	2	2	0	0	0	0	$—	$—

(*continued*)

State	1984								1988							
	Rep. E.C. Strategy	Dem. E.C. Strategy	Rep. Pres. Visits	Dem. Pres. Visits	Rep. VP Visits	Dem. VP Visits	Rep. Spot Buy Spending (2020$)	Dem. Spot Buy Spending (2020$)	Rep. E.C. Strategy	Dem. E.C. Strategy	Rep. Pres. Visits	Dem. Pres. Visits	Rep. VP Visits	Dem. VP Visits	Rep. Spot Buy Spending (2020$)	Dem. Spot Buy Spending (2020$)
Alabama	2	0	1	2	3	0	$1,353,586	$948,570	2	2	0	0	2	0	$—	$—
Alaska	2	2	0	0	0	0	$—	$—	2	2	0	0	0	0	$—	$—
Arizona	2	2	0	0	0	0	$—	$—	2	2	0	0	1	0	$3,955	$—
Arkansas	2	0	1	1	1	1	$247,128	$227,658	0	1	1	1	2	2	$1,127,462	$79,819
California	2	0	6	9	4	19	$4,989,736	$7,339,571	0	0	23	27	3	25	$19,759,026	$9,438,394
Colorado	2	2	0	0	0	0	$—	$—	0	1	5	4	3	0	$2,113,699	$629,616
Connecticut	0	0	2	0	1	3	$5,695,173	$7,114,286	0	0	6	5	0	0	$101,136	$579,577
Delaware	−2	1	0	0	1	0	$—	$—	2	1	1	0	0	0	$—	$50,913
D.C.	−2	−2	9	7	14	2	$—	$—	−2	−2	3	2	9	9	$—	$—
Florida	2	1	0	1	1	0	$511,105	$—	2	2	0	0	5	2	$—	$—
Georgia	2	0	1	3	3	0	$3,701,863	$3,407,742	2	2	1	1	5	1	$1,493,427	$—
Hawaii	2	−2	0	0	0	0	$—	$—	−2	−2	0	0	0	0	$—	$31,521
Iowa	0	0	4	7	2	4	$543,682	$199,200	−2	−2	0	1	1	1	$138,836	$465,693
Idaho	2	2	0	0	0	0	$—	$—	2	2	0	0	1	0	$—	$—
Illinois	0	0	6	5	13	11	$8,732,318	$6,156,229	0	0	21	14	7	4	$6,237,233	$2,721,342
Indiana	2	2	0	0	1	1	$283,073	$—	2	2	1	0	5	0	$3,916	$—
Kansas	2	2	0	0	0	0	$1,370,436	$—	2	2	0	0	0	0	$—	$—
Kentucky	2	0	1	2	3	0	$2,499,360	$2,219,658	0	2	3	3	4	2	$1,865,382	$433,195
Louisiana	2	1	0	0	1	0	$1,640,873	$—	2	1	0	1	4	3	$402,833	$80,279
Maine	0	0	0	0	3	2	$—	$474,285	0	1	1	1	0	0	$386,636	$52,770
Maryland	−2	−2	1	2	1	1	$—	$—	−2	−2	1	2	4	0	$—	$574,200
Massachusetts	−2	1	1	1	0	2	$—	$—	−2	−2	2	4	0	0	$—	$411,821
Michigan	0	0	6	6	3	4	$3,390,145	$1,909,001	0	0	10	10	9	2	$4,596,143	$1,588,352
Minnesota	−2	−2	1	3	2	1	$—	$—	−2	−2	0	1	0	0	$—	$427,503
Mississippi	2	0	1	1	1	0	$574,010	$521,715	2	2	0	0	1	0	$—	$—
Missouri	0	0	2	4	2	2	$1,847,983	$1,422,858	0	0	9	9	9	9	$3,929,322	$1,634,888
Montana	2	2	0	0	0	0	$—	$—	2	2	1	1	2	1	$6,592	$182,322

Nebraska	2	2	0	0	0	0	$—	$—	2	2	1	0	2	1	$—	$—
Nevada	2	2	0	0	0	0	$—	$—	2	2	0	0	1	0	$—	$—
New Hampshire	2	2	0	0	0	0	$—	$—	2	2	0	0	0	0	$—	$—
New Jersey	0	0	2	2	2	4	$7,253,763	$4,695,428	0	1	10	3	1	1	$9,165,847	$3,174,114
New Mexico	2	0	0	0	0	0	$—	$278,643	2	2	1	0	1	3	$871,771	$172,730
New York	−2	0	6	6	7	22	$4,953,790	$154,24,721	−2	0	2	7	2	4	$8,204,145	$3,567,705
North Carolina	2	0	1	0	2	0	$4,784,592	$1,048,170	2	2	1	2	2	2	$2,468,205	$328,778
North Dakota	2	2	0	0	0	0	$—	$—	2	2	0	0	1	1	$—	$88,360
Ohio	0	0	11	9	5	9	$7,436,300	$3,547,657	0	0	17	9	20	3	$5,910,507	$1,127,440
Oklahoma	2	2	0	0	1	0	$—	$—	2	2	1	0	4	1	$20,743	$—
Oregon	2	0	2	1	1	5	$2,173,601	$1,208,243	0	0	1	2	0	0	$—	$253,210
Pennsylvania	0	0	3	5	2	11	$2,594,841	$2,548,099	0	0	4	7	5	4	$8,036,641	$2,833,083
Rhode Island	−2	−2	0	0	0	2	$—	$—	−2	−2	0	0	0	0	$—	$273,809
South Carolina	2	1	1	0	2	0	$—	$—	2	2	0	0	4	1	$9,042	$—
South Dakota	2	2	0	0	0	0	$—	$—	2	2	1	2	1	1	$—	$219,291
Tennessee	2	0	1	3	1	2	$2,521,827	$1,795,039	2	2	1	1	5	2	$818,792	$191,012
Texas	2	0	3	5	6	1	$9,452,640	$8,891,670	2	0	5	8	5	44	$751,626	$2,980,010
Utah	2	2	1	1	0	0	$—	$2,015,003	2	2	0	0	0	0	$—	$—
Vermont	0	1	0	0	2	1	$25,836	$—	2	1	1	0	0	0	$3,235	$203,359
Virginia	2	2	0	0	2	0	$39,315	$—	2	2	0	0	4	1	$2,843	$—
Washington	2	0	1	2	2	3	$2,813,887	$—	0	0	3	4	0	1	$2,411,704	$685,586
West Virginia	−2	−2	1	1	0	0	$258,360	$—	−2	−2	0	0	2	1	$1,864,389	$407,270
Wisconsin	−2	0	2	4	1	6	$—	$903,845	0	1	1	2	3	0	$535,008	$993,222
Wyoming	2	2	0	0	0	0	$—	$—	2	2	0	1	1	0	$—	$—

(*continued*)

	1992								1996							
State	Rep. E.C. Strategy	Dem. E.C. Strategy	Rep. Pres. Visits	Dem. Pres. Visits	Rep. VP Visits	Dem. VP Visits	Rep. Spot Buy Spending (2020$)	Dem. Spot Buy Spending (2020$)	Rep. E.C. Strategy	Dem. E.C. Strategy	Rep. Pres. Visits	Dem. Pres. Visits	Rep. VP Visits	Dem. VP Visits	Rep. Spot Buy Spending (2020$)	Dem. Spot Buy Spending (2020$)
Alabama	2	1	1	0	1	1	$495,117	$—	2	2	1	1	0	1	$489,974	$210,778
Alaska	2	2	0	0	0	0	$78,031	$—	2	2	0	0	0	0	$—	$—
Arizona	2	1	0	0	3	0	$503,234	$—	1	0	3	3	2	0	$1,660,984	$1,658,707
Arkansas	−2	−2	0	4	0	2	$—	$10,330	−2	−2	0	3	0	0	$—	$62,122
California	−2	−2	2	4	9	2	$—	$—	0	−1	25	8	24	5	$12,287,724	$7,091,806
Colorado	0	0	2	3	3	6	$830,853	$3,033,267	1	0	3	4	2	0	$2,776,088	$1,812,536
Connecticut	0	−2	1	2	0	2	$851,329	$1,832,172	−2	−1	2	2	4	0	$1,442,746	$1,411,891
Delaware	1	−1	1	1	1	1	$152,741	$—	−2	−2	1	0	0	1	$—	$—
D.C.	−2	−2	2	4	12	5	$—	$—	−2	−2	6	7	6	10	$—	$—
Florida	1	1	6	7	5	8	$2,043,559	$—	1	0	9	11	6	7	$8,605,565	$6,647,391
Georgia	0	0	5	9	6	12	$1,277,086	$5,367,729	1	0	4	2	4	3	$4,623,725	$3,158,016
Hawaii	−2	−2	0	0	0	0	$—	$—	−2	−2	0	0	0	0	$—	$—
Iowa	−1	0	1	3	2	1	$273,569	$131,712	−2	−1	3	2	0	2	$915,297	$938,780
Idaho	2	2	0	0	2	0	$—	$—	2	2	0	0	0	0	$—	$—
Illinois	−2	−2	3	2	6	2	$508,768	$2,422,724	−2	−1	5	2	1	3	$436,643	$833,789
Indiana	1	2	0	1	4	0	$488,292	$—	2	1	1	0	0	0	$1,531,248	$1,300,061
Kansas	2	1	0	0	0	1	$177,829	$—	2	2	1	0	0	0	$245,875	$578,659
Kentucky	1	0	4	3	4	2	$676,083	$1,777,462	1	0	4	2	3	2	$1,916,014	$2,379,437
Louisiana	0	0	5	3	1	5	$1,043,731	$3,006,952	0	0	5	3	4	4	$2,688,492	$2,955,671
Maine	0	0	0	1	0	3	$356,949	$441,307	−2	−1	0	2	0	1	$—	$213,610
Maryland	−2	−1	1	2	0	4	$—	$846,777	−2	−2	0	0	0	0	$—	$—
Massachusetts	−2	−2	1	1	0	0	$—	$—	−2	−2	0	3	0	1	$—	$—
Michigan	0	0	19	13	6	4	$2,188,183	$5,539,416	−1	−1	15	3	6	4	$5,907,610	$4,644,493
Minnesota	−2	−2	0	0	0	0	$—	$—	−2	−2	0	1	0	4	$—	$549,120
Mississippi	2	2	1	1	0	0	$248,297	$—	2	2	0	0	0	0	$637,653	$558,013
Missouri	0	0	7	8	4	4	$1,713,726	$3,258,771	−1	−1	5	3	2	2	$507,226	$1,183,344
Montana	0	0	1	1	3	0	$317,288	$606,814	1	1	0	0	4	0	$364,758	$421,405

Nebraska	2	2	0	0	0	1	$—	$—	2	2	1	0	0	0	$165,120	$—
Nevada	2	1	0	1	1	0	$—	$—	0	0	2	1	2	3	$1,287,239	$1,395,274
New Hampshire	1	1	0	1	0	1	$966,807	$—	−1	2	1	2	0	2	$89,760	$—
New Jersey	0	0	7	6	1	3	$5,263,851	$6,271,334	−1	0	11	4	3	3	$8,668,197	$7,618,562
New Mexico	0	0	2	2	3	4	$522,788	$2,085,990	0	0	2	2	1	1	$1,050,334	$974,534
New York	−2	−2	1	0	1	3	$—	$—	−2	−2	1	4	4	4	$5,587,932	$5,533,960
North Carolina	1	0	7	10	3	12	$1,922,546	$5,172,078	2	0	0	2	0	0	$—	$2,006
North Dakota	2	2	0	0	0	0	$—	$—	2	2	0	0	0	0	$—	$20,736
Ohio	0	0	14	9	11	5	$2,817,410	$6,764,965	−1	0	19	5	8	4	$6,156,150	$7,339,513
Oklahoma	2	2	2	0	2	1	$364,697	$490,961	2	1	0	0	1	0	$—	$—
Oregon	−2	−2	1	2	0	0	$—	$387,018	−2	−1	1	1	1	2	$266,285	$817,859
Pennsylvania	0	−1	4	4	2	4	$1,683,473	$7,325,654	−1	−1	5	3	3	3	$4,760,726	$5,817,506
Rhode Island	−2	−2	0	0	0	0	$—	$—	−2	−2	0	1	0	0	$—	$—
South Carolina	2	1	2	2	1	0	$226,714	$—	2	1	0	0	0	0	$345,149	$190,954
South Dakota	0	1	2	1	2	1	$212,509	$384,028	1	1	1	2	0	1	$252,730	$226,243
Tennessee	0	−1	7	2	1	4	$1,085,790	$1,901,240	1	0	4	2	8	13	$3,534,163	$7,341,206
Texas	1	1	8	3	5	6	$3,132,116	$571,934	2	1	3	5	0	4	$—	$149,222
Utah	2	2	1	1	0	0	$—	$—	2	2	1	0	0	0	$—	$—
Vermont	−1	−2	0	1	0	1	$—	$76,002	−2	−2	0	0	0	0	$—	$—
Virginia	2	2	2	2	0	4	$1,058,858	$—	2	1	2	1	0	0	$1,490,602	$405,734
Washington	−2	−2	1	1	1	2	$—	$—	−2	−1	0	7	1	7	$—	$801,103
West Virginia	−2	−2	0	0	0	0	$—	$—	−2	−2	0	0	0	0	$—	$707,290
Wisconsin	0	0	8	6	4	6	$1,054,431	$2,599,769	−2	−1	1	1	1	3	$—	$1,255,444
Wyoming	2	2	0	1	1	0	$—	$—	2	2	0	0	0	0	$—	$—

(continued)

State	2000								2004							
	Rep. E.C. Strategy	Dem. E.C. Strategy	Rep. Pres. Visits	Dem. Pres. Visits	Rep. VP Visits	Dem. VP Visits	Rep. Spot Buy Spending (2020$)	Dem. Spot Buy Spending (2020$)	Rep. E.C. Strategy	Dem. E.C. Strategy	Rep. Pres. Visits	Dem. Pres. Visits	Rep. VP Visits	Dem. VP Visits	Rep. Spot Buy Spending (2020$)	Dem. Spot Buy Spending (2020$)
Alabama	2	2	4	0	0	0	$—	$—	2	2	0	0	0	0	$—	$—
Alaska	2	2	0	0	0	0	$—	$—	2	2	0	0	0	0	$—	$—
Arizona	1	1	0	0	0	0	$—	$—	1	1	2	3	0	1	$544,527	$—
Arkansas	0	0	0	1	4	4	$3,453,093	$3,074,759	1	1	0	0	0	0	$283,583	$—
California	−2	−2	12	7	9	8	$8,889,409	$—	−2	−2	0	0	0	2	$—	$—
Colorado	0	2	0	0	2	0	$—	$—	1	1	4	3	3	2	$5,063,108	$3,406,782
Connecticut	−2	−2	0	0	1	7	$—	$—	−2	−2	0	0	0	0	$—	$—
Delaware	−2	−1	0	0	1	1	$558,354	$526,513	−2	−2	0	0	0	0	$—	$—
D.C.	−2	−2	0	7	4	5	$—	$—	−2	−2	6	3	5	0	$—	$—
Florida	0	0	22	14	15	19	$25,056,047	$12,351,789	0	0	22	21	16	25	$29,126,007	$20,170,044
Georgia	1	2	0	1	1	0	$—	$—	2	2	0	0	0	0	$—	$—
Hawaii	−2	−2	0	0	0	0	$—	$—	−2	−2	0	0	1	0	$—	$—
Iowa	0	0	4	10	4	3	$5,992,365	$5,145,137	0	0	8	9	10	11	$5,271,801	$3,840,879
Idaho	2	2	0	0	1	1	$—	$—	2	2	0	0	0	0	$—	$—
Illinois	−1	−1	5	4	15	7	$4,142,907	$2,235,752	−2	−2	0	0	1	1	$—	$—
Indiana	2	2	2	0	0	2	$—	$—	2	2	0	0	0	0	$—	$—
Kansas	2	2	0	0	0	0	$—	$—	2	2	0	0	0	0	$—	$—
Kentucky	1	1	1	2	8	4	$—	$—	2	2	0	0	0	1	$—	$—
Louisiana	1	1	1	5	3	0	$5,698,321	$4,569,732	2	1	0	1	1	0	$—	$—
Maine	0	0	1	1	1	2	$2,651,531	$1,614,350	0	−1	1	0	0	2	$1,961,452	$1,218,788
Maryland	−2	−2	0	2	0	1	$—	$—	−2	−2	0	0	0	1	$—	$—
Massachusetts	−2	−2	1	2	0	0	$—	$—	−2	−2	0	5	0	0	$—	$—
Michigan	0	0	18	17	13	4	$18,382,258	$16,073,796	0	−1	7	3	9	6	$9,636,025	$4,612,806
Minnesota	−1	0	2	1	2	3	$2,366,609	$1,216,062	0	0	7	3	6	5	$5,946,648	$3,108,126
Mississippi	2	2	0	0	1	0	$—	$—	2	2	0	0	0	0	$—	$—
Missouri	0	0	9	8	9	5	$13,488,846	$10,993,199	0	1	4	2	2	1	$1,164,767	$—
Montana	2	2	0	0	0	0	$—	$—	2	2	0	0	0	0	$—	$—

Nebraska	2	2	0	0	0	0	$—	$—	2	2	0	0	0	0	$—	$—
Nevada	0	0	0	1	2	1	$3,288,889	$1,412,005	0	0	3	3	3	1	$3,932,434	$2,141,887
New Hampshire	0	0	1	1	1	2	$1,973,702	$420,246	0	−1	4	4	1	3	$3,116,598	$1,545,730
New Jersey	−1	−2	1	1	1	6	$—	$—	−2	−2	1	0	1	3	$—	$—
New Mexico	0	0	3	2	5	2	$3,133,555	$2,571,686	0	0	3	6	3	1	$2,051,674	$2,491,803
New York	−2	−2	2	2	0	9	$—	$—	−2	−2	3	0	0	5	$—	$—
North Carolina	1	2	2	1	1	0	$—	$—	2	1	1	1	0	3	$—	$—
North Dakota	2	2	0	0	0	0	$—	$—	2	2	0	0	0	0	$—	$—
Ohio	0	1	3	6	16	8	$13,595,827	$11,766,225	0	0	17	17	13	16	$15,148,104	$10,483,759
Oklahoma	2	2	0	0	0	0	$—	$—	2	2	0	0	1	0	$—	$—
Oregon	0	0	2	2	5	2	$7,671,282	$6,274,646	−2	−1	1	0	2	4	$3,423,662	$2,268,288
Pennsylvania	0	0	13	17	19	4	$20,103,516	$17,118,648	0	0	13	6	8	9	$18,123,138	$11,444,975
Rhode Island	−2	−2	0	0	0	0	$—	$—	−2	−2	0	0	0	1	$—	$—
South Carolina	2	2	0	0	0	0	$—	$—	2	2	0	0	0	1	$—	$—
South Dakota	2	2	0	0	0	0	$—	$—	2	2	0	0	0	0	$—	$—
Tennessee	0	−1	4	7	3	7	$3,271,173	$2,739,195	2	2	0	0	0	0	$—	$—
Texas	2	2	3	2	2	6	$—	$—	2	2	7	0	0	1	$—	$—
Utah	2	2	0	0	0	0	$—	$—	2	2	0	0	0	0	$—	$—
Vermont	−2	−2	0	0	2	1	$—	$—	−2	−2	0	0	0	0	$—	$—
Virginia	2	2	0	0	0	0	$—	$—	1	1	0	0	0	0	$—	$—
Washington	0	0	4	2	3	5	$12,544,534	$8,713,214	0	−2	0	0	0	0	$956,363	$1,583,583
West Virginia	0	−1	2	2	3	0	$2,736,715	$1,219,993	2	2	1	0	3	6	$5,084,470	$2,096,744
Wisconsin	0	0	9	7	4	12	$9,017,176	$8,018,897	0	0	9	15	11	5	$6,825,395	$5,382,272
Wyoming	2	2	0	0	1	0	$—	$—	2	2	0	0	0	0	$—	$—

(continued)

State	2008								2012							
	Rep. E.C. Strategy	Dem. E.C. Strategy	Rep. Pres. Visits	Dem. Pres. Visits	Rep. VP Visits	Dem. VP Visits	Rep. Spot Buy Spending (2020$)	Dem. Spot Buy Spending (2020$)	Rep. E.C. Strategy	Dem. E.C. Strategy	Rep. Pres. Visits	Dem. Pres. Visits	Rep. VP Visits	Dem. VP Visits	Rep. Spot Buy Spending (2020$)	Dem. Spot Buy Spending (2020$)
Alabama	2	2	0	0	0	0	$452,340	$731,188	2	2	0	0	1	0	$—	$—
Alaska	1	1	0	0	1	0	$660	$9,275	2	2	0	0	0	0	$—	$—
Arizona	2	2	0	0	0	0	$1,118	$1,32,809	2	1	0	0	0	0	$—	$—
Arkansas	2	2	1	0	0	0	$551	$2,138	2	2	0	0	0	0	$—	$—
California	−2	−2	6	4	2	2	$2,223,106	$29,540	−2	−2	5	4	4	0	$—	$—
Colorado	0	0	8	6	5	2	$6,695,615	$8,900,152	0	0	6	7	12	4	$10,457,995	$14,487,402
Connecticut	−2	−2	0	0	0	0	$—	$—	−2	−2	0	0	3	1	$—	$—
Delaware	−2	−2	0	0	0	6	$—	$—	−2	−2	0	0	0	0	$—	$—
D.C.	−2	−2	0	0	0	0	$—	$—	−2	−2	0	0	0	0	$—	$—
Florida	0	0	7	8	4	4	$17,638,865	$32,041,292	0	0	18	11	14	11	$36,744,029	$45,950,567
Georgia	1	1	1	1	0	0	$416	$1,591,229	2	2	1	0	1	0	$—	$—
Hawaii	−2	−2	0	1	0	0	$37	$—	−2	−2	0	0	0	0	$—	$—
Iowa	0	0	6	3	3	1	$3,111,468	$2,834,374	0	0	8	7	11	8	$10,880,642	$13,088,224
Idaho	2	2	0	0	0	0	$506	$322	2	2	0	0	0	0	$—	$—
Illinois	−2	−2	2	10	0	3	$460,435	$2,792,690	−2	−2	1	2	1	1	$—	$—
Indiana	0	0	2	6	3	2	$2,718,803	$7,619,908	0	1	0	0	1	0	$—	$—
Kansas	2	2	0	0	0	0	$1,361	$3,569	2	2	0	0	0	0	$—	$—
Kentucky	2	2	1	0	0	1	$126,564	$770,096	2	2	0	0	1	1	$—	$—
Louisiana	2	2	1	0	0	0	$9,264	$3,282	2	2	0	0	1	0	$—	$—
Maine	−1	−2	1	0	1	0	$280,067	$808,252	−2	−2	0	0	0	0	$—	$—
Maryland	−2	−2	1	0	0	1	$—	$—	−2	−2	0	1	0	0	$—	$—
Massachusetts	−2	−2	1	1	0	1	$—	$—	−2	−2	0	0	0	0	$—	$—
Michigan	0	−1	7	7	2	3	$5,288,258	$9,304,265	−1	−2	0	0	1	2	$—	$667,850
Minnesota	−1	−2	6	1	3	0	$4,453,640	$2,593,393	−1	−1	0	0	3	0	$253,149	$1,719,712
Mississippi	2	2	2	1	1	0	$1,534	$1,644	2	2	0	0	0	0	$—	$—
Missouri	0	0	8	8	6	5	$5,818,330	$7,918,188	1	2	0	0	0	0	$—	$—
Montana	1	1	0	2	0	1	$158,539	$1,132,847	2	2	0	0	0	0	$—	$—

Nebraska	2	1	1	0	1	0	$573,390	$385,084	2	2	0	0	1	0	$—	$—
Nevada	0	0	4	6	3	1	$4,269,422	$7,411,547	0	0	4	4	5	2	$7,831,453	$9,935,657
New Hampshire	0	0	5	4	1	2	$1,371,767	$4,354,241	0	0	4	5	2	5	$6,101,045	$13,597,761
New Jersey	−2	−2	2	1	0	0	$—	$—	−2	−2	0	1	1	0	$—	$—
New Mexico	0	−1	6	4	2	1	$2,180,594	$3,134,168	−2	−2	0	0	0	0	$—	$—
New York	−2	−2	9	4	2	0	$4,800	$2,939	−2	−2	3	4	2	1	$—	$—
North Carolina	0	0	4	8	4	4	$7,421,713	$9,075,916	0	0	1	1	1	4	$9,575,144	$8,806,543
North Dakota	2	1	0	1	0	0	$581	$98,089	2	2	0	0	0	0	$—	$—
Ohio	0	0	16	13	12	9	$16,300,033	$18,143,570	0	0	25	17	30	18	$36,086,710	$34,588,006
Oklahoma	2	2	0	0	0	0	$3,127	$5,004	2	2	0	0	0	0	$—	$—
Oregon	−1	−2	0	0	0	0	$420	$2,417	−2	−2	0	0	1	0	$—	$—
Pennsylvania	0	0	19	8	12	8	$20,836,963	$25,171,744	−1	−1	6	1	1	3	$1,855,174	$34,101,152
Rhode Island	−2	−2	0	0	0	1	$—	$—	−2	−2	0	0	0	0	$—	$—
South Carolina	2	2	0	0	0	0	$728,460	$767,737	2	2	0	0	1	1	$—	$—
South Dakota	2	2	1	0	0	0	$616	$318	2	2	0	0	0	1	$—	$—
Tennessee	2	2	2	1	0	0	$403,502	$483,680	2	2	0	0	2	0	$—	$—
Texas	2	2	1	1	1	1	$1,083,524	$781,309	2	2	1	0	1	0	$—	$—
Utah	2	2	0	0	0	0	$209	$79	2	2	1	0	1	0	$—	$—
Vermont	−2	−2	0	0	0	0	$—	$1,120,532	−2	−2	1	0	0	0	$—	$—
Virginia	0	0	6	13	4	6	$10,470,203	$21,853,440	0	0	17	8	15	5	$27,146,143	$34,101,152
Washington	−1	−2	0	0	0	1	$1,733	$3,230	−2	−2	0	0	1	0	$—	$—
West Virginia	2	2	1	0	0	1	$929,683	$933,103	2	2	0	0	0	0	$—	$—
Wisconsin	0	0	5	5	2	2	$5,928,821	$10,803,924	0	0	1	5	15	7	$8,859,582	$11,488,965
Wyoming	2	2	0	0	0	0	$3,059	$—	2	2	0	0	0	0	$—	$—

(*continued*)

State	2016								2020							
	Rep. E.C. Strategy	Dem. E.C. Strategy	Rep. Pres. Visits	Dem. Pres. Visits	Rep. VP Visits	Dem. VP Visits	Rep. Spot Buy Spending (2020$)	Dem. Spot Buy Spending (2020$)	Rep. E.C. Strategy	Dem. E.C. Strategy	Rep. Pres. Visits	Dem. Pres. Visits	Rep. VP Visits	Dem. VP Visits	Rep. Spot Buy Spending (2020$)	Dem. Spot Buy Spending (2020$)
Alabama	2	2	0	0	0	0	$369,330	$776,547	2	2	0	0	0	0	$1,478,784	$1,293,373
Alaska	2	2	0	0	0	0	$—	$—	2	2	0	0	0	0	$—	$—
Arizona	2	1	2	1	2	2	$—	$3,323,862	0	0	5	1	5	3	$11,027,673	$26,632,975
Arkansas	2	2	0	0	0	0	$—	$—	2	2	0	0	0	0	$—	$—
California	–2	–2	0	0	1	0	$—	$—	–2	–2	1	0	0	2	$—	$11,500
Colorado	0	0	7	1	3	1	$4,895,920	$1,286,103	–2	–2	0	0	0	0	$—	$55,160
Connecticut	–2	–2	0	0	0	0	$—	$—	–2	–2	0	0	0	0	$—	$—
Delaware	–2	–2	0	0	0	0	$—	$—	–2	–2	0	0	0	0	$—	$—
D.C.	–2	–2	2	3	1	1	$—	$—	–2	–2	0	0	0	0	$—	$78,511
Florida	0	0	21	15	8	11	$21,313,437	$28,811,023	0	0	10	7	4	5	$26,950,552	$42,165,956
Georgia	2	2	0	0	0	0	$—	$12,420	1	1	3	2	0	2	$7,922,410	$3,538,027
Hawaii	–2	–2	0	0	0	0	$—	$—	–2	–2	0	0	0	0	$—	$—
Iowa	0	1	3	4	6	2	$1,666,883	$2,461,802	2	2	2	1	2	1	$—	$2,518,501
Idaho	2	2	0	0	0	0	$—	$—	2	2	0	0	0	0	$1,490	$—
Illinois	–2	–2	0	0	1	0	$—	$—	–2	–2	0	0	0	0	$—	$—
Indiana	2	2	0	0	0	0	$—	$—	2	2	0	0	1	0	$—	$479,642
Kansas	2	2	0	0	0	0	$—	$—	2	2	0	0	0	0	$—	$—
Kentucky	2	2	0	0	0	0	$—	$—	2	2	0	0	0	0	$—	$—
Louisiana	2	2	0	0	0	0	$—	$—	2	2	0	0	0	0	$—	$—
Maine	–2	–2	3	0	0	0	$559,559	$497,226	–2	–2	0	0	0	0	$824,541	$1,125,073
Maryland	–2	–2	0	0	0	0	$—	$—	–2	–2	0	0	0	0	$—	$—
Massachusetts	–2	–2	0	0	0	0	$—	$—	–2	–2	0	0	0	0	$—	$7,54,948
Michigan	–1	–2	5	3	5	4	$992,307	$1,791,798	0	0	8	5	4	6	$9,381,681	$18,219,250
Minnesota	–1	–1	1	0	1	1	$—	$77,555	0	–1	3	2	2	1	$3,731,461	$7,125,604

Mississippi	2	2	0	0	0	0	$—	$—	2	2	0	0	0	0	$1,593	$—
Missouri	1	2	0	1	0	0	$—	$—	2	2	0	0	0	0	$—	$—
Montana	2	2	0	0	0	0	$—	$—	2	2	0	0	0	0	$—	$—
Nebraska	2	2	1	0	1	0	$565,807	$428,890	2	2	0	0	0	0	$108,662	$1,662,894
Nevada	0	0	4	2	1	5	$5,306,637	$8,111,813	0	−1	5	1	1	3	$1,552,812	$4,411,489
New Hampshire	0	0	8	3	2	2	$4,461,680	$3,010,689	−1	−2	1	0	1	0	$—	$—
New Jersey	−2	−2	0	0	0	0	$—	$—	−2	−2	0	0	0	0	$—	$—
New Mexico	−2	−2	0	0	1	0	$214,321	$123,306	−2	−2	0	0	0	0	$—	$—
New York	−2	−2	4	2	0	0	$—	$—	−2	−2	0	1	1	0	$—	$26,330
North Carolina	0	0	15	9	9	10	$5,150,043	$10,733,709	0	0	10	3	5	4	$12,368,569	$18,444,470
North Dakota	2	2	0	0	0	0	$—	$—	2	2	0	0	0	0	$539,390	$362,701
Ohio	0	0	9	9	7	5	$6,253,846	$10,408,461	1	1	4	6	3	2	$602,367	$3,981,897
Oklahoma	2	2	0	0	0	0	$—	$—	2	2	0	0	0	0	$—	$—
Oregon	−2	−2	0	0	0	0	$—	$—	−2	−2	0	0	0	0	$—	$—
Pennsylvania	−1	−1	15	11	11	9	$6,917,475	$13,756,830	0	0	8	19	7	3	$10,684,273	$35,946,706
Rhode Island	−2	−2	0	0	0	0	$—	$—	−2	−2	0	0	0	0	$—	$—
South Carolina	2	2	0	0	0	0	$399,858	$1,031,260	2	2	0	0	1	0	$1,980,457	$1,539,828
South Dakota	2	2	0	0	0	0	$—	$—	2	2	0	0	0	0	$2,425	$—
Tennessee	2	2	0	0	0	0	$79,434	$79,434	2	2	0	0	0	0	$4,970	$—
Texas	2	2	1	0	0	1	$—	$35,575	2	1	0	0	0	3	$—	$1,371,019
Utah	2	2	0	0	1	0	$—	$—	2	2	0	0	0	0	$1,500	$—
Vermont	−2	−2	0	0	0	0	$—	$—	−2	−2	0	0	0	0	$—	$—
Virginia	0	0	5	1	8	5	$1,081,770	$2,755,774	−2	−2	1	0	1	1	$—	$537,840
Washington	−2	−2	0	0	0	0	$—	$—	−2	−2	0	0	0	0	$—	$—
West Virginia	2	2	0	0	0	0	$109,906	$143,829	2	2	0	0	0	0	$—	$3,060
Wisconsin	0	0	3	0	1	5	$2,334,452	$1,530,517	0	0	7	3	3	1	$3,407,412	$14,461,238
Wyoming	2	2	0	0	0	0	$—	$—	2	2	0	0	0	0	$4,280	$—

Electoral College strategies are coded as follows: -2=base Democratic, -1=lean Democratic, 0=battleground, 1=lean Republican, 2=base Republican. Spot buy spending is the estimated amount of money, translated into 2020 dollars, spent on TV spots in all markets in a state across the general election campaign. Visits are the total number of public appearances made in a state across the general election campaign.

Notes

Chapter 1

1. From Helmuth Karl Bernhard Graf von Moltke's "On Strategy" (1871) (Hughes and Bell, 1993).
2. Our focus is on Electoral College strategy rather than messaging strategy or targeting strategy. The reasons for this are discussed later in this chapter.
3. For an analysis of why campaigns tend to avoid substance and dialogue in their messaging, see Simon (2002).
4. For an exception, see Erikson and Wlezien (2012).
5. Meta-analyses of this research, however, can allow a broader statement about the magnitude of these effects on average (Kalla and Broockman, 2018).
6. The Federal Election Campaign Act of 1971 (FECA, Pub. L. 92–225, 86 Stat. 3, enacted February 7, 1972, 52 U.S.C. § 30101 *et seq.*).
7. But see Cohen et al., 2008.
8. Bipartisan Campaign Reform Act of 2002 (BCRA, Pub. L. 107–155, 116 Stat. 81, enacted March 27, 2002, H.R. 2356).
9. And indexing them to inflation.
10. *Citizens United v. Federal Election Commission*, 558 U.S. 310 (2010).
11. The precise number of media markets varies slightly over time and across the monitoring organization (e.g., Nielsen versus Arbitron). We use Nielsen definitions and attempt to achieve consistency across time in our analyses.

Chapter 2

1. The main change to this formulation since the days of the Constitutional Convention is that presidents have been limited to two terms starting in 1951 with the passage of the twenty-second amendment to the U.S. Constitution.
2. Wisconsin Center for the Study of the American Constitution, https://csac.history.wisc.edu/document-collections/constitutional-debates/executive-branch/.
3. Ibid.
4. Alexander Hamilton, who had little use for Adams, surreptitiously encouraged South Carolina electors to withhold their votes from Adams, which would have made Charles Pickney president, with Adams becoming vice-president. But electors from the New England states, learning of the scheme, withheld their votes from Pinckney to counter Hamilton's ploy. As a result, Jefferson compiled more votes than Pickney for second place and became vice-president (see Chernow, 2004).
5. This logic, and the attendant machinations, are described in detail in Larson's *A Magnificent Catastrophe* (2007).

6. Jefferson's party dominated the election of 1800. Adams presided over a split among Federalists because of his refusal to go to war with France. In contrast, Jefferson and others were united in opposition to Adams: most notably they opposed his controversial Alien and Sedition Acts, which Adams championed to curb Democratic-Republican opposition to his foreign policy.
7. https://www.motherjones.com/politics/2012/02/historic-price-cost-presidential-elections/. Original estimates of campaign spending are from Thayer, 1974.
8. https://www.fec.gov/updates/2008-presidential-campaign-financial-activity-summarized-receipts-nearly-double-2004-total/
9. https://www.opensecrets.org/2020-presidential-race/joe-biden/candidate?id=N00001669
10. Even as we posit that presidential campaigns emphasize candidate characteristics and experience, we do not wish to suggest that voters necessarily cast their ballots based on candidate characteristics over issue positions or party identification. There is some evidence that candidate traits have considerable explanatory power (see Miller and Shanks, 1996), but the independent effect of trait evaluations on voters is a matter of serious dispute.
11. Of course, over the scope of American history specific presidential candidates have offered detailed policy programs. Democratic candidate William Jennings Bryan, for example, famously proposed in 1896 that the United States should move away from the gold standard to improve the money supply and help farmers and industrial workers who were beset by debt. Such candidacies, however, have been the exception rather than the rule. It was not until the American news media began to demand specificity—whether due to their own professional standards or due to a perceived shift in the needs of voters—that candidates consistently provided it (Patterson, 1994). Most scholars date this shift to changes in the nature of the relationship between journalists and politicians in the wake of Vietnam and Watergate (Graber and Dunaway, 2014).
12. https://www.politifact.com/truth-o-meter/promises/biden-promise-tracker/?ruling=true
13. See also Geer (2006) and Haselmayer (2019) for a review.
14. From Silber, 1971: 36.
15. In addition to documentaries like *The War Room* (about the 1992 Bill Clinton campaign) or *Travels with George* (about the 2000 George W. Bush campaign), there are films offering dramatized versions of recent presidential campaigns ranging from *Primary Colors* (about the 1992 Bill Clinton campaign) to *Game Change* (about the 2008 Barack Obama and John McCain campaigns) to *The Front Runner* (about Gary Hart's 1988 campaign). With respect to music, songs praising candidates (such as "Crush on Obama" and "Real Women Vote Trump") or trashing them (including the memorable "My Brain is Hanging Upside Down (Bonzo Goes to Bitburg)" and "Land of Confusion") have been a part of the scene for several decades.
16. The late-night comedy show *Saturday Night Live* has produced some especially memorable comedic impersonations of presidential and vice-presidential candidates, including Chevy Chase as Gerald Ford, Dan Akroyd as Jimmy Carter, Phil Hartman as Ronald Reagan and Bill Clinton, Dana Carvey as George H. W. Bush, Will Ferrell as George W. Bush, Tina Fey as Sarah Palin, Kate McKinnon as Hillary Clinton, Alec Baldwin as Donald Trump, and Woody Harrelson as Joe Biden.
17. This assumption may seem trivial to scholars of American politics, but in other countries election campaigns are often about advancing policies or winning enough votes to influence a governing coalition rather than seeking outright victory (Duverger, 1954; Kirchheimer, 1966).

18. This has been the goal since 1964, the first election in which the total number of electoral votes reached 538 (the District of Columbia was granted electors with the passage of the twenty-third amendment in 1961; Alaska and Hawaii were granted statehood in January and August 1959, respectively).
19. For 2004, see Thomas and Newsweek Staff (2005); for 2000, see Milbank (2001); for 1960, see White (1961).
20. We say "major party" for a reason. Minor party and independent candidates may have other goals besides winning the election. They may wish to advance an issue position, or they may seek to position themselves or their party for a (more successful) future campaign.
21. https://www.cnn.com/election/2020/exit-polls/president/national-results
22. But see Campbell (2000), Vavreck (2009), Hersh (2015) and Sides, Vavreck, and Warshaw (2022).
23. This expectation is consistent with Stromberg (2008), who develops a "probabilistic voting model" under the Electoral College and finds that the probability of a state being decisive is influenced by (among other things) the closeness of the race in the state and the size (or "voting power") of the state. More to the point, Stromberg also suggests that underdog candidates have greater incentive to increase variance in the electoral vote by going on the offense and campaigning in large states where they are behind.
24. Both the Barack Obama and Hillary Clinton campaigns referred to "lean Republican" states as "stretch" states.
25. The importance of non-competitive states on shaping Electoral College strategies is explored by Brams and Kilgour (2017), who point out that foreseeable outcomes in non-competitive states can create a "loading of the dice," by requiring the candidate with fewer expected easy victories to do remarkably well in competitive states to win (see also Cervas and Grofman, 2017). In the extreme, a candidate could have enough "safe" states to make competitive states irrelevant. This insight is consistent with our notion that competitiveness is imperfectly related to battleground or pivotal states.
26. By "net effect of persuasion," we mean the sum of pro-Republican and pro-Democratic persuasion, such that there is an estimated directional effect favoring one side. For example, if the Republican candidate persuades 2% of voters to vote for her, while the Democratic candidate persuades 4% of voters to vote for him, the net effect of persuasion is +2 Democratic. This directional effect is almost certainly smaller than the absolute effect of persuasion, which would sum all persuasive effects without regard to whom they favor.
27. Our thanks to Matthew Dowd, Tucker Eskew, (the late) John Gorman, Karl Rove, Robert Shrum, and Fred Steeper.
28. The resultant inter-coder reliability score for the five-fold categorization (base Republican, lean Republican, battleground, lean Democratic, base Democratic) as measured by Cohen's kappa is a robust 0.82. For a simpler three-fold designation (base Republican, battleground, base Democratic), it is an even stronger 0.87.
29. Although modern presidential campaigns begin earlier than Labor Day, this is the traditional start of the general election campaign. More substantively, focusing on September through Election Day campaigning allows us to analyze properly the dispensation of resources in battleground states across years.
30. During an investigation of federal election campaign financing, Congress subpoenaed records on television and radio buys for the 1952 and 1956 cycles from the Federal Communication Commission. We accessed these records through the National Archive and use them in this project. To our knowledge, this is the first time these data have been analyzed by political scientists.

31. Media markets are sometimes referred to as designated market areas (DMAs), their Nielsen name, or Areas of Dominant Influence (ADIs), their Arbitron name prior to the 1970s. To ensure comparability over time, whenever appropriate we transform the spending data for each election into 2020 dollars. Ideally, we would use gross rating points (GRPs) as our unit of analysis. One hundred GRPs is the amount of TV advertising necessary for each voter in the market (or state) to see the ad one time. GRPs are thus a measure of audience reach, which is comparable across markets. Unfortunately, until recently campaigns tended to keep expenditure records solely of dollars spent and not of GRPs purchased. We are decidedly less enamored with the number of airings of advertisements as a unit of analysis. Airings account for neither pricing discrepancies across markets nor the size of the electorate within a market.
32. Most famously, votes in Alabama in 1960 are often assigned erroneously to John Kennedy even though "these votes were cast for electors who were unambiguously not supporters of the Senator from Massachusetts" (Gaines, 2001: 71).

Chapter 3

1. Some scholars have argued that the fundamental strength of the post-war economy made Truman's "comeback" predictable, irrespective of the whistle-stop campaign (Holbrook, 2002).
2. In doing this, we endeavor to provide extensive notes about subtleties in the strategic thinking of the campaigns. Not all base states or battleground states are equal, as the reader shall see from our rendering of the plans.
3. The twenty-second amendment to the U.S. Constitution limited presidents to being elected twice, or once if they had already served more than two years.
4. The Eisenhower campaign was largely shaped by Sherman Adams, governor of New Hampshire, and Robert Humphreys, who had served as a public relations director for the Republican Congressional Campaign Committee. The Republican Party "loaned" Humphreys to the campaign in July 1952, and Humphreys wrote an extensive strategic plan that was known within the campaign by its cryptic title: "Document X." As far as we can tell, this is the first time a campaign put on paper such a detailed and extensive plan. And in our review of the archival material, no other such strategic plan in the years since has been so dramatically named as this one.
5. For the 1952 and 1956 elections, there were 531 total electoral votes available, such that 266 constituted an Electoral College majority. By 1960, those numbers jump to 537 and 269 (respectively) with the addition of Alaska and Hawaii. By 1964, they jump to 538 and 270 (respectively) with the addition of the District of Columbia and reapportionment.
6. Among other nicknames, Bernays was referred to as "the father of spin" in a biography (Tye, 1999).
7. We are not sure why the Republican campaign failed to designate Illinois as a "priority 2" state. It did so with California and several other consequential base states.
8. Excluding Gallup, the only other publicly available general election survey from September 1–November 5, 1952, is one conducted by the University of Chicago's National Opinion Research Center.

9. As implied in the text, these early strategies were simply applying the strategic logic of radio advertising to television. In this sense, there was nothing new under the sun, just with pictures rather than with sound alone. Same game, same logic (at least so it was thought in those early days). Our archival material from the 1952 and 1956 campaigns is clear about the sophisticated uses of radio that had already been in place in the presidential campaigns of the 1930s and 1940s, including detailed audience data and so on. We return to this topic in later chapters when we discuss buy patterns.
10. https://news.gallup.com/interactives/185273/presidential-job-approval-center.aspx
11. Based on transcript of Eisenhower's conversation with Republican national chairman, Leonard Hall. https://www.nytimes.com/1979/10/04/archives/eisenhower-papers-cast-new-light-on-nixon-in-1956.html
12. Once again, the absence of polling data in the archival record reflects both the early state of campaign adaptation to this kind of strategic information as well as the widespread pessimism of the time that opinion polls could usefully predict election outcomes, as evidenced in the 1948 polling fiasco that predicted a Dewey landslide (Converse, 1987). This was a revisionary period for political polling methods, which were transitioning from older quota-based sampling frames to newer random probability sampling methods that would eventually provide the higher quality insights that campaigners have relied on ever since.
13. In part this almost certainly reflected a sense among Stevenson aides that Eisenhower's weak speaking skills were being "papered over" with image-based and highly edited TV spots. Democrats preferred the longer form "let's hear an entire speech" approach both because it was the standard mode for radio campaigning and because Stevenson was good at it. In this sense, they sincerely did not "get it" with respect to television.
14. https://www.nytimes.com/1964/02/16/archives/political-evolution-of-nelson-rockefeller-in-less-than-six-years-he.html
15. Nixon apparently approached Rockefeller about being on the ticket, but the New York governor refused.
16. Zeleny, Jeff, and Julie Bosman. 2008. "Obama Rejects Idea of Back Seat on Ticket." *The New York Times*, March 11. https://www.nytimes.com/2008/03/11/us/politics/11clinton.html
17. https://www.npr.org/templates/story/story.php?storyId=16920600.
18. Lawrence, W. H. 1960. "West Virginia Poll Finds Kennedy Gain." *The New York Times*, May 6. Retrieved February 1, 2023.
19. The issue of Kennedy's religion recurred in the general election. On September 12, Kennedy gave an extended response to questions about whether he could exercise "independence" from the Catholic Church and the pope. This response was replayed in its entirety as special program television ad buys made by the Kennedy campaign all over the country.
20. There is considerable debate among historians about how Johnson's nomination came about. Robert Kennedy claimed that his brother offered the spot on the ticket as a courtesy to Johnson, never expecting LBJ would accept it. Most historians dispute this account, however, and it seems that Kennedy wanted Johnson on the ticket due to the calculation that he would greatly enhance Kennedy's electoral prospects by delivering Texas into the Democrats' column. The main complication, setting side Robert Kennedy's disdain for Johnson, appears to be that organized labor objected vociferously to Johnson, causing

Kennedy to hold several meetings and make several substantive concessions before holding fast to his insistence that Johnson was his man (Caro, 2012).

21. In contrast, North Carolina is also a "priority 2" state for Kennedy but was clearly regarded as leaning toward Kennedy.
22. Rockefeller divorced in 1962 and remarried in the spring of 1963.
23. Barry Goldwater. 1964. "Presidential Nomination Acceptance Speech at the Republican National Convention" (https://www.4president.org/speeches/1964/barrygoldwater1964acceptance.htm).
24. The "Daisy Girl" ad (http://www.livingroomcandidate.org/commercials/1964/peace-little-girl-daisy) was only one of the "nuclear threat" ads used by Johnson against Goldwater (another, shorter, one can be seen here: http://www.livingroomcandidate.org/commercials/1964/merely-another-weapon). Bill Moyer's made for television documentary "The 30-second President" (https://billmoyers.com/content/30-second-president/) includes a detailed interview with Tony Schwartz—creative talent behind the Johnson ads—explaining that Johnson's use of television ads was designed to primarily elicit strong emotional responses to the political environment, and the use of over-the-top scare tactics seemed to fit right in with this approach.
25. http://www.livingroomcandidate.org/commercials/1964/kkk
26. Goldwater's best advertisement was a half-hour speech, but it was delivered by Ronald Reagan.
27. Gallup Presidential Job Approval Center https://news.gallup.com/interactives/185273/presidential-job-approval-center.aspx.
28. During this time, the Republican party also moved in parallel to usher in its own nomination reforms that prioritized primary wins over proverbial "smoke filled rooms" of party insiders. By 1976 both parties had committed to nomination systems that chose candidates mainly based on primary and caucus wins (which selected over 80% of convention delegates for both parties), with a smaller set of delegates representing the preferences of party insiders.
29. Behind the scenes, the Nixon campaign worked connections with the South Vietnamese to undermine this peace deal/October surprise. For details, see https://www.nytimes.com/2016/12/31/opinion/sunday/nixons-vietnam-treachery.html?_r=0 and https://www.nytimes.com/2017/01/02/us/politics/nixon-tried-to-spoil-johnsons-vietnam-peace-talks-in-68-notes-show.html.
30. Has American politics ever produced a better acronym?
31. There is appreciable evidence that Nixon and his team were obsessed with Kennedy and the possibility that he would challenge Nixon in 1972. Nixon's supporters clearly engaged in efforts to keep the Chappaquiddick story alive, and to investigate other potentially damaging stories about the feared younger brother (Matthews, 2011).
32. The Canuck letter was reputedly a fake produced by the "dirty tricks" operation of the Nixon campaign.
33. Gallup Organization, Gallup Poll # 857, Question 7, USGALLUP.857.Q004B, Gallup Organization, Cornell University. Ithaca, NY: Roper Center for Public Opinion Research, 1972.
34. For a then-contemporary description of the project see Pool and Abelson (1961); for a retrospective look at the project from the lens of present-day targeting technologies, see https://www.newyorker.com/magazine/2020/08/03/how-the-simulmatics-corporation-invented-the-future.

Chapter 4

1. The name "plumbers" referred to their original purpose, which was to ascertain the source of White House "leaks" to the press (most notably, information associated with the Vietnam War).
2. The FECA distinguished between primary elections and general elections, so that an individual could give $1,000 to a candidate for the primary election and then give another $1,000 for the general election.
3. These multi-candidate committees are better known as political action committees or PACs. In recognizing and regulating these groups, the FECA legitimized them, and interest group organization and activity exploded in the aftermath of the act's passage.
4. https://www.fec.gov/introduction-campaign-finance/understanding-ways-support-federal-candidates/presidential-elections/public-funding-presidential-elections/
5. Soft money is campaign money raised and spent in unlimited increments to engage in "party building" and "voter information" activities. By the 1990s, the Democratic and Republican parties were raising soft money in amounts equal to—and, in 1996 and 2000, more than—the presidential campaign public funds. This created some (relatively minor) asymmetries between the major party candidates, but nothing like the differences seen in 1972 and earlier election campaigns.
6. Strategic memo for Bush Campaign, September 20, 1992 (from the first author's personal papers from the 1992 Bush-Quayle campaign).
7. We came across the plan among the papers of Edwin Meese, counselor to Reagan and later his attorney general.
8. We found these among the papers of Richard Wirthlin, Reagan's pollster.
9. Part of the effort to discredit Dukakis pushed the bounds of propriety and arguably veered into racist imagery and rhetoric. Most famously, an independent expenditure committee, the National Security PAC, aired an advertisement called "Weekend Passes," produced by Larry McCarthy, which bashed Dukakis's record on crime. The ad emphasized Massachusetts's experimental "weekend prison furlough" program. More pointedly, they cited the example of Willie Horton, an African-American man who was released as part of the program on June 6, 1986, but did not return. On April 3, 1987, in Oxon Hill, Maryland, Horton twice raped a White woman after pistol-whipping, stabbing, binding, and gagging her fiancé. He then stole the car belonging to the man he had assaulted. The ad used not only the example but images of Horton and emphasized racial aspects of the incidents to play to white voters' fears of Black people. For example, Mr. Horton was known by his friends or family as "William"; "Willie" was an invention of the ad team to emphasize racial aspects of the case (see Kathleen Hall Jamieson's (1992) detailed analysis of the Horton ad and its integration into the larger George H. W. Bush campaign's emphasis on crime as a wedge issue). The so-called "Willie Horton" ad was aired only in regional markets in Connecticut but received national attention (and viewership) when the network news broadcasts questioned its use of what came to be known as "dog whistle" racial appeals. The Bush campaign denied coordinating with the PAC, but the candidate and his campaign never shied from referring to Dukakis's record on crime or his supposed support of the prison furlough program. The controversy is not only emblematic of the negativity we referenced earlier but also continues to echo in today's politics, with Democrats often accusing Republicans of clandestine racial appeals in their campaigns.

10. Quote from author's personal conversation with Mr. Steeper.
11. https://content.time.com/time/subscriber/article/0,33009,984423-1,00.html
12. Morris resigned on August 30, 1996, after a story broke linking him with a New York call girl, but still advised Clinton on an informal basis throughout the campaign.
13. As indicated in the notes to Table 4.6, Reed offered his own account of the campaign's electoral strategy (Woodward, 2007). This account, based on a quote, has several factual errors, though, raising the possibility that Reed was speaking off the cuff.
14. As he raised funds in California in 1999 and early 2000, Bush's campaign had promised Golden State party officials not to "abandon" the state, which Californians claimed George H.W. Bush had done in 1992. Bush therefore made an early October swing through California on his way back east after campaigning in Washington and Oregon. He appeared on NBC's popular *Tonight Show*, and the campaign publicized the swing as evidence that Bush was competing everywhere. He was not.
15. Gore and Clinton endured a "political divorce" after the 2000 election (Branch, 2009). Clinton was mystified and hurt that Gore had not used him more to campaign in the closing days of the race. Gore was hurt that Clinton had never apologized to him for the Lewinsky affair and blamed the president for his loss to Bush (Branch, 2009).
16. Ironically, the Supreme Court decision in *Bush v Gore* involved two separate decisions. In the first, the court ruled 7–2 in favor of Bush's claim that the Florida Supreme Court had erred in ruling that there could be a select recount only in four heavily Democratic counties. The oft-cited 5–4 vote referred to the second question of whether a full statewide recount was justified and necessary at the risk of Florida not getting its slate of electors counted in the official Electoral College tally. It turns out that if the Gore campaign had initially demanded a full statewide recount, or if the Florida courts had ultimately ordered one, Gore might have won the presidential election. So concluded a consortium of news organizations examining the full set of 175,010 rejected ballots that had never been officially recounted (e.g., Fessenden and Broder, 2001). The lesson for future presidential campaigns: Be careful what you ask for.

Chapter 5

1. https://www.nytimes.com/2004/12/04/politics/kerry-left-14-million-unspent-in-campaign.html
2. http://www.cfinst.org/pdf/federal/HistoricalTables/pdf/CFI_Federal-CF_18_Table1-07.pdf
3. https://www.propublica.org/article/everything-we-know-so-far-about-obamas-big-data-operation
4. https://slate.com/news-and-politics/2012/07/the-romney-campaigns-data-strategy-theyre-outsourcing.html
5. Turnout estimates are from the U.S. Elections Project (https://www.electproject.org/2012g).
6. https://newrepublic.com/article/110597/exclusive-the-polls-made-mitt-romney-think-hed-win
7. The name ORCA was a chosen because the 2012 Obama get-out-the-vote effort was called Project Narwal, and orcas are the only known natural enemies of the narwal. Although we

appreciate their native intelligence, the obsession with marine mammals in 2012 escapes our comprehension.

8. Forecasts are from the *New York Times* website (https://www.nytimes.com/interactive/2016/upshot/presidential-polls-forecast.html).
9. https://www.politico.com/magazine/story/2016/09/hillary-clinton-data-campaign-elan-kriegel-214215/
10. https://www.opensecrets.org/pres16
11. https://www.nytimes.com/2018/03/17/us/politics/cambridge-analytica-trump-campaign.html
12. https://www.opensecrets.org/news/2021/02/2020-cycle-cost-14p4-billion-doubling-16/

Chapter 6

1. For example, see https://projects.fivethirtyeight.com/2020-election-forecast/.
2. Once again, we thank Matthew Dowd, Tucker Eskew, (the late) John Gorman, Karl Rove, Robert Shrum, and Fred Steeper.
3. See note 28 of chapter 2 for details on the reliability of this measure.
4. Regarding the Obama campaign's 2008 placement of campaign ads inside video games like the then-popular Madden 09 football game, see Gorman (2008).
5. This is particularly true for elections after the 2002 Help America Vote Act (HAVA), which mandated that states maintain updated registered voter files.
6. This is consistent with the notion of "the neglected majority" (see Panagopoulos, 2004).
7. As Table A6.1 presents the first of the book's statistical models, it is important to observe that we adhere to the convention of noting effects that reach specified levels of statistical significance. That is, we mark effects where likelihood that they are due to statistical noise or random error falls below a certain level. In so doing, we follow a long tradition of political science scholarship. But it is important to point out that there is nothing sacrosanct about this approach to "statistical significance"; some of the effects that fall just below these thresholds may be impressive substantively, while others that meet them are shaky substantively and could just as soon melt away with slightly different specifications or modeling assumptions (this point is often made by scholars who bemoan what they call "p-hacking" in the discipline). The book's discussions make an effort to be transparent about these issues and to account for them in the interpretations of data analyses.

Chapter 7

1. The text of the full speech can be found at the website for The American Presidency Project: https://www.presidency.ucsb.edu/documents/address-accepting-the-presidential-nomination-the-republican-national-convention-chicago.
2. According to Barr, Pascarella, and Pappas (2023), "Because of his leg wound, Nixon developed chronic DVTs in that limb, including a severe thrombus in 1974 that embolized to his lung, required surgery, and prevented him from testifying at the Watergate Trial."
3. These percentages from 1952 and 1956 are totals for major party campaigns at all levels, not just presidential campaigns, and include network buys as well as spot ad purchases.

4. Regional advertisements have also existed since 1952. However, these have never been especially popular among campaign consultants.
5. When aggregating TV spot buy spending numbers to the state level, we attribute them to the state the campaign intended to reach. This is usually a simple matter. For example, spending in the Washington, D.C., market has never been intended to reach voters in the District; rather, it has invariably been intended to reach voters in either Virginia or Maryland. An example of a more difficult decision (historically) is whether TV ad spending in Philadelphia is intended to reach voters in Pennsylvania or New Jersey. Campaign documents and memos typically clarify these calls and are most often the basis for our choices with respect to statewide aggregation.
6. The FCC data is an outstanding but previously neglected source of historical spot television ad buy records. To ensure station compliance with Fairness Doctrine regulations, it produced a census of station-level spot ad buy and network time records detailing advertising expenditures by candidates for federal and state-wide office. In a search of National Archive and Records Administration files, we found partial records of these station-level survey forms from 1952 and complete sets from 1956 and 1972. State-level compilations of these FCC-mandated station surveys appeared biennially in the records of various congressional hearings related to Fairness Doctrine compliance as well as in the FCC's own *Survey of Political Broadcasting* reports published each year following a federal election from 1960 through 1970 (e.g., Federal Communication Commission 1961).
7. Campaigns typically paid their advertising companies not only for their own advertising, but also to keep tabs on their opponent's spot buys.
8. Alexander's volumes occasionally include estimates of statewide television ad spending and usually include estimates of aggregate television spending. We find that his aggregate figures correlate highly with data estimates from the campaigns, although there is almost never a perfect match. This is unsurprising given that the time frame and exact nature of TV ad spending is all but impossible to replicate identically.
9. Licensed stations are obliged by FCC regulations to offer the lowest unit rate to candidates for political office.
10. If the network cannot sell their five or so minutes to national advertisers, the remainder of the ad time reverts to the local station for local ad sales.
11. The use of advertisements aired is a common metric in more recent elections, as additional contextual data has allowed us to adjust our overall estimates of the volume of TV advertising (see, for example, Fowler et al., 2021; Sides, Vavreck, and Warshaw, 2022).
12. From a practical perspective, it is also the case that earlier presidential campaigns measured television advertising in dollars spent more consistently and comprehensively than in advertisements aired.
13. In our later analysis of TV advertising data at the media market level, we transform these county-level data to measure candidate appearances at the market level since media markets are aggregations of counties.
14. "Soft money" refers to unregulated contributions made to parties or groups for "party building" activities, such as registering voters of issue advocacy.
15. McConnell v. Federal Election Commission, 540 U.S. 93 (2003); Citizens United v. Federal Election Commission, 558 U.S. 310 (2010).
16. See https://www.fec.gov/data/ for updated data on this claim.
17. The 1952 Eisenhower spot buy strategy, outlined in what was known as the Levin Plan after its author, Michael Levin, could not be found in the Eisenhower presidential library

by our research team, probably because Eisenhower ordered significant campaign documents burned after his 1952 victory according to library staff. But we discovered a purloined copy of the Levin Plan in Adlai Stevenson's papers (Box 229, Folder 7—Reports, Eisenhower, Dwight D. "How to Insure an Eisenhower Victory in November," n.d.). It turns out the Democrats had a mole in the Republican camp and were able to obtain an advance copy of the entire plan from a disgruntled advertising strategist long before the first Eisenhower ad ever aired. The list of twelve states targeted for the Eisenhower spots shifted somewhat over the course of the campaign, but the actual ad spending targeted forty-nine key counties in Arizona, Colorado, Connecticut, Delaware, Illinois, Massachusetts, Michigan, New Mexico, Nevada, New York, Pennsylvania, Texas, and Wyoming, with the lion's share spent in New York alone. The Stevenson campaign bought television spots in nineteen states, but only weakly counter-programmed on television against the GOP buy.

18. In addition, while Super PAC spending by conservative and liberal groups was roughly even over this period, one should bear in mind that Republican party spending allowed GOP candidates to appreciably reduce some of these spending deficits.

Chapter 8

1. https://www.opensecrets.org/news/2021/02/2020-cycle-cost-14p4-billion-doubling-16/
2. Estimates are based on presidential election data from David Leip's "Election Atlas." https://uselectionatlas.org/.
3. The average is calculated as follows: R Vote AVG = (.5*R Vote in election t−1) + (.3*R Vote in election t−2) + (.2*R Vote in election t−3), where t = the current election and R Vote is the Republican share of the major party vote. Using the Republican share of the two-party vote eliminates the impact of third-party or independent candidates in each election. Later, when we focus on media market results (which are a little more volatile), we use a slightly different measure that takes an average of only the two most recent presidential elections.
4. There is no natural log of zero, so when there is no TV ad spending, we set the variable's value equal to 1. Since the natural log of 1 is zero, this means our explanatory variable takes on a value of zero when there is no TV ad spending.
5. We explored estimating the models with variables capturing incumbency (Democratic, Republican, and open-seat elections) and for the individual states (additional fixed effects, with California serving as the base category). Incumbency, however, loses almost all explanatory power once year-by-year fixed effects are introduced. As for state fixed effects, these were almost all statistically insignificant (with the odd exception of Utah). We therefore proceed without these variables in the models.
6. Because the spending variable is logged, it is important to point out that additional increases in spending do not produce linear increases in the vote shift. We use the $0 to $100,000 increases because they are illustrative and plausible in the context of statewide presidential campaigns.
7. We also tested coefficients associated with vice-presidential appearances, which are indistinguishable from zero for both the Republicans and the Democrats. Although we are not convinced these efforts produce zero effects (more on this soon), this result is only mildly surprising. It is certainly plausible that vice-presidential appearances simply do not receive the local news media attention that presidential appearances do.

8. The presence of third-party candidates in the southern states might also have limited the Republicans' ability to over-perform two-party vote share expectations in those states.
9. We are using Nielsen's designated market areas (DMAs) as our guide for media markets. Currently, there are 210 media markets in the United States, ranging in population from New York City (7.7 million individuals) to Glendive, Montana, (3,920 individuals).
10. As noted in chapter 7, we have TV spot buy data at the media market level for 1956 and 1972. However, media markets (and their boundaries) changed significantly from 1956 and 1972 to 1988, such that comparisons are extremely fraught. We therefore confine our analyses here to the 1988–2020 era, where we are more confident in the analyses.
11. Oftentimes, the outside tracking organizations are the source for the campaign's reports.
12. For our media market analysis, we found that market boundaries change often enough to make a three-election average inappropriate (for example, the geographic boundaries—and the attendant voter populations—of the Denver media market in 1988 are quite different than they are in 2000). The assumption of geographic stability, however, holds for the most recent election and even for the second most recent election. We therefore use a weighted average of the two most recent elections: 2 × the R share of the two-party vote in the previous election (t–1) + 1 × the R share of the two-party vote in the election before that (t–2) ÷ by 3.
13. We use 1988 and 2000 as our baseline years, with dummy variables for 1992, 1996, 2004, 2008, 2012, 2016, and 2020. As the most distant year for which we have data, 1988 is a conventional choice as a baseline year. The inclusion of 2000, though, is less obvious. We find that including a dummy variable for 2000 causes significant changes in the parameter estimates and the model's diagnostic statistics. Put simply, the 2000 dummy variable dominates all other explanatory variables and causes heretofore stable coefficient estimates to reverse in sign and standard errors to increase significantly. We speculate that this is because there was a shift in the 2000 vote compared to the expected vote (based on 1992 and 1996 results), which is larger than those in other elections and is not strongly correlated with campaigning differentials. It is also possible that the inclusion of the 2000 dummy variable with the incumbency variable produces these effects. At any rate, given the destabilizing effect of the 2000 dummy variable on the entirety of the data, and with no theoretical reason to insist on its inclusion, we think it appropriate to exclude it.
14. It is unclear how this bias might play out. If no campaigning is correlated with vote results that look exactly like predicted, then we could overstate the "effects" of campaigning. If, on the other hand, no campaigning is uncorrelated with expected vote results, then we could understate the "effects."
15. These aggregate tendencies suggest that the closest elections of the era—1960 and 1968—might not have been affected in the expected ways by the presidential campaigns, although we admittedly do not have television ad data for 1960.

Chapter 9

1. The 2000 George W. Bush campaign had committed to spending money in California to appease west coast contributors and fundraisers, who were still smarting over the failure of George H. W. Bush to campaign in their state in 1992 (see Shaw, 2006).

References

Abramowitz, Alan. 2010. *The Disappearing Center: Engaged Citizens, Polarization and American Democracy*. New Haven, CT: Yale University Press.

Alesina, Alberto, and Alex Cukierman. 1990. "The Politics of Ambiguity." *The Quarterly Journal of Economics* 105 (4), 829–850.

Alexander, Herbert E. 1976. *Financing the 1972 Election*. Lexington, MA: Lexington Books.

Alexander, Herbert E. 1992. *Financing Politics: Money, Elections, and Political Reform*. 4th ed. Washington, DC: Congressional Quarterly Press.

Allen, Jonathan, and Amy Parnes. 2021. *Lucky: How Joe Biden Barely Won the Presidency*. New York, NY: Crown Publishing.

Althaus, S. L., P. F. Nardulli, and D. R. Shaw. 2002. "Candidate Appearances in Presidential Elections, 1972–2000. *Political Communication* 19 (1), 49–72.

Alvarez, R. Michael. 1997. *Information and Elections*. Ann Arbor, MI: University of Michigan Press.

Anderson, Patrick. 1994. *Electing Jimmy Carter: The Campaign of 1976*. Baton Rouge, LA: LSU Press.

Ansolabehere, Stephen, and Shanto Iyengar. 1995. *Going Negative: How Political Advertisements Shrink and Polarize the Electorate*. New York, NY: The Free Press.

Barr, Justin, Luigi Pascarella, and Theodore N. Pappas. 2023. "Richard Nixon's Left Knee and Its Impact on American History." *American Surgeon* March (3), 31348231161769. doi: 10.1177/00031348231161769. Epub ahead of print. PMID: 36867122.

Bartels, Larry M. 1984. "Resource Allocation in a Presidential Campaign." *Journal of Politics* 17 (3), 571–577.

Beckett, Lois. 2012. "Everything We Know (So Far) About Obama's Big Data Tactics: A New Look at What the Obama Campaign Did With Its Much-Heralded Data Operation." ProPublica. November 29, 2012. https://www.propublica.org/article/everything-we-know-so-far-about-obamas-big-data-operation.

Bennett, W. Lance. 2016. *News: The Politics of Illusion*. 10th ed. Chicago, IL: University of Chicago Press.

Berelson, Bernard R., Paul F. Lazarsfeld, and William N. McPhee. 1954. *Voting: A Study of Opinion Formation in a Presidential Campaign*. Chicago, IL: University of Chicago Press.

Bergan, Daniel E., Alan S. Gerber, Donald P. Green, and Costas Panagopoulos. 2005. "Grassroots Mobilization and Voter Turnout in 2004." *Public Opinion Quarterly* 69 (5), 760–777. https://doi.org/10.1093/poq/nfi063.

Berke, Richard, with Janet Elder. 2000. "Poll Shows Gore Overcoming Voter Concerns over Likability." *Los Angeles Times*, September 13.

Berkin, Carol. 2003. *A Brilliant Solution: Inventing the American Constitution*. New York, NY: Mariner Books.

Bird, Kai. 2012. *The Outlier: The Unfinished Presidency of Jimmy Carter*. New York, NY: Crown Publishing.

Blake, David Haven. 2016. *Liking Ike: Eisenhower, Advertising, and the Rise of Celebrity Politics*. New York, NY: Oxford University Press.

Boller, Paul. 2004. *Presidential Campaigns: From George Washington to George W. Bush*. Rev. ed. New York, NY: Oxford University Press.

Brady, John. 1996. *Bad Boy: The Life and Politics of Lee Atwater*. New York, NY: Addison-Wesley.

Brams, Stephen J., and D. Marc Kilgour. 2017. "Paths to Victory in Presidential Elections: The Set-Up Power of Non-Competitive States." *Public Choice* 170 (2), 99–113.

Branch, Taylor. 2009. *The Clinton Tapes: Wrestling History with the President*. New York, NY: Simon and Schuster.

Broockman, David E., and Joshua L. Kalla. 2022. "When and Why Are Campaigns' Persuasive Effects Small? Evidence from the 2020 US Presidential Election." *American Journal of Political Science* 67 (4), 833–849.

Brownstein, Ronald. 2016. "Is Donald Trump Out-Flanking Hillary Clinton?" *The Atlantic*, November 2.

Bruschke, Jon, and Divine, Laura. 2017. "Debunking Nixon's Radio Victory in the 1960 Election: Re-analyzing the Historical Record and Considering Currently Unexamined Polling Data." *The Social Science Journal* 54 (1), 67–75. DOI: 10.1016/j.soscij.2016.09.007.

Campbell, Angus, Philip E. Converse, Warren E. Miller, and Donald E. Stokes. 1960. *The American Voter*. Chicago, IL: University of Chicago Press.

Campbell, James. 1992. "Forecasting the Presidential Vote in the States." *American Journal of Political Science* 36 (2), 386–407.

Campbell, James. 2000. *The American Campaign: U.S. Presidential Campaigns and the National Vote*. College Station, TX: Texas A&M Press.

Caro, Robert. 2012. *The Passage of Power: The Years of Lyndon Johnson*. New York, NY: Knopf.

Cervas, Jonathan R., and Bernard Grofman. 2017. "Why Noncompetitive States Are so Important for Understanding the Outcomes of Competitive Elections: 1868–2016." *Public Choice* 173 (3\4), 251–265.

Chandler, D. Aaron. 1998. "A Short Note on the Expenditures of the McKinley Campaign of 1896." *Presidential Studies Quarterly* 28 (1), 88–91.

Chen, Lanhee J., and Andrew Reeves. 2010. "Turning Out the Base or Appealing to the Periphery? An Analysis of County-Level Candidate Appearances in the 2008 Presidential Campaign." *American Politics Research* 39 (3), 534–556.

Chernow, Ron. 2004. *Alexander Hamilton*. New York, NY: Penguin Press.

Chester, Lewis, Godfrey Hodgson, and Bruce Page. 1969. *An American Melodrama: The Presidential Campaign of 1968*. New York, NY: Dell.

Clinton, Hillary Rodham. 2017. *What Happened?* New York, NY: Simon and Schuster.

Cohen, Marty, David Karol, Hans Noel, and John Zaller. 2008. *The Party Decides: Presidential Nominations Before and After Reform*. Chicago, IL: University of Chicago Press.

Collins, Robert M. 1996. "The Economic Crisis of 1968 and the Waning of the 'American Century.' " *American Historical Review* 101 (2), 396–422.

Converse, Jean M. 1987. *Survey Research in the United States: Roots and Emergence 1890–1960*. Berkeley, CA: University of California Press.

Cook, Rhodes. 2012. "When the Whole Map Was in Play." Larry Sabato's Crystal Ball, University of Virginia Center for Politics. https://centerforpolitics.org/crystalball/articles/when-the-whole-map-was-in-play/.

Coppock, Alexander, Seth J. Hill and Lynn Vavreck. 2020. "The Small Effects of Political Advertising Are Small Regardless of Context, Message, Sender, or Receiver: Evidence from 59 Real-Time Randomized Experiments." *Science Advances* 6 (36), eabc4046. doi: 10.1126/sciadv.abc4046.

Cramer, Richard Ben. 1993. *What It Takes: The Way to the White House*. New York, NY: Random House.

De Tocqueville, Alexis. 1835. *De la démocratie en Amérique*. Vol. I. 1st ed. Paris: Librairie de Charles Gosselin.

Debenedetti, Gabriel. 2016. "They Always Wanted Trump," *Politico*, November 7.

Devine, Christopher J. 2018. "What If Hillary Clinton *Had* Gone to Wisconsin? Presidential Campaign Visits and Vote Choice in the 2016 Election." *The Forum* (16) 2, 211–234. https://doi.org/10.1515/for-2018-0011.

Devine, Christopher J. 2023. *I'm Here to Ask for Your Vote: How Presidential Campaign Visits Influence Voters*. New York, NY: Columbia University Press.

Dickerson, John. 2017. *Whistlestop: My Favorite Stories from Presidential Campaign History*. New York, NY: Twelve Publishing.

Downs, Anthony. 1957. *An Economic Theory of Democracy*. New York, NY: Harper.

Drew, Elizabeth. 1981. *Portrait of an Election: The 1980 Presidential Campaign*, New York, NY: Simon & Schuster.

Drew, Elizabeth. 1995. *On the Edge: The Clinton Presidency*. New York, NY: Touchstone.

Duverger, Maurice. 1954. *Political Parties*. Paris: Armand Colin.

Edwards, George C. 2005. *Why the Electoral College Is Bad for America*. New Haven, CT: Yale University Press.

Enos, Ryan D., and Anthony Fowler. 2018. "Aggregate Effects of Large-Scale Campaigns on Voter Turnout." *Political Research and Methods* 6 (4), 733–751.

Epstein, Joseph. 1968. "Adlai Stevenson in Retrospect: Why Adlai Stevenson's Campaign Still Draws Special Feelings." *Commentary*. December. https://www.commentary.org/articles/joseph-epstein/adlai-stevenson-in-retrospect/.

Erikson, Robert S., and Christopher Wlezien. 2012. *The Timeline of Presidential Elections: How Campaigns Do (and Do Not) Matter*. Chicago, IL: University of Chicago Press.

Evers-Hillstrom, Karl. 2021. "Most Expensive Ever: 2020 Election Cost $14.4 Billion." *Open Secrets*, February 11, 2021. https://www.opensecrets.org/news/2021/02/2020-cycle-cost-14p4-billion-doubling-16

Fair, Ray C. 1978. "The Effect of Economic Events on Votes for President." *The Review of Economics and Statistics* 60 (2), 159–173.

Federal Communication Commission. 1961. *Survey of Political Broadcasting: September 1–November 8, 1960*. Washington, DC: Federal Communications Commission.

Fessenden, Ford, and John M. Broder. 2001. "Examining the Vote, the Overview: Study of Disputed Florida Ballots Finds Justices Did Not Cast the Deciding Vote." *New York Times*, November 12. Section A, Page 1.

Finkel, Steven E. 1993. "Reexamining the 'Minimal Effects' Model in Recent Presidential Campaigns." *The Journal of Politics* 55 (1): 1–21.

Fiorina, Morris P. 1981. *Retrospective Voting in American National Elections*. New Haven, CT: Yale University Press.

Fleegler, Robert. 2023. *Brutal Campaign: How the 1988 Election Set the Stage for Twenty-First Century American Politics*. Chapel Hill, NC: University of North Carolina Press.

Fowler, Erika Franklin, Michael M. Franz, Gregory J. Martin, Zachary Peskowitz, and Travis N. Ridout. 2021. "Political Advertising Online and Offline." *American Political Science Review* 115 (1), 130–149.

Fowler, Erika Franklin, Travis N. Ridout, and Michael M. Franz. 2016. "Political Advertising in 2016: The Presidential Election as Outlier?" *The Forum* 14 (4), 445–469.

Franz, Michael M., Paul B Freedman, Kenneth M. Goldstein, and Travis N. Ridout. 2008. *Campaign Advertising and American Democracy*. Philadelphia, PA: Temple University Press.

Freedman, Paul, Michael Franz, and Kenneth Goldstein. 2004. "Campaign Advertising and Democratic Citizenship." *American Journal of Political Science* 48 (4), 723–741.

Garcia, Gilbert. 2012. *Reagan's Comeback: Four Weeks in Texas that Changed American Politics Forever*. Dallas, TX: Trinity Press.

Geer, John G. 2006. *In Defense of Negativity: Attack Ads in Presidential Campaigns*. Chicago, IL: University of Chicago Press.

Gelman, Andrew, and Gary King. 1993. "Why Are American Presidential Election Campaign Polls So Variable When Votes Are So Predictable?" *British Journal of Political Science* 23 (4), 409–451.

Gerber, Alan S., James G. Gimpel, Donald P. Green, and Daron R. Shaw. 2011. "How Large and Long-Lasting Are the Persuasive Effects of Televised Campaign Ads? Results from a Randomized Field Experiment." *American Political Science Review* 105 (1), 135–150.

Germond, Jack W., and Jules Witcover. 1981. *Blue Smoke and Mirrors: How Reagan Won & Why Carter Lost the Election of 1980.* New York, NY: Viking Press.

Germond, Jack W., and Jules Witcover. 1985. *Wake Us When It's Over: Presidential Politics of 1984.* New York, NY: Macmillan Press.

Germond, Jack W., and Jules Witcover. 1989. *Whose Broad Stripes and Bright Stars: The Trivial Pursuit of the Presidency 1988.* New York, NY: Grand Central Press.

Germond, Jack W., and Jules Witcover. 1993. *Mad as Hell: Revolt at the Ballot Box, 1992.* New York, NY: Grand Central Press.

Goldmacher, Shane. 2016. "Hillary Clinton's 'Invisible Guiding Hand.'" *Politico Magazine.* September 7, 2016. https://www.politico.com/magazine/story/2016/09/hillary-clinton-data-campaign-elan-kriegel-214215/.

Goldman, Peter, Thomas M. DeFrank, Mark Miller, Andrew Murr, and Tom Matthews. 1994. *Quest for the Presidency 1992.* College Station, TX: Texas A&M University Press.

Goldstein, Kenneth, and Travis N. Ridout. 2004. "Measuring the Effects of Televised Political Advertising in the United States." *Annual Review of Political Science* 7, 205–226.

Gordon, Brett R., and Wesley R. Hartmann. 2013. "Advertising Effects in Presidential Elections." *Marketing Science* 32 (1), 19–35. http://www.jstor.org/stable/23361432.

Gorman, Steve. 2008. "Obama Buys First Video Game Campaign Ads." *Reuters*, October 17. Accessed March 24, 2024. https://www.reuters.com/article/idUSTRE49EAGL/#:~:text=LOS%20ANGELES%20(Reuters)%20%2D%20Barack,ads%20in%20online%20video%20games.

Graber, Doris, and Johanna Dunaway. 2014. *Mass Media and the American Politics.* 9th ed. Washington, DC: CQ Press.

Graf, J., Reeher, G., Malbin, M., & Panagopoulos, C. 2006. "Small Donors and Online Giving." *Report Issued by the Institute for Politics, Democracy and the Internet.* Washington, DC: Institute for Politics, Democracy and the Internet. http://www.cfinst.org/president/pdf/IPDI_SmallDonors.pdf.

Green, Donald P., and Alan S. Gerber. 2023. *Get Out the Vote! How to Increase Voter Turnout.* 5th ed. Washington, DC: Brookings Institute.

Halperin, Mark, and John Heilemann. 2013. *Double Down: Game Change 2012.* New York, NY: Harper Perennial.

Heilemann, John, and Mark Halperin. 2010. *Game Change: Obama and the Clintons, McCain and Palin, and the Race of a Lifetime.* New York, NY: Harper Perennial.

Haselmayer, M. 2019. "Negative Campaigning and Its Consequences: A Review and a Look Ahead." *French Politics* 17, 355–372.

Heard, Alexander. 1962. *The Costs of Democracy: Financing American Political Campaigns.* New York, NY: Doubleday Anchor Publishing.

Hersh, Eitan D. 2015. *Hacking the Electorate: How Campaigns Perceive Voters.* New York, NY: Cambridge University Press.

Hill, Seth J., James Lo, Lynn Vavreck, and John Zaller. 2013. "How Quickly We Forget: The Duration of Persuasion Effects from Mass Communication." *Political Communication* 30 (4), 521–547.

Hillygus, D. Sunshine, and Todd G. Shields. 2008. *The Persuadable Voter: Wedge Issues in Presidential Campaigns.* Princeton, NJ: Princeton University Press.

Holbrook, Thomas M. 1996. *Do Campaigns Matter?* Thousand Oaks, CA: Sage Press.

Holbrook, Thomas M. 2002. "Did the Whistle-Stop Campaign Matter?" *PS: Political Science and Politics* 35 (1), 59–66. http://www.jstor.org/stable/1554764.

Hollitz, John E. 1982. "Eisenhower and the Admen: The Television Spot Campaign of 1952." *The Wisconsin Magazine of History* 66 (1): 25–39.

Huber, Gregory A., and Kevin Arceneaux. 2007. "Identifying the Persuasive Effects of Presidential Advertising." *American Journal of Political Science* 51 (4), 957–977.

Hughes, Daniel J., and Harry Bell. 1993. *Moltke on the Art of War: Selected Writings*. Toronto, Ontario: Presidio Press.

Institute of Politics, John F. Kennedy School of Government, Harvard University. 1997. *Campaign for President: The Managers Look at '96*. Hollis, NH: Hollis Publishing.

Institute of Politics, John F. Kennedy School of Government, Harvard University. 2002. *Campaign for President: The Managers Look at 2000*. Hollis, NH: Hollis Publishing.

Institute of Politics, John F. Kennedy School of Government, Harvard University. 2006. *Campaign for President: The Managers Look at 2004*. Lanham, MD: Rowman and Littlefield.

Institute of Politics, John F. Kennedy School of Government, Harvard University. 2009. *Campaign for President: The Managers Look at 2008*. Lanham, MD: Rowman and Littlefield.

Institute of Politics, John F. Kennedy School of Government, Harvard University. 2013. *Campaign for President: The Managers Look at 2012*. Lanham, MD: Rowman and Littlefield.

Institute of Politics, John F. Kennedy School of Government, Harvard University. 2017. *Campaign for President: The Managers Look at 2016*. Lanham, MD: Rowman and Littlefield.

Institute of Politics, John F. Kennedy School of Government, Harvard University. 2022. *Campaign for President: The Managers Look at 2020*. Lanham, MD: Rowman and Littlefield.

Issenberg, Sasha. 2012. *Victory Lab: The Secret Science of Winning Campaigns*. New York, NY: Crown Publishing.

Jamieson, Kathleen Hall. 1992. *Dirty Politics: Deception, Distraction, and Democracy*. New York, NY: Oxford University Press.

Jamieson, Kathleen Hall. 1996. *Packaging the Presidency: A History and Criticism of Presidential Campaign Advertising*. New York, NY: Oxford University Press.

Jamieson, Kathleen Hall. 2006. *Electing the President 2004: The Insiders' View*. Philadelphia, PA: University of Pennsylvania Press.

Jamieson, Kathleen Hall. 2009. *Electing the President 2008: The Insiders' View*. Philadelphia, PA: University of Pennsylvania Press.

Jamieson, Kathleen Hall. 2013. *Electing the President 2012: The Insiders' View*. Philadelphia, PA: University of Pennsylvania Press.

Jamieson, Kathleen Hall, and Paul Waldman. 2001. *Electing the President 2000: The Insiders' View*. Philadelphia, PA: University of Pennsylvania Press.

Johnston, Richard, Michael Hagen, and Kathleen Hall Jamieson. 2004. *The 2000 Presidential Election and the Foundations of Party Politics*. New York, NY: Cambridge University Press.

Jordan, Hamilton. 2001. *No Such Thing as a Bad Day: A Memoir*. New York, NY: Gallery Books.

Judis, John B., and Ruy Teixeira. 2004. *The Emerging Democratic Majority*. New York, NY: Scribner.

Kalla, Joshua, and David E. Brookman. 2018. "The Minimal Persuasive Effects of Campaign Contact in General Elections: Evidence from 49 Field Experiments." *American Political Science Review* 112 (1), 148–166.

Kearns Goodwin, Doris. 2006. *Team of Rivals: The Political Genius of Abraham Lincoln*. New York, NY: Simon and Schuster.

Kenski, Kate, Bruce W. Hardy, Kathleen Hall Jamieson. 2010. *The Obama Victory: How Media, Money and Message Shaped the 2008 Election*. New York, NY: Oxford University Press.

Kernell, Samuel. 2000. Life before Polls: Ohio Politicians Predict the 1828 Presidential Vote. *PS: Political Science and Politics* 33 (3), 569–574.

Kilgore, Ed. 2023. "There Could Be a New Batch of Battleground States in 2024." *New York Magazine*. May 2. Accessed July 12, 2023. https://nymag.com/intelligencer/2023/05/2024-election-battleground-states.html.

Kirchheimer, O. 1966. "The Transformation of the Western European Party System." In *Political Parties and Political Development*, edited by J. La Palombara and M. Weiner. Princeton, NJ: Princeton University Press: 177–200.

Klarman, Michael. 2018. *The Framers' Coup: The Making of the U.S. Constitution*. New York, NY: Oxford University Press.

Krasno, Jonathan S., and Donald P. Green. 2008. "Do Televised Presidential Ads Increase Voter Turnout? Evidence from a Natural Experiment." *The Journal of Politics* 70 (1), 245–261.

Kraus, Sidney. 1996. "Winners of the First 1960 Televised Presidential Debate between Kennedy and Nixon." *Journal of Communication* 46 (4), 78–96. https://doi.org/10.1111/j.1460-2466.1996.tb01507.x.

Larson, Edward J. 2007. *A Magnificent Catastrophe: The Tumultuous Election of 1800, America's First Presidential Campaign*. New York, NY: Free Press.

Lau, Richard R., and David P. Redlawsk. 1997. "Voting Correctly." *American Political Science Review* 91 (3), 585–598.

Lepore, Jill. 2020. "How the Simulatics Corporation Invented the Future." *The New Yorker*. July 27. Last accessed on March 24, 2024. https://www.newyorker.com/magazine/2020/08/03/how-the-simulmatics-corporation-invented-the-future.

Lewis-Beck, Michael, and Tom Rice. 1982. "Presidential Popularity and the Presidential Vote." *Public Opinion Quarterly* 46: 534–537.

Longley, Lawrence G. and Alan G. Braun. 1972. *The Politics of Electoral College Reform*. New Haven, CT: Yale University Press.

Longley, Lawrence D., and James D. Dana, Jr. 1984. "New Empirical Estimates of the Biases of the Electoral College for the 1980s." *Western Political Quarterly* 37, 157–175.

Longley, Lawrence D., and James D. Dana, Jr. 1992. "The Biases of the Electoral College in the 1990s." *Polity* 25, 123–145.

Longley, Lawrence D., and Neal R. Peirce. 1999. *The Electoral College Primer 2000*. New Haven, CT: Yale University Press.

Malbin, Michael, ed. 2006. *The Election after Reform: Money, Politics, and the Bipartisan Campaign Reform Act*. Lanham, MD: Rowman & Littlefield.

Mann, Irwin, and Lloyd S. Shapley. 1960. "Values of Large Games, VI: Evaluating the Electoral College by Monte Carlo Techniques." The Rand Corporation, Memorandum RM-2651.

Mattes, Kyle, and David P. Redlawsk. 2015. *The Positive Case for Negative Campaigning*, Chicago, IL: University of Chicago Press.

Matthews, Chris. 2011. *Kennedy & Nixon: The Rivalry that Shaped Post-War America*. New York, NY: Free Press.

McClurg, Scott D., and Thomas M. Holbrook. 2009. "Presidential Campaigns and Fundamental Predictors of Vote Choice." *Political Research Quarterly* 62 (3), 495–506.

McDonald Michael P. 2008. "The Return of the Voter: Voter Turnout in the 2008 Presidential Election." *The Forum* 6 (4), Article 4.

McGerr, Michael. 1988. *The Decline of Popular Politics: The American North, 1865–1928*. New York, NY: Oxford University Press.

McGhee, Eric, and John Sides. 2011. "Do Campaigns Drive Partisan Turnout?" *Political Behavior* 33, 313–333.

McKenna, Elizabeth, Hahrie Han, and Jeremy Bird. 2014. *How Obama's 2.2 Million Volunteers Transformed Campaigning in America*. New York, NY: Oxford University Press.

Meacham, Jon. 2008. *American Lion: Andrew Jackson in the White House*. New York, NY: Random House.

Medvic, Stephen K. 2011. *New Directions in Campaigns and Elections*. New York, NY: Taylor & Francis.

Merolla, Jennifer, Michael Munger, and Michael Tofias. 2005. "In Play: A Commentary on Strategies in the 2004 U.S. Presidential Election." *Public Choice* 123 (1/2), 19–37.

Merolla, Jennifer, Michael Munger, and Michael Tofias. 2006. "Lotto, Blotto, or Frontrunner: U.S. Presidential Elections and the Nature of 'Mistakes.'" Paper presented at the Annual Meeting of the American Political Science Association.

Merrill, Irving R. 1954. "Campaign Expenditures and Their Control: A Study of Expenditures for Television Time in the 1952 Federal Election." PhD dissertation, Mass Communications, University of Illinois Urbana-Champaign.

Middendorf, J. William. 2006. *Glorious Disaster: Barry Goldwater's Presidential Campaign and the Origins of the Conservative Movement*. New York, NY: Basic Books.

Milbank, Dana. 2001. *Smashmouth: Two Years in the Gutter with Al Gore and George Bush, Notes from the Campaign Trail*. New York, NY: Basic Books.

Miller, Warren E., and J. Merrill Shanks. 1996. *The New American Voter*. Cambridge, MA: Harvard University Press.

Moore, Jonathan and Janet Fraser (eds.). 1973. *Campaign for President: The Managers Look at '72*. Cambridge, MA: Ballinger Publishing Company.

Moore, Jonathan, and Janet Fraser (eds.). 1977. *Campaign for President: The Managers Look at 1976*. Cambridge, MA: Ballinger Publishing Company.

Moore, Jonathan (ed.). 1981. *Campaign for President: 1980 in Retrospect*. Institute of Politics, Harvard University. Cambridge, MA: Ballinger Publishing.

Moore, Jonathan (ed.). 1986. *Campaign for President: The Managers Look at '84*. Institute of Politics, Harvard University. Dover, MA: Auburn House Publishing.

Newman, Bruce I. 1994. *The Marketing of the President: Political Marketing as Campaign Strategy*. Thousand Oaks, CA: SAGE Publications.

Nie, Norman, Sidney Verba, and John R. Petrocik. 1976. *The Changing American Voter*. Cambridge, MA: Harvard University Press.

Oliphant, Thomas, and Curtis Wilkie. 2017. *The Road to Camelot: Inside JFK's Five-Year Campaign*. New York, NY: Simon & Schuster.

Panagopoulos, Costas. 2004. "The Neglected Majority: Unequal Distribution of Campaign Resources. *Campaigns & Elections* 25 (7), 44–47.

Panagopoulos, Costas. 2006. "Vested Interests: Interest Group Resource Allocation in Presidential Campaigns." *Journal of Political Marketing* 5 (1–2), 59–78. DOI: 10.1300/J199v05n01_04.

Panagopoulos, Costas. 2009. "Campaign Dynamics in Battleground and Nonbattleground States." *The Public Opinion Quarterly*, 73 (1), 119–129. http://www.jstor.org/stable/25548065.

Panagopoulos, Costas. 2009. *Politicking Online: The Transformation of Election Campaign Communications*. New Brunswick, NY: Rutgers University Press.

Panagopoulos, Costas. 2013. "Positive Social Pressure and Prosocial Motivation: Evidence from a Large-Scale Field Experiment on Voter Mobilization." *Political Psychology* 34 (2): 265–275.

Panagopoulos, Costas. 2017. *Political Campaigns: Concepts, Context and Consequences*. New York, NY: Oxford University Press.

Panagopoulos, Costas. 2021. *Bases Loaded: How U.S. Presidential Campaigns Are Changing and Why It Matters*. New York, NY: Oxford University Press.

Panagopoulos, Costas, and Daniel Bergan. 2009. "Clicking for Cash: Campaigns, Donors and the Emergence of Online Fund-Raising." In *Politicking Online: The Transformation of Election Campaign Communications*, edited by Costas Panagopoulos. New Brunswick, NY: Rutgers University Press: 127–140.

Panagopoulos, Costas, and Benjamin Farrer. 2014. "Polls and Elections: Preelection Poll Accuracy and Bias in the 2012 General Elections." *Presidential Studies Quarterly*, 44 (2), 352–363.

Patterson, Thomas E. 1994. *Out of Order*. New York, NY: Vintage Books.

Petrocik, John R. 1981. *Party Coalitions: Realignment and the Decline of the New Deal Party System*. Chicago, IL: University of Chicago Press.

Phillips, Kevin. 1969. *The Emerging Republican Majority*. Washington, DC: Arlington House.

Plouffe, David. 2009. *The Audacity to Win: The Inside Story and Lessons of Barack Obama's Historic Victory*. New York, NY: Viking Books.

Pogue, Dennis. 2011. *Founding Spirits: George Washington and the Beginnings of the American Whiskey Industry*. Pender Harbour, British Columbia: Harbour Books.

Pool, Ithiel De Sola, and Robert Abelson. 1961. "The Simulmatics Project." *The Public Opinion Quarterly* 25 (2), 167–183.

Pooley, Eric. 1996. "Clinton's Stealth Campaign." *Time Magazine*, April 22, 1996. Last accessed on March 24, 2024. https://content.time.com/time/subscriber/article/0,33009,984423,00.html.

Popkin, Samuel. 1994. *The Reasoning Voter: Communication and Persuasion in Presidential Campaigns*. Chicago, IL: University of Chicago Press.

Powell, L., and Clowart, J. 2002. *Political Campaign Communication: Inside and Out*. New York, NY: Allyn and Bacon.

Prior, Marcus. 2007. *Post-Broadcast Democracy: How Media Choice Increases Inequality in Political Involvement and Polarizes Elections*. New York, NY: Cambridge University Press.

Rainie, Lee, Michael Cornfield, and John Horrigan. 2005. "The Internet and Campaign 2004." Report by the Pew Research Center for the People and the Press.

Rakich, Nathaniel. 2020. "Why Minnesota Could Be the Next Midwestern State to Go Red." Fivethirtyeight.com, August 31. Accessed August 1, 2023. https://fivethirtyeight.com/features/why-minnesota-could-be-the-next-midwestern-state-to-go-red/.

Ridout, Travis M., and Michael M. Franz. 2011. *The Persuasive Power of Campaign Advertising*. Philadelphia, PA: Temple University Press.

Ridout, Travis N., Michael Franz, Kenneth M. Goldstein, and William J. Feltus. 2012. "Separation by Television Program: Understanding the Targeting of Political Advertising in Presidential Elections." *Political Communication* 29 (1), 1–23.

Riker, Wiiliam H. 1962. *The Theory of Political Coalitions*. New Haven, CT: Yale University Press.

Rogers, Mary Beth. 2016. *Turning Texas Blue: What It Will Take to Break the GOP Grip on America's Reddest State*. New York, NY: St. Martin's Press.

Rosenberg, Matthew, Nicholas Confessore, and Carole Cadwalladr. 2018. "How Trump Consultants Exploited the Facebook Data of Millions." *New York Times*, March 17. https://www.nytimes.com/2018/03/17/us/politics/cambridge-analytica-trump-campaign.html.

Rove, Karl. 2010. *Courage and Consequence: My Life as a Conservative in the Fight*. New York, NY: Threshold Editions.

Rove, Karl. 2016. *The Triumph of William McKinley: Why the Election of 1896 Still Matters*. New York, NY: Simon & Schuster.

Royer, Charles T. 1994. *Campaign for President: The Managers Look at '92*. Institute of Politics, Harvard University. Hollis, NH: Hollis Publishing.

Runkel, David R. 1989. *Campaign for President: The Managers Look at '88*. Institute of Politics, Harvard University. Dover, MA: Auburn House Publishing.

Saad, Lydia. 2000. "Average Convention 'Bounce' Since 1964 Is Six Points: Clinton Set the Record in 1992 with 16 Points." Gallup News Service. Accessed February 21, 2024. https://news.gallup.com/poll/2704/average-convention-bounce-since-1964-six-points.aspx.

Schram, Martin. 1976. *Running for President 1976: The Carter Campaign*. New York, NY: Stein and Day.

Schudson, Michael. 1998. *The Good Citizen: A History of American Civic Life*. New York, NY: Free Press.

Shadegg, Stephen. 1965. *What Happened to Goldwater? The Inside Story of the 1964 Campaign*. New York, NY: Holt, Rinehart, and Winston.

Shaw, Daron R. 1999. "The Effect of TV Ads and Candidate Appearances on Statewide Presidential Votes, 1988–1996." *American Political Science Review* 93 (2), 345–361.

Shaw, Daron R. 2006. *The Race to 270*. Chicago, IL: University of Chicago Press.

Shaw, Daron R., and James G. Gimpel. 2012. "What if We Randomize the Governor's Schedule? Evidence on Campaign Appearance Effects from a Texas Field Experiment." *Political Communication* 29 (2), 137–159.

Shields-West, Eileen. 1992. *The World Almanac of Presidential Campaigns*. New York, NY: Pharos Books.

Sides, John, Chris Tausanovitch, and Lynn Vavreck. 2022. *The Bitter End: The 2020 Presidential Campaign and the Challenge to American Democracy*. Princeton, NJ: Princeton University Press.

Sides, John, Michael Tesler, and Lynn Vavreck. 2018. *Identity Crisis: The 2016 Presidential Campaign and the Battle for the Meaning of America*. Princeton, NJ: Princeton University Press.

Sides, John, and Lynn Vavreck. 2013. *The Gamble: Choice and Chance in the 2012 Presidential Election*. Princeton, NJ: Princeton University Press.

Sides, John, Lynn Vavreck, and Christopher Warshaw. 2022. "The Effect of Television Advertising in United States Elections." *American Political Science Review* 116 (2), 702–718.

Sifry, Micah. 2011. "From Howard Dean to the Tea Party: The Power of Meetup.com." CNN Business. November 7. Last accessed on March 24, 2024. https://www.cnn.com/2011/11/07/tech/web/meetup-2012-campaign-sifry/index.html.

Silber, Irwin. 1971. *Songs America Voted By*. Harrisburg, PA: Stackpole Books.

Simon, Adam. 2002. *The Winning Message: Candidate Behavior, Campaign Discourse, and Democracy*. New York, NY: Cambridge University Press.

Smith, Eric R. A. N., and Peverill Squire. 1987. "Direct Election of the President and the Power of the States." *Western Political Quarterly* 40, 29–44.

Snyder, James M., and Hasin Yousaf. 2020. "Making Rallies Great Again: The Effects of Presidential Campaign Rallies on Voter Behavior, 2008–2016," NBER Working Paper 28043.

Spenkuch, Jorg L., and David Toniatti. 2018. "Political Advertising and Election Results." *Quarterly Journal of Economics 133* (4), 1981–2036.

Stacks, John F. 1981. *Watershed—The Campaign for the Presidency 1980*. New York, NY: Times Books.

Stevens, Stuart. 2001. *The Big Enchilada: Campaign Adventures with the Cock-Eyed Optimists from Texas Who Won the Biggest Prize in Politics*. New York, NY: Free Press.

Stimson, James A. 2004. *Tides of Consent: How Public Opinion Shapes American Politics*. New York, NY: Cambridge University Press.

Stone, Walter J., and Ronald B. Rapoport. 2007. *Three's a Crowd: The Dynamic of Third Parties, Ross Perot, and Republican Resurgence*. Ann Arbor, MI: University of Michigan Press.

Stromberg, David. 2008. "How the Electoral College Influences Campaigns and Policy: The Probability of Being Florida." *The American Economic Review* 98 (3), 769–807.

Sundquist, James. 1983. *Dynamics of the Party System: Alignment and Realignment of Political Parties in the United States*. Washington, DC: Brookings Press.

Taylor, Paul, and David S. Broder. 1988. "Dukakis Electoral Strategy Set." *Washington Post*, October 16, 1988.

Thayer, George. 1974. *Who Shakes the Money Tree: American Campaign Financing Practices from 1789 to the Present*. New York, NY: Simon & Schuster.

Thomas, Evan, Karen Breslau, Debra Rosenberg, Leslie Kaufman, and Andrew Murr. 1997. *Back from the Dead: How Clinton Survived the Republican Revolution*. New York, NY: Atlantic Monthly Press.

Thomas, Evan, and Newsweek Staff. 2005. *Election 2004: How Bush Won and What You Can Expect in the Future*. New York, NY: Public Affairs.

Thompson, Hunter S. 1973. *Fear and Loathing: On the Campaign Trail '72*. New York, NY: Straight Arrow Books.

Toner, Robin. 1992. "The 1992 Campaign: Primaries; Tsongas Abandons Campaign, Leaving Clinton with Clear Path Toward Showdown with Bush." *New York Times*, March 20, Section A, Page 1. Last accessed on March 24, 2024. https://www.nytimes.com/1992/03/20/us/1992-campaign-primaries-tsongas-abandons-campaign-leaving-clinton-clear-path.html.

Troy, Gil. 1996. *See How They Ran: The Changing Role of the Presidential Candidate*. Cambridge, MA: Harvard University Press.

Truman, Harry S. 1960. *Mr. Citizen*. New York, NY: Bernard Geis Associates.

Tufte, Edward R. 1978. *Political Control of the Economy*. Princeton, NJ: Princeton University Press.

Tye, Larry. 1998. *The Father of Spin: Edward L. Bernays and the Birth of Public Relation*. New York, NY: Crown Books.

Tynan, Daniel. 2004. "GOP Voter Vault Shipped Overseas." *PC World*. September 24.

Urofsky, Melvin I. 2020. *The Campaign Finance Cases: Buckley, McConnell, Citizens United and McCutcheon*. Lawrence, KS: University of Kansas Press.

US News and World Report, 1964. "Barry's Chances against LBJ: Issues Abound Once Goldwater Takes on Johnson in Presidential Campaign." *US News and World Report* 56 (June 22, 1964), 31–33.

Vavreck, Lynn. 2009. *The Message Matters: The Economy and Presidential Campaigns*. Princeton, NJ: Princeton University Press.

Wainstock, Dennis Dean. 1984. "The 1968 Presidential Campaign and Election." Ph.D. Dissertation, West Virginia University.

Webster, James G., Lawrence W. Lichty, and Patricia F. Phalen. 2005. *Ratings Analysis: The Theory and Practice of Audience Research*. Hillsdale, NJ: Lawrence Erlbaum.

Wentworthy, E. W. 1964. "Campaign—Goldwater's Strategy Takes Shape." *New York Times*, August 2, 1964.

West, Darrell M. 2018. *Air Wars: Television Advertising and Social Media in Election Campaigns, 1952–2016*. 7th ed. Washington, DC: Congressional Quarterly Press.

White, Phil. 2015. *Whistle Stop: How 31,000 Miles of Train Travel, 352 Speeches, and a Little Midwest Gumption Saved the Presidency of Harry Truman*. New York: ForeEdge Press.

White, Theodore S. 1961. *The Making of the President, 1960*. New York, NY: Atheneum.

White, Theodore S. 1965. *The Making of the President, 1964*. New York, NY: Atheneum.

White, Theodore S. 1969. *The Making of the President, 1968*. New York, NY: Atheneum.

White, Theodore S. 1973. *The Making of the President, 1972*. New York, NY: Atheneum.

Witcover, Jules. 1992. "Clinton Campaign Credits Success to Early Start, Careful Targeting of States." *Baltimore Sun*, November 5.

Wolak, Jennifer. 2006. "The Consequences of Presidential Battleground Strategies for Citizen Engagement." *Political Research Quarterly* 59 (3), 353–361.

Woodward, Bob. 1996. *The Choice: How Bill Clinton Won*. New York, NY: Simon & Schuster.

Woodward, Bob, and Carl Bernstein. 1974. *All the President's Men*. New York, NY: Simon & Schuster.

Wright, John R. 2009. "Pivotal States in the Electoral College, 1880–2004." *Public Choice* 139 (1), 21–37.

Index

For the benefit of digital users, indexed terms that span two pages (e.g., 52–53) may, on occasion, appear on only one of those pages.

Tables and figures are indicated by an italic *t* and *f* following the page number

abortion, 91
Access Hollywood, 158
Adams, John
  campaign letters attacking, 23–24, 28
  Democratic-Republican Party representation, 20
  vs. Jefferson, 20
Adams, John Quincy, 25–26, 28–29
Adams, Sherman, 66–67
advertising
  candidate appearance effects and, 212–15
  door-to-door, 7–8
  emails and text messages, 7–8
  micro-targeted campaigning era, 16–17
  online, 7–8
  radio advertising, 7–8, 9, 13–14, 46, 50–52, 54, 63–64, 97, 103, 168–69, 171–72, 190
  resource allocation for, 42
  studies/surveys of, 7–8
  television, data analysis, 5–6, 7–8, 37, 47
  wholesale campaigning era, 9, 16, 49–54, 62–64, 70, 73, 77, 89–90, 93
  zero-sum campaigning era, 99, 113–16, 129, 137–38, 198–99
  See also spot television advertisements; television/television advertising
Advertising Analytics, 190–91
Affordable Care Act (2010), 152–53
Alexander, Herb, 190–91
Alexander, Lamar, 128
Allbaugh, Joe, 132
allocation of resources. *See* resource allocation
American National Election Study (ANES), 36
Annenberg Conference (2008), 149–52
Annenberg School of Public Affairs (University of Pennsylvania), 4
Antifederalists, 19
anti-war sentiment/protests (Vietnam War), 84–85, 91
Articles of Confederation, 19
The Art of War (Sun Tzu), 31–32, 33, 34
Atwater, Lee, 117, 120, 123
Axelrod, David, 4, 154

Bacall, Lauren, 70
Baker, James A., III, 123
battleground status frequency data (1952–2020), 175*f*
Batton, Barton, Durstine, & Osborn (BBD&O) advertising firm, 62
Bayh, Evan, 148–49
BCRA. *See* Bipartisan Campaign Reform Act
Begala, Paul, 122
Benenson, Joel, 158–59
Bennet, Michael, 162
Biddle, Larry, 143
Biden, Hunter, 162
Biden, Joe, 21–22, 117–20, 148–49
  COVID-19 related promises by, 26
  exit poll data (2020), 36
  fundraising by, 24
  limited campaign appearances, 188, 201–2
Biden, Joe-Trump, Donald election (2020)
  Biden's choise of Harris for VP, 162–63, 188
  Biden's electoral strategy, 163–66, 164*t*
  record election spending, 163, 209
  Trump's electoral strategy, 163–66, 164*t*
Bipartisan Campaign Reform Act (BCRA) (2002), 11, 139–40, 143–44, 166–67, 194–95
Bird, Jeremy, 153
Black, Charlie, 149
Bloomberg, Michael, 162

blue wall states, 158–59, 241–42, 244–45
Boller, Paul, 3–4
Booker, Cory, 162
Bradley, Bill, 132
Breckinridge, John C., 71
broadcast news, vii
Brown, Jerry, 121
Bryan, William Jennings, 193
Buchanan, Patrick, 123, 128
Buckley v. Valeo (1976), 100
Bush, George H. W., 43
  candidacy advantages, 117
  obstacles to reelection, 116–17
  post-Gulf War popularity, 121, 142–43
  service as Reagan's VP, 116–17
Bush, George H. W.-Clinton, Bill election (1992), 121–27, 124*t*
  Bush's election strategy, 118*t*, 120–21, 126
  Clinton's election strategy, 102–3, 122–26
  obstacles facing Clinton, 121–22, 126–27
  Perot's complex impact on, 122–23, 126, 127
  post-election victory challenges, 127–28
Bush, George H. W.-Dukakis, Michael election (1988), 116–21
  Bush's election strategy, 117, 118*t*, 120–21
  Dukakis's election strategy, 118*t*, 120
Bush, George W.
  declining approval ratings, 143, 148
  Iraq War, "shock and awe" campaign, 142–43
  post-9/11 popularity of, 142–43
  signing of Bipartisan Campaign Reform Act, 139–40
Bush, George W.-Gore, Al election (2000), 132–37
  Bush's electoral strategy, 132–33, 134*t*
  Gore's electoral strategy, 133–36, 134*t*
Bush, George W.-Kerry, John election (2004), 142–48
  Bush's campaign strategy, 144–48, 146*t*
  Bush's "swift boating" of Kerry, 144
  Kerry's campaign strategy, 145
Buttigieg, Pete, 162

Caddell, Pat, 104, 112, 137
Cain, Herman, 152–53
Callender, James, 23–24, 28
campaign effects, 36–38
  analysis of opinion surveys for, 13–14
  ANES study findings, 36
  constraints of, 41
  cross-sectional/panel polling data findings, 5–6, 37, 38
  description, 42
  field experiment findings, 37
  impact of negative advertisements, 37
  micro-/macro-level assumptions, 41
  micro-targeted campaigns and, 142
  mobilization/persuasion effects, 41–42
  possible variance with a state, 213
  resource allocation and, 17–18
  role of studies for understanding, 7–8, 15, 37
  "rolling cross-section" survey analysis, 5–6
  term description, 42
  usefulness of opinion surveys, 13–14
  use of innovative analytic techniques, 37
  volume *vs.* quality of campaigning, 38
  vote outcomes and, 17–18, 31, 97, 210, 213–14
  zero-sum campaigning and, 101–2, 103, 138
Campaign Finance Institute, 149
campaign finance laws
  Alexander's work on, 190
  evolution of, 240
  impact of BCRA, 166–67
  impact of FEC oversight, 10, 100–2
  spot television advertising and, 207
  targeting of slush funds, dirty tricks, 93–96
  Watergate's impact on, 99–100, 103–4
  zero-sum campaigning and, 10
Campaign for President book series, 4
Campaign Media Analysis Group (CMAG), 46–47, 190–91
campaign songs, 29
campaign spending. *See* presidential campaigns, expenses
Campbell, James, 5, 7
candidates. *See* presidential candidates, appearances by
Carter, Jimmy-Ford, Gerald election (1976)
  Carter's campaign strategy, 104–5, 106*t*
  Ford's campaign strategy, 105–8, 106*t*
Carter, Jimmy-Reagan, Ronald election (1980), 109–12
  Carter's electoral strategy, 110*t*, 112
  Reagan's electoral strategy, 108–12, 110*t*
Carville, James, 4, 122
Castellanos, Alex, 129, 137
Castro, Julian, 21–22

Chappaquiddick car accident, 90
characteristics of presidential campaigns. *See* presidential campaigns, characteristics of
Checkers speech (Nixon), 52–53, 58, 77
Cheney, Dick, 105, 148, 193–94, 220, 232–33
Chisholm, Shirley, 90
Citizens United v. Federal Election Commission (2010), 11, 139–40, 166–67, 194–95, 233
Civil Rights Act (1964), 78
Clay, Henry, 25–26
Clinton, Bill-Bush, George H. W. election (1992), 121–27, 124*t*
  Bush's election strategy, 118*t*, 120–21, 126
  Clinton's election strategy, 102–3, 122–26
  obstacles facing Clinton, 121–22, 126–27
  Perot's complex impact on, 122–23, 126, 127
  post-election victory challenges, 127–28
Clinton, Bill-Dole, Robert election (1996), 128–32
  Clinton's election strategy, 128–29, 130*t*
  Dole's election strategy, 129
  Perot's complex impact on, 128
Clinton, Hillary, 127–28, 148–49
Clinton, Hillary-Trump, Donald election (2016)
  Clinton's electoral strategy, 158, 159, 160*t*
  projections of a Clinton victory, 158
  Trump's electoral strategy, 155–62, 160*t*
Committee to Re-Elect the President (CREEP), 90, 92, 99–100
Congress (U.S.)
  authorization for Bush's war on Iraq, 142–43
  Civil Rights Act passage, 78
  deficit reduction package, 127–28
  Federal Election Campaign Act, 24
  investigation of Trump, 158
Constitutional Convention, 19
Constitution (U.S.), 20
contested elections, 210–11
Continental Congress, 19
conventions
  anti-war protests at, 84–85
  Constitutional Convention, 19
  Democratic, 65–66, 71–72, 77–78, 84–85, 90, 91–92
  GOP (Republican), 55–57, 63, 71, 78–79, 84, 85, 187
  nominations at, 50–52
Cook, Rhodes, 188
COVID-19 pandemic, 26, 36, 162, 168–69, 188, 244–45
Cramer, Richard Ben, 3–4
CREEP. *See* Committee to Re-Elect the President
Cruz, Ted, 155–58
Cuomo, Mario, 121

Daley, Richard, 84–85
Davidsen, Carol, 153
Davis, Rick, 149
Dean, Howard, 22–23, 143–44
Delaney, John, 21–22
Democratic National Committee (DNC), 50, 190–91, 233
Democratic Party
  anti-war constituency, 84, 91
  appearances by candidates, 202–7, 204*f*
  blue wall states, 158–59, 241–42, 244–45
  candidacy declarations, 21–22
  embrace of television advertising, 70
  impact of activities on vote outcomes, 222–25
  New Deal Democrats, 49
  passage of Affordable Care Act, 152–53
  problematic relationship with White South, 92
  spot television ad spending across the eras, 190–92, 194–200, 196*f*, 197*f*, 198*f*, 215–21, 215*t*, 223–24
  targeting of voters by, 141–42
  television advertising data, 220
  television spot buy spending, 197*f*
  2004, cash flow problems, 22–23
  2010, midterm losses, 152–53
  See also Democratic-Republican Party; Republican Party
Democratic-Republican Party (Jeffersonian Democrats), 20, 21
Devine, Christopher, 8
Dewey, Thomas, 49, 52, 55–56, 62
Dewey-Warren ticket (1948), 49
DiBlasio, Bill, 162
Dickerson, John, 3–4
digital news, vii
discipline of presidential campaigns. *See* presidential campaigns, discipline of
Dodd, Chris, 148–49

Dole, Robert-Clinton, Bill election (1996), 128–32
  Clinton's election strategy, 128–29, 130*t*
  Dole's election strategy, 129
  Perot's complex impact on, 128
Dowd, Matthew, 132
Dukakis, Michael-Bush, George H. W. election (1988)
  Bush's election strategy, 117, 118*t*, 120–21
  Dukakis's election strategy, 117–20, 118*t*

Eagleton, Thomas, 91–92
economic and forecasting models, 7–8
economic recession, 65, 71, 121
Edwards, John, 148–49
Eisenhower, Dwight D., 25–26, 43
  call for Lodge's candidacy (1963), 78–79
  heart attack's impact on campaigning, 65
  landslide victorries (1952, 1956), 97
  Nixon's vice-presidency with, 56–57, 71
  Truman's lobbying for, 55–56
Eisenhower, Dwight D.-Stevenson, Adlai election (1952)
  Eisenhower's electoral strategy, 59–64, 60*t*
  Stevenson's electoral strategy, 58–63, 60*t*, 64
Eisenhower, Dwight D.-Stevenson, Adlai election (1956)
  criticisms of Stevenson's performance, 66
  Eisenhower's electoral strategy, 66–67, 68*t*
  Eisenhower's health complications, 65
  Stevenson's electoral strategy, 66–67, 68*t*, 70
"Eisenhower Answers America" TV commercials, 64
Electoral College strategies, 170–73
  analysis of, 173–76
  bias in charge of large states, 170
  building blocks, 31–36
  competitive states classification as battlegrounds, 172–73
  determination of state political leaning, 170–71
  electoral closeness factors, 176–78, 177*f*
  evolving sophistication of campaigns, 171–72
  factors predicting battleground status, 176–83, 185*t*
  five-category categorization scale, 44, 171, 176
  how to think about, 170–73
  impact of varying a state's electoral vote count, 177*f*, 179–81, 180*f*
  1952-2020, percentage of states classified as battlegrounds, 182–83, 182*t*
  percent of states with fifteen or more electoral votes classified as battlegrounds, 181*f*, 181–82
  "pivot"/tipping point" assessment, 170
  rank-order states, 32, 170–71
  Republican *vs.* Democratic campain plans, 173
  role of electoral votes/past competitiveness, 175–76, 178–81
  sorting of states into categories, 170–71
  states frequency of battleground status (1952-2020), 175*f*
  target determination, 170
  time-related strategic adjustments of, 173–75
email, 7–8, 144, 158, 171–72
Erikson, Robert, 5
Estrich, Susan, 120
expenses of presidential campaigns. *See* presidential campaigns, expenses

Fabrizio, Tony, 129
Facebook, 149, 159–62
FEC. *See* Federal Election Commission
Federal Communication Commission (FCC), 46–47, 190–91
Federal Election Campaign Act (FECA) (1971)
  description, 10, 16
  passage/success of, 24
Federal Election Campaign Act (FECA), amendments (1974)
  critical provisions of, 100–2
  description, 100–1
Federal Election Commission (FEC), 21–22, 100–2
  Citizens United v. FEC decision, 11, 139–40, 166–67, 194–95, 233
  McConnell v. FEC decision, 194–95
  SpeechNow.org v. FEC decision, 11, 139–40, 166–67, 194–95, 233
Federalists
  battles with Democratic-Republicans, 21
  defense of newly redesigned presidency, 19–20
  response to attack campaign letters, 23–24
Feingold, Russ, 139–40
Ferraro, Geraldine, 112–13

Financing the 1960 Election (Alexander), 190–91
focus groups, 10, 12, 102, 103, 122
Forbes, Steve, 128, 132–33
Ford, Gerald-Carter, Jimmy election (1976)
  Carter's campaign strategy, 104–5, 106*t*
  Ford's campaign strategy, 105–8, 106*t*
fundraising
  BCRA's impact on, 11
  Campaign Finance Institute data, 149
  Committee to Re-Elect the President and, 90
  by corporations, 24
  donors/donations, 22–23, 149, 153, 163, 167, 207
  impact of Bipartisan Campaign Reform Act, 11
  impact of falling behind, 24–25
  Internet/social media's impact, 167
  by McKinley, 24
  1972 excesses, 93–96
  public funding system, 10, 101, 149, 153, 163
  transparency of, 24–25
  by Trump (2016), 159
  See also presidential campaigns, expenses

Gallup, George, 59
Garfield, James, 57
Gephardt, Richard, 117–20
Germon, Jack, 3–4
Gillespie, Ed, 154
Gillibrand, Kirsten, 162
Gingrich, Newt, 152–53
Giuliani, Rudy, 148
Glassner, Michael, 163–66
Goldwater, Barry, 4, 78–79
  acceptance of GOP nomination, 79
  de-emphasis on tv spot ads, 83
  Ku Klux Klan's endorsement of, 79–82
  1963, seeking of GOP nomination, 78
Goldwater, Barry-Johnson, Lyndon election (1964), 77–83
  Goldwater's electoral strategy, 80*t*, 82–83
  Johnson's electoral strategy, 79–83, 80*t*
Gore, Al-Bush, George W. election (2000), 132–37
  Bush's electoral strategy, 132–33, 134*t*, 136
  Gore's electoral strategy, 133–36, 134*t*
Gramm, Phil, 128
Gravel, Mike, 148–49, 162
Greenberg, Stanley, 122, 128–29
Greenfield, Edward L., 96
Grunwald, Mandy, 122, 128–29
Guggenheim, Charles, 93
Gulf of Tonkin Resolution, 78
Gulf War (1991), 121, 142–43

Haldeman, Bob, 76
Halperin, Mark, 3–4
Hamilton, Alexander, 20, 23–24
Hannah, Mark, 21, 24
Harkin, Tom, 121
Harris, Kamala, 162, 188
Harris, Lou, 96
Harrison, William Henry, 29, 192–93
Hart, Gary, 112–13
Harvard, Kennedy School of Government, 4
Hechler, Ken, 59, 60*t*, 67, 68*t*
Heilemann, John and Hersh, Eitan, 3–4, 6, 7
history of presidential campaigns. *See* presidential campaigns, historical background
Hoover, Herbert, 24
  campaign expenditures (1932), 24
Huckabee, Mike, 148
Hughes, Charles Evans, 57
Hughes, Karen, 132
Humphrey, Hubert, 4, 71–72
  backers of, 85
  campaign expenditures (1968), 24
  Carter's campaign comparison, 104–5
  declaration of candidacy, 84
  efforts of unseating Nixon, 90
  fight for nomination, 91
  as Johnson's choice for running mate, 77–78, 83
  support for candidacy of, 85
Humphreys, Robert, 58–59, 60*t*
Huntsman, Jon, 152–53
Hussein, Saddam, 142–43

Internet
  candidate announcements on, 148–49
  Dean's use of for fundraising, 143–44, 167
  email communication, 7–8, 144, 158, 171–72
  email/text messages, 171–72
  impact on fundraising, communications, 167
  impact on micro-targeted campaigning, 11
  Kerry/Edwards, use of for fundraising, 143–44

Internet (*cont.*)
- micro-targeted campaigning and, 11, 139, 143–44, 148–49
- prominence in Democrat/Republican campaigns, 143–44
- registered voters use of, 143
- zero-sum campaigning and, 101–2
- *See also* social media

Iran-Contra Affair scandal, 116–17
Iraq War, 144, 148, 149

Jackson, Andrew, 21, 25–26, 116–17
Jackson, Jesse, 112–13, 117–20, 121
Jefferson, Thomas, 20, 23–24
Jeffersonian Democrats (Democratic-Republican Party), 20
Jim Crow laws, 78
Johnson, Lyndon
- attack on Goldwater's extremism, 79–82
- choice of Humphrey as running mate, 77–78, 83
- decision to not rerun, 84
- elevation to presidency, 77–78
- falling approval ratings, 84
- legislation passed by, 78
- reliance on polling data, 96–97
- vice-presidency to Kennedy, 77–78

Johnson, Lyndon-Goldwater, Barry election (1964), 43, 77–83, 97
- Goldwater's electoral strategy, 80*t*, 82–83
- Johnson's electoral strategy, 79–83, 80*t*

Jones, Eugene, 89–90
Jones, Jerry, 105
Jordan, Hamilton, 104, 105, 106*t*, 112, 122–23

Kaine, Tim, 155, 221
Kantar Media, 190–91
Kasich, John, 155–58
Kefauver, Estes, 65–66
Kemp, Jack, 116–17
Kennedy, Edward "Ted," 90
Kennedy, John F., 43
- assassination of, 77–78
- electoral strategies of, 72–77
- emergence as front-runner, 71–72
- impact on presidential campaigns, 70
- 1960 nomination strategy, 49
- obstacles in seeking the nomination, 72
- presidential campaign plans, 74*t*
- reliance on polling data, 96–97
- Truman's opinion of, 72
- use of spot television ads, 77

Kennedy, John F.-Nixon, Richard election (1960), 3–4, 52, 70–77
- Kennedy's electoral strategy, 71–73, 74*t*, 201–2
- Nixon's electoral strategy, 72–73, 74*t*, 76, 187–88

Kennedy, Robert F., 73, 77–78
- assassination of, 84
- backers of, 85
- declaration of candidacy, 84

Kennedy School of Government (Harvard University), 4
Kerrey, Bob, 121
Kerry, John-Bush, George W. election (2004)
- Bush's campaign strategy, 144, 145–48, 146*t*
- Bush's "swift boating" of Kerry, 144
- folding of Kerry's campaign, 241–42
- Kerry's campaign strategy, 145, 146*t*
- Kerry's heroism status, 144

Klobuchar, Amy, 162
Knight, Peter, 128–29
Kopechne, Mary Jo, 90
Korean War, 55, 57, 65
Kriegel, Elan, 153, 159
Kucinich, Dennis, 148–49
Ku Klux Klan, 79–82

labor unions, 85
Landon, Alf, 62
LBJ Library, viii
lengthiness, of presidential campaigns, 20–23
libraries. *See* presidential libraries
Liddy, G. Gordon, 99–100
Lincoln, Abraham, 21, 24, 25–26
Lodge, Henry Cabot, 56–57
Lodge, Henry Cabot, Jr., 71, 78
low-information rationality, 6
Lugar, Richard, 128

macro-targeting strategies, 6–7, 8
Magruder, Jeb, 92. *See also* Committee to Re-Elect the President
"Make American Great Again" campaign (Trump), 155–58
Marshall, George, 58
Matalin, Mary, 4
McCain, John, 24, 132, 141
McCain, John-Obama, Barack election (2008)
- McCain's choice of Palin for VP, 149

McCain's electoral strategy, 149, 150*t*
Obama's electoral strategy, 148–49, 150*t*, 152, 174
McCain-Feingold Act. *See* Bipartisan Campaign Reform Act
McCambridge, Mercedes, 70
McCarthy, Eugene
backers of, 85
battle *vs*. R. Kennedy, 84
declaration of candidacy, 84
efforts at unseating Nixon, 90
support from liberal, anti-war Democrats, 91
McCarthy, Joseph, 58
McConnell v. FEC (2003), 194–95
McGinnis, Joe, 3–4
McGovern, George, 4
Carter's campaign comparison, 104–5
choice of Eagleton as vice-president, 91–92
efforts of unseating Nixon, 90, 92
fight for nomination, 91
McGovern, George-Nixon, Richard election (1972)
McGovern's electoral strategies, 91–93, 94*t*
Nixon's electoral strategies, 90, 92, 94*t*
McGovern-Fraser Commission, 85
McInturff, Bill, 149–52
McKinley, William, 21, 24
The Message Matters (Vavreck), 6
messaging strategy, 6–7
messaging themes, 6–7
Messina, Jim, 154
micro-targeted campaigning era (2004-2020), 11–13, 139–67
"battle of the bases" approach, 140–41
Bush, George W., reliance on, 144–45
campaign finance reforms, 139–40
candidate-centric strategies, 27
description, 11–13, 16–17
discipline in candidate appearances, television advertising, 189
execution of, 12, 141
expectations in the era, 141–42
impact of evolving technology impact, 140
impact on partisan polarization, 140–41
Internet/social media's transformative impact, 139, 140–41, 143–44, 148–49, 167
micro-targeting strategies, 7, 9, 11–13, 16–17, 27, 35–36
promise of, to campaigns, 140
resource allocation, 140, 141, 189
roll of rank-order of states, 38–41, 39*t*
targeting goals, tactics, 12, 141–42
use of television advertising, 16–17
midterm elections
1858 midterms, 21
1994, Clinton's losses, 127–28
2010, Democratic losses, 152–53
2022, Republican wins, 244–45
Miller, William E., 79
Moffatt, Zac, 153
Moltke, Helmuth von, 1, 184
Mondale, Walter-Reagan, Ronald election (1984)
Mondale's choice of Ferraro as VP, 112–13
Mondale's electoral strategy, 112–13, 114*t*, 116
Reagan's electoral strategy, 113–16, 114*t*
Mook, Robby, 158–59
Morse, Wayne, 71–72
Moyers, Bill, 82
Muskie, Edmund, 90, 91

New Deal, 57–58, 59, 66–67, 97, 228
New Deal Democrats, 49, 85
"New Democrats" (of Clinton), 152
Newhouse, Neil, 154
Newsweek magazine, 3–4
Newton, Carrol, 77
Nixon, Richard, 43
campaign expenditures (1968), 24
Checkers speech, 52–53, 58, 77
Democratic efforts and unseating, 90
efforts at rebuilding his reputation, 85
fundraising by, 71
impact of health-related issues, 187–88
impact on presidential campaigns, 70
pioneering campaign approach of, 77
presidential campaign plans, 74*t*
promises at 1960 Republican Convention, 187
refusal to leave Eisenhower's ticket, 65
reliance on polling data, 96–97
Republican nomination, 71, 85
role in GOP campaigning, 58
role of November Group advertisements, 93
running mate with Eisenhower, 56–57
slush fund scandal, 52–53, 58, 93–96
use of spot television ads, 77
Watergate break-in scandal fallout, 52–53, 139–0

Nixon, Richard-Kennedy, John F. election (1960)
  Kennedy's electoral strategy, 71–73, 74*t*, 201–2
  Nixon's electoral strategy, 72–73, 74*t*, 76, 187–88
Nixon, Richard-McGovern, George election (1972)
  McGovern's electoral strategies, 91–93, 94*t*
  Nixon's electoral strategies, 72–77
  Nixon's landslide victory, 93, 97
Nixon-Agnew ticket (1972), 52–53
nomination (nominating processes)
  benefits of winning, 27–28
  control of, by political parties, 9–10, 21–22
  exploratory committees and, 21–22
  importance for candidate's national viability, 50–52
  intra-party battles, 22–23
  Kennedy's 1960 strategy, 49
  rules changes, 10
  2004 Democratic cash flow problems, 22–23
November Group (advertising firm), 93

Obama, Barack
  The Cave, 2012 data war room, 153
  eight-point victory over McCain, 141
  fundraising by, 24, 148–49
  Internet candidacy announcement, 148–49
  positioning strategy of, 27
  pros/cons of incumbent presidency, 153–54
  token opposition for 2012 nomination, 152–53
Obama, Barack-McCain, John election (2008)
  McCain's choice of Palin for VP, 149
  McCain's electoral strategy, 149, 150*t*
  Obama's electoral strategy, 148–49, 150*t*, 152, 174
Obama, Barack-Romney, Mitt election (2012), 152–55
  Obama's electoral strategy, 153, 154–55, 156*t*, 173, 174–75
  Romney's electoral strategy, 153, 154, 156*t*, 173, 174–75
Obama for America campaign, 153
ORCA (mobile-optimized web application) oral strategy, 153, 154

Palin, Sarah, 149
Parscale, Brad, 163–66
partisanship, 36–37, 97, 240
Paul, Ron, 148
Pawlenty, Tim, 152–53
Pence, Mike, 155–58
Perot, Ross
  impact on Clinton-Bush, George H. W. election, 122–23, 126, 127
  impact on Clinton-Dole election, 128
Plouffe, David, 4, 149–52, 154
Podesta, John, 158–59
political action committees (PACs), 139–40, 153, 233. *See also* super PACs (political action committees)
political polarization, 97, 101–2, 141–42, 174, 181, 207
polls/polling
  candidate use of on polling data, 96–97
  Clinton's 1992 polling strategy, 122
  cross-sectional/panel polling data, 37, 38
  extensive/innovative use of data, 96–97
  method of contemporary campaigns, 172–73, 174, 240
  micro-targeted campaigning era, 141, 148, 153–55, 158, 162
  1948 polling debacle, 52
  1952-2008, polling data book, 5
  1960 election data, 76, 97
  1968 election data, 97
  1972 election data, 92
  1980s/1990s, data, 36–37
  ongoing development of, 9–10, 52–53
  pre-election polls, 7
  public opinion polling, 52, 67–70, 102
  tracking of, 13–14
  2000/2004 election data, 37
  2012 election data, 153–54, 174–75
  2020 exit polls, 36
  use of television for, 93–96
  value of, 10
  wholesale campaigning era, 96
  zero-sum campaigning era, 102–3, 105, 112–13, 117, 122–27, 133
Popkin, Sam, 6
positioning strategies, 15, 29
pre-election polls, 7
presidential campaigns
  academic studies of, 1
  ads and appearances as mesures of, 189–94
  ads and appearances effects, 212–15

books written about, 4–6
candidacy declarations, 21–22
candidates *vs.* issues focus, 25–27
characteristics of, 12, 20, 23, 25, 27–28, 30–31
Clinton-Bush-Perot (1992), 30–31
continuing evolution of, 240
discipline of, 187–89
1800 campaign, 20, 28–29
1840 campaign, 28–29
1860 campaign, 28–29
1876 campaign, 28–29
1888 campaign, 28–29
expensiveness of, 23–25
FECA's establishment of public finance system for, 100–1
historical background, 19–31
historical review of, 30–31
impact of close elections, 17–18
impact of partisanship, 240
impact on Electoral College tally, 3
insider memos, 3
Kennedy-Nixon (1960), 3–4
length of, 20–23
mid-nineteenth *vs.* twenty-first century, 29
1912 campaign, 28–29
1936 campaign, 28–29
1984 campaign, 32–33
1992 campaign, 28–29
1960s campaigns, 70
Nixon-McGovern (1972), 3–4
partisanship's impact on, 36–37, 97, 240
previous studies of, 3–9
primary goal of candidates, 25
related personalities of, vii
rolling cross-section surveys of, 5–6, 37
1788, 1792, 1796, 21
as spectator sport, 1–2
statewide impact of differential activities, 225–28
tell-all books about, vii
theoretical perspectives on, 38–42, 39*t*
2016 election, 28
2020 election, 28
video-conferencing, televised town halls, 189
of Washington, George, 20, 23
See also micro-targeted campaigning era; presidential campaigns, characteristics of; presidential campaigns, discipline of; presidential campaigns, expenses; presidential campaigns, historical background; wholesale campaigning era; zero-sum campaigning era; specific campaigns
presidential campaigns, characteristics of
big, noisy, context-dependent, 30–31
candidate *vs.* issues centered, 20, 25, 50–52
expensiveness, 20, 23
lengthiness, 20, 30
negative, 20, 27–30
presidential campaigns, discipline of, 187–89
micro-targeted campaigning era, 189
wholesale campaigning era, 189
zero-sum campaigning era, 189
presidential campaigns, expenses, 23–25
advantage of incumbent presidents, 128
banning corporate money, 24, 139–40
continuing evolution of, 240
cost of political pamphlets/newsletters, 23–24
FECA's oversight on, 10, 100
Federal Election Campaign Act and, 24
1968, Nixon, Humphrey, Wallace, 24, 88, 97
1972, Nixon and Agnew, 52–53
overturning banning corporate money, 139–40
public funding and, 101
self-financing/wealthy contributors, 24
"soft money" spending, 101
super PACs and, 139–40
television spot ad spending across the eras, 194–200
Tillman Act and, 24
2008, Obama and McCain, 149
2012, Obama and Romney, 153
2016, Clinton and Trump, 159
2020. Biden and Trump, 163, 209
Washington's use of liquor for payment, 23
zero-sum campaigning era, 16
See also advertising; fundraising; resource allocation; spot television advertisements
Presidential Campaigns: From Washington to George W. Bush (Boller), 3–4
presidential campaigns, historical background, 19–31
early battlegrounds, swing states, 21
elector choice inter-party conflicts, 21
formation of Democratic-Republican party, 20

presidential candidates, appearances by
  advertising and appearance effects, 212–15
  Democratic *vs.* Republican campaigns, 202–7, 204*f*
  history of, 192–93
  impact on donations, volunteers, 15
  impact on vote outcomes, 33
  importance of, 194
  in-person appearances, 46
  micro-targeted campaigning era, 16–17
  1952-2020 data/visits across the eras, 42, 201*f*, 203*f*, 204*f*, 264
  pandemic era limitations, 168–69
  re-election bid travel records, 46
  resource allocation of, 42, 46, 47
  state-by-state differences, 14, 38, 54
  statewide appearance differentials, 226
  television appearances, 14–17, 38, 46
  TV ad spending and appearance effects, 215–22, 215*t*
  2004-2020, decline of, 202
  wholesale campaigning era, 16, 97, 189
  zero-sum campaigning era, 102–3
presidential libraries, 43, 54–55
primary elections (contests)
  contesting of, by potential candidates, 71–72
  McGovern's domination of, 91
  Minnesota, 56–57
  New Hampshire, 56–57, 84, 121–22, 123, 148
  Republican (1896), 21
  role in candidate national viability, 50–52
  Wallace's domination in southern primaries, 91
"The Prospect Before Us" pamphlet (Callender), 23–24
public opinion polling, 52, 102

radio advertising, 7–8, 9, 13–14, 46, 50–52, 54, 63–64, 97, 103, 168–69, 171–72, 190
Rafshoon, Gerald, 104, 137
rank-order of states, 38–41, 39*t*
Raoul-Duval, Michael, 105
Reagan, Ronald-Carter, Jimmy election (1980), 32–33, 43, 104
  Carter's electoral strategy, 110*t*, 112
  Reagan's electoral strategy, 108–12, 110*t*
Reagan, Ronald-Mondale, Walter election (1984), 29–116
  Mondale's electoral strategy, 112–13, 114*t*, 116
  Reagan's electoral strategy, 113–16, 114*t*
The Reasoning Voter (Popkin), 6
recession (U.S.), 65, 71, 121
Reed, Scott, 129
Reeves, Rosser, 63
Renteria, Amanda, 158–59
Republican National Committee (RNC), 62
Republican Party
  appearances by candidates, 202–7, 204*f*
  1896 primaries, 21
  hypothetical state rank order, by estimated presidential vote potential, 39*t*
  impact of activities on vote outcomes, 222–25
  1952 presidential campaign, 13
  pioneering the use of television advertising, 62
  spot television ad spending across the eras, 190–92, 194–200, 196*f*, 197*f*, 198*f*, 215–21, 215*t*, 223–24
  targeting of voters by, 141–42
  2020 presidential campaign, 13
  vetting of Goldwater, 78–79
  Voter Vault program, 144–45
  See also Democratic Party; Democratic-Republican Party
resource allocation
  ads and appearances as mesures, 42, 46–47, 189–94
  campaign discipline and, 187–89
  candidate appearances by strategic categories, 200–6, 203*f*
  era-related variability, 188
  impact of COVID-19 pandemic, 188
  impact on campaigning, 15
  importance of careful planning, 188
  measures of, 46, 47
  micro-targeted campaigning era, 140, 141, 189
  relation to strategic planning, 41
  television spot ad spendig across the eras, 194–200
  types/limitations of, 34
  vote outcomes and, 209–34, 215*t*–39*t*
  wholesale campaigning era, 15, 16, 67, 97
  zero-sum campaigning era, 10, 16, 102–3, 109–12, 137–38, 189
  See also fundraising; presidential campaigns, expenses

Rhoades, Matt, 154
Richard, Ann, 132
Richardson, Bill, 148–49
Robertson, Pat, 116–17
Rockefeller, Nelson, 71, 78
Rogers, Ted, 77
rolling cross-section surveys, 5–6, 37
Romney, George, 154
Romney, Mitt, 148
Romney, Mitt-Obama, Barack election (2008), 152–55
  Obama's electoral strategy, 153, 154–55, 156*t*, 173
  Romney's electoral strategy, 153, 154, 156*t*, 173
Roosevelt, Eleanor, 72
Roosevelt, Franklin D., 24, 116–17
Roosevelt, Theodore, 122–23, 193
Rove, Karl, 4, 132, 144–45
Rubio, Marco, 155–58

Salter, Mark, 149
Sanders, Bernie, 155, 159, 162–63
Santorum, Rick, 152–53
Sasso, John, 120
Schweiker, Richard, 104
Scott, Hugh, 56–57
Scranton, William, 78
September 11, 2001, terrorist attack, 142–43
Sides, John and Vavreck, Lynn, 3–4, 5–7
Simulmatics Corporation, 96
Slaby, Michael, 153
slush fund scandal (Nixon), 52–53, 58, 93–96
Smathers, George, 71–72
Smith, Margaret Chase, 78
social media
  Clinton's candidacy announcement on, 148–49
  Dean's innovative use of, 143–44, 167
  micro-targeted campaigning and, 11, 139, 141
  Obama's candidacy announcement on, 148–49
  Sanders' strong presence on, 155
  transformative impact on campaigning, 140–41, 144, 167
  user communications on candidates, 1–2
  See also email; Facebook; Internet; text messages; Twitter
soft money, 101, 139–40, 143–44, 194–95
Sparkman, John, 57–58, 59–62
spot television advertisements
  advertising differentials, 226
  Democratic *vs.* Republican spending, 194–200, 196*f*, 197*f*, 198*f*, 215*t*, 223–24
  Eisenhower-Stevenson campaign, 64, 70, 97
  Johnson-Goldwater campaign, 79–82, 83
  Kennedy-Nixon campaign, 77
  1952-2020 data analysis, 190–92, 196*f*, 197*f*, 198*f*
  wholesale spending by strategic categories, 197*f*
Stassen, Harold, 78
Stephanopoulos, George, 122, 128–29
Stevens, Thomas E., 66–67
Stevenson, Adlai, 43
  effort at being a "compromise" candidate, 71–72
  embrace of television advertising, 70
  meeting with Truman, 57
  Roosevelt, Eleanor, backing of, 72
  use of television spot ads, 29, 64
Stevenson, Adlai-Eisenhower, Dwight D. election (1952)
  Eisenhower's electoral strategy, 59–64, 60*t*
  Stevenson's electoral strategy, 58–63, 60*t*, 64
Stevenson, Adlai-Eisenhower, Dwight D. election (1956)
  criticisms of Stevenson's performance, 66
  Eisenhower's electoral strategy, 66–67, 68*t*
  Eisenhower's health complications, 65–54
  Stevenson's electoral strategy, 66–67, 68*t*, 70
Steyer, Tom, 162
Stone, Roger, 4
strategy/strategy building blocks, 31–36
  campaign effects, 36–38
  campaign execution, 33–34, 102–3
  campaign strategy, 31–33
  campaign targeting, 34–36
  data and design, 43–47
  micro-targeted tactics, 7, 9, 11–13, 16–17, 27, 35–36
  1952-2020 strategies, 44–47, 45*t*
  wholesale campaigning, 12
  zero-sum campaigning, 12
Sun Tzu, 31–32, 33, 34
super PACs (political action committees), 139–40, 153, 233

Supreme Court (US)
Buckley v. Valeo (1976), 100
Citizens United v. FEC, 11, 139–40, 166–67, 194–95, 233
McConnell v. FEC, 194–95
SpeechNow.org v. FEC, 11, 139–40, 166–67, 194–95, 233
Swift Boat Veterans for Truth (527 organization), 144
Symington, Stuart, 71–72

Taft, Robert, 56–57
targeting goals, tactics
micro-targeted campaigning, 12
wholesale campaigning, 12
zero-sum campaigning, 12
Teachout, Zephyr, 143
Ted Bates Company, 63–64
Teeter, Robert, 105, 123, 137
television/television advertising
ABC network, 54
advantages of, 232
allocation shifts in battleground states, 17–18
analysis of, 5–6, 7–8, 37, 47, 211–12
campaign resource allocation and, 46
candidate appearance effects, 14–17, 38, 46, 211–12, 215–22, 215t
CBS network, 54, 126
Democratic Party embrace of, 70
development of 30-second ad, 29
"Eisenhower Answers America" commercials, 64
gross rating points (GRPs), 192
impact on campaigns, 1–2, 9, 10, 50
Kennedy/Nixon, use of spot ads, 77
logarithmic/"ceiling effect" of spending, 222
micro-targeting campaigning era, 16–17
NBC network, 54, 191
"Optimizer" project (Obama), 153
penetration data (1953-1960), 51f
Perot's use of infomercials, 126
Republicans' pioneering the use of, 62
resource allocation for, 46, 192
rise of advertising on, 1, 7–8, 13–14, 16, 18, 99
role/importance of, 190, 213–14
spot ad spending, across the eras, 190–92, 196f, 197f, 198f
state-level Republican Presidential voting advantages, 215t
Stevenson's embrace of, 70
televised town halls, 189
wholesale campaigning era, 16, 50–54, 62, 70, 72, 83, 93
zero-sum campaigning era, 99, 102–3, 118t, 129
See also spot television advertisements
tell-all books, vii
text messages, 7–8, 168–69, 171–72
Thompson, Fred, 148
Thompson, Hunter S., 3–4
Tillman Act (1907), 24
The Timeline of Presidential Elections (Erikson and Wlezien), 5
tracking
allocation of resources over time, 187–208
changes over time, 13–14
electoral strategy over time, 17, 168–86
in-person campaign appearances, 46
media-tracking organizations, 229
trial ballots, 7
Trippi, Joe, 143
Truman, Harry
lobbying for Eisenhower to run, 55–56
meeting with Stevenson, 57
1948 "whistle stop" campaign tour, 49, 50f
opinion of Kennedy's nomination, 72
Trump, Donald
Access Hollywood video tape and, 158
accusations of collusion with Russia, 162
candidacy declaration by, 21–22
COVID-19 and, 36
fundraising by, 24
impact of celebrity of, 25–26
"Make American Great Again" campaign, 155–58
positioning strategy of, 27
shocking 2016 victories, 136–37
Trump, Donald-Biden, Joe election (2020), 162–66
Biden's electoral strategy, 163–66, 164t
impact of global pandemic, 169
record election spending, 163, 209
Trump's consistent planting of doubt, 163
Trump's electoral strategy, 163–66, 164t
Trump, Donald-Clinton, Hillary election (2016), 155–62
Clinton's electoral strategy, 158, 159, 160t
projections of a Clinton victory, 158
Trump's electoral strategy, 155–62, 160t, 174–75

Tsongas, Paul, 22–23, 121
Twitter, 155–58

University of Pennsylvania, Annenberg School of Public Affairs, 4

Van Buren, Martin, 29
Vavreck, Lynn and Sides, John, 3–4, 5–7
Vietnam War, 78, 83–84, 89, 90, 121–22, 144, 211
Vilsack, Tom, 148–49
Virginia House of Burgesses, 23
vote outcomes
  campaign ad/candidate appearance effects, 212–15
  campaign effects and, 17–18, 31, 97, 210, 213–14, 229
  contested elections, 210–11
  growth of predictability over time, 234
  impact of small shifts in critical states, 210–12
  media market impact of differential activities, 228–31, 238*t*, 239*t*
  resource allocation and, 209–34
  statewide impact of differential activities, 225–28
  statewide impact of Republican/Democratic activities, 222–25, 235*t*, 236*t*
  TV ad spending/candidate appearance effects, 215–22, 228, 235*t*, 236*t*
Voter Vault program (Republican Party), 144–45

Wagner, Dan, 153
Wallace, George
  backers of, 85
  campaign expenditures (1968), 24
  domination in southern primaries, 91
  efforts at unseating Nixon, 90
  fight for nomination, 91
Warren, Elizabeth, 21–22, 162
Washington, George, 20, 23–24
Watergate break-in scandal (Nixon), 52–53
  fallout from, 99–100
  impact on federal campaign finance laws, 99–100, 103–4
weapons of mass destruction (WMDs), 142–43
"whistle stop" campaign tour (Truman, 1948), 49, 50*f*
White, Theodore, 3–4
wholesale campaigning era (1952-1972), 9–13, 49–98
  advances in public opinion polling, 52
  advertising, 9, 15, 16, 49–54, 62–64, 70, 73, 77, 89–90, 93
  allocation of resources, 189
  description, 9, 16
  discipline in candidate appearances, television advertising, 189
  Eisenhower-Stevenson elections, 55–70
  execution of strategic plans, goals, 12, 54
  expectations in targeting goals, tactics, 12, 54
  Kennedy-Nixon campaign (1960), 3–4, 52
  Kennedy's 1960 nomination strategy, 50–52
  money, heightened importance of, 52–53
  resource allocation, 15, 16, 67, 97
  strategy, 12
  television advertising, 50–54, 62, 70, 72, 83, 93
Witcover, Jules and Wlezien, Chris, 3–4, 5

Yang, Andrew, 162–63

zero-sum campaigning era (1976-2000), 10–11, 99–138
  advertising, 99, 113–16, 129, 137–38, 198–99
  campaign finance laws and, 10
  Carter-Ford election, 103–8
  description, 10–11, 16
  discipline in candidate appearances, television advertising, 189
  execution, 12
  expectations in, 102–3
  fallout from Watergate, 99–100
  Federal Election Campaign Act and, 100–2
  historical context of, 103
  individual-level impact of campaigns, 103
  resource allocation, 10, 16, 102–3, 109–12, 137–38, 189
  strategy, 12
  targeting goals, tactics, 12
  television advertising, 99, 102–3, 118*t*, 129

Printed in the USA/Agawam, MA
September 27, 2024

873496.013